ESEA

The Office of Education Administers a Law

ESEA
The Office of Education Administers a Law

STEPHEN K. BAILEY AND

EDITH K. MOSHER

SYRACUSE UNIVERSITY PRESS

FIRST EDITION

Library of Congress catalog card number: 68–27692

Manufactured in the United States of America

TO FRITZ—

husband of one, friend and teacher of both

PREFACE

This is a study in public administration. It is the story of the role of a Federal agency in developing and administering a law. The law—The Elementary and Secondary Education Act of 1965 (hereafter ESEA) [1]—is an important watershed in the history of American education. It set in motion a series of fiscal, political, and administrative forces that cannot help but have profound consequences for American education and for the American Federal system generally. Some of these broader implications of ESEA will be examined in the concluding chapters. The body of the study, however, is directed not at the possible or probable long-range consequences of a particular law; it is focused on the administrative behavior of a government agency during a brief period of policy gestation and organizational crisis.

The time period is artificially circumscribed. It covers a two-year span—roughly spring, 1964 to spring, 1966. Like all case studies, this one is long on "uniquities," short on ubiquities. But in a general sense it deals with a series of relationships and tensions that are probably characteristic of most Federal agencies charged in recent years with the responsibility of administering new grants–in–aid to and through State and local public authorities.

Both in the innovative and administrative aspects of public policy, a grant–in–aid agency must operate in a complex political environment. It must function in an intricate web of tensions spun by historical circumstance and by both coordinate and cross purposes: congressional, presidential, judicial, group interest, intra-agency, inter-agency, intergovernmental, personal, societal, and even international. When, as is the case with aid to education, the magnitude of Federal involvement is increased with dramatic suddenness, these tensions are particularly illuminated and exacerbated.

Federal aid to education is not a new phenomenon, but the growth in Federal investment in education in the past half decade has been explosive. In the single year 1965–66, for example, largely as a result of the passage of the Elementary and Secondary Education Act, Federal funds

[1] Public Law 89–10, 89th Cong., 1st sess., April 11, 1965.

supporting elementary and secondary education almost tripled (from $890,685,000 in 1965 to $2,408,209,000 in 1966).[2]

It may be wondered at the outset by what constitutional authority the Federal government has moved massively into areas of educational support formerly deemed the exclusive province of State and local governments. The fact is that once the General Welfare Clause (Article I, Section 8) of the United States Constitution is interpreted liberally, it is impossible to set limits to the extent of Federal involvement in public education. Under Supreme Court decisions of the past third of a century, it is clear that questions of the future of American federalism do not revolve around the constitutional authority of the Federal government; they revolve around questions of political values and administrative prudence. In effect, the only constitutional provisions which limit the nature of Federal policies in the field of education are to be found in the establishment clause of the First Amendment.[3] Clearly, Congress cannot finance religious instruction in parochial schools, however much indirect support is given to church-related education under "shared-time" and "child benefit" formulae. It is ironical but probably true that Congress can legitimately support the teaching of religion in public and private education only when the society becomes sufficiently secular to accept religion as an object of scholarship rather than as a subject of dogma.

If, then, most questions of Federal involvement in education are political and prudential rather than constitutional, it is important to ask what are the legitimate interests of the wider national community in the conduct of local educational enterprises. There is, of course, a corollary of this question: what self restraints should be exercised by the Federal government in order to avoid the dangers to liberty of a monolithic, central control of educational policies and programs?

It is trite but true that, in the broadest sense, the legitimate interests of the Federal government in education are encapsulated in the equality clause of the Declaration of Independence and in the Preamble and the Fourteenth Amendment to the Constitution. The Declaration and the Preamble are not legally binding in the same sense as the equal protection clause of the Fourteenth Amendment; but they provide an ethical logic for the development of public policy. Granted these ethical premises of equality of opportunity, the Federal government is logically concerned with education whenever questions arise about disparities in publicly supported educational opportunity, and whenever it can be shown that

[2] U.S. Department of Health, Education, and Welfare, *Projections of Educational Statistics to 1975–76* (Washington, D.C., 1966), 111.

[3] U.S. Const. Amend. I: "Congress shall make no law respecting an establishment of religion, or prohibiting the free exercise thereof; . . ."

educational activity bears significantly upon such issues of national value as unity, justice, domestic tranquility, the common defense, the general welfare, and the liberties of present and future generations. In this framework the Tenth Amendment of the Constitution [4] becomes less a limitation upon the Federal prerogative than a reminder of the effective administrative and political limits of Federal competence.

However much some may differ with this analysis, it is to the authors the only possible interpretation of modern constitutional reality. From 1937 to the present, the Supreme Court has built a doctrine of Federal supremacy that, while it may not have relegated the Tenth Amendment to a minor codicil to the national will, has certainly curtailed traditionally-assumed autonomies and monopolies of State and local authorities. It is conceivable that the time may come when the Supreme Court will find the Tenth Amendment a useful and necessary instrument to limit the extension of the authority of the Federal government in such a field as education. One can conceive of this happening, for example, if Congress should grant to Federal administrators the power to assign nationally-approved text books or curricula. But at present such developments seem both remote and improbable.

The ethical and constitutional framework of education is fundamental, but it is also ambiguous, malleable, and evolving. What the Federal government does in the way of supporting, modifying, or regulating education is directly related to perceived current and prospective national problems. The Fourteenth Amendment was on the books for almost ninety years before the Supreme Court invoked the Equal Protection Clause to attack segregated schools. The Civil Rights Act of 1964, prohibiting Federal assistance to activities marked by racial or religious discrimination, has achieved only uncertain results, despite the passage of more than a decade since the Supreme Court decision in *Brown v. Board of Education of Topeka.*[5] Historically, the Federal interest in education has been more clearly marked in areas like agriculture, vocational training, and defense than in such fields of recent concern as justice (racial equality), domestic tranquility (urban unrest), welfare (unemployment and poverty), and liberty (interpreted as self-fulfillment). The linkages between education and these latter issues of national concern have only

[4] U.S. Const. Amend. X: "The powers not delegated to the United States by the Constitution, nor prohibited by it to the States are reserved for the States respectively, or to the people."

[5] 347 U.S. 483 (1954): The Due Process Clause of the fifth amendment was interpreted in Bolling v. Sharpe, 347 U.S. 497 (1954), (a companion case to Brown v. The Board of Education) to apply the same kinds of restrictions against the Federal government that the Brown case applied through the 14th amendment to the States.

recently evolved as guides and rationales for Federal educational policy-making.

Why these recent concerns have emerged and why Federal support and regulation of education has been an accepted means of attacking these broader social issues are complex matters of historical interpretation. Suffice it to say that depressions, wars, population growth, tax pressures, economic and technological inter-dependencies, a mobile population, academic insights, political anachronisms like mal-apportioned legislatures, and a suddenly emerging consciousness on the part of minority groups of the disparity between the promise and the reality of American democracy, have combined to induce justices, officials, and politicians to seek new solutions to both ancient and emerging problems. Education has increasingly been recognized as a key to the solution of these problems for the obvious reason that human skills, attitudes, and behavior are in part a product of educational in-puts. Because of the inadequacies and inequities of State and local educational resources and endeavors, national money has been needed to supplement local resources in overcoming what have become patently national—even international—problems.

This recognition has led to an explosive proliferation of Federal education programs in recent years—three dozen statutes applicable to the Department of Health, Education, and Welfare (hereafter HEW) under President Johnson alone. The Elementary and Secondary Education Act is only one of these; but it is significant in scope, in funding, and especially in the lessons that can be derived from its implementation to date. This is why an examination of its origins and execution seemed to the authors of considerable current importance.

The following study is neither an apologia nor a carper. It attempts simply to describe a complex administrative reality of contemporary significance. The authors hope, however, that the reader will come away with a new appreciation for the extraordinary vitality and adaptability of the American democratic system and for the safeguards against error and tyranny that a highly pluralistic, interactive administrative process provides in the formulation and execution of important public policies.

Those who fear Federal government domination of American education should be reassured by the study. Those who deplore untoward and inequitable atomization of educational policy-making should be equally comforted. The administrative apparatus of a separation-of-powers, Federal, and politically diffuse polity, is too cumbersome for tyranny; too interdependent for anarchy. On divisive issues like civil rights and church-state relations, the system is too weak to enforce total conformity to national principles and standards, too strong to permit pockets of bigotry or intransigence to enjoy an uninterrupted self-indulgence. What T. V. Smith once called "the promise of American democracy" is manifest in the experiences and behaviors herein described. For the essence of the story is the slow and intermittent increase of broad, just, humane, and rational perspectives over parochialism, inequity, indifference, and temper. If the millenium is not proximate, neither is the likelihood of an atavistic reversion. The bargaining process of public administration in the American society permits and promotes marginal and incremental approximations to generally accepted and evolving national norms—including the norms of a continuing pluralism. The process makes reformers restive; but it also disturbs the satisfied from their callous slumbers. It diffuses responsibility, but maintains responsiveness. If it leaves vast room for discontent and impatience, it also undermines the hopelessness of the cynics.

If the net reaction at this moment is one of restiveness and concern, it is largely because of the magnitude of the educational problems affecting the nation—especially in urban ghettos—and the sense that Congress is as yet unwilling to make the quantum jump in appropriations required for their solution.

These, at least, are the conclusions of the authors who remain alternately disconcerted and impressed.

Extended interviews and extensive reading are the base of the study. The material gleaned from interviews is not reflected in the footnotes in order to protect the confidentiality of sources. But major informants are listed alphabetically in Appendix E. The opinion sampling of local educational officials, summarized and interpreted largely in Chapter V, and compiled and described methodologically in Appendix C, was conducted and computerized with the help of Dr. Eleanor P. Godfrey of the Bureau of Social Science Research in Washington, D.C. The survey could not have been conducted without the understanding and assistance of Dr. Forrest E. Conner, Executive Secretary of the American Association of School Administrators. Some of the findings in Chapters IV and V are based upon responses to a letter to chief state school officers (see Appendix C), sent out with the encouragement and endorsement of Dr. Edgar Fuller, Executive Secretary of the Council of Chief State School Officers.

Our gratitude is extended to scores of informants in the U.S. Office of Education; in the White House; in Congress; in professional societies; in universities; in State departments of education; and in schools; and to some in private life—who gave willingly of their time and knowledge. Special thanks are due to Gordon Ambach, Charles S. Benson, Douglass Cater, Wilbur Cohen, Lawrence A. Cremin, Harold Howe II, Herbert Jasper, Norman Karsh, Laurence Iannaconne, Francis Keppel, and especially to Samuel Halperin for advice, criticism, and a variety of indispensable services.

Finally, particular acknowledgment must be given to Raoul Kulberg, leg-man extraordinary; to Cornelia Bailey, Joel S. Berke, J. Martin Rochester, and James Carroll, conscientious and perceptive critics and editors; to Marian Borst, Virginia Moran, and Marianne Lombardo, expert secretaries; to Syracuse University, for permitting a leave of absence; and to the University of California, Berkeley, the Brookings Institution, and to the Carnegie Corporation of New York for indispensable financial and logistical support.

In the case of joint authorships it is sometimes easy to define the precise contribution of each partner. In this case it is impossible. It is true that Chapters I, II, and IV represent modifications of material originally prepared by the west coast author and that Chapters III, V, and VI were originally drafted by the east coast author. But each author felt free to tear the other's work to pieces, and did so. The exchange of correspondence and manuscript drafts between the two was voluminous. Sentences, such as "Surely you did not mean to say that." were countered with questions like the following, "Why have you inverted what is obviously a rational ordering of sequence?" What has emerged is a product of spirited exchanges, hard questioning, and collaborative insight. Delightfully, friendship has been maintained and mutual respect has been enhanced.

Responsibility for all errors of fact and judgment are assumed jointly and solely by the two authors.

STEPHEN K. BAILEY
EDITH K. MOSHER

May, 1968
Syracuse, New York
Berkeley, California

CONTENTS

TABLES

ESEA

The Office of Education Administers a Law

I. The Historical Setting

The notion that education is a necessary and proper concern of government is as ancient as classical political theory. Aristotle wrote that "the education of youth ought to form the principal part of the legislator's attention . . . since education first molds, and afterwards sustains the various modes of government." He went on to note that "the better and more perfect the system of education, the better and more perfect the plan of government it is intended to introduce and uphold." For this reason, Aristotle deduced that ". . . education ought to be regulated by the general consent, and not abandoned to the blind decisions of chance, or to idle caprice." [1]

In America, government interest in education dates back at least to the "old deluder Satan" law in the colony of Massachusetts in 1642. Intermittently at first, but with increasing consistency in the nineteenth and twentieth centuries, public education came to be considered a matter of government interest and concern. However, for most of American history, the view prevailed that education was primarily a function of local authority and control—even though both State governments and the Federal government had a substantial impact upon the course and direction of American educational development. Until the twentieth century, the Federal government's main impact was through land grants for educational purposes. The influence of State governments came to be felt increasingly during the nineteenth century in the standardization of minimal educational requirements and services. The fact remains, however, that up to the end of World War II, local educational programs were financed and determined in large part by local school systems.

This is not to say that local educational systems were immune to standardizing or directive influences. Economic, professional, religious, commercial, social, and political forces in the society at large have always conditioned local educational policy. But so long as school revenues were largely raised locally, substantial autonomy was permitted to those who

1. Quoted in U.S. Department of Education, *Report of the Commissioner of Education* (Washington: U.S. Government Printing Office, 1868), 331. For a more recent rendition of these same points, see William Ellis (trans.), Aristotle's *Politics* (New York: E. P. Dutton & Co., Inc., 1912), 238.

controlled school governance at the local level. In the nineteenth and early twentieth centuries, State legislatures began to establish minimum standards for school attendance and teacher certification, to mandate courses in American or State history, to induce or require school consolidation, and to establish standards for the awarding of school diplomas. Despite these new factors, local educational authorities continued in large measure to determine the size, shape, and content of school programs. The rise of categorical Federal and State grants for vocational education and for the handicapped unquestionably influenced local resource allocations for education, but substantial latitude was left to local school districts in the implementation of such measures—granted always the intrusion of the power of municipalities in the shaping of the budgets of dependent school systems. Dramatic increases in general State aid in the thirty-year period after 1925 still left the programmatic power of local school boards substantially intact. The fact that the persistence of local power has not brought about a series of totally atomized and disparate educational programs has been due far more to basic cultural similarity and to the homogenizing influence of church, college, and textbook manufacturers than it has to legal arrangements.

American education, in short, has been a highly diffused enterprise over most of the course of its history. The role of the Federal government, particularly, has been minimal and any suggested increase in that role has been generally feared and fought.

In the scant period of 13 years (1954–67), however, a sea change has occurred. The Federal government's interest in stimulating change and improving quality in public education at the pre-collegiate level has been increasingly visible in four fields: (1) desegregation; (2) education related to defense and to vocations; (3) aid to research; and (4) education of the economically and culturally disadvantaged, and of the handicapped. Federal activity—judicial, legislative, and executive—in these four areas has unquestionably affected the traditional, decentralized autonomies of American education. This is especially true when one adds the fact that Federal aid to parochial school children was an important corollary, even a precondition, of many of these new Federal thrusts, and that Supreme Court decisions on the place of religion in the schools had widespread impact. Quality and equality of opportunity in education have become matters of national concern. All levels of government, and a variety of branches and agencies at each level, are now deeply involved in a complex and uneasy partnership whose collective aims are transforming educational priorities and methods. Education, like so many other governmental services, has now become involved in a "marble cake," not a "layer cake," of federalism.

The Irony of ESEA

That the recent emergence of substantial Federal involvement in education has taken the form of an active partnership, rather than that of a passive and distant financial patron, is not without irony. For, as late as the early 1960's, most of the pressures for extensive Federal aid to education were couched in terms of general relief to local school budgets through unrestricted Federal grants for school construction and/or teachers' salaries, and in public schools only. When the first great breakthrough in Federal school aid occurred, as it did in the Elementary and Secondary Education Act of 1965, it involved a series of programmatic and innovative imperatives which plunged the Federal government smack into the middle of the total educational enterprise—public and private.

ESEA was not a form of general relief to the local education agency (hereafter LEA) for operating and capital budgets. Its provisions were directive and categorical, yet far more flexible than those, say, in the Smith-Hughes Vocational Education Act or in the National Defense Education Act of 1958 (hereafter NDEA). Title I of ESEA dictated the use of massive Federal funds for the general purpose of upgrading the education of children who were culturally and economically disadvantaged, but it left vast discretion of LEA's in developing local programs to achieve this goal. Title II had no "poverty" formula, but it did focus upon a particular rather than a general need of schools—public and private: the improvement of school libraries, textbooks, and instructional materials; but even here the organizational nature of Title II was far broader than similar materials provisions in the original version of NDEA. Title III funds were earmarked not for the general support of existing programs, but for innovative or supplementary educational centers and services approved by the U.S. Commissioner of Education. Once again, categorical aid was stressed, but it did provide enormous flexibility in scope and emphasis. Title IV grants for research and development and for regional educational laboratories were to be directly allocated from Washington. Under Title V, Federal funds were to be made available for the strengthening of State education agencies (hereafter SEA) according to criteria established in the act.

In sum, ESEA was not just a Federal handout to ease State and local educational budgets. It mandated a series of programs and priorities which involved a massive shift in the locus of policy-making power in American education.

A further irony of ESEA was that those in the traditional educational establishment who had fought longest and most vociferously for Federal aid to education saw victory achieved at the price of allowing the traditional bugaboos, "Federal control" and "aid-to-non-public-schools," to haunt the victory banquet. Their solace was in the fact that the new Federal categories provided substantial discretion to State and local educational agencies in designing specific projects under the various titles.

How and why this happened constitutes the historical setting of our story. It is an involved scenario, for it is composed of the interaction over a 20-year period of new educational demands, limited and inadequate resources, often heroic but essentially expediential responses, and political inventiveness and compromise stimulated by frustration.

Perhaps, in a generic sense, this is the evolutionary pattern of all major policy innovations in a democratic polity.

THE NEW EDUCATIONAL DEMANDS

The postwar years in the United States were marked by a series of demands upon the educational system that were unprecedented in scope and magnitude. Any one of the new demands would have produced disquiet and concern. Together they constituted an explosive admixture.

The Postwar Explosion in the Learning Force

An unanticipated increase in the birth rate, and an equally unanticipated growth in school attendance through high school and beyond, placed unprecedented strains on the staff and facilities of American education.

In 1946, only 2,200,000 pupils were enrolled in the first grade of the nation's schools. By 1953, this number had jumped to 3,700,000.[2]

In 1949–50, there were 6,453,000 students enrolled in grades 9–12, including post-graduate studies below the collegiate level. By 1965, this number had almost exactly doubled.[3]

In the single decade 1954–55 to 1964–65, the number of students graduating from high school leapt from 1,351,000 to 2,567,000.[4]

These and similar statistics show the ruthless pressure of numbers upon

2. *Statistics of State School Systems, 1961–62,* U.S. Department of Health, Education, and Welfare (Washington: U.S. Government Printing Office, 1962), 42.

3. *Progress of Public Education in the United States of America 1963–64,* U.S. Department of Health, Education, and Welfare (Washington: U.S. Government Printing Office, 1964), 10. cf., *Projections of Educational Statistics to 1975–76,* U.S. Department of Health, Education, and Welfare (Washington: U.S. Government Printing Office, 1964), 5.

4. *Trends,* U.S. Department of Health, Education, and Welfare (Washington: U.S. Government Printing Office, 1965), 20.

the American school system in the two decades following the end of World War II.

How were these additional students to be housed? Who would teach them? Who would pay for the facilities and staff needed to serve them? If no other educational demands had existed in the postwar years, the sheer volume of responsibility for teaching millions of additional children would by itself have produced extraordinary claims upon the educational system.

The Knowledge Explosion

Concomitant to the school population explosion was an intellectual and technological explosion. The postwar rate of technological invention and economic growth; breakthroughs in electronic communications, and in the speed and ease of publishing and disseminating information; the heightened mobility of people and ideas; the intractability and unprecedented responsibilities of the cold war; the vast outpouring of research findings in the social and behavioral sciences; and the rising expectations of the dispossessed at home and abroad—all combined to challenge the adequacy of the American educational system. How could it produce the skills needed to understand, and ultimately manage, these new forces? Sputnik dramatized the dilemmas and the shortfalls, but widespread awareness of the basic problem presaged as well as followed the Russian triumph of 1957. Scholars and pamphleteers, often working with funds provided by major private foundations,[5] addressed themselves with increasing fervor to the patent inadequacies of the educational system and to possible new directions. Studies of public education by former Harvard President James B. Conant had a pervasive impact upon public thinking.[6] Books, articles, monographs, and speeches emerged in profusion asking why Johnny could not read; why curricula and pedagogical techniques were outmoded; why the talents of gifted children were inadequately cultivated in the schools; why teachers' colleges were mired in mediocrity; why vast discrepancies seemed to exist between education for the middle-class suburban children on the one hand and education for children of the urban and rural poor on the other. Research and clinical experiments dealt with such areas as the nature of learning, innovation

5. Rene A. Wormser, *Foundations: Their Power and Influence* (New York: Devin Adair Co., 1958). See also, Richard W. Saxe, *The Fund for the Advancement of Education and Teacher Education* (Unpublished Ph.D. dissertation, Dept. of Education, University of Chicago, 1964).

6. James B. Conant, *The American High School Today* (New York: McGraw-Hill, 1959); *Slums and Suburbs* (New York: McGraw-Hill, 1961); and *The Education of American Teachers* (New York: McGraw-Hill, 1963).

in education, education for the culturally deprived, and the evaluation of educational performance. The work of scholars like Bettleheim, Bloom, Bruner, Callahan, Clark, Deutsch, Hersey, Pettigrew, Riesman, Tyler, and Zacharias were symptomatic of a growing concern with traditional educational philosophies and practices.[7]

Other scholars and intellectual brokers brought other points of view to America's educational problems. Economists like Professors Harold F. Clark and Theodore W. Schultz began to point out that education was a nation's most important investment in sustaining and promoting a viable economy in a highly technological culture.[8] John W. Gardner, then President of the Carnegie Corporation, became chairman of the Task Force on Education of President Eisenhower's 1960 Committee on National Goals. Gardner contended that education was the key to improving the "quality of life" in the American society. Government administrators and international commentators pointed out that technical assistance programs to the developing nations were foundering because of inadequate educational resources of both donor and recipient nations.

This vast increase in concern and analysis led reformers to wonder whether anything short of substantial Federal infusions of money could move the educational system off its traditional dead center. Were pupils being educated well enough and fast enough to adapt to a world in massive flux? Could new knowledge be controlled by a new wisdom?

The notion that demands for substantial help from the Federal treasury might well be feasible grew as the fiscal performance of the Federal tax system showed increasing resiliency—especially in the early 1960's. Between 1961 and 1965, the country had experienced economic expansion of extraordinary length, strength, and balance. This expansion was generating an automatic growth in Federal revenues of over $6 billion a year. Walter Heller, former chairman of the President's Council of Economic Advisors, saw in this growth the following:

7. For a list of some of the pertinent publications of these authors, see the bibliography at the end of this book.

8. Theodore W. Schultz, *The Economic Value of Education* (New York: Columbia University Press, 1963); Harold F. Clark, *Cost and Quality in Public Education* (Syracuse: Syracuse University Press, 1963).
For earlier brief statements of the Clark and Schultz theses, see *Education—An Investment in People,* Education Department, Chamber of Commerce of the United States (Washington: The Chamber, 1954); and Theodore W. Schultz, "The Emerging Economic Scene and its Relation to High School Education," as published in F. S. Chase and H. A. Anderson, eds., *The High School in a New Era* (Chicago: University of Chicago Press, 1958). See also *Paying for Better Public Schools,* Committee for Economic Development (New York: Committee for Economic Development, 1959).

> At the federal level, economic growth and a powerful tax system, interacting under modern fiscal management, generate new revenues faster than they generate new demands on the federal purse. But at the state-local level, the situation is reversed. Under the whiplash of prosperity, responsibilities are outstripping revenues.[9]

Many educators, politicians, academicians, and industrialists [10] found very attractive his conclusion that the huge, and presumably controllable growth in the national economy provided the opportunity to declare "generous dividends" in the form of transfer of more funds to State and local governments. If Heller's pre-Vietnam optimism was premature, it was a powerful incentive to educational reformers and interests groups to attempt to tap the Federal treasury for the nation's hard-pressed schools.

Segregation

A major catalyst to the educational ferment of the 1950's and early 1960's, and a source of new demands on the educational system, was the Supreme Court's historic decision of 1954 on school segregation. In *Brown* v. *Board of Education of Topeka, Kansas,* the court overturned the long-standing *Plessy* v. *Ferguson* ruling that racial segregation was permissible if schools were "separate but equal." The 1954 decision held that ". . . in the field of public education the doctrine of 'separate but equal' has no place. Separate educational facilities are inherently unequal." Recognizing the traumatic consequences of its ruling for existing mores, the Court in a second *Brown* decision, in 1955, ordered a "prompt and reasonable start toward full compliance" but left to Federal district courts the supervision of the desegregation process in the local communities.[11] In any case, a beginning was made toward the elimination of school segregation, at least *de jure*.

In terms of the dynamics of national educational policy, *Brown* v. *Board of Education* had a number of other consequences. Perhaps the most impressive of these was that it made visible the condition of Negro

9. Walter W. Heller, *New Dimensions of Political Economy* (New York: W. W. Norton & Company, Inc., 1967), 118.

10. As the promise of large Federal spending for education increased in the 1960's, a number of industries formed divisions and subdivisions devoted to supplying the educational market: e.g., Time, Inc. and General Electric (General Learning Corporation), Radio Corporation of America and Random House, Xerox, International Business Machines, Litton, Raytheon, CBS.

11. *Brown* v. *Board of Education of Topeka, Kansas,* 347 U.S. 483 (1954), 349 U.S. 294 (1955); *Plessy* v. *Ferguson,* 163 U.S. 537 (1896).

education in America and thereby highlighted the social and economic costs and consequences of prejudice, cultural deprivation, and poverty. These costs and consequences were being felt increasingly outside of the American South. During the 1950's, approximately a quarter of a million Negroes a year moved from rural southern farms to northern and western industrial cities. By and large miserably educated, they found themselves relegated to welfare rolls, forced by prejudice and income to live in segregated slum housing, and unrelated to existing job markets. Negro children constituted the largest percentage of "drop-outs" from the schools. Too frequently their unutilized energies and their frustrations led to delinquency and crime. Altogether, Negroes constituted the most intractable element in hard-core poverty across the land.

Although the impact of the Negro migration was uneven, hundreds of school districts—particularly in large cities—found themselves facing the postwar years with an influx of pupils from a tragic sub-culture largely unrelated to the middle-class orientation of urban education. The educational demands prompted by this in-migration were insistent and almost cruelly complex, especially since it was accompanied by a flight of middle-class whites to the suburbs.

Poverty and Cultural Deprivation

Closely tied to the segregation issue was the question of the relationship of education to the nation's economic health. By the early 1960's, two issues had become particularly prominent. First, although over-all national productivity had been steadily increasing since the end of World War II, marked disparities in income and in employment opportunities persisted. Large pockets of unemployment and poverty remained, especially in the large cities and in dispersed rural slums. These disparities came to be viewed not only as a deterrent to regional prosperity and a violation of the individual's right to the dignity of gainful employment, but as a blot on America's international reputation as a humane democracy.

The second issue related particularly to young people. Although their numbers were increasing in proportion to the total population, they accounted for a disproportionately high percentage of the unemployed. As noted earlier, problems such as school drop-outs and juvenile delinquency were all parts of the same picture. It was becoming more obvious that ignorance, unemployment, and dependency were interrelated and self-perpetuating. High incidence of unemployment and dependency invariably correlated with low educational achievement. Traditional educational programs appeared to be both unable to hold such young people for a sufficient training period, and unable to train effectively those who did stay aboard.

During the mid-50's, the superintendents and board members of the country's largest cities formed a Great Cities Program for School Improvement to study the special problems of urban areas.[12] One of their basic concerns was the needs of educationally disadvantaged children, especially Negroes. It was becoming obvious that conventional educational designs were inadequate to meet the learning problems of the culturally deprived, and it seemed that desegregation alone was not the answer. By early 1963, the Research Division of the National Education Association (hereafter NEA) listed 42 experimental projects underway for disadvantaged children in the country's largest school systems.[13] These projects were variously sponsored by cities, States, and professional associations including NEA itself. New York City's "Higher Horizons" program was one example. Even some of the smaller school systems became involved in this kind of activity.

These experiments differed widely in scope and financing, and the results of these efforts were rarely evaluated with sufficient rigor to make them conclusive. Often the experiments were too short-lived. Nevertheless, these projects provided an important testing ground for many different kinds of experimental activities, and once again reflected new and unprecedented demands upon the nation's schools.

Parochial Schools

Church-state controversies in the field of education have been caused basically by uncertainties over the meaning of two interrelated phrases in the first amendment of the U.S. Constitution: (1) "Congress shall make no law respecting an establishment of religion"; (2) "or prohibiting the free exercise thereof . . ." The first phrase has served as the basis of argument for those who wish to prevent Federal aid to parochial schools; the second phrase has served as a reference point for those who defend the existence of parochial schools and the public support of their secular and auxiliary activities. Federal courts have been reluctant to set clear guidelines, partly because of the inherent ambiguities in the Constitution, partly because the issue is laden with deep and divisive political controversy.

Until the post-World-War-II years, the issues were largely moot.

12. Later on, the Research Council of this organization was active in getting the Title I formula revised to count families receiving Aid to Dependent Children.

13. National Education Association, *School Programs for the Disadvantaged Children,* Educational Research Service Curricula No. 2 (February, 1963).

Parochial school teachers were almost entirely composed of members of various Orders. The church was able from its own resources to carry the capital and operating costs of parochial education.

But after the war, inflation, the explosion in the learning force (which affected parochial schools quite as much as public schools), and a shortage of teaching staff placed an enormous financial burden upon parochial schools. Increasingly, church fathers went to public sources to find funds for supplementary services like transportation and school health. The justification was that such services were for the benefit of the child and did not support religious instruction. The Supreme Court upheld this position in *Everson* v. *Board of Education.*[14] But Justice Hugo Black in a dictum for the majority in this case had the following to say about the meaning of the first amendment:

> Neither states nor the federal government can set up a church. Neither can pass laws which aid one religion, aid all religions, or prefer one religion over another . . . no tax in any amount, large or small, can be levied to support any religious activities or institutions.

The *Everson* case, in consequence, has been cited by both friends and enemies of extending certain types of public assistance for the benefit of the children of parochial schools. The key issue has been: when does a public grant under the child-benefit doctrine actually support a religious institution?

Two other Supreme Court cases on the church-state issue followed in 1948 and 1952. In *McCollum* v. *Board of Education,* the Court ruled that children released 30 minutes a week for religious instruction could not receive such instruction in public school facilities. Four years later, in *Zorach* v. *Clauson,*[15] the Court ruled that "released-time" was permissible if religious instruction took place on private property.

These Court decisions were both the cause and the effect of increased parochial school demands upon public resources in the post-war years. The demands were often subtle and indirect, but they were persistent and politically powerful. And the fact that many States had strict constitutional prohibitions against direct or indirect aid to parochial schools gave a special impetus to asserting church claims upon Federal largess.

LIMITED AND INADEQUATE RESOURCES

This congeries of new demands fell upon an educational system woefully shy of institutional, human, and fiscal resources. Some of these

14. *Everson* v. *Board of Education,* 330 U.S. 1 (1947).

15. *McCollum* v. *Board of Education,* 333 U.S. 203 (1948); *Zorach* v. *Clauson,* 343 U.S. 306 (1952).

inadequacies were long-standing, but some at least were traceable to World War II and its aftermaths, and to the great depression which preceded it.

Deferred Investment and Postwar Inflation

A major war inevitably produces massive shifts in any society's allocation of resources. The war machine is a great maw that consumes enormous quantities of human and physical goods and services. The effects of World War II upon the American school system were manifold but one of its most profound effects was to defer capital outlays for schools. This deferment came on top of ten years of depression during which time capital outlay for public elementary and secondary schools had dropped from $370 million in 1929–30 to only $258 million in 1939–40.[16] By the late 1940's, America's school plant was by and large old, dilapidated, and overcrowded. And the prospect of necessary new construction and refurbishing came at a moment of mounting postwar inflation. Between 1946 and 1953 the value of the dollar—including the tax dollar—was cut by 40 per cent. And a special kind of inflation hit the educational labor market. At a time of prosperity and full employment, school systems had to compete in the open market for teachers, school administrators, and maintenance personnel who began to shun school employment unless salaries and wages were pushed to what once would have been considered dizzying heights.

Heroic measures were taken by State and local governments and local school districts to adjust tax levies and tax assessment policies to help close the inflationary gap. Revenue receipts of State and local governments for education jumped from just over $2 billion in 1939–40 to over $5 billion in 1949–50, to $7.5 billion in 1953–54, and to $11.7 billion in 1957–58.[17] But the demands for new buildings, equipment, staff, and services continued to outrun revenues. As local school districts and their property-tax payers came to feel the fiscal pinch, both local and professional educational interests pressured State governments to increase both general and categorical aid to education. But States were also suffering from fiscal rigidities and inadequacies and were forced increasingly to turn toward the Federal government.

This upward pressure for tax relief was made even more acute by the simple reality that education was only one among many claimants for additional government revenues. The capital deferment enforced by the demands of World War II affected all aspects of government: highways,

16. *Statistics of State School Systems 1963–64,* U.S. Department of Health, Education, and Welfare (Washington: U.S. Government Printing Office), 21.

17. *Progress of Public Education 1963–64, op. cit.,* 16.

hospitals, public works equipment, public office buildings, water works, sewage disposal plants, recreational facilities, etc. Urbanization and the increasing metropolitanization of the American population placed particular burdens upon the governments of larger cities which were deluged with demands for new services and facilities of all kinds—demands often accompanied by a crumbling tax base in the central city.[18] At the national level, new demands for domestic services were superimposed upon international commitments which had become truly global, and which imposed then, as later, cruel constraints upon the Federal government's ability or courage to meet new and insistent domestic demands.

Traditionalism and Educational Balkanization

It is conceivable that the American educational system could have weathered the fiscal storms and the winds of change of the postwar period without undue strain, if its own ship had been in order. But it was not. Conservative in outlook and fragmented in structure, the American school system had developed an entrenched neglect of efforts to improve educational productivity. It was both too ponderous and too Balkanized to be regenerative.

Local Autonomy. In a legal sense, all local authorities are creatures of State governments. But, as already noted, State control over local school districts has been traditionally weak. The basic units of effective control of the American public schools have generally been the local school boards, even when these boards have been fiscally dependent upon general units of local governments. The basic organizational unit has been the local school district. In 1947–48, America was pock-marked with more than 90,000 separate school districts, most of them tiny.

Most authorities agree that small school districts (less than 6,000 pupils) are unable, because of size and lack of facilities, to provide an adequate educational program. In the small districts, inadequate funding is accompanied by inadequate organization, staffing, leadership, and community involvement. As McClure has stated:

> A modern school requires more than a principal and a coterie of teachers for full-time instruction, augmented by a complement of

18. Philip Meranto, *The Politics of Federal Aid to Education in 1965: A Study in Political Innovation* ("Education in Large Cities Series" [Syracuse: Syracuse University Press, 1967]), 20–28. For more detailed studies of growing metropolitanism and city schools see other volumes of "Education in Large Cities Series" under the general auspices of Alan K. Campbell and Seymour Sacks (Syracuse: Syracuse University Press, 1967–68). See also Alan K. Campbell and Seymour Sacks, *Metropolitan America: Fiscal Patterns and Governmental Systems* (Glencoe: The Free Press, 1967).

> custodians, cooks, and bus drivers; an adequately organized school system requires more than a school or a mere organization of schools. It requires additional staff who supplement and integrate the leadership of the schools into a system which can use professional skills and the potential of the community most effectively.[19]

The historic Balkanization of the American school system into tens of thousands of districts—most of them of a patently inefficient size—was unlikely to produce talents and economies of a scale relevant to the educational demands of the postwar years. Little scope was afforded for innovative activities, and almost none for project-planning aimed at external sources of aid. And even though a combination of state-mandated reorganization laws, financial incentives, and increased pupil mobility (buses and autos) produced a rapid consolidation of school districts from 1950 on, 25,000 separate districts still existed in 1965, and almost half of the nation's pupils were still in districts enrolling less than 6,000.

At the State level, not more than a half dozen State educational agencies had either the resources, the leadership, or the quality of staff needed to give spirited direction to grass roots educational improvement for meeting the extraordinary demands of the postwar years.

Fiscal Disparities. The scatteration of local school districts had for generations produced glaring financial, and consequently educational, inequities. As long as schools were almost entirely supported from a local property tax base, the quality of education tended to vary in direct proportion to the availability of local tax revenues. Even though States increased their percentage contribution to local school districts from 30 per cent in 1940 to 40 per cent in 1964,[20] and in the process evened out some of the more glaring intra-state financial disparities, grim differences in school-district revenues continued to exist. Urban school districts were almost consistently short-changed in State allocation formulae —a morbid manifestation of mal-apportioned and rurally dominated State legislatures. Some State equalization grants have been so low that differences in local fiscal capacity have produced mammoth differences in per pupil expenditures from one district to another. Finally, of course, economic disparities *among* the several States have produced egregious educational inequities in the nation as a whole. In the school year 1959–

19. William P. McClure and Van Miller, *Government of Public Education for Adequate Policy Making* (Urbana: Bureau of Educational Research, College of Education, University of Illinois, 1960), 33. See also Charles S. Benson, *The Cheerful Prospect* (Boston: Houghton Mifflin, 1965).

20. *Estimates of School Statistics,* Research Report, National Education Association, Research Division, 1964–R17, 15.

60, for example, one State spent as little as $3,645 per classroom unit, while another spent $12,215.[21]

Roald F. Campbell has summarized the reasons for the disparities in provision of resources for schools: (1) the relative wealth of States and localities; (2) their differential access to funds due to statutory restrictions [e.g., local or State limitations on taxing power and bonded indebtedness]; and (3) variations in the level of aspiration of different sectors of the population.[22] Such factors are deeply imbedded in the American social structure and economy. In the postwar years, the persistence of a large degree of disparity in local economic resources, educational requirements, and tax effort, was another indication of the gap which existed between new educational demands on the one hand and the capacity of the educational system to respond effectively and equitably to them.

Non-Fiscal Consequences of Traditional Autonomies. The traditional autonomies in the American educational system had other than fiscal consequences. They made it difficult if not impossible, for example, for school districts and for the several States to cooperate among themselves, or to relate educational programs and policies to other human resource questions in such fields as health, welfare, housing, and recreation—especially in large urban agglomerations. Linkages with such cognate problems would involve compromising the traditional independence of education in the political and governmental systems. In the postwar years, emerging social needs cried out for coordinated governmental planning, but American education was largely deaf to the cries.

Even within the educational systems narrowly conceived, functional autonomies—often tied to categorical grants from the States and the Federal government in such fields as vocational education or education for the handicapped— set up a variety of internal tensions within State and local educational agencies, and made it difficult if not impossible for these agencies to develop goals and plans for education as a whole, even within their own jurisdictions.

Interest Groups and Federal Aid to Education

The highly decentralized character of American education, and its accompanying ethos of local control, were reflected in the postwar years

21. *State Variations in Support of Public Schools,* U.S. Department of Health, Education and Welfare (Washington: U.S. Government Printing Office, May, 1965), 5. *Syracuse Post Standard,* September 8, 1967: In terms of per pupil expenditure in 1966, New York paid out $912 for each student in average daily attendance while Mississippi—the national low—paid out $315.

22. Roald F. Campbell, Luverne L. Cunningham, Roderick F. McPhee, *The Organization and Control of American Schools* (Columbus: C. E. Merrill, 1965).

in the nature and philosophy of education's major professional associations and interest groups.

By far the largest of the interest groups is the National Education Association, founded in 1857.[23] With a million members, both teachers and administrators, NEA is both a national membership association and a loose confederation of State and local affiliates, variously active in their respective areas and supporting an elaborate overhead structure of divisions, committees, and commissions to serve educational specialists and to formulate general policy positions. The NEA national headquarters at 1201 Sixteenth Street, N.W., Washington, D. C., serves as a voice for its national membership and as a vast holding company for the Association's constituent divisions. Some of these divisions or departments are organized by educational level: elementary, secondary, higher. Others are organized by function: administration, teaching, research. Still others are organized by subject matter: social studies, science, English, mathematics.

The striking thing about NEA is the virtual autonomy of its constituent parts. The American Association of School Administrators (hereafter AASA), for example, serves the interests of more than 12,000 local superintendents. It is patent that the views of these administrators cannot be identical with those of NEA's teachers. The interests of the Association of Higher Education have little in common with those of the Department of Elementary School Principals.

And yet NEA is a single system. It does take positions on national educational policy through its mammoth representative assembly of over 6,000 delegates who give voice to the common interests of a highly diverse constituency. Until recently, the policy agenda was set by the interaction of a semi-autonomous Educational Policies Commission, a Legislative Commission, and the top layers of NEA's formal structure: a Board of Directors and an 11-man Executive Committee. NEA's Executive Secretary serves as the top administrative coordinator of this far-flung empire. Communications are maintained through a variety of publications, the most important of which is the *NEA Journal* published monthly.

Ever since the end of World War I, NEA had pressed—at least intermittently—for Federal aid to schools. In the post-World-War-II years, NEA's philosophy on Federal aid to education was marked by two attitudes: first, Federal aid should be general rather than categorical—leaving decisions on specific resource allocations to State and local edu-

23. Although it forms the largest lobby, NEA is not the most powerful interest group. The vocational education lobby, the audio-visual lobby, the publisher's lobby, and the library lobby have been, in their respective fields, more effective forces in shaping Federal educational legislation than has NEA.

cational agencies; second, no Federal aid should be given to parochial schools. On these two positions, NEA found itself in general harmony with America's other major educational groups: its militant rival, the American Federation of Teachers; the Council of Chief State School Officers (hereafter CCSSO); the National School Boards Association (hereafter NSBA); and the National Congress of Parents and Teachers (hereafter PTA). Each of these national educational groups reflected the concerns of highly dispersed, decentralized, and often internally divided constituencies. Over-all agreement on general Federal aid for public schools actually hid a series of disputes on questions of amount, timing, distribution formulae, and locus of effective decisions on detailed resource allocation questions. The ponderousness and the internal divisions within education's major professional associations weakened their capacity to press their case for Federal aid even though they enjoyed, on the church-state issue, the support of powerful organizations like the National Council of Churches, the American Jewish Congress, and Protestants and Other Americans United for the Separation of Church and State (hereafter POAU).

In fairness, however, it is necessary to point out that they faced a phalanx of outside opposition which would have been formidable even if the education groups themselves had been internally united. Opposed to any NEA-type Federal aid were the U.S. Chamber of Commerce, the National Association of Manufacturers, and the American Farm Bureau Federation, who were generally against additional Federal spending for general welfare purposes. More serious was the opposition of the National Catholic Welfare Conference (hereafter NCWC), the powerful legislative voice of the American bishops, and the related organization, the National Catholic Education Association (hereafter NCEA). NCWC took the simple position that no substantial Federal aid to education, general or categorical, should be supported unless it included aid to parochial school children.

These opposition groups enjoyed at least tacit support from a substantial number of Congressmen who feared that general aid, especially for teachers' salaries, would open Congress to annual lobbying campaigns by teachers' associations and teachers' unions similar in intensity to those mounted by postal employees. They feared that each Congressman would be subject to a continuing barrage of letters and telegrams from teachers in his district—letters and telegrams stating or implying that unless the Congressman voted for additional aid for teachers' salaries he had better not count on teachers' support at the next election.[24]

24. A variety of other interest groups have taken positions in favor of, or in opposition to, Federal aid to education: e.g., The National Farmers Union and the

The policy confrontation symbolized by the NEA and the NCWC was, as we shall note later on, the most serious contretemps in the whole field of Federal aid to education in the late 1950's and early 1960's. As the postwar years continued, a direct clash became inevitable and, in fact, occurred. At this point it is important only to note that the rival positions made an early and substantial Federal response to new educational demands effectively impossible. Adequate resources to meet the postwar needs of education were certainly delayed, and in part denied, because of this extended feud between major interest groups. To many, the feud was particularly maddening because the rising levels of national productivity were giving both the reality and the promise of substantially increased Federal revenues. If the feud could be overcome, some of these new revenues could obviously be used to assist State and local educational agencies in meeting the accumulated educational demands of the postwar years. Resources were limited and inadequate in part because of a family squabble within education itself—a squabble which left the cover to the Federal "cookie jar" largely undisturbed.

The Old United States Office of Education

Even if the stars had been propitious during the postwar years for a dramatic response of the Federal government to the new educational demands, there would have been a serious question about the administrative capacity of the U.S. Office of Education to adjust imaginatively and effectively to its vast new educational responsibilities. USOE had lived most of its life since 1867 as a stepchild of other Federal departments and agencies—notably the Department of the Interior and HEW's forerunner, the Federal Security Agency—dominated by non-educational concerns. Until the late 1950's, limited largely to the collection and dissemination of educational statistics, and to technical consultancies, the Office was almost entirely service-oriented rather than operations-oriented. Even USOE's statistical services were limited in scope. The U.S. Bureau of the Budget, for example, never approved USOE budget items for statistical data on teachers' salaries. Such data as existed on teachers' salaries was compiled by NEA. Aside from grants-in-aid for vocational education and to Land Grant Colleges under automatic, non-discretionary formulas, USOE managed next to nothing. It had few friends apart from the National Education Association, the American

American Veterans Committee, in favor; the American Legion, and the DAR, in opposition. For a fuller array and the interesting history of switches in alignment over the last few decades, see Philip Meranto, *op. cit.,* 52–55. In the case of ESEA, the important actors symbolically and actually were the NEA and the NCWC.

Association of School Administrators and the Council of Chief State School Officers, whose Washington staffs and whose constituencies found the statistical and advisory services of USOE of direct value. There was at least some validity to the widely-held assumption that USOE was, in fact, the "kept" Federal agent of these major private educational associations.

Over the decades, Congress had virtually ignored USOE—occasionally criticizing it for "meddling" if it showed initiative; for ineptitude if it did not. Financially it was starved; administratively it was victimized. As Kursh has written, ". . . for years after its creation, the Office was held in such low esteem that it was continually pressed to find adequate if not permanent office space for staff, facilities, and a growing library." [25] John Eaton, the Second Commissioner of Education, recalled the administrative indignities and harassments of the early years in the following words:

> When I first went into that office [a rented building on G Street, N.W.], we had two rooms and then we were driven out of that building into another and another and back to where the office is at present, and then not allowed all of that small building. Go there today and see how . . . the books of the library have to be put in rooms where work is going on all the time. It has been said that there is not interest enough in education in the United States to furnish that office a proper home, a proper working plan and proper means.[26]

Commissioners were chronically underpaid. The first Commissioner, Henry Barnard, actually suffered the indignity of having his salary reduced by $1,000 his second year in office. As late as 1948, Commissioner John Studebaker resigned partly because he could not afford to live in Washington any longer. Actually, the total appropriation for the United States Office of Education did not reach the $1 million mark until the 1930's, and even then three quarters of this amount was specifically awarded for educating Eskimos in Alaska. Even when vast new responsibilities were added to the work of the Office in the 1950's, and its visibility was increased by the word *Education* appearing in the title of its new departmental home (HEW, 1953), it received inadequate authorizations and appropriations for staff and for effective program management. Commissioner Sterling M. McMurrin commented in his farewell speech on September 8, 1962, "I feel that very often Congress

25. Harry Kursh, *The United States Office of Education* (Philadelphia: Chilton Co., 1965), 13.
26. *Ibid.*, 14.

is inclined to withhold funds from the Office of Education, those very resources that are necessary to make it possible for the Office of Education to do the things that Congress rightly expects of it." [27]

It is not surprising, in view of this history, that well into Francis Keppel's incumbency as Commissioner in the early 1960's, USOE was marked by a number of institutional characteristics which branded it an "old line" bureau.[28] (These characteristics will be more fully explained in Chapter III.) It is only necessary to comment at this point that during most of the postwar period, USOE was both a symbol and a manifestation of the general inadequacy of the American educational system, and was an added reason why that system found it so difficult to respond effectively to new and insistent educational demands.

Expediential Responses

The irresistible force of new educational demands was not exactly stopped by the immovable object of limited and inadequate resources—for the latter turned out not to be totally immovable. But the irresistible force was enormously slowed, and in the two decades following World War II the gap between need and response was, if anything, widened. It is true that local and State property taxes turned out to be more elastic than taxpayers' leagues were wont to admit; local and State revenues for educational purposes grew dramatically. But the fact remains that the pace had to be forced just to keep the educational system from falling impossibly behind. Needed educational investment continued to be deferred. Expensive remedial work for educationally disadvantaged children was finessed in favor of preserving as much as possible in the way of quality services for the population of school achievers.

At the national level, a few developments occurred incrementally in the late 1940's, notably the GI Bill and the creation of the National Science Foundation (hereafter NSF). Although addressed largely to the needs of

27. *Ibid.*, 22.

28. For critical descriptions of these inadequacies, note especially *Federal Relations to Education,* National Advisory Committee on Education (Washington: U.S. Government Printing Office, 1931); *The Federal Government and Education,* U.S. Advisory Committee on Education (Washington: U.S. Government Printing Office, 1938); *Staff Study Number 2,* U.S. Advisory Committee on Education (Washington: U.S. Government Printing Office, 1938–39); *Research—A National Resource,* U.S. National Resources Planning Board (Washington: U.S. Government Printing Office, 1938–41); Francis S. Chase, *Report on Administrative Survey of the U.S. Office of Education of the Federal Security Agency* (Chicago: Public Administration Service, 1950); and *A Federal Education Agency for the Future,* U.S. Office of Education, Committee on Mission and Organization (Washington: U.S. Government Printing Office, 1961).

higher education, these provided spin-offs for elementary and secondary education in terms of teacher training and/or support for curricular revisions—especially in the sciences. And NSF was a harbinger of later Federal programs addressed directly to the support of educational research.

A Federal program was passed in 1950, solidifying World War II legislation that was passed to provide financial aid to school districts impacted by Federal defense plants and other Federal establishments. These plants and establishments were tax exempt, yet they inevitably involved a substantial increase in the local labor force and in the need for schools for the children of federally sponsored workers. Aid to impacted areas followed the NEA formula, i.e., it was general aid for school construction and operating expenses and it was for public schools only. But it affected only a tenth of the nation's school districts. Nonetheless, it became a politically powerful and untouchable program, with bipartisan support.

In 1954, a Cooperative Research Act was passed which ultimately funnelled modest grants into educational research.

Following the dramatic orbiting of Sputnik by the Russians in the fall of 1957, Congress, with presidential backing, passed the National Defense Education Act of 1958. The Act provided for substantial Federal support to secondary-school and higher-education programs to increase the quantity and quality of scientists, engineers, and foreign-language specialists throughout the American educational system. It established fellowships and supported curricula-revision aimed at a major transformation of defense-related aspects of the American educational system. It also provided for student loans, guidance counseling, grants for audio-visual aid and for various additional types of technical assistance. Although NDEA was later criticized for warping the educational curriculum away from the humanities and the social studies, it was nonetheless an important harbinger of the kinds of Federal support for American education that blossomed in the mid-1960's. It was categorical aid; it affected both secondary and higher education; it was substantial in the volume of funding; some of its titles included religious affiliated institutions among NDEA's beneficiaries; and it proclaimed that education was a matter of national concern. But it was still a far cry from general Federal aid for the nation's elementary and secondary schools. And even within its own limited domain, the Act tended to strengthen superior and wealthier secondary schools that had the staff, the equipment, the matching funds, and the students to profit from marginal infusions of Federal money for science, mathematics, and foreign languages. Poorer schools in the countryside and in the urban ghettos were left largely untouched. Like the renewals of impacted area legislation, extensions of NDEA went forward with almost no effect upon the substantive concerns of those seeking some answer to education's general need for massive Federal support.

It is true, of course, that in the late 1940's and in the 1950's, general school aid bills were introduced every session of congress—as they had been since the 1880's. Some of them, like Senator Lister Hill's attempts to earmark for education the royalties from off-shore oil, were highly imaginative. But all of them foundered on the three "R's" of Race, Religion, and Reds (Federal control). Even before he became President, Dwight Eisenhower had gone on record as opposing ". . . any grant by the federal government to all states in the Union for educational purposes." He warned ". . . unless we are careful even the great and necessary educational processes in our country will become yet another vehicle by which the believers in paternalism, if not outright socialism, will gain still additional power for the central government." [29] As President, aside from promoting national conferences and surveys, and a few abortive and complicated bills for underwriting school bonds for construction purposes (dubbed by Democratic opponents as "banker bills"), Eisenhower's hostility to ". . . the simple remedy of federal intervention" was an added blanket to the fires of national concern.[30] In the decade of the 1950's, the Cooperative Research Act and NDEA were the national government's only significant legislative contributions to the cause of Federal aid to education; and in both cases, the President's leadership was minimal.[31] General education bills sponsored in Congress faced the threat of Presidential veto, and were in any case cut to pieces by conflicts over the church-state issue and by controversies over desegregation amendments added regularly in the late 1950's and early 1960's by Representative Adam Clayton Powell.[32] A school construction bill

29. As quoted in *Congress and the Nation 1945–64* (Washington: Congressional Quarterly Service, 1965), 1203.

30. *Ibid.*, 1206.

31. In fairness, tribute should be paid to Secretary of HEW, Marion Folsom, and to President Eisenhower for their sponsorship of the first major White House Conference on Education. This 1956 meeting of national leaders gave voice to increasing national concern about American education and pressed for substantial Federal support.

32. The "Powell Amendment" stipulated that funds appropriated for any Federal aid program could not be used by States engaging in racially discriminatory practices in the administration of such a program. The provision was recurrently offered as an amendment to social legislation. Perversely, it was often supported by conservative opponents of social legislation who knew that attaching the Powell Amendment to a measure would bring solid opposition from the southern bloc, even from those who might otherwise have favored the particular aid program.

almost passed in 1960, but was pigeonholed by the House Rules Committee.

In spite, then, of heroic responses on the part of some States and many thousands of local school districts to keep the nation's educational deficits from getting worse, and in spite of a few innovative responses from the Federal government, America left the decade of the 1950's with a vast educational agenda still unfinished.

POLITICAL INVENTIVENESS AND LEGISLATIVE FORERUNNERS

In the field of Federal school aid, the half-decade 1960–64 was filled with political inventiveness and some major breakthroughs in cognate legislative areas; but it was a period of massive frustration in regard to the central target issue.

The decade began with a presidential campaign which pitted the Eisenhower-Nixon philosophy of indirect aid-for-school-construction-only against the Kennedy-Democratic-congressional philosophy of general aid for both school construction and teachers' salaries. The presidential victory of Senator John F. Kennedy, Democrat of Massachusetts, in November, 1960 presaged the beginning of a struggle whose resolution was ultimately to be the Johnson Administration's triumph of ESEA. But for Kennedy himself, attempts to crack the issues of race, religion, and fear of Federal control with traditional NEA-type legislation were bitterly unsuccessful.

The Kennedy Education Bill of 1961

The struggle peaked early. In what the President called "probably the most important piece of domestic legislation of the year," he asked in early 1961 for grants of $2.3 billion over three years to be used by the States primarily for construction of public elementary and high school classrooms and for boosting public teachers' salaries; and an even greater amount over a five-year period for higher education facilities, and for construction loans and student scholarships to both public and private colleges. The Kennedy school aid bill specifically contained provisions to extend the expiring portions of the impacted areas laws in the hope that the inclusion of this popular program of long standing would swing votes for the new aspects of the legislation.

But under the Kennedy proposal, aid to private elementary and secondary schools was barred, and the Catholic hierarchy issued a pronouncement that unless the public school bill included private school loans, it should be defeated.

It did not, and it was.

The tangled legislative history of the 1961 school aid bill need not detain us here. The story has been extensively reported elsewhere.[33] But the successful forces against the bill were so powerful and pervasive as to make thoughtful analysts predict that no breakthrough in substantial Federal aid to elementary and secondary education would likely occur for years or even decades.[34] These predictions seemed borne out by the fate of similar or extended Kennedy recommendations in 1962 and 1963. In each case, an alliance of Southern Democrats, conservative Republicans, and Catholic congressmen was triumphant. But the fate of the 1962 and 1963 school bills was almost anticlimactic. The bruising struggle and dismal defeat in 1961 dramatized the increasingly obvious reality that if new approaches to Federal aid to schools were not invented, such aid was a dead issue.

To the observant, however, the phoenix of new ideas and directions could be discerned in the very ashes of defeat. These new ideas and directions that emerged over a four year period, can be classified as follows: (1) the shift toward program aid; (2) attempts to improve the quality of education; (3) emphasis on "educationally disadvantaged" children.

Increasingly Categorical Limits on Federal Grants

From 1961 on, there was a gradual shift in Congress from aid proposals for teachers' salaries and school construction under general State administration, to proposals with a specific program emphasis under federally set standards.

The first evidence of this trend is to be found in one part of President Kennedy's 1961 twenty-four-part school and college aid proposal (S.1021). For in addition to calling for a three-year program of $2.3 billion for school construction and teachers' salaries, the bill mandated "special projects" of an experimental or demonstration nature.[35] Ten per cent of the grants was to be reserved for the latter purpose. The abortive struggle for S.1021 presaged some of the issues that had to be

33. Frank J. Munger and Richard F. Fenno, Jr., *National Politics and Federal Aid to Education* (Syracuse: Syracuse University Press, 1961); Robert L. Bendiner, *Obstacle Course on Capitol Hill* (New York: McGraw-Hill, 1964); and Hugh Douglas Price, "Race, Religion, and the Rules Committee: The Kennedy Aid-to-Education Bills," as published in Alan F. Westin, ed., *The Uses of Power* (New York: Harcourt, Brace and World, 1961).

34. Philip Meranto, *The Politics of Federal Aid,* 2.

35. Experience in legislation designed to improve quality in the health and welfare fields may also have been influential.

faced in the drafting of ESEA in 1965. For example, Senator Winston L. Prouty, Republican of Vermont, then as in 1965 a minority member of the education subcommittee, recommended a permissive rather than mandatory 10 per cent allocation for experimental programs, claiming that the State educational agencies needed more freedom. In support of this position, he cited the testimony of Dr. Edgar Fuller, Executive Secretary of the Council of Chief State School Officers. Said Prouty: "People at the grass-roots are more likely to accept Federal aid if they are not bound and gagged by regulations." [36] Senator Joseph S. Clark, Democrat of Pennsylvania, spoke in opposition, expressing the concern that the effect of the Prouty amendment would be to dissipate aid too widely for it to have a major impact. In the House, Representative Carl D. Perkins, Democrat of Kentucky, Chairman of the General Subcommittee of Education, introduced his own version of the Kennedy bill which would have been more restrictive of State distribution of Federal grants, requiring them to allocate funds to local districts with the greatest needs and the least ability to finance them.

The 1962 and 1963 Kennedy education proposals again included aid for experimental programs. The 1962 special-program bill failed to reach the floor in either House. Many of Kennedy's proposals in 1963 for special programs to aid vocational, adult, and higher education; education for the handicapped; and libraries did in fact pass. But aside from extensions of NDEA and impacted areas legislation, nothing of significance happened in the field of aid to general elementary and secondary education. Suffice it to say that by 1964, general Federal aid for teachers' salaries and for school construction had reached a dead end. Emphasis was shifted almost entirely to bills which specified other uses of, and limitations on, Federal grants.

Improving the Quality of Education

Early in the 1962 session, President Kennedy's bill (S.2826) proposed a series of programs which "pin-pointed the basic requirements for upgrading the educational system." [37] The Administration hoped that Congress might pass the "developmental" programs, which closely followed the NDEA model with respect to inclusion of private colleges and schools. Both education subcommittees held hearings, but the two versions of the bill died in the House Rules Committee and in the Senate Education Committee respectively. Nonetheless, several provisions influenced subsequent legislation.

36. *Congressional Record,* May 23, 1961, 8605.
37. S. 2826 and H.R. 10165, 87th Cong., 2nd sess.

Title I of S.2826 called for grants to colleges and universities to conduct institutes for teachers and to upgrade programs for teacher preparation. It also provided scholarships for individual teachers to pursue their study on a full-time basis for a year. Title II provided $50 million annually for grants to State educational agencies to carry on pilot, demonstration, or experimental projects designed "to improve the quality of instruction in public elementary and secondary schools." At least 90 per cent of the funds were to be expended to support local school district activities for this purpose, under plans submitted by them and approved by the State agency. The remaining 10 per cent of the State's allocation could be spent by the State educational agency to assist in its own task of "developing, evaluating, and promoting the broader application of improved instructional practices in such schools." [38] Two types of pilot programs were suggested. These provided precedents for two separate provisions subsequently included in Title I of ESEA:

> (vi) programs or services for adapting curriculums to the needs of deprived or disadvantaged pupils;
>
> (vii) programs for coordinating the school system planning and programming . . . with that of other public and private non-profit agencies dealing with problems related to the alleviation of deteriorated or depressed communities . . . and of the families and children residing therein.[39]

The strengthening of State agencies for these purposes was partially offset by an additional section which amended the Cooperative Research Act. This section extended the authority of the Commissioner of Education to make research contracts directly with local educational agencies (if the State agency concurred) and with other public and non-profit private organizations to pay part of the cost of establishing and operating educational research centers.[40]

As might have been predicted, Monsignor Hochwalt of the National Catholic Welfare Conference approved of the Title I grants and scholarships for which Catholic colleges and parochial school teachers were eligible, and protested the confinement of the Title II grants to public schools. Dr. Fuller of CCSSO took the opposite view on Title I and objected to the enlargement of the discretionary authority of the Commissioner of Education under the provisions of Title II. The witnesses supporting the bill included a number of professors and representatives of organizations interested in educational research. They placed stress

38. *Ibid.*, Sec. 201.
39. *Ibid.*, Sec. 201(c) (1) (B).
40. *Ibid.*, Sec. 202.

on the need to break away from old instructional practices and to utilize research results in the schools. These voices were to be echoed later in testimony defending Titles III and IV of ESEA.

Perhaps the most seminal of the bills for improving the quality of education was introduced by Representative Carl Perkins as "the Elementary and Secondary Education Improvement Act of 1964." [41] This was a massive Federal aid proposal providing $1 billion per year for four years to States in proportion to the numbers of school age children who were members of families having an annual income less than $1,000, leaving to the State agencies the intra-state allocation of funds for the neediest school districts. One of its featured programs was to "meet more effectively the special educational needs of educationally deprived children in slums or similarly depressed urban or rural areas having a particularly high incidence of school drop-outs and having serious problems of youth delinquency and unemployment." [42] The Perkins bill never got off the ground. Its importance lay not in its mentioning low-status children, for these were in large measure simply a device for developing an equalizing allocation formula. The stated goal of the bill was "to strengthen and improve educational quality." Programs specifically targeted on disadvantaged children accounted for only one out of eight very broad categories for allowable expenditures. But the poverty formula for allocations under the Perkins bill was an important harbinger of ESEA.

Concentration on Educationally Disadvantaged Children

President Kennedy's 1963 omnibus education bill included a proposal for general aid, with 10 per cent to 20 per cent of each State's grant requested for educationally deprived children in economically depressed areas and slums. When the bill was split up by Congress, this proposal was dropped. The remainder became: the Higher Education Facilities bill of 1963; an omnibus bill with familiar components such as vocational education, impacted areas aid, and NDEA expansion; and the Library Services and Construction bill of 1964. All three bills emerged from conference-committee deadlock only after Kennedy's assassination. Hearings on the Higher Education Facilities Act are important to our story because they demonstrated the first melding of interest-group opinion before Congress—the first successful fruits of Commissioner Francis Keppel's careful labors to find a common meeting ground between NEA and NCWC on the church-state issue. Furthermore, the

41. H.R. 10253, 88th Cong., 2nd sess.
42. *Ibid.,* Section 6(a) (b).

Higher Education Facilities Act and the remaining parts of the omnibus education bill broke the logjam of educational measures that had piled up for nearly two decades. Educational reformers, both in and out of the government, tasted success; and success begets success. If elementary and secondary education was still caught in an eddy, other big timber had successfully been pried loose and was coursing down the mainstream of legislative enactment and administrative implementation.

The 1964 amendments to NDEA included Federal grants to institutes for the advanced work of teachers in the instruction of disadvantaged children—another relevant precurser to sections of ESEA.

Concurrently (February, 1964) in the Senate, the culturally deprived among the nation's school population became the central focus of a significant legislative proposal spearheaded by Senator Wayne Morse, Democrat of Oregon, and called the Morse-Dent bill.[43] In essence, the Morse-Dent bill attempted to add poverty, welfare payments, and unemployment to the definition of "impaction" in order to enlarge massively the scope of the traditionally popular aid-to-impacted-areas legislation which had been on the books for 15 years and which had resisted both Eisenhower's and Kennedy's efforts at reform. Senator Morse has given the following version of the importance of S.2528 as a major forerunner of ESEA:

> Last year my subcommittee had a brainstorm. We were working on impacted areas legislation. I felt that we neded a new section to this impacted area legislation to provide Federal funds for another type of impact—namely the impact of poverty and deprivation upon youngsters in the low-standard school districts of the country and in rural and urban slums. We talked about it for quite a while as an amendment to the impacted area legislation. Finally we introduced a separate bill.
>
> We didn't think that we had a chance of getting it passed last year, but we felt we could get some hearings. That's how the Morse Bill of last year came into being. Unless you understand this bill and its history, you can't possibly understand Title I of the Perkins-Morse bill (Public Law 89–10).[44]

Senator Morse's description of subsequent events illuminates the tensions (and the forms of gamesmanship) that frequently characterize relations between Congress and the Executive Branch, even when all relevant actors are working for a common goal:

43. S.2528 and H.R.10159, 89th Cong., 2nd sess.
44. As quoted in *School Management,* June, 1965, 87.

I will never forget those hearings last summer. To my astonishment the Administration, speaking through the mouth of the Commissioner of Education, pleaded against the enactment on the grounds that my bill cost too much and on the grounds that there would be administrative difficulties in working out the formula provided.

Now I conduct my hearings in the form of a seminar, with term papers assigned to the Administration witness. So I told the Commissioner, more in sorrow than in anger, that, in my judgment, he had flunked the course. And I made him my emissary to the Administration to tell it, all the way to the top, that they had failed it, too. But I held out hope. I told the Commissioner that he could repeat the course for make-up credit in this session.

Last fall during the signing of the Powell-Morse-Perkins National Defense Education Act Amendments of 1964 (Public Law 88–665), the Commissioner came over to me and said, "Senator, the President wants us to tell you that we are for your bill. We are even going to expand it. We don't know by how much, but we are going to expand it."

The rest is history. Instead of my little $218 million a year bill, they took me at my word and increased it five fold, when they sent up S.370 and H.R.2362 (ESEA). When we talked with the HEW people and the Office of Education people about their bill prior to its introduction last January, we had a great deal of fun with them, pointing out how much time and effort they could have saved themselves. But seriously, the key point consisted in finding a formula which was (1) objective, (2) verifiable from independent sources without too great an investment in personnel, and (3) most importantly, which was based on forerunner legislation which was known to Congress, so that the strawmen such as the myth of Federal control could be laid to rest. This helped us to build a bridge across the chasm which had swallowed up every Federal aid bill since 1947.[45]

Members of the NEA Educational Policies Commission might disagree privately with Senator Morse's version of the origins of the aid formula in S.2528. One official has stated that "the NEA staff, once NEA itself had broken away from its long-standing commitment to general aid only,"[46] came up with the idea that Federal aid could be

45. Excerpts from the comments of Senator Wayne Morse to the American Association of School Administrators, May 13, 1965 (mimeo.).

46. Some observers give credit for this shift after 1963 to the influence of James E. Russell, Executive Secretary of the Educational Policies Commission, who had attempted for years to convince a stubborn NEA leadership that race and religion would continue to stop general aid.

expanded along lines of "impaction" of areas with low employment and poverty, where the national interest was involved, and that the Morse-Dent bill embodied an NEA design. However, interest groups working with congressional brokers are not likely to insist that by-lines be attached to draft legislation. Investigators find it generally impossible to track down a single source of the ideas in legislative proposals; there may be either a multiplicity of claimants, or none at all, depending on the circumstances. It is probably a pretty good indication of the political glamor of ESEA that those who contributed to its formulation are not reluctant to be so identified.

Commissioner Keppel subsequently acknowledged that the administration had learned from S.2528, and had been able to use it as the "essential foundation" for the Title I provisions of ESEA. He graciously overlooked the scolding he had received from Senator Morse and the Senator's slight misrepresentation of the Commissioner's testimony. Keppel did not attempt to publicize his vital role as homogenizer of group interests or as the key catalyst in drafting ESEA. Keppel had, in fact, at no time stated that the S.2528 proposal "would cost too much"; but he had described the many administrative complexities that his office had uncovered in the bill and he had asked for more time to come up with recommendations. He indicated that there were more educational policy decisions involved than getting a bill through Congress: for example, the possibly deleterious effects of requiring a school to seek information on the welfare status of a child, or the employment status of his parents, by means of pupil-parent surveys recommended in the Morse-Dent bill to determine federally-connected employment. And there was the added issue of the ephemeral nature of unemployment data. The interchange between Morse and Keppel at the subcommittee hearings on S.2528 is notable, in retrospect, as much for what was not said as what appears in the record. All present were fully aware that it was not the Administration, but the House of Representatives, which had stalled so long on Federal school aid and that Keppel recognized the lack of viability in grant programs which merely reinforced existing local practices and were unlikely to stimulate change and improvement.

It is impossible to judge how much Morse's pressure on Keppel and on the Administration resulted from earlier inputs of key group interests and of executive branch experts—notably Wilbur Cohen, then Assistant Secretary of HEW and one of Washington's most creative policy innovators. The policymaking maze in Washington is almost infinitely complex. Morse's implied admonition to Keppel, "Bring back something to us next year in this format," was an important but by no means exclusive factor in promoting Title I of ESEA. And in spite of its dedication to the problems of disadvantaged youngsters, the impacted-area type allocation formula would have given fairly general aid to poor school districts without insisting that money be targeted on the educational needs of the disadvantaged within such districts.

COGNATE DEVELOPMENTS

While these various shifts in forces were occurring in the field of school aid, other domestic legislation was being developed and passed in the areas of civil rights and poverty, and precedents were being set for liberalizing Federal aid to church-related institutions. These cognate developments were important antecedents to the emergence of the Elementary and Secondary Education Act of 1965.

Civil Rights

In the Federal legislative arena, civil rights legislation had traditionally been aborted by the southern minority in coalition with northern conservatives. Through seniority, southern conservatives were able to hold key committee positions so that civil rights legislation was pigeonholed in the Senate, in the Judiciary committee, and in the House, in the Rules Committee. And, of course, there was always the ultimate weapon of Senate filibuster; there was an unbroken tradition that no civil rights measure could ever pass this hurdle.

In 1957, however, civil rights laws did start to emerge from Congress. Not all of these acts are pertinent to this study. In fact, only the 1964 Civil Rights Act is directly connected to the present narrative, but the modest developments in civil rights legislation between 1957 and 1964 helped to weaken some of the traditional centers of power and hostility in both the House and the Senate.[47] These modest breakthroughs were abetted in 1963–64 by increased racial demonstrations, the murder of two civil rights marchers, and President Kennedy's recommendation for strong civil rights legislation. One of the sweeping new Kennedy provisions required administrators to cut off Federal grants-in-aid for any State programs administered discriminatorily. This was the heart of the civil rights bill which, under President Johnson, became the powerful Civil Rights Act of 1964;[48] and although the provision applied to discrimination in several fields, it had very special educational consequences. By outlawing discrimination in all federally-aided programs, the Civil Rights Act of 1964 added full presidential and congressional

47. Stephen K. Bailey, *The New Congress* (New York: St. Martins Press, 1966), Ch. V.

48. Public Law 88–352, 88th Cong., 2d sess.

authority to the Supreme Court's school desegregation mandate of 1954. The judicial machinery set in motion by the 1954 Supreme Court decision had largely eliminated *de jure* segregation—at least on paper. But, in fact, much *de jure* segregation continued or was simply replaced by *de facto* segregation. Hopefully, the mobilization of the legal, fiscal, and administrative resources of the Federal government under the 1964 Act would be more effective and quicker than litigation alone. The Attorney General was given authority to intervene in school desegregation suits or to initiate such suits. And a threat of withdrawal of funds from States with discriminatory practices was a powerful weapon—a weapon that became even more powerful as Federal aid to education increased.

One of the most important aspects of the Civil Rights Act of 1964 was the fact that it eliminated the danger of attaching a "Powell Amendment" to each separate education bill. In this sense, the race issue was removed from the political calculus of those supporting or attacking increased Federal aid to education. As we shall have reason to note, the issue of race has continued to affect Federal school aid legislation, but the passage of ESEA in 1965 was testament to the fact that the civil rights issue vis-a-vis education had been at least temporarily blunted by the previous passage of the Civil Rights Act of 1964.

Poverty Legislation

Before the Anti-Poverty Program of the Johnson Administration, a number of laws were passed to up-grade the job skills of the unemployed in the cities and in depressed rural areas. The Area Redevelopment Act of 1961; the Manpower Development and Training Act of 1962 (hereafter MDTA), and its amendments of 1963; the Trade Expansion Act of 1963; the Public Welfare Amendments of 1962; and the Vocational Educational Amendments of 1963 were all geared, in whole or in part, to helping economically-dependent segments of the population become self-supporting through job training and extended vocational education. Since a growing percentage of the nation's unemployed were in fact school drop-outs, the Kennedy legislation had necessary implications for education. At that time, however, there was little admission of the fact that educational failures manifested in adolescent drop-outs were inexorable consequences of educational failures during pre-school and early-school experience.

In his first State of the Union message, President Johnson called for heroic measures to abolish poverty wherever it existed in the United States. Recommendations had been drafted by the President's Task

Force on the War Against Poverty. The resulting Economic Opportunity Act of 1964 (hereafter EOA)[49] created a number of programs such as the Job Corps, the Neighborhood Youth Corps, and Adult Basic Education. Some of these programs were logical extensions of past Federal experiments. Conceptually, however, the Act leapt beyond the goals of vocational education. Its overriding purpose was to mobilize "the human and financial resources of the Nation to combat poverty by opening to everyone opportunity for education and training and opportunity to work." The Office of Economic Opportunity (hereafter OEO), created by the Act, was given independent status and placed directly in the Executive Office of the President with a mandate to carry out a coordinated national effort involving all possible resources, both public and private. OEO, in addition to directly implementing a series of programs, was charged with the responsibility of working through several established agencies responsible for a number of separate anti-poverty programs. At least 15 Federal agencies and 156 separate Federal programs were involved. These programs dealt with education, manpower training, health, welfare, social security, housing, urban renewal, migrants, and economic development.

Given the pluralistic traditions of American life and the vested interests of persons and organizations already working in these undertakings, the problems of such a coordinated enterprise were staggering. However, some new approach was necessary, since the long sequence of uncoordinated, intermittent, palliative measures had largely failed. Innovation as well as agency coordination was patently needed. The appointment of R. Sargent Shriver to head OEO indicated the Johnson Administration's premium on new ideas and energy. Shriver's administration of that novel approach to foreign aid—the Peace Corps—had been highly successful. It was hoped that this success could be duplicated in the domestic field.

The most original, far-reaching, and controversial endeavors of the "War on Poverty" involved the local Community Action Programs (hereafter CAP). Over 600 had been established by early 1966. The CAP's were to be "umbrella agencies," with the role of binding together at the local level the fragmented public and private resources available for fighting poverty. In this experiment, OEO largely bypassed State agencies, making grants directly to the local CAP for projects which seemed promising.

In administering EOA, high priority was given to two policies: the

49. Public Law 88–452, 88th Cong., 2d sess.

CAP's should have personnel, status, and management resources independent of existing public and private community welfare and education programs; and the poor themselves should engage in planning and working to meet their own needs.

It was inevitable that local agencies concerned with these problems, including the public schools, should tangle with the Community Action Programs. Extraordinary preventive measures were taken by OEO and USOE to preclude head-on collisions between the CAP's and the public school systems, but side-swipes have been common. Title I of the Elementary and Secondary Education Act mandated cooperation between the local school agencies and the CAP's. But the mandate itself was to become a source of friction, even though some joint endeavors between USOE and OEO have been highly successful.[50]

The Economic Opportunity Act presaged the Elementary and Secondary Education Act of 1965 in at least two respects: its stress upon the importance of variety and innovation; and its acknowledgement of the special needs of educationally disadvantaged children. And, of course, both acts reflected in turn the influence of scholarly evidence that the handicaps of poverty are translated into educational disadvantage at a very early age, and that those who come to adulthood without adequate schooling will have at best a future of uncertain, unskilled employment and low income. It should also be noted that "the church-state settlement" in Title II of the Economic Opportunity Act provided a strategic precedent for ESEA.

Church-State Relations

The judicial tight-rope walking that marked church-state relations in the post-war years was accompanied by legislative actions and pressure-group détentes that had the effect of liberalizing traditional concepts of appropriate public assistance to church-related institutions. The GI Bill, the National Defense Education Act, the National Science Foundation Act, college housing loans, the National School Lunch Act, and the Hill-Burton Hospital Construction Act all involved Federal assistance to sectarian institutions. And an increasing number of people came to argue that the very fact of tax exemption for religious property, including parochial schools, was a tacit acceptance of the notion that certain kinds of public assistance for parochial schools had in fact been accepted for generations as within the legitimate sanctions of the Constitution. Fur-

50. See, for example, *Education: An Answer to Poverty,* a joint USOE-OEO publication describing school programs eligible for Federal aid.

thermore, in the postwar years, a number of State legislatures and local school systems had authorized the practice of "shared-time"—allowing parochial school children to attend public school classes during certain hours on certain days each week.

With this background of ambiguous judicial sanctions and legislative and administrative permissiveness, it is little wonder that the Catholic church entered the debates on increased Federal aid to education in the early 1960's in a spirit of tough legislative bargaining. Believing that public support for the secular aspects of parochial education was within the spirit and letter of the Constitution, the National Catholic Welfare Conference pressed vigorously for the inclusion of such support in Federal aid legislation. As we have already noted, the NEA and its allies pressed equally hard against such support. More than any other single issue, the church-state controversy precluded the formation of a workable coalition to pass the Kennedy general-aid-to-education bills in 1961 and 1963.

From the ashes of these two defeats there emerged two realities which were to have important effects upon the future of Federal aid: first, a new grasp of political realities on the part of both Catholic [51] and professional public educational associations,[52] and a recognition that intransigencies on both sides had in fact denied children the benefit of extensive Federal resources for education; and second, the realization on the part of key policy makers in Washington that if substantial Federal aid to elementary and secondary education were to emerge, compromises such as those which had insured passage of the 1963 Higher Education Facilities Act would have to be reached between the forces centered in NEA and those centered in the National Catholic Welfare Conference. The environment for such a rapprochement was undoubtedly enhanced by the public admiration for America's first Catholic President, and the shock of his martyrdom.

51. Important in this change was the younger and less tradition-bound leadership brought into NCWC at this time, notably Monsignor (now Bishop) Mark Hurley.

52. In 1962, the defeat of the higher education bill on the floor of the House demonstrated an open split between the ACE and the NEA when the latter publicly opposed the final compromise measure. This open split seemed to shock many in the educational community, and early in 1963 both organizations sought ways to collaborate. The omnibus bill of 1963 was in part designed with the goal of uniting the educators. A gentleman's agreement was developed among the educational associations to support the whole package and not to oppose sections that were unsatisfactory to any particular group. The result of this strategy, which lasted throughout 1963, 1964, and 1965, was to make it exceedingly difficult for opponents to play off one part of the educational constituency against another.

United States Commissioner of Education: Francis Keppel

No one understood the political preconditions of new Federal aid to education better than Francis Keppel who had been brought to Washington as Commissioner of Education by President Kennedy in 1962, and who was quick to absorb the political briefings given to him by experienced hands like Wilbur Cohen, Theodore Sorensen, Lawrence O'Brien, and key interest group leaders. Keppel had, of course, arrived in the nation's capital after the 1961 Federal aid debacle. His major concern was to find a path which would avoid the tangled thicket of race, religion, and fear of Federal control that had combined to defeat the Kennedy proposals (and for that matter, all previous attempts at massive Federal aid to education over the course of a century).

Keppel's assumption of the Commissionership in December, 1962 was itself a harbinger of change and innovation. Unlike most of his predecessors, Keppel had not come out of the public school system. Quick, bright, articulate, Keppel had been Assistant Dean of Harvard College at the age of 23. In his early 30's he had become Dean of the Harvard Graduate School of Education, and through enormous skill and energy had transformed sleepy, institutional mediocrity into a vibrant center of educational innovation. Kennedy called Keppel to Washington charging him to do for the U.S. Office of Education and for Federal educational policy what he had done for the Harvard School of Education. Passionate in his belief that American education could not move dramatically ahead without substantial Federal support, but equally sure that the Federal government should remain a junior partner in the educational enterprise, Keppel devoted his energies to finding a legislative formula that would permit massive Federal assistance of a kind that would at the same time strengthen state and local initiative. A tireless broker, negotiator, and salesman, Keppel became one of the key agents of the new Federal aid. It was he more than any other single person who found the compromises acceptable to both NEA and its allies on the one hand, and to the National Catholic Welfare Conference on the other. His personality and the fact of his incumbency were intimately associated with the creation, passage, and implementation of the Elementary and Secondary Education Act of 1965.

Overview

These were the forces and developments that led to the passage of the Elementary and Secondary Education Act of 1965. Explosive postwar demands; inadequate institutional, human, and financial resources at all levels of government; a series of expediential, if sometimes heroic, responses; and political inventions born of frustration—all of these had combined to set the stage for a new legislative breakthrough. But the breakthrough would be a far cry from the general aid bills, for school construction and teachers' salaries for public schools only, that had dominated the congressional educational agenda during the postwar years.

The legislative logjam in the field of Federal aid to education was effectively broken in 1963, but not in terms of elementary and secondary education. However, educational forces inside the Government and in outside professional groups and interest groups tasted success in such fields as higher education and vocational education. This gave them confidence. But before an effective breakthrough could occur for elementary and secondary education, a political campaign, an election, and patient brokerage among divergent educational innovators and interest groups had to occur.

II. The Enactment of Public Law 89-10

The Democratic landslide in November, 1964 strengthened all of the elements favorable to the early passage of Federal school aid legislation: a President elected in his own right by an overwhelming margin; heavy democratic majorities in both the Senate and the House; experienced chairmen and a predominance of well-disposed members of relevant legislative committees and subcommittees; and a liberalized Rules Committee.

To these factors must be added the strong impetus attributable to the personality, convictions, and abilities of President Johnson. During the campaign in the summer and fall of 1964, he repeatedly stated that improvement of educational quality and opportunity was crucial to the attainment of Great Society objectives. His personal effort to obtain a college education, and his early experience as a school teacher, gave a special authenticity to his strong commitment to education. He could refer to an impressive record of legislative accomplishments during his pre-election tenure, calling the 88th Congress the "Education Congress." Even if some of his electoral support was more anti-Goldwater than pro-Johnson, he had good reason to believe that his statement of Great Society aspirations was in some measure responsive to public demand when he polled 61 per cent of the popular vote, as compared with Kennedy's narrow margin of 50.1 per cent in 1960.

But prior to his election, Johnson had not tackled the toughest educational problem of all: the provision of massive Federal aid to elementary and secondary schools. His election victory removed any necessity to settle for legislation of minimal impact. From the outset it was clear that he intended to oversee the passage of a landmark law and that he was ready to use every personal and official resource to achieve his ambition. To this task he brought an unparalleled combination of personal drive, legislative know-how, and presidential prestige.

The election results also presaged a high order of congressional accomplishment on education legislation. The Senate Democratic membership gained by two, making a partisan split of 68–32; the strength of its liberal wing was assured by the return to office of all of its members who had been "new look" freshmen senators in 1958.

With respect to the issue of Federal aid to schools, the 1964 change in House membership was a crucial factor. The Democrats gained 38 seats, making the division in the House 295–140. Moreover, they traded some conservative seats in the South for some liberal votes elsewhere. This enabled the majority party to curtail the coalition of conservative Southern Democrats and Republicans which had so frequently thwarted the passage of key legislation between 1960 and 1964. Evidence of a new party consensus is the fact that during the 1965 session the freshmen Democratic House members supported the President's program on 82 per cent of the roll-call votes, in comparison to 74 per cent for all their fellow Democrats.[1] At the organization meeting for the 1965 session, the Democrats further trimmed the power of the House Rules Committee, the nemesis of Federal school aid measures, by adopting a rule which permitted the Speaker to by-pass the Committee on bills reported out of legislative committees for three weeks or more.

All experienced and liberal chairmen of the education committees and subcommittees remained in office: Senators Hill and Morse and Representatives Powell, Perkins, and Green. One Democrat was added to both the Senate Committee on Labor and Public Welfare and the House Committee on Education and Labor, making the division 11–5 and 21–10 respectively. Based on an analysis of their 1963 and 1965 voting records in support of, or opposition to, the measures endorsed by the bi-partisan conservative coalition that persisted in both Houses, the membership of the two committees included a high percentage of liberals or moderates and a relatively low percentage of the most conservative members of Congress. Conservatives on the education committees and subcommittees were destined to fight a rear-guard battle, since the friends of Federal school aid had virtually safe majorities.

Preparations for the 1965 legislative session moved into high gear after the November election. With President Johnson's encouragement, the transformation of ideas into programs was carried out rapidly by aides who displayed unusual talent, timing, and teamwork. For ESEA, the process was even more accelerated than for most of the other Great

1. It is interesting to note that while the presidential and congressional election results were key elements in facilitating passage of ESEA, opinion polls reflected little evidence of a specific mandate for the new federal aid to education or for the inclusion of parochial schools in federal education programs. For a collection of poll results and an intelligent discussion of their meaning and shortcomings, see Meranto, *op. cit.*, 43–50. For another view, see Frank J. Munger, "The Politics of Federal Aid to Education," paper, delivered at the 1965 annual meeting of the American Political Science Association.

Society proposals, owing to the previous legislative spadework described in Chapter I and to a priority on the congressional agenda second only to the Appalachia bill. In rough chronological order, the following steps took place in the development of the education bill: (1) preparation of the President's task force proposals; (2) incorporation of the proposals into the President's legislative program; and (3) preparation of draft legislation, budget projections, and Presidential messages.

The Work of the Task Force on Education

On May 22, 1964, at the University of Michigan, President Johnson first spoke of his intention to develop the Great Society program by assembling, in a series of working groups, "the best thought and broadest knowledge from all over the world to find the answers." [2] Budget Director Kermit Gordon, Walter Heller of the Council of Economic Advisors, and Special Presidential Assistants Bill Moyers and Richard Goodwin were assigned responsibility for recruiting 14 task forces, averaging 9 members each, from both government and academic institutions. Each group had an executive secretary drawn, in most cases, from the Bureau of the Budget, and a liaison officer appointed from the White House staff. Task force deliberations began toward the end of June, with completed reports scheduled for November 15. "Problem-status" papers prepared by the Bureau of the Budget were the basis for initial task force discussions.

President Kennedy had also used task forces for program formulation, but President Johnson set distinctive guidelines for the groups appointed in 1964. The Johnson groups were instructed to leave questions of political feasibility to the President and the Cabinet, and to devote task force efforts to generating ideas of real merit. Members were pledged to prepare recommendations without any publicity, since premature release of the task force reports in 1960 had given opponents of the Kennedy program a chance to organize against task force recommendations. Indeed, eighteen months after the Johnson groups had completed their work, neither their reports nor the names of the members had been made public.

The Task Force on Education was composed of 13 members, most of them from outside the government, with William B. Cannon of the Bureau of the Budget as Executive Secretary. Clearly one of the most productive of the Johnson task forces, the education group owed its success primarily to the dynamic, experienced leadership of its chair-

2. William E. Leuchtenberg, "The Genesis of the Great Society," *The Reporter,* April 22, 1966, 36–39.

man, John W. Gardner, then President of the Carnegie Corporation. After a first round of gathering, circulating, and sifting a wide range of ideas from a variety of sources,[3] the group agreed to keep its proposals in the realm of the possible and to limit them to elementary and secondary education. Two criteria were used to judge proposals: their contribution to the equalizing of educational opportunity and their prospects for the improvement of educational quality. Despite the diversity in ideology and temperament of the task force members and the difficulty of the matters they considered, by the time of the third task force meeting (Labor Day, 1964) the group had narrowed its focus to the specific problems that became chapters in the final report drafted by Chairman Gardner.

FORMULATING THE PRESIDENT'S LEGISLATIVE PROGRAM

Upon completion, task force reports were circulated to relevant government agencies for comment, and were then evaluated in the light of general objectives and feasibility by panels of top Federal officials. Presidential Assistant Bill Moyers presided over this review process, meeting with the various panels and consulting with the White House congressional liaison staff. Results of the review were then presented to President Johnson for decision as to whether particular proposals were to be included in the administration's legislative program.

In the case of the education program, the review process was modified and accelerated. Commissioner Keppel, as well as a representative of the National Science Foundation, had been meeting as ex officio members with the Gardner task force.[4] Keppel was concurrently working with HEW and USOE planning staffs on the promise made to Senator

3. In the summer of 1963 the USOE partially underwrote a 2-week seminar on education for the deprived and segregated. This conference, held at Endicott House in Dedham, Mass., reenforced a number of seminal ideas which were beginning to burgeon throughout the country. The Dedham conference proposals may have had a substantial impact on the Gardner task force, most notably in regard to the development of both Titles III and IV. See C. Philip Kearney, *The 1964 Presidential Task Force on Education and the Elementary and Secondary Education Act of 1965,* unpublished Ph.D. dissertation, University of Chicago, 1967.

4. In the welter of forces which produce legislative innovation, it is quite impossible to factor out individual influences. In the case of the Gardner task force, for example, it is difficult to judge its status as an independent variable. Some observers claim that apart from Title III, where the impact of the task force was clear, the main function of the task force was to legitimize the legislative planning already underway in USOE—HEW. In any case, Keppel's role as broker between USOE and the task force was of key significance in keeping these twin efforts consistent.

Morse to look for a way to channel Federal school aid into areas "impacted" with low-income families. At the same time Keppel was consulting with various professional groups and interest groups in an attempt to resolve the issues dividing them—especially the issues of church-state relations and the degree of Federal control. In short, Keppel performed a key role as an intermediary broker of ideas, moving among various arenas: the task force; HEW and USOE planning staffs; the White House; the Congress; the Press; professional associations, and interest groups. One of his principal staff aides paid him a tribute by saying, "Who else could possibly have been a bridge between Gardner and Morse?" And because of this background work, Commissioner Keppel was able to prepare a memorandum immediately upon completion of the task force report that translated the broadly worded task force thinking into a package of specific legislative proposals.

Other officials who had become involved in the deliberations of the new Federal aid to education program included: Douglass Cater, a Presidential assistant and speech writer, who became the focal point in the White House for overseeing the education program; Wayne Reed, Deputy Commissioner of Education; Philip H. des Marais, Deputy Assistant Secretary of HEW; and two principal staff members of the Bureau of the Budget: Michael S. March, Assistant Chief of the Education, Manpower, and Science Division, and Emerson J. Elliott, the Budget Examiner for HEW education programs. Keppel continued to consult with HEW Assistant Secretary (later Under Secretary), Wilbur Cohen. This was not only because of the latter's extraordinary experience in the formulation of social legislation over three decades; it was also an expression of Keppel's determination to bring the Office of Education into the HEW team in order to get its help and protection. Samuel Halperin took over as Keppel's principal aide on legislative development and liaison late in 1964, when Peter Muirhead moved into full-time direction of USOE's Bureau of Higher Education. The various persons responsible for formulating ESEA had a common task, but differing vantage points within the bureaucracy. All worked intensively on the new legislation during the fall of 1964 and the early winter of 1965.

In November, 1964, President Johnson held preliminary talks at his ranch with each member of his Cabinet. The President personally read the task force reports, and soon after the Thanksgiving weekend met with Secretaries Celebrezze and Wirtz, HEW Assistant Secretary Cohen, Commissioner Keppel, Bill Moyers, and William Cannon who, by this time, had become Chief of the Education, Manpower, and Science Division of the Bureau of the Budget. The President approved the tentative plans for ESEA and instructed his legislative staff to start the necessary legislative and budget preparations. The target dates became January 4, 1965 for the State of the Union Message, January 12 for the President's special message on education and for recommended bill drafts, and January 25 for the budget submission to Congress.[5]

PREPARATION OF DRAFT LEGISLATION, BUDGET PROJECTIONS, AND PRESIDENTIAL MESSAGES

At the White House level, steps were taken to give the President's Great Society program maximum exposure and impact. For the first time, the State of the Union address was delivered to Congress at a prime television hour. In a series of one-sentence proposals, the message outlined the entire Great Society package, and in subsequent weeks special messages with accompanying bill drafts gave substance to each State of the Union proposal, all carefully dovetailed with the summary program and budgetary documents. The education message was the second in this series of messages delivered in such rapid succession that they were called "a drumbeat summons" to congressional action.

This multiplicity of new programs complicated the process of budgetary preparation in 1964. Midway in Fiscal Year 1965 (hereafter FY'65) the level of Federal expenditure was running at $97.2 billion. It was clear that substantial additional costs of the Johnson programs already enacted in that year would have to be budgeted in FY'66 in addition to the new programs not yet authorized and priced. Yet the President had worked hard to establish the public image of a frugal man. If he recommended a greatly expanded budget, the business community which he had won to his support would consider him a turncoat. On November 8, the *New York Times* reported that the President's instructions were to keep the FY'66 figure under $100 billion. Three weeks later he stated in a press conference that there was nothing magical in this round figure, and that urgent program needs would likely push the budget total above it.[6]

When the updated agency estimates were collated during December and totalled some $108 billion, President Johnson set in motion a round of cabinet-level negotiations that eventuated in a final budget figure of $99.7 billion. Reductions in the budgets of Agriculture, Defense, and the Agency for International Development (hereafter AID), plus money obtained through the increase in social security taxes and anticipated

5. The budget is normally due by January 19, but was postponed by Congress in 1964 at the President's request because of his added duties in connection with the inauguration on January 20.

6. *New York Times,* November 29, 1964.

revenues from the continued expansion of the economy, were allocated to the new programs.

The amount of money available, however, was limited when measured against the President's visionary objectives. Economic and political considerations as well as existing programmatic requirements had been factors in the decisions made on the recommended level of appropriations, and the *New York Times* concluded, "the expenditure problems were as much psychological and political as economic." [7]

In ESEA the appropriation for Title I was set at more than $1 billion. This amount, while in line with the Perkins bill of the previous year, was less than the $1.5 billion proposed by the NEA and even more out of line with the wishes of a number of liberal and labor groups who considered even the NEA figure insufficient.[8] Yet $1 billion was several times larger than any previous annual authorization requested for elementary and secondary education in an administration bill, and President Johnson took full advantage of the Federal financing procedures of separating authorization from appropriation estimates which permit the Chief Executive to take credit for initiating a popular program without incurring an immediate backlash of blame for higher costs. While the Administration's total requested authorizations for ESEA grant programs amounted to $1.255 billion, the expenditure estimates were set at less than half that much: $600 million. Similarly, the administration's total authorization requests for all educational programs for FY'66 were $4.03 billion, while expenditure estimates were $2.66 billion. The higher authorization figures served a public relations purpose and established a level of aspiration; the lower expenditure estimates reflected the reality that the new programs would not be in full operation during their entire first year.

Preparations for developing both the authorization and first year budget figures had been initiated in earnest after completion of the task force report, with officials of the Bureau of the Budget, HEW, and USOE working closely together. Initiative for recommended authorizations was carried chiefly by Bureau of the Budget personnel; responsibility for development of administrative budgets to implement the new programs lay primarily with the USOE and HEW fiscal staffs.

Establishment of the Title I formula was the most intricate portion of the budgetary task. It involved finding a combination of factors that

7. *Ibid.,* December 27, 1964.

8. See, for example, testimony of Andrew J. Biemiller, Director, Department of Legislation, AFL-CIO: *Hearings before the General Subcommittee on Education, on Aid to Elementary and Secondary Education,* 89th Cong., 1st. sess., House, 971.

would produce both the desired distribution of funds on a geographical basis and a total grant authorization figure at the $1 billion level. Given the focus of the program on the needs of educationally disadvantaged children, the variables considered relevant were: numbers and locations of school-age children, family income levels, and State average per-pupil expenditures. Various trial combinations of these measures produced a wide range of fiscal effects. The formula adopted used the age levels 5 to 17; a family annual income level of $2000 to define poverty, and indirectly, "educational disadvantage"; and 50 per cent as the "Federal percentage" of the State average per-pupil expenditure figure. The percentage term of the equation is a constant in that it preserves existing interstate variations in school expenditures. However, the choice of the "poverty level" affects the relative numbers of children to be counted in rural and urban areas and in various regions of the country because of wage and cost-of-living differentials. Under the Economic Opportunity Act, a family annual income of less than $3000 is used to define the poverty level. The lower figure of $2000 was adopted for ESEA, partly because of its over-all budgetary effects when combined with the other measures, and partly because there could be little disagreement that a $2000 yearly income identifies the hard core of impoverished families.

Two other ESEA funding provisions, both of which were enacted without controversy, were largely the contribution of the Budget Bureau staff. One was a limitation on the amount to be paid to any school district. The figure arrived at was 30 per cent of the district's budget for the previous year, on the grounds that no more than this increase could be efficiently managed during the initial year of the program. The other, a last-minute addition to the bill, was a plan for "incentive grants" to those school districts that increased their expenditures after the first year of the program.[9]

Explanations of administration planning for ESEA were given by HEW and USOE officials to the top policy staffs of such interest groups as the NEA, CCSSO, and NCWC during December, 1964. It was clear that general aid would remain in the background, but suggestions and opinions were solicited, especially concerning the poverty impaction terms of the Title I formula. Douglass Cater also conducted a round of conferences with interest group representatives at the White House. By the time the President's education program was made public on January 12, the path for ESEA had been effectively smoothed by prior consultation with all relevant groups.

9. No further mention will be made in the book of the "incentive grant" program. It was withdrawn, with great difficulty, by the administration a year later as a technical and policy blunder. Its main effect would have been to help the rich get richer—a goal inconsistent with the basic design of ESEA.

The White House announcement of the special message was skillfully managed. The President briefed the Cabinet on the legislative program for education on January 11th, and the press reported that Cabinet members emerged from the two-hour closed session using expressions like "revolutionary," "exciting," and "exhilarating" to describe what they had heard.[10] A special press conference was held at the White House the next morning, just before the message was sent to Congress. Reporters were told that President Johnson hoped to be known as "the education President." [11]

Immediately after the press briefing at the White House, reporters were invited to an NEA press conference. NEA spokesmen, fresh from a January 9 and 10 meeting of their Legislative Commission concerning ESEA, expressed support of the President's bill, even though some of their members had adopted a "wait and see" attitude.[12] Later that day, Msgr. Hochwalt of NCWC issued a statement favorable to the bill. The astute brokerage of Frank Keppel on the church-state issue had paid off.

The reception of the President's FY'66 budget message on January 25 was quiet and perfunctory. There was not even mild criticism of the proposed expansion of health, education, and welfare expenditures. The President and his aides had been successful in drafting a fiscal plan that accorded with Johnson's own conviction that "the budget should be the area of broadest consensus, not of most partisan controversy." [13] At a time when cutbacks in the previous levels of government spending for certain domestic and international programs could be justified, Johnson displayed a sensitive awareness that public opinion would not demand over-all budget reduction, but would even support a modest degree of expansion, including an unprecedented amount for Federal school aid.

The Politics of Bill Drafting

Problems and Strategies for Building Consensus

Except for minor changes made by the House Committee on Education and Labor, the Act signed by President Johnson on April 11, 1965, was the same document introduced three months earlier. This extraordinarily rapid and cooperative congressional behavior can be attributed largely to factors already described: antecedent Federal school-aid groundwork, the election outcome, and presidential drive. But the drafting strategies for insuring favorable congressional action also played an

10. *New York Times,* January 12, 1965.
11. *Education Digest,* February 1965.
12. *Education USA,* National Education Association, January 14, 1965.
13. *New York Times,* November 20, 1964.

important part in expediting passage of ESEA. Draftsmen in HEW, USOE, the White House, and the Bureau of the Budget devised provisions that all important interest groups accepted in advance, thus circumventing conflict and obviating the need for changes during the enactment stage. What made this form of consensus building possible was the fact that various "inside" participants were conversant with the interest of key individuals and groups: congressional liaison staffs knew the concerns of legislators, committees, and factions; intellectuals on the task-force were aware of the hopes of educational researchers; old line education specialists in USOE were sensitive to the attitudes of state and local administrators and professional organizations; and the staff agencies of the President, on occasion, provided what Neustadt calls the "binding forces" of Federal program planning and fiscal management.[14]

The focus on educational problems was delimited and sharpened by antecedent events and legislative efforts. The attack on racial segregation in the schools was relegated, at least temporarily, to authority under the Civil Rights Act of 1964. Educational activities of great scope and variety had become accepted methods for waging a national war on poverty. The pivotal issues on the legislative agenda remained: (1) the purposes and distribution schemes for Federal school aid funds; (2) the inclusion of parochial school students in federally aided programs; (3) the respective responsibilities of Federal, State, and local authorities; (4) the special problems of the urban schools; (5) the reform and improvement of educational practices.

These issues were negotiated in a pliable interest-group milieu. The wide range of viewpoints and priorities held by important educational interests provided elbow room for those seeking compromise solutions. Proponents of identical positions on one issue were not necessarily in agreement on others, and strong feelings on one or two issues were coupled with relative indifference on others. Although there was a broad area of agreement that Federal school aid should be distributed on a geographical basis with some type of equalization for the areas of lower economic status, differences over the mode of distributing funds cut across all issues and produced a recognizable split between an "old guard" and a "new guard" on matters of educational and administrative policy.

Among the "old guard" were educators with a state and local orientation, including many USOE staff members responsible for the existing grant programs. They favored reliance on a formula enacted by Con-

14. Richard E. Neustadt, in David B. Truman (ed.), *Congress and America's Future* (Englewood Cliffs, N.J.: Prentice-Hall, Inc., 1965), 111–12.

gress that would be automatic in application, preserving intact the structure of intergovernmental responsibilities to which they were accustomed, and restricting funds to programs controlled by professional educators. USOE would serve merely as a conduit through which funds would flow to the State or local agencies, or to both.

On the other hand, reformist groups and individuals regarded such arrangements, even when hedged with categorical program requirements, as likely to reinforce the educational status quo. The "new guard" urged a more aggressive Federal leadership role and favored detailed statutory provisions designed to produce specific, measurable results. The strongest position was taken by the staff of the Bureau of the Budget who had long considered the fragmentation of Federal school aid an inefficient use of public funds. Bureau staff argued that educational programs, like other Federal programs, should be funded and assessed according to their success in achieving explicit goals. Improvements could be expected only when it became possible to finance activities that had demonstrated their productivity, and to eliminate those that had not. Those holding this view doubted that educators would voluntarily apply tight standards and favored federal requirements that would force school people to develop and adhere to measures of program efficiency.

The avant-garde professional and academic educational reformers agreed with fiscal experts that traditional school practices had been uncritically perpetuated. They too favored an injection of research and experimentation and of rational evaluation procedures. But they envisioned more fundamental changes that could not be imposed by Federal fiat. They diagnosed the country's educational system as (1) attuned to middle-class values, (2) unrelated to the equalitarian pressures of the civil rights movement, and (3) ineffective in utilizing the full range of local resources and peer group influences in the educational process. In place of existing schools they advocated, for example, "learning centers" or "educational parks" enrolling large populations of children to provide a wide range of educational, cultural, and scientific services for an entire community.[15] Coincidentally, these more comprehensive school units would provide the means to eliminate neighborhood segregation of pupils by race and social class, and through supplementary offerings, could enrich the educational experience of children who continued to attend religious-connected schools.

The advocates of such far-reaching changes were convinced that lasting inducements to innovation and improvement of educational quality

15. As of this writing the "educational park" notion is being considered by a number of urban school districts, notably New York, Chicago, Pittsburgh, and Syracuse.

had to flow from a variety of sources: local communities, Federal and State governments, universities, and private enterprise, as well as from the education profession itself. They argued that a new breed of educational leaders should be equipped to deal creatively with the interplay of factors affecting education at every level of government.[16] That such men would ultimately require a large measure of local autonomy and fiscal flexibility was acknowledged. In the short run, however, the reformers were willing to agree that Federal grants should be tied to requirements that would promote longer range operational objectives.

The drafters of ESEA, working in this context of multiple counterpressures, were singularly successful in "pre-forming" their bill to anticipate and head off potential opposition. ESEA has been appropriately described by an experienced observer of Federal educational politics as both "subtly drawn" to give something to everyone, and as "forward-leaning" in its policy implications.

A package format of five separate titles for the bill was one of the devices employed by the architects of ESEA to grant a variety of benefits, while denying to each protagonist his full range of demands. At the same time, viewed as a whole, the product was a closely woven tapestry of educational objectives and program proposals that Congress could not greatly alter without a serious impairment of substance or political appeal. It is useful at this point to look closely at the origins, purposes, and consensus-building properties of each of the five titles, as well as at the projected impact of the Act as a whole.[17]

TITLE I—BETTER SCHOOLING FOR EDUCATIONALLY DEPRIVED CHILDREN

Statement of Purpose (Section 201) ". . . to provide financial assistance . . . to local educational agencies serving areas with concentrations of children from low-income families; and to expand and improve their educational programs by various means . . . which contribute particularly to meeting the special educational needs of educationally deprived children."

Amount and Methods of Support (Sections 202 and 205) The Act establishes a three-year program of Federal grants to the States for allocation to school districts. The maximum amount that can be granted to a school district is based on the number of school age children (5–17) from low-income families multiplied by the "Federal percentage" of the State average per pupil expenditure. For FY'66, "low-income" families are those with earnings less than $2,000 annually, and those who receive more than $2,000

16. See Francis Keppel, *The Revolution in American Education* (New York: Harpers, 1966), Chapter IX. See also Allan R. Talbot, "Needed——A New Breed of School Superintendent," *Harpers' Magazine* (February, 1966), 81–87.

17. The full text of Public Law 89–10 is to be found in Appendix A. The following summary refers to the Act itself rather than to the administration's bill as introduced.

in aid to dependent children under the Social Security Act. A "Federal percentage" of 50 per cent is specified. For the two subsequent fiscal years, Congress is to establish the "Federal percentage" and the "low-income" factors to be applied.

Local school districts are required to develop proposals for projects to be funded under their allotments which the State education agencies are to approve under regulations and guidelines established by the U.S. Commissioner of Education. The SEA must weigh such factors as the scope and quality of the proposed project, its promise of success in meeting the needs of educationally deprived children, its provision of services for deprived children attending private schools, and the degree to which the local agency has complied with requirements to establish procedures for evaluating its projects, disseminating information about improved practices, and coordinating its program with any community action program operating under EOA in its district. The SEA must give "assurances" to USOE that it has taken such factors into account.

Title I, accounting for five-sixths of the total funds authorized for ESEA, was the predominant preoccupation of school administrators at all levels, members of Congress, and those involved in Federal fiscal management. Based on the apparent consensus that the use of Federal funds to meet the needs of educationally disadvantaged children was appropriate and urgent, a novel grant provision allocated such funds to states and localities by formula, subject to the approval of specific programs and projects by State authorities. As indicated above, the formula was devised by legislative and statistical technicians of USOE, who tested various quantitative measures of child population, family poverty, and statewide school expenditures by trial-and-error to find a combination both fiscally feasible and politically viable. Wide geographical distribution of funds and a semblance of "general aid" were ensured by counting all school age children in poverty, and by requiring that a school district have only 3 per cent eligible children to qualify for a grant. In order to obviate church-state difficulties and to provide the widest possible national coverage, no matching funds were involved. All payments to the county level were computed on the basis of nationally uniform demographic and economic data, and subcounty allocations for which such data were not available were determined by State officials in accordance with basic criteria set at the Federal level. In the distribution of funds, this procedure left practically no discretion to the individual states, except within counties, but it did assign to them specific project approval. Once the formula was applied, the amounts were assured to each county. School districts were not required to compete with other school districts for funds, as was the case under NDEA and Titles II and III of ESEA.

Census data to measure relative school district Title I need for funds, collected in 1959, were outdated. But their use obviated any need for school officials to base requests for funds on "means test" data obtained by direct inquiry on the income of specific families and students, as under the Morse bill.

The provision for national equalization among school districts on an intrastate, rather than an interstate, basis was a highly significant part of Title I. This provision had a surer appeal for individual Congressmen than forms of Federal aid allocated primarily to the State level, since it *guaranteed* Federal funds to hundreds of communities throughout the country. And, in the eyes of key USOE officials, it tended to put the money where educational quality most needed upgrading. The allocation formula also worked to favor the most urbanized school districts on the one hand, and the most rural school districts on the other. Legislative strategists were not unaware that the effect of the formula tended to revive the Roosevelt coalition of Northern cities and the rural South. The fact that the bulk of ESEA money was to be distributed to two types of school districts with widely dissimilar characteristics and problems was to create administrative headaches for USOE later on. But administrative prescience is not often a marked characteristic of legislative strategists.

Title I established a pattern of intergovernmental relations which gave influence and responsibility to every level—local, state and federal. But it also set limits on that influence. The USOE by-passed the States in determining the initial allocation of grants. State officials had inherent supervisory power over the performance of local officials, but they were constrained in this case by criteria established at the Federal level. Local districts were given access to earmarked funds and latitude in designing programs to meet local conditions, but they remained circumscribed by State supervision.

Not surprisingly, local school administrators endorsed the design of the grant formula in Title I more enthusiastically than they did its program approval requirements, since they could not receive funds until they had submitted acceptable proposals. They inferred that the provision of Section 205 requiring that SEA's review and approve projects to insure appropriateness in "size, scope, and quality" was likely to become a major constraint on their activities, yet they could not readily protest these broad criteria for program approval stated in the Act. This section of Title I exemplifies a common legislative technique for dissipating political opposition in the enactment phase of controversial laws. Congress created an undefined area of administrative discretion for the Commissioner of Education and the States far more extensive than mere supervision of fiscal accountability and probity, and delayed to the implementation stage of Title I the job of dealing with unresolved issues.

Policy architects knew that Section 205 called for a performance that was probably beyond the existing capabilities of most State and local educational agencies. For various reasons, the evaluation mandate, even if ambiguous and ambitious, was considered not only important, but necessary:

> Sec. 205. (a)(5) that effective procedures, including provision for appropriate objective measurements of educational achievement, will be adopted for evaluating at least annually the effectiveness of the programs in meeting the special educational needs of educationally deprived children;

Major proponent of the provision, Senator Robert F. Kennedy, at whose suggestion it was supported by OE and accepted as an amendment at the House Committee stage, regarded it as a protection against the infusion of Title I funds into on-going school programs unlikely to upgrade the achievements of educationally disadvantaged children. Top OE officials, frustrated in attempting to design programs for the educationally deprived without adequate educational data, welcomed the provision.

A politically significant aspect of Title I was the requirement that local schools make special arrangements to include in their projects services for children enrolled in private, non-profit schools. Based on "child-benefit," "shared-services" concepts, the provision of benefits for these students, while not as specific as in Titles II and III, expressed a definite move to conciliate the protagonists of Federal aid for religious-connected education. And to the drafters of ESEA, there seemed more likelihood of developing effective church-state educational cooperation on the local scene than there was in Washington. The requirement that public school officials take into account the needs of educationally disadvantaged children not attending public schools also advanced the reformist objective of improving both public and private education.

In summary, Title I offered an ingenious balance of power among levels of government, an interweaving of specific and ambiguous program parameters, and a mingling of short- and long-range objectives. Even so, its authors concluded that it alone would fully satisfy neither the Administration's policy objectives nor the concerns of all interest groups. In consequence, Title I was supplemented by four additional Titles—grant programs for different purposes with different formats.

Title II—School Library Resources, Textbooks, and Other Instructional Materials

Statement of Purpose (Section 201) . . . "to provide grants for the acquisition of school library resources, textbooks, and other printed and published materials for the use of children and teachers in public and private elementary and secondary schools."

Amounts and Methods of Support (Sections 202 and 203) the Act establishes a five year program of grants to the States, with a total of $100 million authorized for FY'66. Allotments are made to the States on the basis of the number of children enrolled in their public and private schools. Up to 5 per cent of the first year's allotment may be used by the SEA's for administering the State plans, with 3 per cent authorized for this purpose thereafter.

Each State must submit a plan for the operation of its program which conforms to its laws; but the plan must provide (1) for consideration of the relative need of all children and teachers for additional instructional materials, (2) for limiting materials supplied to those which have been approved for use in the public schools, and (3) for their ownership by public authorities.

Where a State cannot legally provide materials for children and teachers in non-public schools, the U.S. Commissioner of Education is empowered to make the same kinds of materials available to them as are provided under Title II to public school students and teachers, paying the costs out of the State's allotment.

Title II represented the major effort of Federal policymakers to win support for ESEA as a whole from the parochial school interests and their congressional friends. The funding was modest, but the authorization can be construed as a concrete expression of the national interest in improved education for all children, and as a precedent for greater Federal aid to those enrolled in church-related schools. As finally enacted, Title II contained strong wording on public control and ownership of all supplementary materials provided. On this basis, the Justice Department asserted that the title did not violate Federal law. But the intent of Title II was clear: children of private, church-related schools were to benefit substantially from Federal funds for education.

The relationship of Title II to State laws and to both Federal and State court decisions was and is unclear. Most State constitutions contain prohibitions on the use of public funds for religious-connected schools. The child-benefit theory has been tested in a few court cases, but the constitutional status of the theory is unresolved. The NEA representatives merely offered the congressional subcommittees the assurance that Title II did not violate the organization's then current position on the separation of church and State in school affairs.[18] The cross-pressures to which educators were subject under this legislation were particularly evident in the experience of the Council of Chief State School Officers.

18. *Hearings Before the General Subcommittee on Education, op. cit.*, House, 274.

Their national spokesman, Dr. Edgar Fuller, reported to the congressional subcommittees that the CCSSO opposed Title II because it provided for an inappropriate expenditure of public funds.[19] Yet with the passage of ESEA, chief state school officers were faced with the task of finding a way under State laws to carry out the title's provisions for aid to non-public school children. Otherwise, the U.S. Commissioner of Education would be empowered to intervene to provide funds directly to local districts. This "escape clause," a concession to the non-public school interests, was regarded by many professional educators and members of Congress as an undesirable extension of Federal authority. It provoked attacks on Title II that were more concerted and determined than opposition offered to the propriety of the proposed program itself.

A few interest groups outside the education profession (e.g., National Council of Churches, Protestants and Other Americans United for the Separation of Church and State, American Civil Liberties Union, Union of American Hebrew Congregations, American Jewish Congress, Unitarian-Universalist Church) also resisted the Title II provisions of residual power to the U.S. Commissioner. Primarily, they feared that the "escape hatch" precedent might encourage parochial school partisans to attempt to liberalize state constitutional prohibitions against church-school aid or to block public school appropriations at the State level in order to force the Federal Government to support programs in which non-public schools could participate.[20] These interest groups also viewed the "child-benefit" theories of aid to parochial school students as a subterfuge that in reality aided the church-related schools by relieving them of the costs of the federally supported activities.[21] Finally, they feared the confusion in the public mind that they felt would result from permitting the Federal government to support activities that State constitutions barred under various provisions relating to the separation of church and state.[22]

Measured politically, however, the interest groups hostile to the pro-parochial school provisions of Title II were far weaker than those in favor.

Title III—Supplementary Educational Centers and Services

Statement of Purpose (Section 301 (a)) . . . "a program for supplementary centers and services, to stimulate and assist in the provision of vitally

19. *Ibid.*, 1126.
20. *Ibid.*, 1690.
21. *Ibid.*, 1507.
22. George R. La Noue, "The Title II Trap," *Phi Delta Kappan* (June, 1966), 503.

needed educational services not available in sufficient quantity or quality, and to stimulate and assist in the development and establishment of exemplary elementary and secondary programs to serve as models for regular school programs."

Amounts and Methods of Support (Sections 302–4) Of the $100 million authorized for the first year of the 5-year program, each State has a basic allocation of $200,000. One-half of the remainder is allocated on the basis of population between the ages of 5 and 17 in each State and the other half on the basis of the state's total population.

Local educational agencies or groups of agencies are to develop program proposals based on their own perceptions of need and interest. Persons or groups broadly representative of the cultural and educational resources of the community must participate in planning and carrying out the programs—for example, State educational agencies, public and non-profit private schools, colleges and universities, regional educational laboratories, libraries, museums, private industry, artistic and musical organizations.[23] An extensive range of activities is permitted. Programs may be relatively small in scope or highly complex, and they may be designed to serve primarily either supplemental or exemplary school purposes.

Applications may be made for either planning or operational grants. Programs may include construction and equipment, and must be submitted exclusively by local educational agencies concurrently to the USOE and the SEA. Final grant awards are made by the former, but only to programs which have been reviewed and approved by the SEA. The programs must be administered or supervised by the LEA and must provide for participation of children in non-public schools whose educational needs are of the type which the program is intended to meet.

More than any other single provision of ESEA, Title III embodied the aspirations and thinking of the educational reformers of the Johnson task force. The draftsmen of ESEA, faced with putting the eloquent and programmatically vague language of the Gardner report into an acceptable legal and administrative format, found this one of their most difficult tasks. The root question was how to promote local educational innovations and special services (even in States with a moribund SEA) while providing for adequate program review and accountability. Would Title III create free-wheeling educational centers impervious to control by the established educational structures at the State level? The dangers were felt to be real, but policy-makers who sought to stimulate educa-

23. The bill as originally drafted would have permitted the making of grants to non-school consortia, thus bypassing formal school systems. The above provisions of the Act, as passed, were the product of negotiations carried out by Samuel Halperin of USOE in consultation with appropriate groups. For instance, the NCWC and members of the Perkins subcommittee were parties to the discussions concerning the non-profit private school provisions.

tional creativity prevailed by retaining in Title III broad flexibility in programming, organization, and funding.

As a result, local communities were to be given an unprecedented opportunity to develop educational centers and services they would not have financed with their own resources. In theory, less wealthy districts were to be aided to carry on innovative activities previously possible only for affluent districts. However, *intra*state allocations of grants were to be determined by Federal officials whose decisions were to be based on programming criteria which might or might not be consistent with the objective of equalizing school district resources. The real standard was quality, not equalization.

The grant approval authority reserved to the USOE was viewed by most State officials as a usurpation of their supervisory responsibilities, in spite of the requirement that applications be submitted to State education agencies for review and recommendations. The church-state issue was also raised vis-à-vis Title III, since it too required that recipients extend supplementary services to eligible non-public school children. In this program, however, the direct channel from the Federal to the local level by-passed State constitutional and statutory constraints.

In spite of pockets of opposition, Title III was inherently attractive to many local school districts, to educationally-minded Congressmen, and to progressive spokesmen across the nation. Not least, it received the wholehearted support of parochial school interests.

Title IV—Educational Research and Training

Statement of Purpose (Sections 401 and 403) . . . "grants to universities and colleges and other public and private agencies, institutions, and organizations and to individuals, for research, surveys, and demonstrations in the field of education . . . for the dissemination of information derived from educational research . . . for the establishment of facilities for conducting educational research, and . . . for developing and strengthening programs for training educational researchers."

Amounts and Methods of Support (Sections 401 and 403) Title IV programs are supported by annual appropriations to USOE under the Cooperative Research Act of 1954, which it amends and extends. In Title IV $100 million is specifically authorized for construction of research facilities over a five-year period, FY'66 to FY'71. Research support under Title IV is provided by grants or by contracts on either a project or program basis, although grants may be made only to non-profit organizations. Proposals are usually originated by applicants and submitted to USOE, which must obtain the advice of specialists concerning the proposals before making awards of grants. (Under subsequent definition, "projects" are generally clearly delineated research activities by individuals directed to solving particular educational problems: "programs" are comprised of the more comprehensive activities of research and development centers (hereafter R & D centers), regional educational laboratories, and educational research training facilities. The research training facilities may distribute funds for fellowships or other forms of support to individual trainees.)

Title IV broadened the authority and resources of USOE to support educational research under the Cooperative Research Act of 1954 (Public Law 83–531). The underlying premise was that education, like agriculture and health, could be improved by pure and applied research. The support of the National Science Foundation over the previous decade evidenced a growing belief that new knowledge was the key to progress in the society generally. A number of leading scholars in education, throughout the country, supported this position. Under the leadership of Francis Ianni, until early 1966, the USOE Acting Associate Commissioner for Research, a base of congressional support for the program had been established. Ianni had asked for authority to use grant as well as contract procedures and to extend the types of recipients eligible to receive research support.[24] These proposals were included in Title IV, which extended contract eligibility to private, profit-making research organizations.

The purposes of the 1954 Act were amplified to emphasize dissemination of research results, training of educational researchers, and the establishment of a national network of two types of research organizations. There were projected an increased number of university-connected R & D centers, like those already in operation. Autonomous regional educational laboratories with close ties to State educational agencies, nearby school districts, institutions of higher education, and Title III supplementary education centers were also authorized. The educational laboratories were the brainchild of Ralph W. Tyler, distinguished educator and member of the Gardner task force. The R & D centers were to concentrate on research on particular educational problems. The laboratories were to engage largely in demonstration and dissemination activities.[25]

As in the case of Title III, State educational officials viewed the development of direct Federal grants to regional research groups and institutions as a form of Federal influence which diluted the leadership responsibilities of the States.

An interesting question is why Title IV was not made a separate bill, or perhaps a section of the Higher Education Act of 1965. Inclusion of the title in ESEA was apparently based on a staff appraisal that if Title

24. See testimony of Samuel Halperin, *Hearings Before the Special Committee on Education, on the U.S. Office of Education,* 89th Cong., 2nd sess., House, 74.

25. For Commissioner Keppel's open-ended plans for these organizations, see *Hearings Before the General Subcommittee on Education, op. cit.,* House, 101.

IV were tied to Title III, it would be more viable politically than as a separate research bill, or as a discrete section of the Higher Education Act. In addition, there was a logical correspondence between the broader research objectives of Title IV and the legislative mandates in Titles I, III, and V. For example, Title I (Sec. 205) required local education agencies to evaluate all projects and to disseminate information about improved educational practices to teachers and administrators—a substantial R & D workload for which the projected regional laboratories would presumably provide consultation and assistance. Furthermore, projects under Title III could presumably be designed to demonstrate the value of innovations developed and tested in Title IV research centers.

TITLE V—STRENGTHENING STATE DEPARTMENTS OF EDUCATION

Statement of Purpose (Section 501) . . . "grants to stimulate and assist States in strengthening the leadership resources of their State educational agencies, and to assist those agencies in the establishment and improvement of programs to identify and meet the educational needs of States."

Amounts and Methods of Support (Sections 501, 502, 503, 505, and 507) A five-year program is established, with $25 million authorized for FY'66 and the authorizations for subsequent years to be set by Congress. The Federal share of expenditures for activities under Title V is set at 100 per cent for FY'66 and '67; thereafter the percentage will range between 67 per cent and 50 per cent.

Of the total annual appropriation, 85 per cent is designated for basic grants to the states, and the remaining 15 per cent for special grants is reserved to the U.S. Commissioner of Education. The State educational agencies are required to submit applications to USOE setting forth how the activities to be financed under the basic grants will implement the basic purposes of Title V. The special grants may be made to the States for experimental projects in developing leadership, or for services that hold promise of contributing to the solution of problems common to State educational agencies. To further intergovernmental cooperation, an exchange of State officials and personnel of USOE is authorized for periods up to two years.

The provision of grants to State educational agencies in Title V was reminiscent of the 1962 Kennedy legislative proposals for upgrading the quality of the country's educational systems. The inclusion of this grant format in ESEA was largely the work of Commissioner Keppel, who believed that State agencies must be helped if they were to play a significant part in the inter-governmental partnership he envisioned for Federal school aid programs.[26] The list of permissible uses for Title V funds in Section 503 was a summary of USOE's conception of what State educa-

26. For Keppel's testimony on the inadequacy of SEA's see *Ibid.*, 121–134.

tion agencies should be doing. However, many of the other architects of Federal educational policy, particularly in the Bureau of the Budget, were less optimistic about the capacity of State agencies to carry out self-reform. The influence of the skeptics was evident in the low level of funding established for the title.

Potential beneficiaries of Title V grants would have welcomed the removal of the requirement for discretionary allocation by the U.S. Commissioner and the provision that state agencies must submit approvable projects proposals to USOE.[27] But State officials did not push strongly for amendments, and the inclusion of Title V in ESEA may well have rendered more palatable to them (and to Edgar Fuller, Executive Secretary of the CCSSO) provisions of other titles which they disliked.

THE "TOTAL LOOK" OF ESEA

In addition to the specific features of each of the ESEA titles, several general provisions of the bill had an important bearing on its acceptance by Congress. These included:

(1) *The Tie-in with Federal Aid to Impacted Areas.* The format of ESEA followed the legislative practice of "pouring new wine into old bottles," combining a popular and familiar type of authorization with a new and more controversial one. Although this strategy had not been effective during the Kennedy Administration, ESEA was written as an amendment to Public Law 874, the "Impacted Areas" law, and was presented as an anti-poverty measure as well as an educational bill.

(2) *Measures Relating to Federal Control.* Title VI of ESEA included a provision that no Federal official could exercise supervision over the curriculum, administration, or personnel of any institution or school system or over the selection of any instructional materials (Section 604). The provision for administrative hearings and for judicial review in Titles I, II, and V, and the participation of advisory panels in Titles I, III, IV, and V further assured protection against Federal control.

In spite of these strictures, other ESEA provisions gave federal officials substantial authority over grant recipients. Federal administrators were guaranteed access to program and fiscal data of State and local agencies to insure adherence to program criteria, to establish eligibility for grants under Titles I, II, III, and V, and to provide for fiscal accountability. Each of these titles provided for broad Federal discretion in prescribing the kinds of reports and records to be required of State and local participating agencies. But at the time of congressional consideration of ESEA, these intrusions loomed less large than the assurances of independence from Federal control featured in Title VI.

27. *Ibid.,* 1122.

(3) *The Church-State Issue.* Section 605 established a general prohibition against payments for religious instruction. This was in addition to the prohibition included in Title IV against research and training in sectarian fields, and the provisions added in the House to Title II restricting ownership and control of instructional materials to public agencies. Inclusion of these provisions propitiated some of those skeptical of the newly authorized dual-enrollment and shared-services procedures for the benefit of parochial school students.

TABLE 1

Policy Areas and Alternatives	Titles of ESEA				
	I	II	III	IV	V
1. *Purposes and Distribution Schemes for Federal School Aid*					
a. Priority in fund distribution based on incidence of educational disadvantage	X	X			
b. Fund distribution primarily based on relative educational workloads		X			X
c. Required matching of Federal funds					X
d. Fund distribution contingent on acceptable program plans	X		X	X	X
2. *Provision of Federal Aid to Parochial School Students*					
a. Inclusion of students in public school programs by use of child-benefit rationale	X	X	X		
b. Consultation between public and private school officials implicit in statutory requirement	X	X	X		
3. *Intergovernmental Responsibilities*					
a. Exclusive program direction by USOE				X	
b. Indirect program supervision by USOE					
(1) by development of guidelines	X		X	X	
(2) by award of grants and contracts			X	X	X
c. Broadened supervisory role for SEA's	X	X	X[28]		X
d. Broadened program planning or leadership role for LEA's	X		X		
4. *Urban School Problems*					
a. Funding provisions favorable to urban areas	X				
5. *Improvement of Educational Practices*					
a. Stimulation of innovative school programs or educational research activities	X	X	X	X	X
b. Statutory requirement to evaluate programs	X				
c. Broadened involvement of local community agencies in educational programs	X		X		

28. Only in some cases.

(4) *The Levels of Funding.* The attribute above all others that quieted the most vocal of ESEA critics was the unprecedented amount of money the Act provided for the nation's schools. It required that State and local education agencies maintain previous levels of spending to be eligible for money under the various titles, thus insuring that Federal funds were a supplement to, not a substitute for, what would otherwise be spent.

ESEA included some provisions long familiar in Federal school aid measures. But taken as a whole it represented a clean break with earlier models characterized by formula-type matching grants made directly to the states with minimal requirements for fiscal accounting. Title I, the core of the measure, showed every aspect of the "new look" which had begun to emerge three years earlier: program controls on project planning and evaluation; provision of fully-funded assistance to groups of children with specified educational needs, including non-public school students; and stimulation of new forms of interorganizational collaboration for supplemental educational activities.

The summary table on page 59 indicates, with respect to the various ESEA titles, the decisions made on the basis of creative compromise by the legislative draftsmen.

ACTIVITIES IN CONGRESS, JANUARY–OCTOBER, 1965

Considerations of Strategy in the Legislative Process

Minority blocs in Congress have a variety of opportunities to delay and amend bills which they oppose, and there are innumerable potential combinations of personal, partisan, and constituent concerns among lawmakers that can be mobilized by determined efforts of a few strategically placed leaders in committees or subcommittees. An important part of the credit for steering ESEA through these shoals must go to its congressional sponsors and managers, who shared, to a remarkable degree, the knowledge of issues and interest groups that had guided draftsmen in the Executive Branch.[29]

Because of the effects of the 1964 elections, both Senator Morse and Representative Perkins were in a stronger position in 1965 than they had been in any previous session since they had become education subcommittee chairmen. But they were faced with two possible threats to the bill: (1) a protracted period of congressional consideration of de-

29. A summary of the legislative progress of ESEA is included in *The Federal Role in Education* (Washington, D.C.: Congressional Quarterly Service, 1965), 34–38. For a full-length study of the legislative politics surrounding ESEA see Meranto, *Aid to Education, op. cit.*

tailed provisions which would permit dissenting factions to rally effective opposition; and (2) widely disparate bills passed by the House and Senate which would necessitate a conference committee and thus risk costly compromise, delay or even defeat. To avoid these dangers, Morse, Perkins, and administration strategists (with key and extensive assists from House Committee Chairman, Adam Clayton Powell), decided to rush the bill through each stage of the legislative process and, once the bill had passed the House, to preclude the possibility of a conference committee. They were armed with a bill pre-formed to neutralize interest group pressures, but their strategy involved the risk of generating opposition within Congress by curtailing normal congressional prerogatives in the law-making process, and by failing to render due respect to the independence of each House.

Proceedings of the House and Senate Committees

Companion bills, S. 370 and H.R. 2362, were introduced by Senator Morse and Representative Perkins on January 12, 1965, the day the President's education message was received on the Hill. In view of the fact that congressional leadership on the key education committees and subcommittees had been virtually ignored during the bill drafting, it was remarkable that their immediate support was forthcoming.[30] An early scheduling of committee hearings was necessary to establish priority for ESEA. Hearings were set to begin on January 22 before the House General Subcommittee on Education, and on January 26 before the Education Subcommittee of the Senate Committee on Labor and Public Welfare. The timetable for the bill was further accelerated by short hearings. In 12 days, the House subcommittee held 10 sessions, with sessions running into evenings and on Saturdays. The eight sessions of the Senate subcommittee were almost as compressed. Since support for the bill by the most influential religious and professional groups had already been publicized, the hearings were relatively routine, but they did include an impressive summary of the broad economic conditions and policy arguments favoring the bill.

Three days after the House hearings were completed, the House subcommittee met to report the bill to the full committee. The six Democratic members approved it, but the three minority party members

30. Keppel, Morse, Carey (Democrat of New York), and Brademas (Democrat of Indiana) had had some private conversations during the gestation period in the fall and early winter of 1964–65, and key staff members of the education committees in both houses were frequently consulted, but most of the key senators and congressmen knew only what they read in the newspapers.

boycotted the meeting to protest the "hasty and superficial" consideration they felt the measure had received.

After seven days of deliberation in executive sessions of the subcommittee and the full committee, the administration bill, with a few changes, was approved by a 23–8 vote of the House committee and was reported on March 8, 1965. The principal amendments served: to require evaluation of the effectiveness of Title I projects; to strengthen the provisions of Titles II and III on the authority of public agencies over parochial school benefits; to count, in the Title I formula, children from families that received more, as well as less, than $2000 in welfare payments; and to increase the authorization for Title V from $10 million to $25 million annually. The committee report included a statement of the minority view of 8 of the 10 Republican committee members. (GOP Representatives Reid and Bell did not join their colleagues in signing the report.) Among the GOP criticisms were: that the Title I formula benefited wealthy areas more than the poorer ones; that money was not concentrated to the best advantage; and that the authority of the Federal government was unduly extended into local school district affairs.

The House report,[31] characterized by one of the legislative staff members as "a masterpiece of fuzzing-over the ticklish areas of controversy," was written primarily by USOE and Representative Perkins' staff. It did, however, incorporate much Senate thinking; and this may have been a factor in precluding the need for a conference committee. During the period of House consideration, the Senate subcommittee suspended all outward signs of activity.

The House committee version of H.R. 2362 was referred to the House Rules Committee, which sets the order for floor consideration of bills and the conditions for their debate. Four days of hearings were held, with testimony from both the proponents and opponents of the bill on the House Education Committee. Since the powers of the Rules Committee had been curtailed, it was not likely that it would fail to grant a rule. Representative Delaney, whose earlier vote against the Kennedy Administration bill had been decisive, announced that he would support ESEA if its provisions for non-public school children were not amended. While the bill was before the Rules Committee, the United States Chamber of Commerce, which had not appeared at the subcommittee hearings on H.R. 2362, distributed to all House members a 10-page statement attacking ESEA, incorporating many of the criticisms made by the minority members of the House Education and Labor Committee. The Counsel for the House General Subcommittee prepared a detailed rebuttal for distribution in Congress and to the press, and later stated

31. House, *Report No. 143,* 89th Cong., 2d sess.

that he doubted that the Chamber's "delayed bomb" technique had any significant influence on subsequent House action.

After the House approved the Education Committee version of the bill on March 26, the action shifted to the Senate Education Subcommittee and its parent Labor and Public Welfare Committee. The President had endorsed the efforts of the congressional leadership to avoid a conference on the House bill, and Senator Morse undertook the delicate task of persuading his committee colleagues to report H.R. 2362 intact to the Senate. His basic argument was that the House might not muster a majority to pass a version of the bill that would fully satisfy the Senate and might refuse to work out differences in conference. Whether this fear was really justified in the 89th Congress or not, the Senate committee members who had fought for Federal school aid could not easily forget that they had repeatedly been frustrated by the past recalcitrance of the House. They acted quickly, and by unanimous vote reported H.R. 2362 to the Senate on April 2. Minority views were submitted, however, by all five Republican members of the full committee, and individual views by three of the five.

Some vigorous behind-the-scenes activity preceded this overt decision to inhibit Senate prerogatives to rewrite or amend the bill. Committee discussions were held in executive session. Much, however, may be inferred from a careful reading of the Senate *Report,* which was liberally cribbed from its House counterpart. The report became the device employed to put a Senate and even a bi-partisan imprint on the proposed legislation. As an adjunct to the statutes, committee reports, along with hearings and floor debates, are an important resource for officials of the Executive Branch, and for the courts, in interpreting legislative intent. The strategy of curtailed debate and the speed of pressing ESEA through the legislative process greatly restricted normal modes of congressional expression. The committee report became, therefore, an indispensable and unusually significant means whereby the Senate exerted influence on future policy.

The format and content of the House and Senate reports on ESEA were largely identical. However, throughout the Senate document there were several additional subsections and interpolations of commentary. That divergencies within the committee were not drawn entirely along partisan lines is indicated by a number of references to the concerns of the Democratic majority on the committee. It is evident that two kinds of tactical moves were made to counter the objections of various members to the House bill and to fend off amendments to it: first, officials of the Executive Branch were asked to supply interpretations of several specific provisions of each title, except Title III. These interpretations would constitute commitments for future administrative practice. An example is to be found in a memorandum from Assistant Secretary Cohen of HEW and Commissioner Keppel responding to questions raised by Senators Javits and Prouty. Specifically, physically handicapped children are stated to be eligible for benefits under the terms "educationally disadvantaged" and "handicapped" in the bill. This departmental interpretation represented a decided shift from previous policy. Previously, services for these children had been considered under specific rather than general categories of "educationally disadvantaged." "Handicapped" was designed to please a number of senators of both parties who had long interested themselves in the problems of the handicapped.

Second, the committee disposed of specific proposals to amend the House bill on the grounds that further study leading to future legislation was a more desirable course of action. For example, the demand for an explicit provision for judicial review of the constitutionality of the Act and its administration was forestalled by the argument that judicial review could be authorized at a later time, but that inclusion of judicial review in the main bill would jeopardize its passage.

The sponsors of H.R. 2362 skillfully brought the administration proposals through their committees. The few changes broadened rather than lessened the bill's political acceptability to various interest groups: urban school districts, advocates of controls on funds for children in non-public schools, and State educational agencies. Opposition to the bill hardened principally against the Title I formula. The church-state issue had apparently been neutralized, although a number of Congressmen (e.g., Quie, Goodell, and Congresswoman Edith Green) tried hard to raise it on the floor. In the House committee, partisan cleavage was more pronounced and more overt than in the Senate committee. The minority party leadership continued to raise issues during the floor debates. But they lacked the votes and they knew it.

House and Senate Enactment of ESEA

The progress of H.R. 2362 through the House and Senate was facilitated by a favorable place on the calendar, well-organized teamwork, and astute floor management, respectively, by Representative Powell, Chairman of the House Committee on Education and Labor, and by Senator Wayne Morse. The President also took an interest in the speed and timing of passage. He let the Senate leaders know that he hoped to sign the bill at his Texas ranch during Easter vacation. The fact that the entire process of floor consideration in the House and the Senate required only

16 days (March 24 to April 9) was testament in part to White House and HEW aggressiveness.

On the House floor, the only notable threat to the committee version of H.R. 2362 proved to be an amendment offered by Representative Edith Green providing for the funding of Title I by flat grants of $200 per low-income-family child. This would have raised the allotment for 35 states and reduced it for 15. Mrs. Green sent to each favorably affected Congressman a plea for his support, accompanied by a statement of the increased amount of support his State would receive under her formula. Her argument was that the administration formula gave too much money to the richest States and not enough to the poorer ones. The supporters of the administration's formula responded that it was much more expensive to educate a child in the "richer" states, primarily in the North, and that the bill would provide greater percentage increases in southern State budgets than in northern State budgets.

Since Mrs. Green was chairman of the Special Subcommittee on Education, her defection from majority ranks was welcomed by the coalition of Republicans and southern Democrats opposing H.R. 2362. The amendment picked up a scattering of other votes, but was defeated 136–202. This was the closest vote of any taken on the 19 rejected amendments, but it represented only a fractional shift in the relative voting strength of the two opposing bipartisan factions.

In the closing hours of the House action, tension mounted as Representative Powell repeatedly succeeded in limiting debate on each section of the bill to the required minimum of five minutes. Proponents of amendments had little time to explain them, and Representative Howard Smith, Rules Committee Chairman, complained that the House was too noisy for amendments even to be heard.[32] "This bill," he said, "has been treated like it was just dropped down from heaven, that it is sacred and must not be touched." [33] His amendment to add a judicial review provision to the bill was among those defeated. Only one minor last minute change was accepted: an amendment offered by Representative Griffin relating to the appointment of advisory councils. The final vote on the bill was 263–153. The solid bloc of 187 northern Democratic supporters was larger than the total opposing votes cast by 96 Republicans and 57 Democrats. All but three of the opposing Democrats were from the South. The bill was also supported by 35 Republicans and 41 southern Democrats.

32. One of the amendments, by a Republican from California, was to change the word "Commissioner," wherever it appeared, to "Commissar," in the interest of truth and candor to the public.

33. *Congressional Record,* March 29, 1965, 5928.

Proceedings in the Senate on H.R. 2362 were a ritual debate, with few Senators present except when called in to cast routine votes against the Republican amendments.[34] However, the Senate managers of H.R. 2362 found that the issue of passing the bill quickly and without amendment had become a basis for attacking the President rather than the bill itself. The efforts exerted by Senators Morse, Randolph, Ribicoff, and Robert Kennedy, to counter the accusations of undue Presidential influence were far from perfunctory. They stressed the significance of the bill as a contribution to the national interest and justified the legislative strategy as constructive and prudent and in no way restrictive of Senate initiative.

Of the eleven amendments that were debated, two offered by Senator Dominick and one by Senator Ervin are of particular interest. The first, which would have made State approval of Title III projects mandatory, was rejected by a vote of 59–39. The second Dominick amendment was substantially the proposal made in the House by Mrs. Green, and it was similarly supported by a coalition of conservative Republicans and southern Democrats. It was defeated 38–53. Senator Ervin's amendment, which would have added a judicial review provision to the over-all bill, was supported by the same number of southern Democrats and six fewer Republicans. It was defeated 32–53. Senator Morse spoke in favor of an independent judicial review measure which would make it possible to clarify the constitutional issues in all the Federal programs of grants and loans to institutions of religious denominations. He promised to introduce a separate bill for the purpose later in the session—a move to quiet doubts that still lingered in the minds of a number of the bill's supporters.[35] In the end, the Senate passed ESEA by a vote of 73–18. The opposition came from 14 Republicans and four southern Democrats.

Although the favorable vote on ESEA was impressive in both Houses, the outcome reflected long-standing differences between the House and Senate. The passage of H.R. 2362 by the House was accomplished by an overt exercise of majority party power used to override a minority that was both more numerous and combative than the opposition in the Senate. As in previous sessions, the Senate demonstrated a greater degree of bipartisan support for Federal school aid.

The 89th Congress enacted an unprecedented volume of important

34. *Congressional Record,* April 8, 1965, 7526–7601 *passim,* April 9, 1965, 7609–7718.

35. On June 7, 1965, Senators Morse, Clark, and Yarborough introduced a bill to provide judicial review of all Federal grant programs likely to be affected by the First Amendment. The Senate passed the measure, but the House failed to act. See Senate, *Report No. 1403,* 89th Cong., 2nd sess.

administration measures, but all except ESEA and the Appalachia bill required a House-Senate conference. These two exceptions may perhaps be explained on the basis of their timing in the early weeks of the new Congress and of their assumed urgency. But this is probably too simple. Had the sponsors of ESEA failed in their carefully charted campaign of persuasion, propaganda, accommodation, and parliamentary strategy, the administration version of ESEA might well have emerged in substantially modified form if, in truth, it had not been completely mousetrapped along the way.

Aftermath to the Enactment of ESEA

President Johnson signed ESEA on April 11, 1965 in a one-room school house he once attended.

With ESEA on the books, both education subcommittees moved on to other legislative priorities. But a footnote to the ESEA proceedings is necessary. In June, after considerable delay, the House General Subcommittee on Education held hearings, promised during H.R. 2362 floor debate, on the availability of statistical data more recent than that contained in the 1960 census. Wide-ranging testimony by Census Bureau and USOE personnel was taken, but no recommendations for immediate action were made.

Two amendments to Title I, however, were added as a result of Senate subcommittee proceedings. Called "clean up" measures by a subcommittee staff member, the amendments were made as riders to the School Disaster Act (Public Law 89–313). One amendment extended coverage specifically to the 50,000 physically handicapped children for whom the States provide funds for institutional care and instruction. The other amendment raised the minimum level of grants to the States for Title I administrative costs to $75,000. The original provision had reserved 1 per cent of the State's grants to local agencies for State administrative costs. This was considered inadequate for proper program supervision, particularly in the West where small numbers of eligible children were distributed over extensive geographic areas. One other subsequent law is pertinent. Public Law 89–750 added an amendment to Title I which allowed consideration to be given to children in institutions for the neglected and delinquent.

Fiscal Year 1966 Appropriations for ESEA

Shortly after the signing of ESEA, President Johnson sent a request to Congress for appropriations to implement the new act for the fiscal year beginning July 1, 1965. The request was for the full amount of funds authorized for Titles II, III, and V, and for administration estimates of the amounts required for Titles I and IV for the balance of the fiscal year. The total was $1.34 billion, and an additional $4.5 million was requested for added salaries and expenses in USOE. The subtotals by ESEA Title are shown in Table 2, together with the subsequent adjustments made by congressional action.

The speed record set by the leaders of authorization committees in the House and Senate for the enactment of ESEA was obviously not a spur to the Appropriations Committees.[36] The ESEA money bill was a supplement to the regular HEW appropriation request and could not precede it on Appropriations Committee calendars. An even more serious barrier to speed was coincidental timing with controversial requests for unrelated programs in the Labor and HEW Departments. These issues were not unsnarled until August 12. By this time ESEA had been on the books for four months, and the new fiscal year was in its sixth week. The only item in the regular HEW appropriation directly related to the implementation of ESEA was $25 million for the prior programs of the Cooperative Research Act, which was amended and expanded by Title IV of ESEA.

The House Appropriations Subcommittee held hearings on the supplemental appropriations request for ESEA on August 25, 1965. Most of the testimony by administration officials was a repetition of that given earlier to the education subcommittee. In addition, the plans for reorganizing USOE were described for the first time. The administration of Title VI of the Civil Rights Act came under scrutiny, as did the prospect of nationwide testing programs financed by USOE. The Senate group registered its disapproval of the latter activity. A specific prohibition against it, reflecting fears of school administrators that nationwide tests would lead to invidious comparisons, was written into the committee report pending further consideration of the matter by the regular legislative committees.

The attitude of the Appropriations Subcommittees toward the ESEA programs was generally friendly. By September 23, funds had been made available approximating the levels requested by the Administration. As Table 2 indicates, Titles II and IV were fully funded. Reductions were made in the case of Titles I, III, V, and USOE administrative costs. The House Appropriations Subcommittee concluded that it would not be possible for USOE to expand or for the State and local educa-

36. *Hearings Before Subcommittee of the Appropriations Committee on Department of Labor-HEW Supplemental Appropriations for 1966,* 89th Cong., 1st sess., House and Senate.

TABLE 2

FY'66 APPROPRIATIONS FOR ESEA (PUBLIC LAW 89–10)
(Amounts in millions of dollars)

Document and Date of Request of Authorization	USOE Salaries and Expenses	Cooperative Research Act	ESEA Titles					Total
			I	II	III	IV	V	
HEW Appropriations Act of 1966 (Public Law 89–156, 8/31/65)		25						
Administration Request (House Document 149, 4/22/65)	4.5		1071	100	100	45	25	1345.5
House Appropriations Committee (Report 818, 8/19/65)	4		775	100	75	45	17	1016
Senate Appropriations Committee (Report 680, 9/2/65)	4		959	100	75	45	17	1200
HEW Supplemental Appropriations Act of 1966, (Public Law 89–199, 9/23/65)	4		775	100	75	45	17	1016
Second Supplemental Appropriations Act of 1966 (Public Law 89–426, 5/13/66)			184					184
Total FY'66 Appropriations for ESEA	4		959	100	75	70*	17	1225

*Combined amounts provided by Public Law 89–156 and Public Law 89–199

tional agencies to mount these particular new programs in the remaining months of the fiscal year, as rapidly as had been planned. In addition, the entitlements provided by formula in Title I were still being computed during the summer of 1965, and neither the administration spokesmen nor the congressional subcommittee members were certain what the precise totals would be. Finally, it was necessary to estimate the extent to which the local educational agencies would qualify for their entitlements once they had submitted approvable programs. To meet these uncertainties, both the House and Senate Appropriations Committee Reports included provision that USOE might make the grant entitlements at the statutory levels. Then, if the costs of the approved local programs eventually exceeded the amount of the appropriations, the USOE should request another supplemental appropriation for FY'66.

As it turned out, the initial amount for ESEA recommended by the Senate Appropriations Committee was finally approved for FY'66. In the Second Supplemental Appropriations Act, USOE was granted an additional amount of $184 million.[37] This brought the total first year cost for Title I to $959 million.

RECAPITULATION

In summary, ESEA was a remarkable legislative achievement. It was shaped by many factors: the commitment of President Johnson to education, a sizeable Democratic majority in Congress, and effective collaboration among officials in the Executive and Legislative branches.

Johnson Administration officials were the principal architects of ESEA. They drew on a reservoir of ideas from many sources, including previous legislative proposals. An analysis of the specific provisions of each of the five titles of the act indicates that skillful compromises were made to meet the objectives and objections of a variety of interest groups. Traditional patterns of intergovernmental relations were altered. The country's educators were nudged into new programs and administrative experiments. ESEA touched areas of high controversy, but the sting was eased by discretionary, even ambiguous, legislative language—leaving much to be worked out in the implementation of the act. The "pre-forming" of the administration bill successfully warded off appeals to Congress for additions and changes in the bill's provisions.

The congressional sponsors of ESEA planned a legislative strategy that resulted in bringing the original bill through Congress unchanged and within three months. When opponents charged that Congress was

37. Public Law 89–426, April 13, 1966.

abrogating its legislative responsibilities by giving inadequate consideration to the bill, advocates replied that there would be ample opportunity to make changes and improvements on the basis of the first year's experience. Congress acted with less dispatch in approving first-year funds to implement ESEA; but by September, 1965, appropriations were made at substantially the levels the President had recommended.

III. The Reorganization of the Office of Education[1]

The job of administering Public Law 89–10 fell to an agency with a long and pedestrian past. As late as the spring of 1965, the basic weaknesses of the Office of Education were sufficiently glaring to cast doubt upon the possibility of its carrying with vigor and effectiveness the additional burdens which the new act would superimpose.[2]

The Status Quo Ante

Atomization and Specialization

Following Commissioner Studebaker's reorganization of USOE in 1947, effective power in the agency was increasingly exercised by virtually autonomous units under the control of technical or professional specialists. This was partly a matter of design, partly of accident. Studebaker wanted to increase the "service" role of the Office by hiring "experts" who could act as consultants to State and local educational specialists, and the administrative price of specialization tends to be atomization. This administrative logic was exacerbated by the shortage of staff in the office of the Commissioner and, in the 1950's, by a decrease in length of tenure of individual Commissioners. Studebaker had been Commissioner from 1934 through 1949. During the subsequent 15 years, there were to be six Commissioners—five incumbents in the single decade 1954–64. During this same decade, office continuity was provided by a dedicated deputy commissioner, Wayne Reed, and by a number of venerable associate commissioners. However suited their leadership was to historically segmented operations and to the expectations of education's major professional associations, it was only in the most general sense supervisory. In a non-invidious sense the "feudal

1. The paucity of footnotes in this Chapter is due to the fact that most of the material came from interviews and from an internal mimeographed document, "Recommendations of the White House Task Force on Education, June 14, 1965," which has never been published but is not classified.

2. For general references to the administrative conditions of USOE before 1965 see Chapter I, Footnote 28.

baronies" of the associate commissioners were only marginally stronger than the "kingdom" of the Commissioner. Real power was lodged in the guilds of professionals who ran the operating sub-units of the major bureaus: library consultants; vocational education experts; reading and curricular specialists; experts on education of the handicapped; specialists in home economics, agricultural education, counselling and guidance—each with a scattering of friends in appropriate professional groups at the regional, State, and local level. This meant, in effect, that aside from the immediate legislative concerns of the Office of Program and Legislative Planning (OPLP), there was no locus in the Office of Education and no machinery for developing a nationwide educational policy; the very phrase created shivers. In fact, there was almost no way of effecting intra-office communications, and few generalist views to counteract and coordinate the views of specialists.

The legislative successes in 1963–64 were largely due to heroic efforts of a few key Keppel appointees, mostly in OPLP. Drawn into ad hoc seminars by Keppel, and basing their judgments, in part, upon the abortive educational legislation of the early 1960's, these officials set about the task of constructing a coherent legislative policy. That this legislative planning process worked as well as it did was a testament to the wisdom and ability of the participants rather than to any structured information base or long-range planning staff in USOE.

Superannuated Personnel and Personnel Systems

In the years prior to reorganization of 1965, the average age of the professional staff of OE was over 50. In new hirings, formal experience had seemed a more valued criterion than either energy or imagination. Recruitment of able people was not helped by what surely must have been one of the most negatively-oriented personnel management branches in the entire Federal establishment. Out of fairness, it must be pointed out that the operating bureaus contributed their share of sand in the personnel machinery. For example, they often waited until they had selected a person before asking that a job be established and classified for that person to fill. But even this doleful practice was testimony to the inability of the Personnel Management Branch to exercise appropriate managerial leadership within USOE. Top personnel officers controlled where they should have let loose; they relaxed where they should have been firm. There was no over-all manpower planning for the Office; no system of career development; and no effective personnel evaluation system.

Archaic Financial and Management Information Systems

The system of financial and management accountability was almost totally decentralized, disparate, and ineffective. Finance officers and accountants were sprinkled like grains of pepper throughout the lower levels of the organization. The result was irritation rather than spice. Some financial records were kept on ledger sheets in longhand. A set of books in one division or branch was not comparable to a set in another division or branch. No one at the Commissioner's level had the financial or management information needed to make wise allocations of manpower and funds across the agency as a whole. The Office lacked a management reporting system adequate to keep top management currently informed on program status.

An Unrationalized Bureau and Field Structure

The bureau structure of USOE had "growed" like Topsy. New legislative mandates were handled by sedimentary accretions to existing bureaucratic divisions. In 1962, following the recommendations of the U.S. Office of Education Committee on Mission and Organization (the so-called Babbidge Report),[3] the then Commissioner, Sterling McMurrin, reshuffled the top-side organization of USOE by creating a new bureau structure. Concessions made in gaining acceptance for this reorganization, however, weakened its effectiveness, and the new structure developed strains and leaks of its own. Under the 1962 reorganization and prior to 1964 when the Bureau of Higher Education was added, the Office was divided into three major operating bureaus: Educational Research and Development; International Education; and Educational Assistance Programs. The latter particularly became an undifferentiated catch-all for any and every new grant-in-aid. As a bureau it had neither functional clarity nor clarity according to educational level. There was, in short, no organizing principle aside from the general notion of "assistance." The Bureau of International Education faced another kind of issue: it was largely a service and brokerage agency for other Federal departments (particularly State and AID). Furthermore, its volume of "business" was miniscule compared to the other two operating bureaus of the Office. For both these reasons it had little justification for being a separate operating bureau of USOE. The Bureau of Educational Research and Development suffered from some of the same catch-all

3. *A Federal Education Agency for the Future,* U.S. Office of Education, Committee on Mission and Organization (Washington: U.S. Government Printing Office, 1961).

problems as the Bureau of Educational Assistance. Conceived particularly as a long-range planning center, it also contained operating programs which could just as easily (and perhaps more logically) have been in the Bureau of Educational Assistance. Finally, the field offices of USOE were weak in staff, confused in purpose and manned in large part by specialists who reported directly to sub-bureau units in Washington.

Anomie Within the Executive Branch

If USOE was plagued with internal problems of organization, management, and personnel, it also suffered from isolation and withdrawal from the rest of the executive branch. The old line civil servants in the Office of Education had an almost pathological suspicion of the department of which USOE was an integral part: HEW. There was no mechanism, formal or informal, for relating OE's work to the educational programs of the other departments and agencies of government (e.g., Veterans Administration, National Science Foundation, Defense, Agriculture, Office of Economic Opportunity). Combined, these non-USOE programs quite over-shadowed the Office of Education in variety and in funding, causing it to become even more ingrown and isolated.

Fear of the Charge of Federal Control

Finally, and perhaps a basic cause of its other problems, the Office of Education operated under a restraining fear of dominating educational policy in the United States. Whatever the dangers of Federal control, and they do exist, the historically- and constitutionally-conditioned reticence of USOE in this area had a crippling effect upon initiative and leadership. Reinforced in their modesty by State and local education offices, by educational professional associations, and by the long-held theology of "local control," USOE officials (most of whom had been raised in this theology) limited their influence over American education to areas of professional specialization in which their advice was "sought."

Francis Keppel and Henry Loomis

This, then, was the old Office: In the eyes of Commissioner Keppel and of the White House, this was the structure that needed substantial overhaul if the Elementary and Secondary Education Act and the other education laws of the 88th and 89th Congresses were to be effectively implemented.

One may of course ask the question, why, after two and a half years as USOE Commissioner, Francis Keppel had not moved more aggressively to put the Office's internal house in order. One reason was the fact that Keppel joined the agency immediately after the McMurrin reorganization and was reluctant to enter immediately upon a new one. Reorganizations are painful at best. During the consideration and development of reorganization plans, staff uncertainty and insecurity become pervasive. Worries about status and tenure interrupt trains of thought and operating agendas. Adjustments to new roles, new supervisors, and new procedures are rarely simple and are frequently confusing. Shake-downs are often extensive and disruptive. Keppel was fearful that a new reorganization superimposed upon a recent one would create more problems than it would cure and that until the Office had a stronger financial and program base to enable it to attract a number of able new people, reorganization by itself would be an exercise in futility.

But there was something else. Whatever skills Keppel had as a forceful and brilliant policy strategist and external negotiator, he was not a tidy administrator. The mundane details of internal structure and process bored his restless and creative mind. The tyranny of time forces busy executives to make hard choices between an inside and an outside role. And in the allocation of time (the administrator's scarcest resource), need, in some objective sense, is inevitably conditioned by temperamental preference. Furthermore, Keppel's essential command from Presidents Kennedy and Johnson had been to catalyze new legislative breakthroughs. This role Keppel performed with distinction, but it was a role that precluded the pouring of extensive energies into solving difficult problems of organization and methods inside USOE itself. Perhaps most important of all, Keppel was reluctant to reorganize USOE before knowing the outcome of major pending legislation. He knew that what Congress passed would, in large measure, determine the character of any meaningful reorganization.

Keppel, however, recognized his own limitations of time and temperament, and as the actual and prospective burdens of USOE increased in 1964 and 1965, he searched for a deputy who could focus upon the internal administrative issues of the Office. Keppel sensed the need to turn USOE from a series of country stores into a modern supermarket, and he was convinced that his inherited career deputy, Wayne Reed—many of whose talents Keppel greatly admired—was too much a part of the older establishment to provide the tough leadership needed to remake the agency.

In March, 1965, after months of trying, Keppel finally attracted to the position of Deputy Commissioner of Education Henry Loomis,

Director of the Voice of America (VOA). With a rich background in the administration of science, defense, and foreign policy, and with national recognition for his public service accomplishments, Loomis seemed ideally prepared for his new role. Upon joining the Office of Education, however, he began what was probably one of the most extraordinary, bruising, controversial, if in some ways effective, administrative operations in the recent annals of the Federal government.

Loomis began under a heavy political cloud. He was an Eisenhower Republican and continued all during his work under Democratic presidents to hang Eisenhower's photograph on his office walls. His transfer from VOA to USOE was marred and nearly canceled by Johnsonian anger. Loomis' farewell address to his colleagues in VOA had been read as an insinuation that White House pressure to make VOA newscasts conform to U.S. State Department policies and interests had markedly increased under Johnson. Word of this farewell address, reported in one of the Washington newspapers, allegedly infuriated the President.

The weekend of Loomis' shift from the U.S. Information Agency to the Office of Education was suspenseful and agonizing to Civil Service Commission Chairman John W. Macy, Jr., HEW Secretary Anthony J. Celebrezze, Commissioner Keppel, and Loomis' friends and admirers in the Executive Office of the President. It came down to the question of whether the White House was going to permit the Commissioner of Education to have a deputy of his own choice. Although the President finally gave in, Loomis' relationships with the White House were cool from then on. Keppel's adamant defense of Loomis, whom he admired for his demonstrated administrative abilities, temporarily weakened Keppel's own rapport with the President.

This contretemps was to have at least one lingering effect upon the efficiency of USOE operations, for it led to a presidential insistence that all new super-grades for the Office (and throughout the government) were to be cleared personally by Presidential Assistant Marvin Watson in the White House. In a hectic attempt to restaff the Office in late 1965 and early 1966, White House clearance, however expeditious, added another hurdle to an already cumbersome process of personnel recruitment.

Loomis' initial difficulties were not entirely external and political. He had replaced Wayne Reed, a career civil servant, as deputy. Reed was given a new position as Associate Commissioner for Federal-State Relations, and he accepted the shift philosophically and loyally. But the pain of status loss was nonetheless acute, and it was felt by all of Reed's friends and colleagues within USOE and the various professional associations and the State and local educational agencies with whom Reed had worked comfortably and sympathetically over the years. Empathy for Reed was reinforced by fear. If Reed could be pushed aside, who would be next?

Finally, there was the issue of personality and background. Loomis, like Keppel, was by speech, manner, and brains patently Ivy League. Furthermore, Loomis' previous career had involved close association with the cream of American scientists and with foreign affairs officers and their urbane polish. Temperamentally a no-nonsense type, Loomis entered his new post with a superb preparation for everything except a sympathetic understanding of the slow speech and sometimes muddled behavior of the non-ivy, mid-western types who peopled the halls and cubicles of USOE. He and his hand-picked assistant, Walter Mylecraine (whom he had brought with him from the Voice of America), were accused of being rougher than necessary. To the traditional educational establishment, Loomis was alien, cold, domineering, and ruthless. This image was never dispelled. In fact, it was reinforced by the attitude and behavior of Walter Mylecraine, who had the unlovely responsibility of wielding the hatchets handed to him almost daily by his superior and who appeared to many to enjoy this nasty administrative activity.

With the unflagging support of the Commissioner, and the backing of White House staff and HEW, Loomis put the Office of Education through the wringer of almost total reorganization of structure and staff. USOE would never be the same.

THE INK COMMITTEE

Loomis took office on March 8, 1965. He was appalled by what he found. He was immediately convinced that only a thorough and complete reorganization of structure and staff would equip USOE to discharge its existing and prospective responsibilities with efficiency and dispatch. Some insiders, notably Russell Wood and Ralph Flynt, had long since developed notions of a desirable reorganization plan—particularly the desirability of a bureau structure based upon educational levels (elementary and secondary, higher education, and adult and vocational), and a staff office structure that would include a separate office for program planning and evaluation.

These notions made sense to Loomis as working hypotheses; the real problem, as he saw it, was political. If Keppel and Loomis were to conduct a mass reorganization by managerial fiat, the internal heat engendered might consume both of them. They recognized that existing bureaus, divisions, branches, and officials had powerful linkages to sub-units of Congress and to external professional groups. To take the full responsibility for dislodging existing patterns and relationships would be to construct a personal lightning rod that would attract all of the electricity of protest latent in disturbing the status quo. One law of survival in Washington is to distribute political heat as broadly as possible. On the other hand, if the responsibility were passed to the Secretary of HEW and his administrative experts, traditional enmities between USOE and HEW might flare up again. Some thought was given to the possible use of private management consultants like McKinsey and Co. or Arthur B. Little and Co., but Loomis was skeptical of their worth for the purposes at hand.

In the meantime, on the basis of staff reports from the Bureau of the Budget, President Johnson had decided that a full-scale review of the administrative organization and procedures of USOE was imperative. With the President's full support, therefore, Keppel and Loomis reached an agreement with Douglass Cater in the White House that the President, immediately following the signing of ESEA, would appoint a special high-level task force from within the government but outside HEW. This would, in effect, pass the political burden of reorganization to the strong shoulders of the President and throw any adverse congressional or group interest reactions to reorganization into the complicated and forbidding arena of presidential relations.

The Chairman of the Civil Service Commission and White House aide on political executive recruitment, John Macy, recommended Dwight Ink, then Assistant General Manager of the Atomic Energy Commission, as chairman of the new task force. Two other members were appointed: Herbert Jasper from the Bureau of the Budget and Nicholas J. Oganovic (almost immediately replaced by Gilbert Schulkind) of the Civil Service Commission.

All these members were relieved of their normal responsibilities for the 60-day period, April 15–June 14, 1965. They took office space in USOE, conducted extensive interviews, read in-house documents, observed, appointed sub-units on financial management and personnel, and carried out exhaustive assessments of problems and alternative solutions. Close liaison was maintained with Loomis and Keppel, HEW, the White House, the Budget Bureau, and with clientele groups like NEA and NCWC.

Recommendations

A report called "Recommendations of the White House Task Force on Education" was completed on June 14, 1965. A 41-page document, the report was divided into eight sections: Personnel Administration; Financial Administration; Planning and Evaluation; Management Reporting and Information Systems; Contracting and Construction Activities; Evaluating Contract Grant Proposals; Organization of the Office of Education; and Follow-Through. The profound disquiet of the task force members was reflected in each section, as was their rationale for recommended change.

The task force recommendations can be easily summarized.

(1) *Personnel Administration.* First priority was given to recommendations for recruiting able personnel and for strengthening personnel programs and procedures. It was obvious that the success of the Office of Education in meeting its new responsibilities would depend in large measure upon the quality of its staff.

To accomplish its various personnel goals, the task force recommended the immediate establishment of a 90-day ad hoc recruiting committee made up of bureau directors or their deputies and chaired by the Deputy Commissioner. The Director of the Personnel Management Branch was to serve as executive secretary. The task of this ad hoc committee was varied, but in essence its job was to rationalize and streamline the whole process of recruiting new and able personnel.

In terms of immediate needs, the task force recommended that an Executive Staffing Specialist be assigned on a temporary basis to assist the Commissioner and the Deputy Commissioner in identifying, interviewing, and clearing prospective candidates for key executive posts. These posts included a score of new USOE super-grade positions (GS–16–18) that were necessitated by the changed organizational structure and were recommended by the task force. These, of course, had to be secured with the help and permission of the United States Civil Service Commission.

On the larger question of overall manpower planning, the task force reflected its awareness of a doubling of the number of authorized positions in USOE in the five-year span 1960–65, and the existence of 500 unfilled slots as of the moment of the study. It recommended an appropriate staff office to establish short- and long-range personnel requirements, criteria for determining the number of positions to be reserved for entrance-level trainees, appropriate career patterns and promotion ladders, the distribution of occupational specialists, and the conditions under which senior specialists might appropriately be recruited.

(2) *Financial Administration.* In no administrative area was the task force more explicitly critical of existing practices than in USOE's system of financial management. The task force noted that the archaic charac-

teristics of the agency's accounting and record-keeping practices had far-reaching effects. For example:

(a) budget formulation was essentially a mechanical process for the "pricing out" of fixed requirements under existing legislation rather than an instrument of program planning;

(b) existing financial planning procedures were inadequate for assessing actual progress and performance in the course of a single fiscal year; and

(c) the multiplicity of financial handbooks, directives, and instructions from various units of USOE to grant recipients lacked direction and synthesis.

To overcome these shortcomings, the task force recommended a series of steps, including: the application of automatic data processing to accounting procedures; the establishment of five-year forward planning in the formulation of budgets; the establishment of Office-of-Administration-sponsored programs for improvement of the financial control system of grantees in order to assure proper program control, accounting, and disbursement of Federal grant and loan funds; and an evaluation of the effectiveness of fiscal and fund accounting controls at the point of expenditures (i.e., local school districts), as deemed necessary to assure proper disbursement of Federal funds.

(3) *Planning and Evaluation.* Well before the task force study—actually dating back to the Babbidge Report of 1961 [4]—the Office of Education had attempted to establish a program planning and evaluation function. Under the reorganization of 1962, these responsibilities had been assigned to an Office of Program and Legislative Planning. Its legislative functions operated effectively, at times brilliantly, but on relatively short-term programs and strategy. The program planning division, however, charged with long-range and general planning, was a bust. In 1964 a separate Office of Legislation was created. Overall, the OPLP lacked clear directives as to function, and it lacked sophisticated and modern leadership. By the time the Ink Task Force was appointed, Keppel and Loomis were in the process of establishing a new staff unit devoted exclusively to program planning and evaluation. The task force members endorsed this move, and prepared an agenda of functions for the new office. These functions included—

(a) identifying the educational needs and goals of the nation and recommending policies for promoting the progress of education;

(b) establishing a program for the annual formulation of detailed but long-range plans for each of the bureaus;

4. *Ibid.*

(c) preparing a long-range plan for the Office of Education by drawing upon the plans prepared by the bureaus;

(d) regularly evaluating and reporting program results against the specific goals of the bureaus as well as the broad goals of USOE; and

(e) preparing evaluative studies, plans, and proposals in depth.

The task force emphasized that the staff of the Office of Program Planning and Evaluation should include individuals with backgrounds in planning, economics, and statistics, as well as some with practical operating experience and an intensive knowledge of USOE programs and policies.

(4) *Management Reporting and Information Systems.* As of spring, 1965, existing and prospective responsibilities of USOE called for the development of both an internal system of reports and a system of acquiring and analyzing national educational data unprecedented in magnitude and complexity. Top USOE management needed prompt and well-ordered information about program operations, in order to answer departmental, legislative, and presidential inquiries, and to exercise appropriate internal management controls. USOE's organic law (requiring it to collect "such statistics and facts as shall show the condition and progress of education in the several States and territories,")[5] demanded, in the context of the 1960's, an information system quite beyond the capacity of anything but the most up-to-date computer technology.

The task force proposed that the problem of improved internal management reporting be assigned to the Office of Administration. On the larger related question of designing a comprehensive and coordinated information system for the agency as a whole and for its external clients, the task force recommended that USOE's National Center for Educational Statistics (NCES) be assigned the responsibility. The Division of Statistical Services of NCES was to be reconstructed as a Division of Data Processing Systems to be responsible for providing agency-wide computer programming and information processing services in accordance with the over-all design for a new information system.

The Ink Committee, performing under an impossible pressure of time, never effectively clarified the jurisdictions of the Office of Administration, the Office of Program Planning and Evaluation, and the National Center for Educational Statistics, in the development and control of an information system capable of serving the management, planning, and program needs of the agency. This is not surprising. The problem, in both concept and organization, was grotesque in its complexity.

(5) *Contracting and Construction Activities.* Two important auxiliary services connected with USOE activities involved the mounting of con-

5. 15 Stat. L. 434.

struction programs and the negotiation of contract and grant projects. The former had been delegated in prior years to the engineers and architects of the Community Facilities Agency of the Housing and Home Finance Agency (presently the Department of Housing and Urban Development); the latter had been saddled upon the separate operating bureaus and divisions of the Office of Education.

Although the task force recommended a continuation in the short run of inspection services for construction programs by the Community Facilities Agency, it determined that USOE needed some architectural and engineering capabilities of its own, and it looked forward to the time when such auxiliary services would be grouped at the department level within HEW.

Contracting was a different story. The legal and technical aspects of negotiating over 3,000 contracts a year were unduly burdensome on program-oriented bureaus and divisions. Furthermore, the decentralization of contract negotiations led inevitably to disparate and colliding standards. Here the task force recommended the establishment of a central contract services office within USOE which, after consultation with relevant program bureaus, would negotiate and administer all agency contracts. The Contracting Service would also develop a uniform covering agreement that would set general standards and obligations for all USOE contracts.

The small architectural and engineering staff and the new contracting services were to be housed together in a separate Contracts and Construction Services Center reporting directly to the Commissioner of Education.

(6) *Evaluating Grant and Contract Proposals.* Recognizing that a large component of the mission of USOE was the support of individuals and institutions involved in educational research, demonstrations, training, information-dissemination, and similar functions, the task force made a careful appraisal of the machinery for screening applications for federal funds for these purposes. USOE, like the National Science Foundation and the National Institutes of Health, had made considerable use of advisory panels composed of outside consultants, charging them with reviewing and screening grant applications. Sometimes legislation mandated the use of such panels; sometimes USOE established them by administrative fiat. Advisory panels have at least three obvious advantages: (a) they provide extra staff for the agency without involving the agency in long-term job commitments; (b) they bring to bear upon grant decisions an expertise not always available within the Office; and (c) perhaps most important from the standpoint of agency or programmatic survival, they spread the political heat engendered by negative

decisions. ("We here in USOE thought your proposal had a lot of merit, but the Advisory Panel was against it.")

The task force members had a number of criticisms to make of the system as they found it. They discovered, for example, that there was uncertainty as to whether an advisory group was being asked for policy views or for evaluation of specific proposals. They found ambiguity in the respective roles of USOE staff on the one hand and advisory panels on the other, in the evaluation process. They discovered overlapping jurisdictions among advisory groups. They identified wide disparities in the size of the various panels. They found that there were excessive sequential evaluations and reevaluations of proposals. They discovered cumbersome procedures for selecting, appointing, and utilizing consultants. The task force saw some urgency in correcting these difficulties, especially in view of the fact that the evaluation work-load was increasing rapidly with the growth in USOE programs. The task force felt that the burden on many consultants and panels would rapidly become too heavy under existing practices.

Besides recommending a series of steps to improve application, evaluation, and screening practices, the task force made an important statement of political philosophy and administrative ethics:

> No matter how important and expert the advice received from an advisory group, the Office of Education—not the advisory group—is accountable to the Congress and the public for the expenditure of federal funds. Therefore, the relationship of panels and staff should be clarified to ensure that panels and readers are understood clearly to be in an advisory position. Responsibility for final decisions must rest with the Office of Education.

(7) *Organization of the Office of Education.* The bulk of the report of the Ink Task Force was devoted to problems of internal organizational structure. Following the Babbidge Report of 1961, Commissioner Sterling McMurrin had grouped USOE functions into three operating bureaus, nine regional offices (matching the nine HEW regions) and four staff offices. For reasons noted earlier, the bureau structure was cumbersome and confusing, and the field offices and staff offices were too weak to clarify the ambiguities of the operating structure. The Higher Education Facilities Act of 1963 and other legislation aimed at strengthening institutions of higher learning had prompted Commissioner Keppel in 1964 to set up a new Bureau of Higher Education, to handle "bricks and mortar" loans and grants. In some ways, however, this simply compounded confusion. Should research and development grants to colleges

and universities be administered by the Bureau of Educational Research and Development or by an expanded Bureau of Higher Education? Should NDEA fellowship grants to higher education be handled through the Bureau of Educational Assistance Programs, or through the Bureau of Higher Education, enlarged to include "people" programs in addition to "bricks and mortar" programs?

The Ink Task Force was too sophisticated to believe that structural formulae existed that could avoid all inter-program and intra-office ambiguities. Actually, the rationale for USOE organization could have been based either upon function (assistance, research, international education) or level (elementary and secondary, higher education, adult). Each option had its strengths; each had its weaknesses. The Babbidge Report had reacted against a USOE organization of the 1950's that was disorderly but that had been weighted toward organization by level rather than by function.

The reorganization of 1962 was functionally-oriented (i.e., bureaus of Educational Assistance, Research and Development, International Education). Each of these "functions" cut across every level of education: elementary, secondary, higher, and adult. In consequence, in order to compensate for the functional orientation of the *bureaus, divisional* and *branch* organization tended to reflect groupings by educational level. (See Table 3.)

This, however, presented obvious difficulties of coordinating a number of separate programs all of which were addressed to a single level of education.

The Ink Task Force concluded that since most Federal laws were directed at specific levels of education, the principal resources of the Office of Education could best be organized by level. They therefore recommended three major operating bureaus: Elementary and Secondary Education; Higher Education; and Adult and Vocational Education. One functional bureau was retained: a Bureau of Research. The Ink Committee justified its recommendations in the following words:

> This type of organization structure will result in the maximum concentration of resources in relation to the several programs authorized by law. It should permit the recruitment of the most outstanding leaders in the nation to serve in positions of great challenge and significance. It will permit the assignment of bureau titles which will clearly convey the responsibilities which they bear. It will also greatly facilitate the relations of the Office with the educational community.

TABLE 3

PRE-1965 ORGANIZATION OF USOE
BY FUNCTION AND LEVEL: TWO EXAMPLES

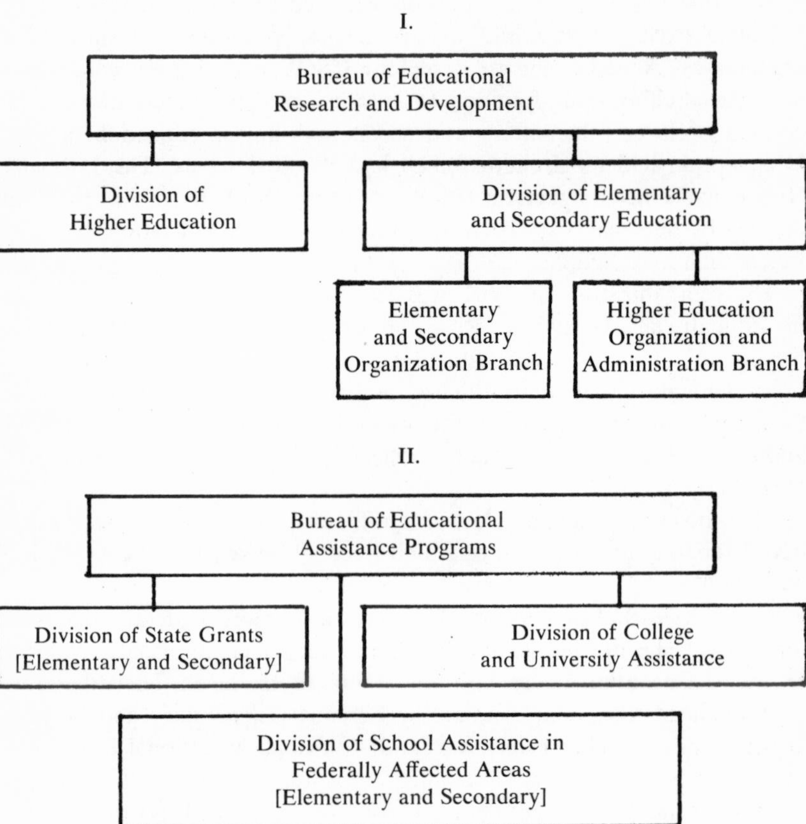

What they did not say was that it would also greatly facilitate the reassignment or the phasing out of old-timers who had developed both internal and external centers of power around isolated functional units. At lower levels of organization, particularly, the new format and the recommended new titles for divisions and branches were tantamount to a nearly total subordination of the role of the traditional specialist. The following example will suffice.

TABLE 4

EXAMPLE OF INK COMMITTEE CHANGES IN DIVISION AND BRANCH TITLES

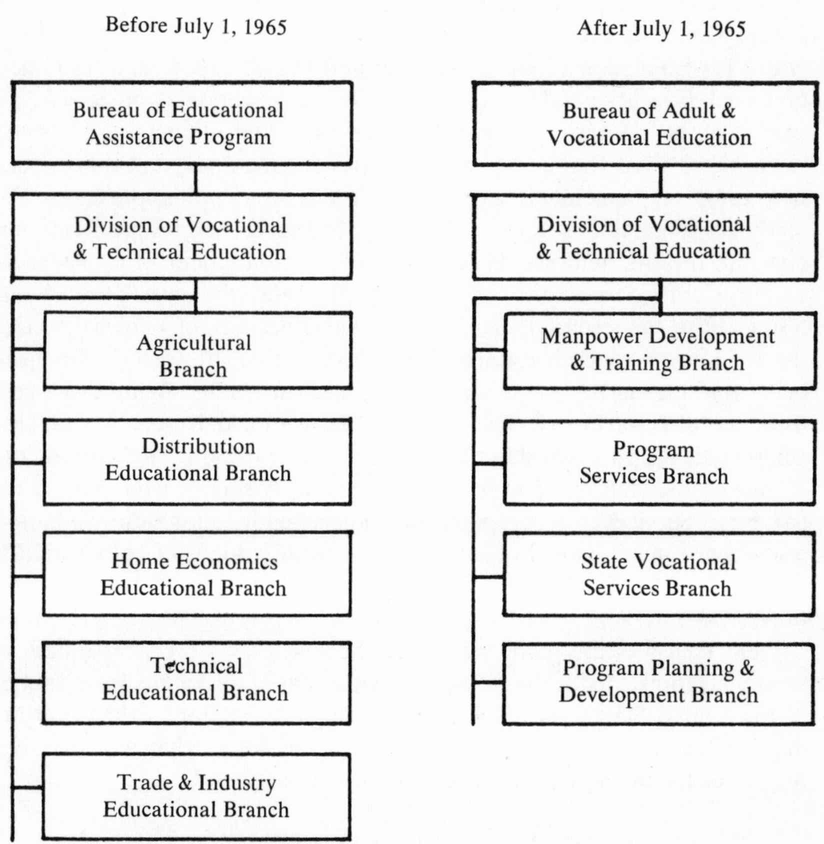

Before Ink, branch management was in the hands of specialists. After Ink, there was a radical shift at this level toward a generalist philosophy.[6]

6. This shift was partly denied, partly defended by Commissioner Howe in testimony before the Green Committee. There was, of course, no wholesale departure or displacement of specialists; but the direction of change was clear. See *Hearings before the Special Subcommittee on Education, on the U.S. Office of Education,* 89th Cong., 2d sess., House, 42–43.

Recommendations for the reorganization of the bureau structure of USOE were accompanied by recommendations for reconstituting the agency's staff offices. By and large these recommendations constituted a reordering of priorities among existing functions rather than the creation of new functions. In addition to the traditional staff offices (before 1962 called Branches and afterwards called Offices) of Program and Legislative Planning, Administration, and Information, the new proposal called for an Office of Program Planning and Evaluation, an Office of Programs for Education of Disadvantaged and Handicapped, and an Office of Equal Educational Opportunities. The last-mentioned office was to handle on an agency-wide basis the mandates and injunctions incorporated in the Civil Rights Act of 1964. Besides these six staff offices, the task force recommended two special Associate Commissionerships directly accountable to the Commissioner: one for Federal-State Relations and one for International Education. The establishment of a new Associate Commissionership for International Education was primarily a testament to the strong desire to retain the continuity of knowledge and the wisdom of venerable Ralph Flynt, rather than the result of a firm belief that the function belonged at that level in USOE. Being dislodged from the directorship of the Bureau of Educational Research and Development, Ralph Flynt deserved a high-status position until retirement. A Special Assistant (in fact he also became an Associate Commissioner) for Field Services was proposed to supervise the up-grading and reorienting of new regional offices and to provide a focus of responsibility close to the Commissioner for the Regional Directors of the reconstituted field offices.

Here then was the grand design of the Ink Task Force. Sweeping in scope, it represented a massive attack upon the traditional shortcomings of the United States Office of Education and an attempt to develop an organizational structure and a managerial philosophy that would equip the Office for the new burdens it was about to assume.[7]

THE TRAUMA OF REORGANIZATION

In order to preclude the formation of hostile counter-pressures inside and outside the Office, Loomis convinced Keppel that implementation of the task force report should be immediate and should be played very close to the chest. In consequence, less than two weeks after submission of the report, the reorganization was effected. The speed of action and the fact that the plan was shattering to *all* vested interests, produced a reaction of numbed, bewildered, bitter acquiescence. Vocational educa-

7. See Appendix D for organization charts of USOE before and after the reorganization of 1965.

tion, with an enormously powerful lobby behind it and dozens of friends on the Hill, had always enjoyed a special autonomy and influence within the Office. Although upgraded by the inclusion of its title at the bureau level, it was denied a separate bureau and faced the indignity of second billing in the title of the new bureau to which it was assigned. The Bureau of International Education was totally abolished. Of 36 traditional divisions of the Office of Education, only two escaped major changes in level or function. Of 25 old super-grade personnel, only eight were unchanged in status or responsibility. Over 20 new super-grade jobs were established—to be filled principally from the outside. At lower levels, generalists superseded specialists throughout the entire USOE pecking-order.

The anguish can only be imagined. The ensuing, if temporary, administrative chaos was shattering. For days and weeks, people could not find each other's offices—sometimes not even their own. Telephone extensions connected appropriate parties only by coincidence. A large number of key positions in the new order were vacant or were occupied by acting directors who were frequently demoralized by status ambiguity and eventual status loss. Those who could not live with the status loss resigned. And all of this came at a time of maximum work load. New guidelines and application forms and procedures had to be developed for the various titles of ESEA. More serious, ambiguities in the enforcement of Title VI of the Civil Rights Act were—at the moment of reorganization—causing a deluge of letters, telegrams, phone calls, congressional threats, and visiting delegations.

That a total breakdown did not occur was a tribute to the dedication of countless professional employees, to the hard-driving efficiency and trouble shooting of Loomis and Mylecraine, and to the tact of Keppel.

Loomis operated through a top-side Executive Group that had been created in March just after his appointment. The Executive Group established an agency-wide communications system, a policy-clarifying system, and a system of rigorously-enforced delegation of powers. Under Loomis' tight reins, this group held the office together and held key officials accountable for getting specific tasks accomplished on time. The months of July through September, 1965, were painful, not to say traumatic, for the entire agency. But if they witnessed the wrecking of an old house, they also saw the creation of the foundations for a new one.

The new one did not automatically bring the millenium. Centralization of some services (e.g., contracting services) provided an acute administrative bottleneck, with the subsequent necessity for re-decentralization. The war against specialists threw out some "babies" with the "bath water," and this policy had to be modified in order to enable

USOE to perform some of its historic and continuing functions of educational advice and data gathering.

But structural reorganization was important—less as an instrument to improve administrative rationality in some abstract sense than as a device for establishing new priorities and for reshuffling and dislodging old-timers and creating vacancies for needed new staff.

The reorganization of USOE in 1965, rough and disruptive as it was in its execution, did establish new management controls, new long-range program and policy planning instrumentalities, and a tidier grouping of functions. If some of these gains created new tensions and new inertias, it is well to be reminded that reorganization is always tentative. USOE has not achieved its final shape. To the extent that it remains vital, it never will.

The Reorganization of HEW

At the same time that the Office of Education was being reorganized, its parent department, HEW, was itself undergoing significant changes in personnel and organization that were to condition USOE administration in subsequent months. The major factor in these events was the appointment of John W. Gardner as successor to Anthony Celebrezze as Secretary of HEW. Widely interpreted as an indication of the heightened importance attached to education both in HEW and in the President's Cabinet, the appointment also reflected President Johnson's desire to upgrade the performance of a department long noted for a lack of coordination and cooperation among its constituent agencies.

For Gardner the job of establishing more effective central control was greatly eased by events already underway at the time he assumed his new post. In late March, Assistant Secretary Wilbur J. Cohen, perhaps the most experienced and talented of the HEW hands, was promoted to the post of Under Secretary. On July 27, 1965, the very day that the President announced the appointment of Secretary Gardner, an act creating three new assistant secretaryships in HEW was sent by Congress to the President for his signature.

In designing the roles and in selecting the personnel to fill these new positions, as well as in redesigning the functions of two of the three existing assistant secretaryships, Gardner made his imprint on departmental operations. He assigned to these new and redesigned posts the staff function of providing, in Gardner's own words, "extra eyes and hands for the Secretary." [8] Without operating responsibilities, this new topside strength was devoted to fostering cooperative interrelationships

8. Cabell Phillips, *The New York Times,* June 21, 1966, 17.

that heretofore had been absent at the department level. Assistant secretaries for Education, Health and Scientific Affairs, and Individual and Family Services, were each responsible for one of the broad tripartite substantive areas of the department's responsibility. To the first of these, Gardner appointed Francis Keppel, who for a number of months carried the double assignment of Assistant Secretary and U.S. Commissioner of Education. In February, 1966 Keppel relinquished his position as U.S. Commissioner of Education and was succeeded by Harold Howe II. An Assistant Secretary for Program Coordination was created to perform for HEW the kinds of modern management, program planning, and budgeting functions that the McNamara "whiz kids" had brought to the Pentagon. William Gorham, a young and talented McNamara protégé, was brought over from the Department of Defense (DOD) to fill this new post. A newly established comptrollership, with rank eventually equal to that of the assistant secretaries, was given the task of developing fiscal controls and analyses of department-wide applicability. Finally, the Office of the Secretary itself was directly strengthened by the creation of the post of Assistant to the Secretary for Civil Rights.

During the last half of 1965 and continuing through 1966, then, a strengthened Secretary's Office, aided by a number of high level and extraordinarily talented assistants, sought to develop the knowledge and control necessary to overcome the department's traditional fragmentation. By March, 1966, a *Wall Street Journal* writer was marvelling at the degree to which these efforts and the personal influence of Secretary Gardner had motivated the HEW operating agencies "to pull together on common problems." [9] USOE, like other HEW components, was affected by the efforts to establish greater uniformity in department-wide policy on such matters as grant-in-aid administration, budgeting and program planning, and professional employment and advancement policies. And with John Gardner as Secretary and Francis Keppel as Assistant Secretary for Education, there was no longer any doubt that the USOE had ready access and support in the highest departmental councils.

Reorganization and the Administration of ESEA

Of special relevance to the administration of ESEA was the structure for the new Bureau of Elementary and Secondary Education (BESE). Arthur L. Harris, a veteran USOE executive, was put in charge of BESE. (Harris had formerly headed the Bureau of Educational As-

9. Jonathan Spivak, *Wall Street Journal,* March 14, 1966, 10.

sistance programs.) The Bureau of Elementary and Secondary Education was assigned five divisions, three of which were directly concerned with the administration of ESEA. A Division of Program Operations was set up to handle the Title I payments to State education agencies for grants to local school districts for the education of children from low-income families.[10] The Division of Plans and Supplementary Centers was assigned the administration of grants under Titles II and III. The Division of State Agency Cooperation was charged with administering Title V money for the strengthening of State Departments of Education.

The administration of Title IV (Educational Research), on the other hand, was assigned to a Division of Laboratories and Research Development in the Bureau of Research. The organizational separation of Titles III and IV within USOE made difficult the effective relating of the experimental activities of the Title IV labs to the dissemination activities of the supplementary education centers under Title III. But it would have been illogical not to have placed Title IV activity under the Bureau of Research, and the ensuing administrative hiatuses were testament only to the impossibility of resolving all coordination problems by structural means.

Actually, according to the Ink Task Force design, problems of lateral coordination among bureaus were to be solved by the new staff offices to the Commissioner (Office of Program Planning and Evaluation, Office of Administration, etc.). Beyond that, these overhead staff offices were expected to absorb a substantial part of the new ESEA workload by providing expanded budget, personnel, information, correspondence, data processing, planning, and statistical services as well as the administrative support needed by a bevy of statutory advisory councils mandated in the law.

Structural reorganization facilitated, but did not obviate the necessity of, new hirings. When Congress passed the FY'66 supplemental appropriations for ESEA, it authorized 330 new positions in USOE, divided as shown in Table 5.

Organization of Title I

The most substantial burden of administering ESEA fell upon the Division of Program Operations (DPO) in the Bureau of Elementary and Secondary Education. DPO was responsible for all Title I grants (by far the largest allotments under ESEA), and for initial review of the programs assigned to the Division of Plans and Supplementary

10. By August 1966, the name of this unit had been changed to the Division of Compensatory Education, in order to define more clearly the purposes of the division.

TABLE 5

NEW ESEA-AUTHORIZED POSITIONS—DIVIDED BY TITLE

Component of ESEA	Bureau or Division	Number of Positions
Title I	Division of Program Operations	82
Title II	Division of Plans and Supplementary Centers	30
Title III	Division of Plans and Supplementary Centers	80
Title IV	Bureau of Research	40
Title V	Division of State Agency Cooperation	28
Supporting Services	Various Central Staff Offices	70

Centers under Titles II and III. DPO was subdivided into units engaged either in program development and evaluation (Policy and Procedures Unit; Programs Branch), or in reviewing grant applications and authorizations and providing services to state and local educational authorities (Operations Branch; Field Services Branch).

Under the direction of John F. Hughes, former chief administrative officer for USOE, DPO through Title I handled over half of BESE's FY'66 appropriations,[11] and over 90 per cent of ESEA's funding.

Perhaps the most troublesome initial difficulty for DPO, and for the rest of the Office of Education, was that of staffing. The Ink Committee had singled out "new blood" as the most important element in revamping the agency. Congress had authorized new positions. But finding the right people quickly was very difficult. It was December, 1965, eight months after the passage of ESEA and three months after its funding, before DPO approached its authorized personnel strength of 82. In the meantime, a variety of expedients was used, and successive waves of recruits were put to work on the tasks at hand with a minimum of briefing and supervision.

The initial professional cadre of the Division of Program Operations consisted almost entirely of a scattering of experienced middle-level staff transferred from a variety of posts in the old USOE organization—mainly from NDEA functions. To these were added a group of seven young college graduates selected from the roster of the Federal Service Entrance Examination. In August, 1965, Division Director Hughes got

11. The remainder was largely for NDEA programs.

badly needed staff support when two assistants were recruited for his immediate office: a Harvard graduate student in Political Economy who was assigned to program development, and a transfer from the National Science Foundation who was made the Division's administrative officer. Specialists, such as psychologists and economists, were obtained on temporary detail from other USOE offices or as part-time consultants from university faculties. Free-lance writers were engaged for temporary writing assignments.

Even these ad hoc arrangements of staffing by transfer and short-term recruitment placed an extraordinary burden on USOE's already overworked Office of Personnel—itself undergoing radical reorganization. And the paper-and-paste nature of covering the DPO table of organization with "something borrowed, something new" led to inevitable confusion and lost motion. It all added up to heavy burdens of over-work for the dedicated, knowledgeable few.

And yet, the very openness of staff relationships put a premium on individual initiative irrespective of employee rank, and the excitement of launching a new program tempered the ordeal of uncertainty and confusion that marked the early months of ESEA. High morale was particularly noticeable among the inexperienced but intelligent Federal Service Entrance Examination recruits whose assignments, as in OEO at the time, far exceeded in variety and responsibility what they would have enjoyed in a more stable situation or agency.

The confusions attendant upon a crash recruitment drive were compounded in the early months by problems of relationships between DPO and other administrative units in USOE. The Ink Committee had reasoned that various school-aid programs of USOE could be most effectively coordinated by grouping the various programs in divisions of parallel status, giving the chief of BESE and his staff the responsibility of providing unified direction. But the job was so big and the need for haste so great that theoretical allocations of responsibility would not stay put. During the first months following the upheaval of reorganization, the machinery of problem-solving and information-sharing was underdeveloped. This was particularly troublesome in relation to Title I because of its size and complexity. In consequence, every ranking official in USOE who had had any initial responsibilities for Title I in the days of the Executive Group, before reorganization, remained entangled in its implementation after reorganization.

It was known in advance that neither DPO nor any of the other divisions could be completely self-contained operations. The USOE staff offices were expected to help with the tremendous initial burdens imposed by ESEA on the operating units. However, the extent to which the Commissioner, the Deputy Commissioner, the Associate Commissioner for Federal-State Relations, the Office of Equal Educational Opportunity, the Office of Legislation, the Office of Administration, the Office of Information, and the National Center for Educational Statistics inevitably became involved in DPO implementation activities was largely unforeseen.

Furthermore, HEW, Congress, the White House, the press and professional interest groups kept up a steady drum-beat of requests for information—requests that flowed into all corners of USOE and then were referred to whomever might be available and knowledgeable inside or outside DPO. All these factors combined to impede the development of routine working relationships at subordinate levels.

And for months the various staff offices at the Commissioner's level were not fully operative. As a result, the effort to obtain the needed supporting services consumed much staff time and energy in DPO during the shake-down period.

Organization for Titles II–V

The administration of Titles II and III was placed under BESE, but in a separate Division of Plans and Supplementary Centers (DPSC) under the direction of Ralph Becker. DPSC was divided into four branches: Instructional Resources, Innovation Centers, Program Development and Dissemination, and Guidance and Personnel Services.

Because Title II involved formula grants to the States, its administration was relatively simple and was confined largely to the preparation of Regulations and Guidelines. Three women with library service background were hired for this purpose. They were placed in the Instructional Resources Branch which also had the responsibility for administering Title III of NDEA (allotments to states for strengthening instructional facilities in science, mathematics, and foreign languages). The staff assigned specifically to ESEA Title II remained small during the first year. After that it was augmented slightly to provide additional services at the field level of USOE, but even then the total professional complement was less than a dozen.

For Title III, another branch in DPSC was created: an Innovative Centers Branch. This took form after considerable bickering as to whether Title III belonged in the Bureau of Research or in BESE. The issue was debated hotly in Executive Group meetings. Keppel himself finally resolved the issue in favor of BESE. The Innovative Centers Branch was subdivided into area units: first, three; later, five; still later, nine. The Branch's table of organization allowed for nearly 50 positions.

By borrowing and stealing personnel from other parts of USOE, the Innovative Centers Branch managed to begin with a dozen full-time staff. By March, 1966, it had approximated its authorized strength. But like DPO, the Innovative Centers Branch of DPSC went through months of traumatic staff shortages, turnover, and work overload.

Title IV was assigned to USOE's new Bureau of Research under Acting Director Francis Ianni. The Bureau was composed of five divisions, three of these parallel to the remaining bureau structure of USOE: Elementary and Secondary Research, Higher Education Research, and Adult and Vocational Research. The other two divisions (Research Training and Dissemination, and Laboratories and Research Development) carried the brunt of the innovative aspects of Title IV: the training of educational researchers, university-based research and development centers, and the new educational laboratories. General research grants of the type previously authorized under the Cooperative Research Act of 1954, were parcelled out to the divisions of the Bureau of Research by an Internal Review Committee consisting of the division chiefs within the Bureau plus program officers from the other bureaus of USOE. This fairly cumbersome mechanism was dictated by the fact that if research were to be related to the on-going needs of the operating bureaus, these bureaus had to be represented on a committee charged with establishing research priorities.

Staffing the new functions of the Bureau of Research turned out to be an horrendous undertaking. Policy and administrative talent in the field of educational research was in short supply in the country at large, and competition for available talent was acute. Almost two years were to go by, for example, before a division chief could be found for the Division of Laboratories and Research Development. In the meantime, acting chiefs came and went with the seasons.

The Research Training and Dissemination Division and the Division of Laboratories and Research Development together were initially allotted a total of 20 positions. In the early months they had to settle for eight or nine. Perhaps no part of USOE faced more traumatic problems of hiring and retaining competent staff during ESEA's first year than the Division of Laboratories and Research Development. A large part of the hostility toward the Bureau of Research that developed among university and educational laboratory personnel during the first year of ESEA can be attributed to the gaps and the turnover in this division's staff during this period. And 70 per cent of the Bureau of Research's FY'66 appropriations were accounted for by Title IV activities alone.

Title V was assigned to a Division of State Agency Cooperation within BESE. The Division was under the direction of Dr. Robert L.

Hopper. Its two branches (State Agency Support and Administrative-Instructional Support) were allotted 78 positions for FY'66. Because of the key role of the States in implementing other titles of ESEA as well as other educational programs administered by USOE, Dr. Hopper's staff was necessarily involved in conversations and collaboration with other divisions of BESE and with the other bureaus of the Office. Special relationships also existed with Wayne Reed, USOE's Associate Commissioner for Federal-State Relations, who maintained close liaison with the Chief State School Officers (CCSO's). But these inter-agency and inter-bureau relationships tended to be intermittent and casual at best.

The Problem of Intra-Agency Coordination

In fact, during the first year, in spite of the work of the Executive Group, little progress was made in coordinating the work for the several parts of USOE concerned with ESEA implementation. This was especially true among and within the several divisions of BESE. Whether these hiatuses were due to the diverse character of staffs and programs, to the low priority given to the problem of inter-divisional coordination in comparison with other management objectives, or to difficulties each division encountered in meeting its own particular responsibilities, the outcome was that each division proceeded to operate in a relatively autonomous fashion. This reality goes far to explain the complaint that began to flow from State and local educational agencies during the fall and winter of 1965–66—that they were being deluged with a flood of diverse application and report requirements related to the various new federal grant programs. In this connection, it should be noted that the strengthening of the USOE regional office staffs that had been recommended by the Ink Committee as a means of coordinating and smoothing agency relations with state and local authorities, was deferred to a second step of reorganization. In consequence, during the hectic, formative stages of ESEA implementation, staff members in the various divisions of BESE carried on direct, independent communications with SEA's and LEA's on details of policy implementation and procedure.

In the face of drastic reorganization, ensuing administrative ambiguities, ad hoc staffing patterns, and operating hiatuses, the wonder is that progress in implementing Title I and the other Titles of ESEA moved as rapidly as it did.

IV. The Process of Implementation

Program execution is at the very heart of the administrative process. An agency's top leaders may participate actively in program formulation, in legislative in-fighting, in making structural changes in the agency's organization; but these activities simply set the conditions and the framework within which the overwhelming majority of the agency's personnel fulfill their operating functions.

The carrying out of a new legislative mandate is rarely simple. Laws are neither self-explanatory nor self-executing in any detailed sense. And laws aimed at providing massive new services in a complex and pluralistic Federal system are particularly difficult to render operational. The process, in David Truman's phrase, of "finding a way of turning the controversial into the routine" [1] is itself far from routine. It involves creative acts of discretionary judgment; an endless interplay with affected clients in the development, interpretation, and modification of ground rules; an elaborate system of data gathering, analysis, and reporting for purposes of administrative and fiscal accountability as well as program execution; a constant sensitivity to demands by executive and legislative superiors, as well as by group interests and the press, for explanations of actions taken or contemplated; resiliency in dealing with the ambiguous functions of statutory or ad hoc advisory committees and panels; and an almost infinite capacity for adjusting to policy modifications imposed by political necessity or induced by administrative experience.

All this must occur within a general framework of predictability, consistency, and equity in the application of the law.

The actions of Federal officials are, of course, partly predictable. They are constrained by specific provisions of enabling and appropriations acts and by statements in congressional hearings, reports, and debates. Related statutes and precedents impose government-wide, standardized procedures for many of the administrative operations. Even when a statute leaves much to administrative discretion, the manner in which it will be executed may be anticipated from a knowledge of the relevant policy issues, the key political actors and interest groups, and the past performance of the agency—especially if its leaders took an active part in drafting and obtaining passage of the legislation.

1. See David Truman, *The Governmental Process* (New York: Knopf, 1960).

Probabilities, however, are not certainties. The accidents and dynamics of administration produce unique and unpredictable developments. When, as in the case of ESEA, a law unprecedented in scope has to be administered through State and local instrumentalities, on an impossible time schedule; by an understaffed agency in structural turmoil, beset by a deluge of complaints and demands for clarification of the legislation at hand, as well as cognate legislation already on the books; the wonder is not that mistakes are made—the wonder is that the law is implemented at all. Those who took delight in pointing out the inadequacies and deficiencies of USOE in carrying out ESEA during the first year of operations rarely stopped to examine the immensity of the task or the complexity of the context.

It is not surprising to find that the initial euphoric reaction of schoolmen to the passage of ESEA gave way, in many cases, to misunderstanding, confusion and disenchantment. Congressional consideration of ESEA had progressed so rapidly that few State and local school authorities understood the Act's specific provisions or its thrust toward certain basic educational changes. Schoolmen were dismayed to learn that ESEA was not "general aid." They were confused by the technicalities involved in eligibility; they were overwhelmed by the amount of paper-work required.

The general task of the USOE staff was to define the options available to the State educational agencies and/or the local educational agencies, or other grantees, and to deal with the technical and political dilemmas posed by the statute in ways that would be likely to enlist the understanding, concurrence, and enthusiasm of these partner-clients. The matters to be considered were themselves likely to create controversy among the partners. For example: how could USOE be specific, even coercive, with regard to fiscal accounting, and at the same time be flexible and permissive in establishing criteria for local project design? How could project criteria be made universally applicable to school districts whose characteristics varied on every conceivable dimension, without stating criteria in terms either too vague or too detailed? What degree of uniformity in applying national standards should be expected or required from SEA officials?

The implementation stage offered Federal officials their most important opportunity to exercise initiative and foresight in exploring policy alternatives, in ventilating controversies, and in testing strategies for obtaining a high degree of voluntary compliance with legislative intent. But implementation was fraught with dilemmas and uncertainties. The problems of implementation differed to some extent from title to title, but some tasks were common to all of the titles: hard and hectic staff work by program officials and legal talent within USOE and HEW, in the preparation of regulations and guidelines, questionnaires, and application and report forms; circuit riding by USOE staff, and both informal and formal "feed-back" colloquies with professional associations and state and local educational officials in the paper planning and modification process; answering thousands of questions and requests for information coming directly by mail, telephone, or personal visitations—or indirectly through congressional or White House channels. All involved, at some point, the cooperation and scrutiny of advisory councils, committees, and/or screening panels—ad hoc and statutory; and ultimately, a series of reviews by congressional subcommittees and by the less formal instruments of a free press and an inquiring academic and professional community.

What varied from title to title were the precise objectives and their attendant and peculiar administrative aspects; the locus of responsibility within USOE; the combination of agencies, public and private, charged with administering each title; the clientele; and the peculiar mix of what Gabriel Almond has called in another context "the attentive public."

In order to avoid undue repetition, major attention is given in this chapter to the implementation of one title only: Title I. Brief mention will be made of the other titles of ESEA and of the peculiar issues surrounding the implementation of Title VI of the Civil Rights Act of 1964. But Title I was by far the largest and most pervasive program under ESEA. The story of its implementation includes processes and problems which were in fact generic to ESEA as a whole.

IMPLEMENTING TITLE I: THE SETTING

The scope of the task of administering Title I of ESEA was unprecedented. Subject to qualifying conditions for approvable projects, nearly 25,000 school districts in 54 States and territories were entitled to spend more than a billion dollars within 15 months, on a specifically targeted group: the educationally disadvantaged. For the initiation of the program to be smoothly integrated with preparations for the school year beginning in September, 1965, the tool-up period for school officials would have been, theoretically, the last three months of FY'65 (April–June) and the first quarter of FY'66, (July–September 1965). But monies for the Act were not even appropriated until September 23, 1965. To launch such an enormous undertaking would take at the very least a number of months. As a result, those responsible were beset not only by the inherent size and difficulties of tasks of implementation but also by mounting pressures to overcome a serious time-lag in putting the funds to work before the statutory deadlines for their expiration. The months spent in gearing up would bring the calendar closer and closer to the end of the fiscal year in which the money was to be spent.

These tight realities were further complicated by the fact that the enactment of Title I found educators, including those in USOE, in a poor state of readiness to move rapidly in carrying out its unfamiliar demands. To begin with, Title I was targeted to the very group of students for which traditional local school services had been least satisfactory. Although a few districts had had special programs to meet the needs of educationally disadvantaged children, these efforts had provided little certainty as to what activities were really effective. Furthermore, there was a widespread shortage of personnel qualified to plan and operate such projects. In fact, many districts entitled to Title I funds had no previous experience in carrying out federally-connected projects of any kind.

These general handicaps were substantial in themselves. However, as knowledge of the provisions of Title I became more widespread, it was apparent to local school administrators that other headaches were involved. The requirements that Title I projects be designed to meet the needs of educationally disadvantaged children, and be of appropriate size, scope, and quality, clearly implied that the services provided would have to be additional to, but not isolated from, the regular school offerings for such children. And the statutory emphasis on measuring the educational achievement of the beneficiaries of Title I projects appeared to lead in the direction of a national assessment of a school's effectiveness—a development long feared and resisted by school administrators throughout the country.

Hope, anxiety, uncertainty, inexperience, and fear at the local level comprised the intellectual and emotional setting within which USOE and SEA's had to implement much of the new experiment in national educational policy represented by Title I of ESEA.

ESEA Task Force Activities, April to June, 1965

Even though the reorganization of USOE was not to be completed before June 15, structural arrangements were made in mid-April to handle the initial tasks of implementing ESEA. The Executive Group set up a special Planning Group under the chairmanship of Russell Wood, then in the Office of Administration, later Acting Director of the Office of Program Planning and Evaluation. Task forces were organized for each of the ESEA titles, with staffs of 10 to 12 persons selected from throughout the agency for their competency in the various areas relevant to each title. In addition, three specialized subgroups were designated to work on services common to the implementation of all the titles: i.e., data sources and needs, form design, and fiscal requirements. The Executive Group assigned the highest priority to the preparations to launch Titles I and V—Title I because of its size and complexity; Title V because of the patent necessity of strengthening the administrative capacity of State educational agencies for their role in implementing new Federal programs including Titles I and II of ESEA.

The specific mission of the Title I Task Force was to develop regulations, guidelines, and the official forms required to administer the largest of the ESEA programs.

Other immediate USOE responsibilities for Title I were handled outside the task forces. For example, the National Center for Educational Statistics was made responsible for working with the Bureau of the Census and the Welfare Administration of HEW in bringing together the data required by the Title I formula. The appointment of the National Advisory Council, required by Section 212 of the Act, received top level attention in the Office of the Commissioner. During May, Associate Commissioner Reed, the former Deputy Commissioner, planned a series of regional meetings of leading school administrators, state and local, at which various high ranking officials of USOE explained the new legislation. As coordinator of the ESEA task forces, Wood periodically reported their problems and progress to the Executive Group, transmitted clarifications of policy decisions to the task forces, and saw to it that they held to specified deadlines.

TITLE I: A SUMMARY OF SEQUENCE

The tasks of the Office of Education in implementing Title I may be grouped under the following classifications: (1) the development of standards and procedures for the funding and control of authorizations; (2) the construction of ground rules and guidelines for educational programming and project design; and (3) the preparation and analysis of reports and other informational and administrative data. These activities are logically sequential in the sense that funding-authorizations and program regulations are essential for subsequent official action, and reports must be based on some period of program execution. However, in the shaping of Title I, anticipatory and unofficial actions became important preludes to official decisions and rule-making. To illustrate, USOE officials held the first round of a series of regional meetings in May, 1965, to provide advance information to, and seek advice from, the educational community at a time when the preparation of official guidelines was just getting started. During the summer of 1965, official guidelines were actually drafted. In November, 1965 a number of USOE officials attended the annual conference of the Council of Chief State School Officers in Honolulu. This participation led shortly thereafter to some official changes in the Title I guidelines. The entire cycle of pre-clearance, official drafts, and post-clearance was reactivated on a small scale when Title I was amended in October, 1965 to include handicapped children in state-supported institutions. Since the activities described under (1), (2), and (3) above were to some extent all going on concurrently, Table 6 has been provided as an aid in clarifying the chronological sequence of implementation in the 15-month period between April, 1965 and July, 1966.

Title I: Authorization Funding and Controls

The first major task to confront those charged with implementing Title I was the development of standards and procedures for the funding and control of authorizations to the States and through the States to the local educational agencies.

The funding of authorizations involved two separate tasks for the implementation architects: first, determination of grant entitlements (i.e., how much money could be allotted to each school district); and second, development of criteria for the design and approval of the local programs. The analytic separation of these interrelated procedures reflected an important policy assumption: that whereas grants were to be made to school districts in accordance with measures of economic need, children were to participate in the program's benefits solely on the basis of relative "educational disadvantage." The result of this policy distinction was to separate the tasks of fiscal and program administration and to create a source of confusion for LEA's. A number of school districts assumed that if they qualified under the Title I formula they could spend Federal money on programs benefitting *all* children. That is, they viewed ESEA as *general aid* distributed on a basis of a "poverty" formula, rather than as *aid to the educationally disadvantaged* distributed according to a "poverty" formula.

The task of developing funding-authorizations and controls was fairly familiar, technical, and relatively non-controversial.

Several sections of the statute dealt almost exclusively with fiscal administration. Section 203 gave the Commissioner of Education the authority to determine both the eligibility of school districts for grants and, if satisfactory data for the purpose were available, the amount of their maximum basic grants.

TABLE 6

Activities	April to June, 1965	July to September, 1965
Funding—Authorizations and Controls	USOE consulted with Census Bureau and Welfare Department of HEW on basic data requirements (May).	USOE sent SEA's suggested form for providing assurances of compliance and Census data for minor governmental subdivisions (July 30). USOE computed maximum grant entitlements to county level and notified SEA's (Aug. 26). Thirty SEA's submitted assurances and received authority to commit FY'66 funds (Sept. 23).
Preparation of Regulations, Guidelines, and Project Application Forms	USOE Title I Task Force appointed (April). CSSO reviewed draft *Regulations* (June 24–25).	Representatives of church groups reviewed the draft *Regulations* (July and August). USOE urged SEA's to prepare for project approval workload and provided draft of *Project Application Form* (July 30). USOE sent final version of *Regulations* to SEA's (August 26) and published them in *Federal Register* (Sept.). USOE compiled draft *Guidelines* (Aug.–Sept.).
Reports		
Administrative and Informational Services	USOE and State officials discussed ESEA implementation at regional meetings (May).	DPO collected informational materials on educationally disadvantaged children; began year-long program of dissemination to SEA's (Sept.).
Related Events	Ink Committee appointed (April); completed survey of USOE (June).	USOE reorganized; DPO made responsible for Title I (July). Congress passed FY'66 appropriations for ESEA (Sept. 23).

Chronological Sequence of Major Implementation Activities for Title I, April, 1965–July, 1966

October to December, 1965	January to July, 1966
Remaining SEA's submitted assurances and received funding authorizations; all SEA's computed sub-county entitlements and notified LEA's (Nov.). USOE requested SEA's to supply basic data for computing grant entitlements under Public Law 89–313 (Nov.). Project design and approval activities got underway in nearly all States (Nov.–Dec.).	USOE sent SEA's instructions for grant applications under Public Law 89–313 (Feb.); sent notifications of their grant entitlements (April). USOE sent cut-off dates for SEA approval of new projects to be funded in FY'66 (April); deadline for all FY'66 project approval was June 30. HEW staff prepared draft *Audit Instructions* (July).
USOE provided SEA's with supply of printed *Project Application Form* and requested copies of SEA approved applications (Sept.–Oct.). USOE draft *Guidelines* discussed at regional meetings (Oct. 14–29), CCSSO conference, and meeting of CCSSO representatives (Nov.). Targeting provisions modified, and final version sent to SEA's (Dec.).	USOE sent SEA's revised instructions for FY'66 *Project Application Form* (Jan.) and a revised *Form* and instructions for FY'67 (June). Revised version of *Regulations,* with Public Law 89–313 amendments published in *Federal Register* (March). USOE asked SEA's to submit complete descriptions of organization and staffing arrangements (July).
USOE sent SEA's instructions for interim annual report (Dec.).	SEA's submitted interim reports which USOE summarized; USOE also compiled *Report on 484 Title I Projects* (Feb.). National Advisory Council completed first report (March) and contracted for consultants to review summer projects (June). USOE published *Chance for a Change* and *Report on the National Conference for Education of the Disadvantaged* (July). USOE sent SEA's instructions for first annual report, due Dec., 1966 (April).
DPO officials conducted regional "roadshows" on Title I implementation (See *Guidelines* item above).	DPO conducted field program reviews and held regional conferences on evaluation (March–May). National Conference on Title I (July).
Congress passed Title I amendments in Public Law 89–313 (Oct.).	Congressional Education subcommittees held hearings on amendments to ESEA (March–April).

Since the collection and analysis of precise demographic data for the purpose of determining a school district's eligibility under the Title I formula was bound in some cases to be an attenuated process, pragmatic bench-marks had to be substituted for refined calibration—at least for FY'66. Otherwise, time taken in establishing eligibility would have denied most LEA's any funds at all. In consequence, a division of labor was worked out between Federal and State officials. In all but 11 States, USOE determined eligibility and aggregate maximum grants only to the county level—using data from the decennial census of 1960 along with records of the payment of aid-to-dependent-children grants during calendar year 1962. The states whose school districts were not coterminous with census-tabulated units were authorized to compute allocations to school districts at the sub-county level.

Congress had settled temporarily on the use of out-of-date national demographic and economic measures on the grounds that they were the best available. However, it soon became apparent that the task of applying uniform criteria for the purpose of making sub-county allocations was complicated (1) by the difficulties of adjusting census-tract data to school district populations; (2) by the inconsistency or incompleteness of other data sources; and (3) by geographical variations in the jurisdiction of different kinds of school districts (e.g., elementary *vs.* K–12 districts). These were among the first problems explored jointly in conferences of USOE and groups of state officials, and a pilot survey was conducted to test the feasibility of alternate methods of procedure. The final decision was that the States could enjoy flexibility in choosing among several bases for computing sub-county allocations, but that the same basis had to be applied throughout the State. Detailed rules were drafted to guide the states in treating uniformly a variety of school district boundary conditions.[2]

The Census Bureau and the Welfare Administration of HEW provided USOE with the requisite statistics, and in July, USOE supplied the State education agencies with the census tract data for their minor governmental subdivisions, alerting the SEA's to their forthcoming task of computing sub-county allocations. The State agencies were also sent instructions on the method of submitting assurances of intent to participate in Title I grants. Such assurances were dictated by Section 206 of ESEA. On August 26, the States were notified of the maximum county-level allocations, and immediately following the approval of the First FY'66 Supplemental Appropriation Act on September 23, the 30 states which had already filed satisfactory assurances were authorized to com-

2. *Code of Federal Regulations,* Title 45, Sections 116.4–116.7.

mit Title I funds upon approval of LEA project proposals. By late October, practically all of the States had submitted assurances, and had notified the LEA's of their entitlements. By that same date, a number of States had actually launched the process of reviewing local project applications.

As to the adoption of grant payment procedures and subsequent fiscal requirements, two factors eased the workload of the implementation period. The first was that "obligation accounting" and "letter of credit" systems for requesting, expending, and reporting on federal grant funds had already became familiar to a number of state and local school administrators under previous legislation and could readily be incorporated into the Title I Regulations and Guidelines.[3] The other factor was related to levels of funding for FY'66. Section 208 provided for "ratable reductions" of total amounts for which LEA's were eligible under the Title I formula in case appropriations were insufficient to pay the full entitlements. As noted in Chapter II, the initial FY'66 appropriations were substantially lower than the Administration's estimate of requirements; but they were also open-ended. That is, USOE did not need to revise the basic entitlements downward. Instead, in March, 1966, USOE simply requested supplemental appropriations to cover revised estimates of the amounts to be obligated by the LEA's during the remainder of FY'66.[4]

When it appeared that substantial amounts could not be used for projects during the regular school term, Commissioner Howe joined OEO officials in an urgent appeal to school administrators to develop Title I programs for the summer of 1966. The SEA's had a special interest in making it possible for the LEA's to claim full entitlement, since the amount of funds available for state administrative purposes was computed on the basis of funds obligated for approved projects.

USOE officials were not only concerned about under-expending FY '66 appropriations; they also feared that a last-minute rush to obligate funds would lower the standards for planning and approving Title I funds. In what school administrators protested as a precipitate and

3. The relevant instructions are to be found in the USOE publication *Financial Management of Federal-State Education Programs,* OE-10019, 1962. There have been some persistent problems in meshing Federal, State, and local accounting and auditing requirements and procedures. See the response to questions on this matter made by Associate Commissioner Harris in *Hearings Before the Special Subcommittee on Education, on the U.S. Office of Education,* 89th Cong., 2d sess., House, 311–12.

4. Title I funding for FY'67 turned out to be much more complicated. *Hearings Before Subcommittees of the Committee on Appropriations,* Supplemental Appropriation Bill, 1967, 89th Cong., 2d sess., House, Part I, 450–463.

arbitrary move, Commissioner Howe issued instructions on April 2, 1966, setting deadlines for project submission and approval. The State agencies were instructed not to approve proposals involving construction, related equipment, or major capital outlay after April 6, and not to approve proposals submitted after May 2.[5]

In spite of (perhaps because of) such strictures, USOE reported that 89 per cent of available funds, or $826 million, was obligated prior to the close of the fiscal year. About $250 million of the $959 million appropriated was approved for projects to be undertaken during the summer of 1966.[6]

With regard to fiscal accountability for the Title I projects, the official Federal issuances became progressively tighter. The earliest regulations referred in general terms only to provision of "proper fiscal controls" at the State and local levels.[7] Six months later, the revised regulations amplified this requirement in a new section on fiscal audits.[8] Further detailed Federal restrictions were issued to ensure SEA uniformity with regard to disbursing and accounting procedures, forms, and impending audits. The SEA's had over-all supervision of LEA fiscal operations, but Federal surveillance was also to be provided both in the form of program reviews by USOE personnel at unspecified intervals, and annual fiscal audits by the HEW staff. Both activities would normally be concerned only with the State level of operation but could be extended to the LEA's if Federal officials found State controls inadequate.

On July 1, 1966 the HEW Audit Agency issued very detailed *Interim Audit Instruction C-10* to apply to the initial review of Title I operations. Auditors were to be concerned primarily with fiscal records and procedures, but they were also to mesh their activities with those of the USOE officials responsible for administrative and program reviews.

During the first year of Title I implementation, Federal officials were seeking to develop systematic compliance by SEA's and LEA's in matters of fiscal accountability and, at the same time, to encourage them to exert initiative in designing their educational programs for disadvantaged children so as to fit local needs and circumstances. These objectives, however, called for different kinds of competency and orientation on the part of school administrators. The FY'66 experience

5. Memoranda from the U.S. Commissioner of Education to Chief State School Officers, April 2 and April 6, 1966; Memorandum of John F. Hughes, Director, Division of Program Operations, to Title I Coordinators, April 14, 1966.

6. *Education USA,* National Education Association, September 8, 1966, 12; December 8, 1966, 90.

7. *Code of Federal Regulations,* Title 45, Section 116.31(d).

8. *Ibid.,* Section 116.48.

indicated that achieving the first objective may be easier than the second. The SEA's and LEA's protested the paperwork imposed by the fiscal accounting, but the requirements were more definite and less troublesome for them than those connected with project design. Students of the administrative process have pointed out that zealous attention to accounting and auditing considerations can subvert flexible and innovative programming.[9] The effects of the Federal fiscal procedures on the educational policy outcomes of Title I were not evident during the early months of the program, but, at an evaluation session in the winter of 1966, urban school officials reported particular difficulty in assimilating Title I projects into their regular programs because of the Federal requirements of entirely separate accounting systems.[10] One of the continuing problems in all systems of public accountability is what Professor Wallace Sayre of Columbia University has called the danger of "the triumph of technique over purpose."

Title I: Ground Rules for Educational Programming and Project Design [11]

Sections 205 and 206 of Title I dealt with program administration and set forth the respective responsibilities of the USOE, and SEA's, and the LEA's. These sections contain the statutory basis for altering the relationships among the three levels of government, for adding new dimensions to federally-funded school aid programs, and for USOE's unprecedented discretionary power in developing administrative ground rules. Specifically, the Commissioner of Education was authorized to establish criteria for State approval of LEA grant applications (Section 205 (a)) and to decide on the details necessary for approval of State applications to participate in the Title I program (Section 206 (a)). USOE officials were, in fact, charged with clarifying ambiguous legislative language relating to some of the most sensitive areas of school management. Just as the drafting of ESEA involved a delicate balance of intergovernmental interests, so the development of ground rules became a matter of vital concern to all the affected groups. Considerations

9. See Frederick C. Mosher, *Program Budgeting: Theory and Practice* (Chicago: Public Administration Service, 1954), 226.

10. See *Education USA,* National Education Association, December 29, 1966, 108.

11. The term "ground rules" refers both to the substance of program rules (whether issued as formal agency regulations or guidelines, supplementary memoranda, or other instructional formats), and to the procedural relationships established by federal officials to govern their negotiations in carrying out their rule-making tasks.

of program administration and educational politics can scarcely be separated in the analysis of the rule-making task.

Development of Regulations and Guidelines

The official promulgation of *Regulations* and *Guidelines* for Title I was given highest priority as soon as the act was passed. From April to December, 1965, this task involved a painstaking process of intra-agency collaboration and of consultations with interested outsiders. A succession of draft documents was prepared. Although the two publications, *Regulations* and *Guidelines,* were interdependent in content and required the joint effort of lawyers and program specialists, they were technically distinct in regard to purpose and mode of preparation.

Under the Administrative Procedures Act of 1946, agency regulations are promulgated by the President and have the status of Federal law. They are the vehicle for specifying how a statute will be put into effect and may include any supplementary rules the statute instructs the agency to establish for this process. The statutory language is closely followed, although it may be amplified, and the sections of the law may be rearranged for greater clarity and for conformity to the government-wide codification scheme of the *Federal Register.* The drafting task calls for a legal counsel highly skilled in administrative law, aided by experienced program specialists. Their work may be somewhat simplified in the case of a statute like Title I of Public Law 89–10, which is technically an amendment to a previous law, because it is then possible to incorporate applicable definitions and other provisions verbatim from previously existing regulations. It is desirable to keep elaborations of policy or details of administrative procedures to a minimum in the Regulations, since a long process of official clearance is required to amend them in any particular.

Guidelines also express binding Federal policy in the sense that they must be completely consistent with the relevant statute and the regulations. But they are issued on the lesser authority of an agency head and may be amended at his discretion. They are a less legalistic and formal set of instructions, and responsibility for their preparation falls largely to program officials directly in charge of the administration of the law. These officials have considerable latitude in the kinds of content that will be included, such as operating standards, required procedures and forms, allowable deviations, hortatory and precautionary statements, etc. In general, Guidelines comprise relatively long-term directives in comparison with more ephemeral materials issued as ad hoc memoranda or as supplementary publications dealing with matters of specific moment.

Largely at the urging of the HEW legal advisors, the *Regulations* were restricted as closely as possible to statutory language and to the statement of concrete fiscal standards, such as those involved in making the sub-county fund allocations. Specific criteria for project approval and for detailed fiscal procedures, on the other hand, were reserved for the *Guidelines*. The *Regulations* were developed swiftly, and they were made ready for a first review by outsiders at all-day meetings of the Council of Chief State School Officers on June 24 and 25, 1965. During July and August subsequent drafts were reviewed by several of the interest groups concerned with the church-state issue, and the final version of the *Regulations* was distributed in typescript to the SEA's on August 26. Official publication of the *Regulations* in the *Federal Register* appeared on September 15.

In the meantime, agency personnel worked on the *Guidelines* and on a proposed project application form. A draft of the latter was also sent to the States on August 26.

A 76–page preliminary version of the *Guidelines* was first distributed and discussed at five regional meetings held between October 14 and 29. These conferences, dubbed "road shows," were first used in connection with the Higher Education Act of 1963. They involved the majority of the DPO professional staff and more than 500 State and local officials, including school administrators, finance officers, OEO field personnel, and a few representatives of private schools. This first draft of the *Guidelines* was vulnerable to criticism. It was long, discursive, and, in some ways, insensitive to State and local fears of "Federal control." The following is one example of tactless phrasing:

> Without these criteria [for ranking] the State educational agency has no basis to judge whether the local educational agency is fulfilling its obligation, and therefore, the State educational agency cannot approve the project applications without violating its assurance to the U.S. Commissioner of Education.[12]

While many State and local conferees found the meetings a useful and constructive experience, others used the opportunity to air various complaints not only to Federal officials but to the press and to members of Congress.

In early November, the Commissioner and a number of top USOE executives attended the CCSSO meeting in Honolulu. On that occasion the CCSSO adopted the following resolution:

12. Draft *Guidelines,* Title I, ESEA.

> . . . We call upon the U.S. Commissioner of Education and all federal officials dealing with state departments of education to curtail federal discretion to that necessary under the laws. We believe state departments of education should assume full responsibility for their increasing functions. Federal administrative power of approval or disapproval should not be used to induce state departments to act or refrain from acting on matters not legally relevant to the matter under consideration for possible approval by the federal officials.[13]

Behind this verbiage lay numerous outspoken expressions of opposition to specific provisions of the Title I draft guidelines—expressions addressed to USOE officials in the conference sessions. In consequence, USOE acceded to a meeting in Washington on November 23, to permit a final review of the document by Chief State School Officers. Seventeen of the CSSO responded to the invitation to send representatives. Following the Washington meeting, the draft guidelines were again rewritten, and typewritten copies of the final version were sent to the States on December 3. With the exception of the targeting issue, which will be discussed below, few changes in substance were made in the final draft, but the document was considerably condensed and revised editorially, especially the sections on project design and evaluation which were placed after, instead of before, the section on fiscal administration—presumably in order to reduce their prominence.

Although the careful drafting and advance clearances of the *Regulations* and *Guidelines* produced documents which, in the main, were generally acceptable, the length of time required for this process caused a delay of several months before reasonably complete Federal ground rules were generally available to educators. An additional complication arose when several of the more aggressive SEA's followed a suggestion in a memorandum from Commissioner Keppel in July, 1965, that they prepare their own guidelines. When these were distributed before the USOE draft guidelines were completed, conflicts arose over differing SEA and Federal interpretations of project design requirements.

On the other hand, the time-consuming process of consultation served several useful, and probably indispensable, purposes in Title I implementation. It moderated the charges of arbitrary action by Federal officials; it increased understanding and acceptance of the new educational policies and objectives; and it garnered the benefits of experience which some of the front-running SEA's had gained in attempting to formulate draft guidelines of their own.

13. Resolution VII, adopted at the Annual Business Meeting of the Council of Chief State School Officers, Honolulu, Hawaii, November 12, 1965. 11 pp, mimeo.

There was, however, one underlying tension which was imbedded in the very nature of the statute. Previous Federal aid to education (notably "impacted areas" and NDEA) had given wide discretion to LEA's and SEA's in devising local or State educational plans and programs.

Section 205 and 206 of ESEA Title I, on the other hand, gave most of the responsibility for detailed rule-making to the Federal government. This was perhaps the inevitable concomitant of a statute drawn in part to by-pass State restrictions on aid to church-related schools, and designed to serve the national interest in overcoming the pathologies of educational disadvantage in large cities whose interests had been systematically short-changed by rural-oriented SEA's. But the problems of Federal-State cooperation in attempting to fulfill the requirements of Sections 205 and 206 were neither fully anticipated nor well understood in advance. The "assurances from States" required in Section 206(a), for example, involved an application

> ". . . *in such detail as the Commissioner* (U.S.) *deems necessary"* and ". . . annual and *such other reports* to the Commissioner, *in such form and containing such information* as may be necessary to enable the Commissioner to perform *his* duties under this Title." (Emphasis supplied.)

Because of the pressure of time and the need to move money out as quickly as possible, the Commissioner permitted quite loose "assurances." The operating effect of this section was, then, to allow States to qualify for funds *before* providing USOE with staffing, organizational, or procedural commitments. But combined with Section 205, which specifically moved the initiative for project approval criteria to the Federal level, the loose construction of Section 206(a) by the Commissioner prompted the States to busy themselves at the outset with the task of computing sub-county allocations under the formula, rather than with developing program instructions. When the Federal *Regulations* and *Guidelines* were finally issued, most States simply reissued them as constituting the State's own standards. A few States added various kinds of supplementary content, but the Federal hand was clearly dominant. It should be remembered, however, that USOE officials took extraordinary steps to insure State reactions to federally established ground rules during the process of their construction. When USOE officials consulted the State staffs, the overriding purpose was to find definitions and procedures of the widest possible applicability and utility. Nonetheless, Federal initiative was paramount.

To maintain influence in this new situation of diminished rule-making authority, the recourse of some SEA's was to work through an interest group structure. Hence, the militancy of the CCSSO effort to reduce the discretionary authority of Federal officials to a minimum. The militancy was largely ineffectual, however. Many of the SEA's welcomed USOE guidance; some felt that it did not go far enough. They recognized that educators would lack guidance for making consistent and uniform interpretations of the statutory purpose to benefit disadvantaged children, irrespective of locale, unless USOE provided operational meanings for terms like "consistent," "sufficient," "show reasonable promise," and "reasonably necessary" in Sections 205 and 206.

An example of the manner in which USOE proceeded to define the criteria for project design is the low priority established for the use of Title I funds to construct school facilities. The rationale for this federal policy was that the most pressing needs of disadvantaged children could, and should, be met during FY'66 by educational and supplementary services in "operational" projects. The *Regulations* and the *Guidelines* both provided that a project application could not cover construction of school facilities except in those exceptional cases in which construction was demonstrated to be essential to a program or project. To the SEA's and LEA's hungry for construction funds, the USOE priority for "operational" programs was viewed as a sorry example of Federal insensitivity to local needs. To USOE staff, constraints upon using federal funds for facilities was simply a prudent way of insuring that ESEA would not become simply a general aid bill for school construction.

Some of these conflicts were in fact foreseen. When the administration bill was initially unveiled, congressional opponents of ESEA mounted an attack on the "unwarranted" expansion of authority given to the Commissioner of Education in connection with Title I. The following exchange occurred during the first day of hearings before the House General Subcommittee on Education in January, 1965:

> Mr. Goodell (Republican from New York) to HEW Secretary Celebrezze: Tell me about "basic criteria" . . . Can you tell me what "basic criteria"—not "control" but "criteria," you are going to impose on the States? . . .
>
> Secretary Celebrezze: We don't impose anything on the States.
>
> Mr. Goodell: They have to submit their plan in conformance to your criteria.
>
> Secretary Celebrezze: They can participate in a program or they don't have to. It is pretty well set out in the Act . . . It is in the law what the States might submit to the Secretary.
>
> Mr. Goodell: You are not telling me when you go to the States now after this law is passed, you are going to say, "Well, now there is the law, and you interpret it the way you want to." You are

going to go to them with some specific criteria, if you will, basic criteria. I would like to know what they are . . . It is not what control or criteria you have written into this law, it is what you are going to do when you go there to the States and tell them what they can get money for. What kind of plans will qualify for money. And you won't impose it on them because if they don't want the Federal money, all right, but they all want it.

Mr. Cohen (HEW Assistant Secretary): May I try to clarify one point that I think is related to this . . . I interpret "basic criteria" here as used to be in effect criteria defining what is in 1 to 6 (of Section 205) . . . Let me put it this way: I want to make this clear for the legislative history. "Basic criteria" doesn't mean here that the Commissioner may establish, just out of the blue, elements that he thinks the States have to comply with. "Basic criteria" here means definitions and explanations or guidelines, whatever you want to call them, of the terms and conditions that are specified here . . .

Mr. Goodell: All right. You are going to define it. That means what programs are eligible for funds. You are saying to the State in effect, "This is which program is eligible and which isn't." You can say it is criteria. I don't care about the term. I would like to know what you have in mind. How much discretion are you going to leave to the States and localities? . . .

Mr. Brademas (Democrat from Indiana): . . . I have the impression we are quarreling about something . . . we don't need to quarrel about. My point is that when we legislate we always talk about criteria.

Mr. Goodell: And that is where we get in trouble. When the Department starts imposing criteria, criteria nobody saw in the law. And it has always happened.[14]

The minority party members of the Senate Labor and Public Welfare Committee succeeded in having incorporated in the Committee report on ESEA a specific constraint on the authority of the Commissioner, as follows:

> The minority pointed out that the language of the bill was ambiguous with respect to the authority of the Commissioner of Education under Title I to establish "basic criteria" beyond those stipulated in Section 205(a) to guide State educational agencies in deter-

14. *Hearings Before the General Subcommittee on Education, on Aid to Elementary and Secondary Education,* 89th Cong., 1st sess., House, 176–7.

> mining whether a local school district's application for aid was satisfactory. The Senate report now acts to restrain the Commissioner from adding criteria beyond those written in the law.[15]

What is clear is that the first year of administering Title I of ESEA dramatized one of the most troublesome issues in Federal-State relations: how to dispense Federal monies for categorical national purposes without undercutting the traditional and decentralized responsibilities of State and local officials.

The Issue of "Targeting"

If the question of the use of funds for school construction dramatized the dilemma, the problem of "targeting" Title I funds (making sure that they were actually addressed to benefiting educationally disadvantaged children) illustrated, in the words of one commentator, how "delicate, difficult, tedious, and quarrelsome" [16] was the business of drawing up regulations and ground rules. During FY'66, "targeting" became a focal issue in the search for viable administrative compromises. USOE officials found themselves in the middle, accused on the one hand of being too liberal in ensuring local autonomy and, on the other, of exceeding their statutory authority.

To ensure that the Federal monies would not be thinly spread over the entire school population and for merely "more of the same" kinds of educational services, the legislative draftsmen of Title I had come up with the following wording for Section 205(a)(1):

> . . . that payments under this title will be used for programs and projects . . . (A) which are designed to meet the special educational needs of educationally deprived children in school attendance areas having high concentrations of children from low-income families and (B) which are of sufficient size, scope, and quality to give reasonable promise of substantial progress toward meeting those needs. . . .

This language constituted a tangled skein of geographic, economic, educational, and institutional constraints, but its twin precepts were obvious: first, to reach the children in need; and second, to spend enough on each beneficiary to get results.

15. *Report No. 146,* 89th Cong., 1st sess., Senate, 84. In the same report (p. 9) HEW contended that it was unnecessary to include a specific constraint on the commissioner's authority to designate criteria.

16. Elizabeth Brenner Drew, "Education's Billion Dollar Baby," *The Atlantic Monthly,* July, 1966, 39.

The first ground rules with regard to the selection of participants appear in the Title I *Regulations* of September 15, 1965:

> The application by a local educational agency for a grant shall designate for each project the project area, which may include one or more school attendance areas with high concentrations of children from low-income families. The project area should, however, be sufficiently restricted in size in relation to the nature of the applicable project as to avoid jeopardizing its effectiveness in relation to the aims and objectives of the project . . . in no event may a school attendance area be designated as a project area if the degree of concentration of such children in the area is less than that of the school district as a whole. In exceptional circumstances, the whole of the school district may be designated as a project area. . . . [17]

The first LEA task in carrying out this rule would be to determine the target pupil populations, whether drawn from one or more school attendance areas; the next step would be to design projects of appropriate "size, scope, and quality" for particular children or groups of children from that population. The interdependent determinants were the degree of educational disadvantage of eligible participants, the kinds and costs of services considered most likely to promise progress in meeting their needs, and the amount of Title I funds available. The more children included in a project, or the lower the expenditure per child, the greater would be the dilution of the supplementary funding, and vice versa.

Federal officials were aware that monetary measures were not entirely satisfactory to indicate the quality of service offered to individual children, since there were many kinds of permissible projects which varied in cost factors. However, the administration had originally estimated that Title I projects would involve approximately 5.4 million children at a cost of about $200 each. This represented a rough professional judgment (based on the results of earlier compensatory programs) on the level of spending that would be required to make any substantial improvement in the educational achievement of the average disadvantaged child. It was also estimated that the incidence of "educational disadvantage" throughout the country was greater than that identified by the measures of hard-core poverty in the Title I formula and, further, that Title I funds could not provide all the services needed for target populations.

17. *Code of Federal Regulations,* Title 45, Section 116.17(b).

In an effort to provide the "saturation of services" for the most needy children, the Federal rule-makers included fairly specific rules in the draft of guidelines for the targeting process. The LEA's were to rank school attendance areas on the basis of the number of children from low-income families and then select their project areas in strict rank order of such concentrations. The SEA's were precluded from approving project applications which failed to state the explicit procedure by which project areas had been indentified, ranked, and selected. The *Guidelines* also stated that the total LEA program, defined as the sum of its projects, should be designed to serve approximately the number of children that had been used to compute its eligibility for funds.

This effort of Federal officials to interpret the legislative intent of Section 205 (a)(1) had a mixed reception from school administrators. Many urged even more specific instructions from USOE concerning the design of projects that would be of appropriate size, scope, and quality. Others expressed a variety of concerns and complaints. For example, many local administrators objected to the formal ranking procedure for selecting project areas and to singling out some children for greatly increased benefits while excluding others of apparently equal need from any benefits. They argued for the long-standing equity principle that schools should make the same investment of funds in each student, perhaps because they could anticipate criticism in their own communities from parents of children excluded from Title I benefits. And, of course, equivalent expenditures are easier to compute.

While the first of the October "roadshows" was still in progress, Commissioner Keppel received numerous expressions of dissatisfaction with the draft *Guidelines* from educators and Congressmen. The Title I staff urged the retention of strict requirements for targeting on the grounds that these requirements would provide backing to school officials in resisting local pressures to dilute the federally-financed services. However, Keppel had become convinced (perhaps under interest-group and congressional pressure) that the mandatory provisions of both the September edition of the *Regulations* and the proposed *Guidelines* violated the commitment made to the Senate Labor and Public Welfare Committee not to add criteria for project design and approval beyond those in the statute. On basic philosophical grounds, Keppel was also unhappy about the degree of Federal authority and dictation written into the first draft of the *Regulations* and *Guidelines* by BESE. He insisted on the immediate elimination of the statement that LEA's should relate the number of Title I participants to the number of children upon which LEA eligibility had been based, and instructed the staff to develop more permissive statements concerning selection of beneficiaries and per capita concentration of funds.

Accordingly, in the revision of the draft *Guidelines* that followed the regional meetings of school administrators, the Honolulu conference of the CCSSO, and the meeting of State representatives in Washington in late November, 1965, Federal officials agreed to an all-out broadening of SEA and LEA discretion on the targeting issue. The final version of the *Guidelines* called for the ranking procedure to establish eligible project areas, but made its use contingent upon State approval. The extent of the concessions made to critics is well illustrated by the following amendment of Section 116.17 in the March, 1966, revision of the *Regulations:*

> . . . A school attendance area for either elementary or secondary schools in which the percentage of children from low-income families is as high as the percentage of such children in the school district as a whole, or in which the number of children from low-income families is as large as the average number of such children in the several school attendance areas in the school districts, may be designated as a project area. *Other areas with high concentrations of children from low-income families may be approved as project areas but only if the State agency determines that projects to meet the most pressing needs of educationally deprived children in areas of higher than average concentration have been approved and adequately funded.* (Italics supplied.)

One USOE official commented on the liberalization of the ground rules, "That is when we gave away the ball-game." However, the effect of the change is difficult to assess. The final FY'66 reports indicate that the number of children participating in Title I projects was 8.3 million with an average per capita expenditure of just under $120. This was a much higher coverage and lower per capita expenditure than had originally been contemplated.[18] And top USOE officials became satisfied that the majority of local school administrators identified target populations and project areas in accordance with congressional and USOE intent. Actually, many States adhered to the detailed ranking procedure for school attendance areas when it was no longer mandatory.

Whatever the final assessment of actual practice, the targeting issue proved that the course of negotiating ground rules, like the course of true love, never does run smooth.

18. *Education USA,* National Education Association, April 3, 1967.

The Trend Toward Standardization: The Case of the Project Application Form

After the issuance of the *Regulations* and *Guidelines,* USOE entered a second stage of Title I policy elucidation. As SEA's and LEA's began to wrestle with the mandates and the meaning of various provisions in the *Regulations* and *Guidelines,* a variety of problems emerged and recurred on a national scale. These were treated in a series of USOE memoranda which were sent to State Title I coordinators and which supplemented *Guidelines.* Taken together, these memoranda clearly exemplified a trend toward increasingly specific Federal instructions aimed at the elucidation and simplification of Title I operations. The subjects ranged from church-state and civil rights matters on the one hand, to less controversial administrative problems, such as the use of consultants, staffing and recruiting, rental of office space, and the avoidance of unsound equipment bargains on the other. Some memos indicated Federal efforts merely to persuade or warn; still others were tied to questions of fiscal accountability and amounted to direct orders; others looked toward standardized and computerized data collection and retrieval. While consultation with state and local officials was continuous and the official communications were tactfully worded, the move to standardize certain types of State and local practices under Title I became increasingly evident as the inevitable ambiguities and gaps in the general *Regulations* and *Guidelines* began to show up.

An example of this trend may be found in the history of the forms provided to the LEA's in applying for Title I funds. Three successive versions of this project application form, accompanied by increasingly elaborate instructions, were developed and distributed by DPO during FY'66. Their purpose and effect was to facilitate compliance with statutory provisions. Yet, unlike the purely fiscal accounting forms, they were not included in the *Guidelines.* Several uncertainties underlay the separate handling of this type of regulatory issuance: lack of precedent for an appropriate division of Federal and State responsibility in the tasks of compiling and reporting program data required on such application forms; technical difficulties of developing, in advance of actual operation, the most serviceable source documents and formats for prescribed reports; and the complicated data collection problems imposed by Section 205. At the outset, USOE officials were even unsure as to whether their authority to establish criteria for project approval should be interpreted as requiring the nation-wide use of a standard form of grant application, or the transmission of copies of approved project applications to Washington—whether prepared in standard form or not. Since such procedures might be equated with unwarranted Federal intervention, the development of a standard project application form was undertaken cautiously.

The matter was broached in discussions with State officials in July, 1965. They acknowledged the need for a standard application form. Actually, their own shortage of time and technical competence may have persuaded state officials to leave this task entirely up to USOE. Consequently, DPO developed a draft version that was sent to the states on July 30, and was printed and widely distributed during September and October. The initial plan provided for a two-part application form:

Part I-Basic Data (OE-4303) (to be submitted once by each LEA applicant) requested information on enrollment, finances, school attendance areas with high concentrations of children from low-income families, and the special educational needs of such children.

Part II-Project Application (OE-4305) (to be submitted for each proposal) requested information on project purposes, participants, staff, budget, and proposed methods of evaluation. An LEA might prepare only one, or several of these applications, depending on the number of projects it submitted to the SEA.

The apparent willingness of the State officials to use this standardized format encouraged Federal officials to believe that forms might serve as a basis for national summaries of Title I activities and progress. On September 27, the SEA's were requested to send to Washington a copy of all portions of the two forms which had not been made discretionary (Part I-A and B, and Part II-A). A sampling of "attachments" relating to LEA project design was also requested. The DPO memorandum was not worded as an order, but as a bid for state cooperation in the USOE task of providing information to Congress and others concerning Title I implementation. The resulting deluge of paper during FY'66 may be estimated from the fact that 17,481 LEA's submitted Part I, and that Part II of the application was returned for 22,173 projects.[19] Part I required three to six pages, and Part II a minimum of six pages. Many project applications were much more voluminous, and the DPO staff found that there was considerable variation in the care and completeness with which their instructions were followed.

The data requirements for the approval of Title I projects were unusually complex, and uniform data inputs on a national basis were at

19. Statement of Harold Howe II, U.S. Commissioner of Education, before the House Committee on Education and Labor, 90th Cong., 1st sess., March 2, 1967, 3 (mimeo).

best difficult to achieve. Quite apart from this, however, the FY'66 version of the project application form had serious deficiencies. Hastily prepared under great pressure of time, the forms were bulky, called for some ambiguous and repetitious entries, and were not well designed for codification of data and automatic processing techniques. Their use for compiling summary reports was onerous and subject to errors of interpretation. In November, 1965, the DPO staff began to work on overcoming some of these deficiencies. A much clearer and more comprehensive set of instructions to accompany the forms was issued in January, 1966.[20] The method of recording the ranking procedure for identifying project areas was spelled out for the first time in detail. Specific data on LEA relationships with Community Action Projects under OEO were required and were made part of the "Part I–Basic Data" section of the application.

Following further consultations with state and local officials, work began early in 1966 on the FY'67 version of the application forms. The package of forms and instructions, distributed to the States in final form in June, 1966, retained the basic design for Parts I and II. However, the data to be submitted by any LEA engaged in cooperative projects became a supplemental form, and a "statement" to be completed by CAP officials was added (where relevant), as a new part of project applications. Provision was made to use codes for many entries which had previously required free-answer responses. Attention was also given to making information about project plans compatible in format with that required in follow-up activity reports. Although few items were eliminated, the forms were reduced in bulk and designed so that an LEA need supply only one Part II including all of its projects—at least for Federal purposes. The States, however, retained authority to establish requirements for supplementary information, such as detailed budgets, equipment lists, and special justifications.

The changes represented considerable progress toward a comprehensive Title I data system, with an efficient input and output of reliable statistics, to meet the informational and planning needs of both State and Federal officials. But this could not be accomplished without imposing a higher degree of standardized requirements on the SEA's and LEA's.

The task of supplying the data required to qualify for the Title I entitlements was beyond the experience of a considerable number of school administrators. The bulk of their complaints to Washington was overwhelmingly directed at the redtape involved in Title I implementation rather than to the substance of the legislative mandates for project

20. *Instructions for Title I Application Forms* (OE 37003), 1966.

design. However, their added paperwork was not all traceable to the federally-designed application form for Title I projects. A number of states added "piggy-back" requests to the LEA's for additional information, and the application forms for Titles II and III were also complex.

In responding to exhortations to reduce Title I red-tape, USOE officials had to consider the statutory mandate for program evaluation. If too little information for this purpose were compiled on a uniform basis nationally, the States themselves would have to require the LEA's to supply it anyway, and the workload would be equivalent. Commissioner Keppel had moved cautiously in dealing with the representatives of the State agencies on these matters. In retrospect, however, it seems clear that USOE had powerful support from the White House, the HEW Secretary, and a growing contingent of educational reformers for standardized interpretations of Title I provisions that would fulfill legislative intent and result in a significant nation-wide educational accomplishment.

The officials who worked on the program directives were imbued with a national perspective. In exercising both their official responsibilities and professional judgment, they sought to maximize Title I's effect on educationally disadvantaged children and to prevent the slippage of funds into programs of general aid. While the ground rules provided scope for SEA leadership and LEA initiations, they also laid the foundation for a standard structure of program administration. The advice and consent of those who would carry out the programs was regularly solicited; but once decided, the program criteria and procedural requirements were spelled out in increasingly specific and definite terms. As Commissioner Howe expressed it, "We have not asked for good intentions, but specific things, done with specific children in specific places." [21] USOE maintained this position even in the face of congressional objections that requirements for Title I projects were being more strictly applied than had been intended. Many specific conflicts and misunderstandings over the application of the Title I regulations were undoubtedly resolved privately and quietly; but only in the case of the targeting issue, did USOE officials back down publicly before organized opposition.

Preparation and Use of Reports

In a complex operation like the implementation of Title I, reports for many purposes must be planned and produced at all levels. Actually, Congress itself had established a fairly elaborate structure for formal reporting: LEA to SEA (Section 205(a)(6)); SEA to USOE (Section

21. *Wall Street Journal,* April 19, 1966.

206(a)(3)); and the National Advisory Council on the Education of Disadvantaged Children to the President and Congress (Section 212(c)). The Act also gave USOE and the SEA's blanket authority to establish procedures for periodic reports deemed necessary in the performance of their respective duties. Several types of record keeping and reporting are explicitly stated: those essential to evaluate the effectiveness of grant payments and particular programs in improving the educational achievement of participating children; those required to determine eligibility for funds and propriety of expenditures; and those required to provide a basis for recommending legislative changes. Both the early deadline for congressional reconsideration of the act, and its novel statutory provisions for program evaluation underlined the importance of the reporting tasks.

More traditional forms of management control, such as mandated personnel standards, had been omitted from the act. Aside from direct auditing requirements and indirect fiscal limitations (such as the percentage ceiling on LEA entitlements to prevent excessively rapid expansion, or the allotment of SEA administrative funds by formula), a mandated reporting system was to be the essential method of continuing federal review and supervision of Title I operations. On the other hand, reporting normally connotes an authority-subordinate relationship. The drafters of ESEA had scrupulously attempted to avoid language which would suggest that reporting requirements were tantamount to Federal control of State and local educational administration. The dilemma of the Federal officials was that they were assigned responsibility to appraise whether SEA program operations were in conformity with announced criteria and advance assurances; and at the same time were constrained by Section 604 from exercising "direction, supervision, or control" over administration. The thorny path between these potentially conflicting mandates was uncharted. USOE officials adopted a form of semantic protection; the term "report" was used as much as possible in combination with the term "evaluation," indicating and emphasizing the legislative intent which justified the reporting process.

The original version of Title I had included a provision giving the Commissioner responsibility for making a comprehensive report to Congress on the Title I programs by December 31, 1967. This was amended by the House Education and Labor Committee. Under their revision, the precise reporting responsibilities of the Commissioner were left ambiguous. Instead, an independent National Advisory Council on the Educationally Disadvantaged was created. This Council was asked to review the operations of Title I as well as other public and private educational programs for disadvantaged children. The Council was to report to Congress each year by March 31st. Vis-à-vis Title I, the Council was to review both the administration and operation of this title, including its effectiveness in improving the educational attainment of educationally deprived children. This instruction presumed that the quality of program administration and the attainment of educational objectives were related and that this relationship could and should be documented and appraised. However, it initiated a reporting policy fraught with controversy, since educators had long resisted the utilization of measures of student achievement (such as standardized test scores) or any form of appraisal not strictly limited to purposes of student instruction and counseling. While Federal evaluation requirements built into Title I projects could be accepted as beneficial educational research if carried out under local and State school jurisdiction, any tie-in with Federal reviews and reports of program operations was sure to be regarded as an unwelcome extension of authority on the part of those who had the power to grant or withhold funds. However, the creation of the National Advisory Council did at least spread some political heat. The bifurcated reporting structure for Title I made it possible for USOE to produce relatively inoffensive national summaries of SEA and LEA self-evaluations, while the National Advisory Council performed more independent and critical program audits. The arrangement finessed the issue of "Federal control" and, at the same time, took account of the demands of those who insisted upon rigorous accountability of State and local performance under the act.[22]

A major technical problem was that the integrated system of project planning, execution, evaluation, and reporting envisioned in the statute theoretically required early attention to the selection of meaningful data for eventual analysis and reporting purposes. For example, it is axiomatic that base line data should be collected at the outset of a new program so that future changes may be accurately measured. Yet there was little opportunity—either in Washington or in SEA's and LEA's—to give early attention to these difficult and novel aspects of educational and administrative planning. All available staff was simply swamped for several months with more pressing implementation tasks. About the best that could be done during the first year was to meet immediate demands

22. As was pointed out in Chapter II, Senator Robert Kennedy was one of the staunchest advocates of evaluation as a step towards upgrading school district administration. During the Senate subcommittee hearings on ESEA he stated repeatedly the conviction that low educational achievement was tied in part to poor school administration and that Title I funds would be wasted under inefficient school operations. See *Hearings Before the Subcommittee on Education, on the Elementary and Secondary Education Act of 1965,* 89th Cong., 1st sess., Senate, 511–516.

for operational reports by interim, ad hoc methods. The development of a comprehensive system was inevitably delayed.

DPO carried out the reporting mandates of Title I in a variety of ways. Some general suggestions for SEA reports were included in the preliminary draft of the *Guidelines,* but the final version contained only brief references to reporting. These brief references alluded to future activity of three types: project reports, fiscal reports, and evaluative reports. To obtain interim data for the first two kinds of reports, DPO relied upon financial and other information included in the approved project applications it had received from the SEA's. DPO also sent out observer-reporters to local school districts, and made several telegraphic canvasses of the SEA's to obtain statistics on current work load and progress. Several studies based on direct analysis of program and fiscal data were produced by DPO during FY'66: (1) *Analysis of 484 Title I Projects;* (2) *A Chance for a Change*; (3) *Survey of Title I Supported Programs*; (4) *1965–66 Statistical Report of Title I Program Activities.*

The first of these reports was a statistical analysis of 484 Title I project proposals which had been submitted to USOE by January 25, 1966. The sample was admittedly biased, since not all States and no large northeastern cities were included. However, the report showed some initial trends and was used by USOE in its testimony before the congressional subcommittees considering the 1966 amendments to ESEA. It was also used as a source document by the National Advisory Council.

The second report, *A Chance for a Change,* was a 64-page slick-paper, lavishly illustrated, narrative intended for general circulation among educators and the public at large. It described in readable style a number of noteworthy Title I projects, classified under headings which indicated the diversity of approaches taken to the problems of the educationally disadvantaged. It also included some updated statistical summaries and a directory of state Title I and CAP officials. First distributed to the participants at the National Conference on Educationally Disadvantaged Children in July, 1966, this report was designed to promote enthusiasm and support for the Title I objectives.

In order to implement the statutory requirement that annual evaluation reports be submitted by LEA's and SEA's, DPO staff consulted with State officials. After review by Title I representatives of several States, instructions were issued in December, 1965 for preparing an initial report according to a special, abbreviated, format. Thirty-seven States responded by the February 15th deadline, and DPO prepared an 89-page mimeographed document, *Summary of the State Interim Evaluation Reports*. The SEA reports provided little information about accomplishments, except those from the few States which had had preliminary work on Title I operations well underway during the previous summer. Comments on current difficulties were voluminous and concrete, and more than a third of the summary report was devoted to "problems and misconceptions." At the time of reporting, most of the SEA's were in the process of reviewing or anticipating the review of, a large volume of pending LEA projects. Their narrative reports included information on the status of their work loads. But the reports also revealed more than was intended. DPO officials noted (privately and ruefully) that several States which first appeared to be making rapid progress in carrying out their Title I responsibilities had done so by an uncritical process of "shoveling out the money."

The SEA reports were made available to the National Advisory Council, but their principal value was to be found in a variety of DPO follow-up activities. As a result of the reports, DPO issued memoranda to all SEA's suggesting various program activities and modifications. It also conducted a full-scale series of field visits to the individual States in ensuing weeks. The Federal officials then held extensive discussions on reporting requirements and problems with State and local officials at several regional conferences devoted exclusively to project evaluation. In April, 1966, DPO sent to the SEA's a comprehensive *Guide for Title I Project Evaluation* to be followed in preparing their FY'66 Evaluation Reports which were due on December 15, 1966.

The first cycle of reports on Title I operations was completed almost two years after enactment of the statute.

In March 1967, USOE released its 128-page summary of SEA reports, entitled *The First Year of Title I.* Commissioner Howe was enthusiastic about the account of the first year's operations, stating that "although the survey covered for the most part programs of only four months duration, it is clear that the Title I concept was soundly conceived and of tremendous benefit to the schools." [23] The report itself contained little interpretive, comparative, or critical comment on the SEA submissions. It was confined to narrative summaries of State administrative operations and local program activities, supplemented by graphic and statistical materials and quotations from the individual State reports. The editors, reflecting the ambivalence of the Federal role, commented as follows:

> This report represents the first national effort at self-evaluation of broad educational programs designed to assist educationally deprived children. Although it falls short of long-range goals for

23. *Education USA,* National Education Association, April 3, 1967, 191.

accurate assessment of progress, it represents an historic first step in building an evaluation model for the future. It provides a guide for state and local agencies to improve their evaluation procedures, and it illuminates the need for more attention to the testing and assessment objectives of the Elementary and Secondary Act of 1965.[24]

The National Advisory Council on the Education of Disadvantaged Children published two reports on the administration and operation of Title I during FY'66. The first was dated March 31, 1966 (actually it was released several weeks later). The second was entitled *Summer Programs for Children of Poverty,* dated November 25, 1966. These two reports were quite distinct. The first was based on a review of the 484 approved project applications and interim reports from the SEA's which USOE had used for its reports to the congressional subcommittees. Obviously the Council relied heavily at the outset on USOE for compilations of data about the activities and problems of the implementation period, although the Council's first report formally represented an independent assessment of the materials. The second report was based on the observations of consultants employed by the Council who visited summer projects in 66 school districts in 43 States. This was a sampling within counties that were spending one-third of the total Title I funds. The document had both the freshness and frankness of first-hand reporting.

Taken together, the reports developed under and about Title I during the first year were useful indices of progress and problems. But as we shall note in more detail in the following chapter, they fell woefully shy of measured and objective evaluations of actual accomplishments. By and large the reports were self-serving and/or subjective. What hard data they included provided at best indices of effort and expenditures. They failed to include even base lines for judging teacher and pupil performance. Their inadequacy was due in part to the brevity of the experience reported; in part to the crushing preoccupation of officials at all levels with getting the program started; in part to the limited state of the art of evaluating educational results of any kind.

TITLE I: INFORMATIONAL SERVICES

Underlying all of the detailed negotiations with State and local educational agencies on questions of implementing Title I was the imperative

24. *The First Year of Title I,* U.S. Department of Health, Education and Welfare (Washington: U.S. Government Printing Office, 1967), 13.

of insuring a widespread and accurate understanding of ESEA's substance and intent. The law was complex. It had been passed and signed only eight weeks after its introduction. It would affect better than 95 per cent of all school districts in America. Effective implementation would depend in large part upon the degree of enthusiasm and commitment which only a pervasive public understanding of the act's provisions and intent could insure. Such an understanding would have to include a new appreciation of the problems of educationally disadvantaged children.

In short, the implementation of Title I involved a massive public relations program. Some of this was undertaken directly by USOE. Much of it was carried out by professional associations, commercial houses, and other government agencies (especially OEO)—each with its own peculiar interest in getting the word around. All told, these activities included publications and publicity on both the educational and administrative aspects of Title I; the dissemination of research and program information concerning the education of disadvantaged children; and a variety of conferences to promote interchange of ideas among educators. Because of the involved procedures in the awarding of grants, special attention was given to non-legalistic, popularized versions of the *Regulations* and *Guidelines,* and to explaining the relationship of the various ESEA titles to one another and to other governmental programs for disadvantaged children. In this latter connection, practical guidance was given on the use of multiple sources of Federal funding for school and community programs. More general publicity was devoted to the over-all goals of Title I—in the perspective of national interests and policies.

USOE made considerable use of information techniques which several other Federal agencies had successfully adopted in recent years, notably the Peace Corps and the various OEO subdivisions. Professional associations worked mainly through trade journals and conferences. Text book and educational hardware manufacturers used their traveling salesmen. A few examples of both official and non-official artistry suggest the range and diversity of techniques and agents.

Initially, USOE distributed 150,000 copies of an eight-page section of its May, 1965 issue of *American Education* entitled "First Work of These Times"—an attractive, slick-paper overview of the purposes and provisions of ESEA. These same plates were also used for several other periodicals, such as *American School and University*. Subsequently the agency issued a series of brief separate brochures on each ESEA program (e.g., *Focus on Title I* and a composite *Profile of ESEA*) designed for mass circulation.

A large audience of educators was reached by the vigorous and expensive campaign which NEA undertook to inform and influence its membership. The campaign included publications, speeches at regular and ad hoc conferences, and visual aids. A single NEA article prepared at the Washington headquarters, "We've Got it Started," was reprinted in the journals of most state affiliates and reached almost a million educators. The American Association of School Administrators kept its influential membership of superintendents and principals up to date with a newsletter called *Hotline.*

The Department of Education of the National Catholic Welfare Conference distributed widely among Catholic educators its own publication, *Understanding the Elementary and Secondary Education Act of 1965.*

In the winter of 1965–66, at the end of the first session of the 89th Congress, a number of official publications appeared under an HEW or USOE imprimatur describing the full gamut of new USOE and HEW programs, such as: *1965, Year of Legislative Achievements* (a summary of articles from the monthly *HEW Indicators*); and *Education, 65, A Report to the Profession.* Another lavishly illustrated brochure, also entitled *The First Work of These Times,* described the educational accomplishments of the Johnson Administration. Since the President's picture and Presidential seal appeared prominently on the end-papers, this publication resembled a piece of campaign literature.

A reflection of the mutual concerns of USOE and OEO was the jointly prepared pamphlet, *Education: An Answer to Poverty,* 200,000 copies of which were distributed by the two agencies. OEO also issued the highly informative and useful 411-page *Catalogue of Federal Programs for Individual and Community Improvement* which described legislation administered by USOE and by more than a dozen other Federal agencies. This publication listed eligibility and application requirements for each program.

USOE programs were also covered by commercial publishers. Doubleday and Company published a handy paperback monograph, *The Doubleday Guide to Federal Aid Programs, 1966–67.* A widely reprinted series of three articles appeared in *School Management* magazine under the title, *A Schoolman's Guide to Federal Aid.* These included lengthy interviews with Senator Morse, BESE Director Arthur Harris, DPO Director Hughes, and Commissioner Howe on both the policy and administrative aspects of Title I.

Business interests displayed a growing awareness of a market for information on Federal school aid procedures and even for assistance in preparing Title I project applications. The National Audio-Visual

Association issued *A Summary of the Titles of the Elementary and Secondary Education Act of 1965: Nothing Matters More* which included a model list of audio-visual equipment and materials for both elementary and secondary schools applying for ESEA funds. One commercial firm launched a loose-leaf reference manual service which included current Federal administrative instructions; another provided copies of Title I project proposals which had received SEA approval. Some vendors of educational equipment supplied completed Title I project applications as a part of a sales contract to LEA's. This was so widely used that the National Advisory Council felt constrained to criticize the practice.[25]

During FY'66 the top HEW and USOE leaders and the new educational programs rated unprecedented coverage in the national news magazines. For example, Commissioner Keppel was the subject of the *Time* cover story on October 15, 1965. Secretary Gardner was similarly featured in *Newsweek* on February 28, 1966. On several occasions, President Johnson utilized his unparalleled resources for gaining space in the mass media to focus attention on educational developments. For example, at a surprise appearance at the AASA meeting in Atlantic City in February, 1966 he made a well-publicized speech on his intentions to enlarge the ESEA programs and work for their extension to 1970.[26]

While not all of the publicity on the Great Society educational programs was accurate or uncritical, it would have been difficult for any educator to remain unaware that his profession was in the national spotlight. In fact, at the operating level, the problem was not a dearth but a surfeit of information—particularly undigested (and often conflicting) information about the education problems of disadvantaged children and the programs which had previously been carried out for their benefit. Mindful that the research and program information which would aid in Title I project development had heretofore received limited national circulation, USOE undertook during FY'66 to make available to SEA's and LEA's a large accumulation of materials of this type. The objective of cross-fertilization was in line with the requirement of Section 205 of Title I that the results of promising Title I projects would be widely disseminated and would contribute to improvements in project design. A major activity of DPO was to prepare listings and make shipments of publications to the SEA's. More than 20,000 copies of the most

25. DPO also warned State Title I Coordinators of the possibility of inaccuracies in materials supplied by commercial enterprises for use in project development. See Memorandum from DPO Director Hughes, December 10, 1965.

26. *Education USA,* National Education Association, February 24, 1966, 113.

useful materials were made available to the entire list of LEA's across the nation. USOE's Bureau of Research issued its own *Disadvantaged Children Series,* and the Educational Materials Center prepared a comprehensive bibliography of current publications updated to August 15, 1966.[27] The most ambitious USOE project was carried out by the Educational Research Information Center (ERIC), which abstracted, indexed, and put on microfilm a total of 1,740 documents on education of the disadvantaged supplied by school districts and universities. The SEA's and a selection of 600 LEA's each received four information packets containing resumes, indexes, and some of the documents themselves. Bell and Howell of Cleveland became the repository from which school administrators could order copies of the documents, for which ERIC published catalogues.[28] To continue the new stream-lined system for compiling and disseminating data on disadvantaged children and youth, ERIC subsequently designated Yeshiva University as one of its subsidized clearinghouses for educational information.

The informational and administrative services provided by USOE to school administrators encompassed much in addition to the flood of written and published materials. DPO staff consultations and field visits have already been mentioned in connection with the preparation of administrative instructions. In addition, State Title I officials were encouraged to communicate freely with Washington on their problems—by telephone or in person. USOE staff participated both officially and unofficially in numerous regional, State, and local conferences on the administration of Title I. A capstone event epitomizing the new attempts to foster intergovernmental and educational interchanges was the two-day National Conference on Education of the Disadvantaged, held in Washington on July 16–18, 1966. Suggested initially by the National Advisory Council as a stimulus for a round of subsequent state-sponsored colloquies, the national conference was carefully planned and conducted by USOE as a top-level conclave for program appraisal and planning for FY'67. President Johnson made a conference appearance with Secretary Gardner. A keynote address was delivered by Vice-President Humphrey. Each State sent four representatives, most of whom were Title I Coordinators, university educational specialists, or administrators or teachers directly engaged in a Title I project. The remaining group of 400 participants consisted of government officials in education

27. *The Education of Disadvantaged Children: A Bibliography,* U.S. Department of Health, Education and Welfare (Washington: U.S. Government Printing Office, 1966).

28. *Catalogue of Selected Documents on the Disadvantaged,* U.S. Department of Health, Education and Welfare (Washington: U.S. Government Printing Office, 1966).

and related fields (community action specialists, civil rights leaders, etc.), and officials of the major professional educational organizations. The report of the conference proceedings vividly reflected the controversies and the common concerns of the eight representative sub-groups of participants. But this was only one of its functions. President Johnson set the tone and the rationale in the following words:

> To reach the disadvantaged child's mind—to tear away the awful shrouds that dim the light of learning, to break barriers built by poverty and fear and racial injustice—this is the most exciting task of our times. . . . I believe the school bill now on the books is the most creative legislation passed by Congress since I came to Washington. But it will be a sterile piece of paper unless you breathe life into the programs that flow from it . . . We hope you will have an opportunity to review your plans, exchange your ideas, describe your problems—and then go back home and work double time on your programs.[29]

The National Conference, like the bulk of the official USOE public relations activities, was designed to unite the educational community behind the purposes of ESEA, to imbue practitioners with a high sense of mission, to gain their support in fulfilling nationally established educational priorities. It helped to establish a climate of professional and public opinion friendly to the act, and also pointed out to harrassed State and local officials the programs and procedures which could make ESEA effective.

In truth, it is difficult to imagine how any bold and pervasive new Federal program could be implemented effectively without a studied attention on the part of administrators to those arts of persuasion which have been the government official's stock in trade since the days of Aristotle's *Rhetoric*.

Implementing Other Titles

Generically, the procedures used in implementing Title I characterized the implementation of the other titles of ESEA and of Title VI of the Civil Rights Act of 1964. Yet each of these other titles had its own peculiar problems. A brief mention of some of these should suffice to suggest the range of issues which USOE had to negotiate in carrying out the provisions of ESEA during its first year.

29. *National Conference on Education of the Disadvantaged,* U.S. Department of Health, Education and Welfare (Washington: U.S. Government Printing Office, 1966).

Title II

As noted earlier, the responsibility for administering Title II was placed in the hands of the Division of Plans and Supplementary Centers in the Bureau of Elementary and Secondary Education. Essentially, the Commissioner's powers over Title II were delegated to the Director of DPSC, Ralph Becker, who, with his staff, assumed the burden of Title II implementation, including the approval of State plans.

For DPSC, the most difficult issue was how to give effective guidance to the States on intra-state allocations.[30] Obviously, the simplest method would have been on a pupil per capita basis. If, for example, School District A had 10,000 public and private school pupils and School District B had only 1,000, then School District A would receive 10 times the amount of money under Title II as School District B. The law provided, however, that "criteria . . . [should] take into consideration the *relative need* of the children and teachers of the State for such library resources, textbooks, or other instructional materials. . . ." [31] (Emphasis supplied.), and that each State should submit a State plan for the approval of the U.S. Commissioner indicating how the State intended to distribute Title II largess, and for what purposes.

Confronting DPSC, then, was the task of formulating *Regulations* and *Guidelines* which would allow maximum flexibility to the States in developing plans, criteria, and standards, but which would give the States sufficient ground rules, procedures and substantives so that they could have some notion as to how to qualify under national legislative intent.

It took DPSC nine double-column pages of *Regulations* and 50 pages of *Guidelines* to spell such matters out. To many of the non-lawyers in SEA's and LEA's responsible for submitting applications for funds, the *Regulations* and *Guidelines* were as maddening as they were indispensable. Part of the task of DPSC was to explain the reasons for the complexity of the ground rules, and to offer whatever help they could to State and local officials in interpreting the meaning of the *Regulations*

30. The interstate allocation was a relatively simple matter. Once the Federal appropriations had been settled for FY'66 ($100 million), the amount each State would receive under the formula was a simple matter of addition and division. California, with the largest number of children enrolled in public and private elementary schools, was, for example, allotted $9,308,483; Alaska, at the other end of the scale, was allotted $118,854. Aside from the fact that some states were unclear about the number of enrolled private school children, the determination of State allotments was strictly mechanical.

31. Public Law 89–10, 89th Cong., 1st Sess., Sec. 203(a) (3).

and *Guidelines* issued. One unexpected source of assistance was the educational textbook, instructional materials, and audio-visual fraternity who took it upon themselves to assist a number of LEA's in preparing application forms under both Title I and Title II—including, of course, "appropriate" lists of books, materials, and equipment.[32] In a survey conducted by the Bureau of Social Science Research, one out of every five school districts received such aid.[33] Two thirds of the school districts surveyed did not receive *Guidelines* and instructions for Title II applications until after January 1, 1966—a third of them not until March and April.[34] This delay was occasioned largely by the "State plan" format of Title II, which required SEA's to prepare proposals and distribute their own particular instructions to LEA's—proposals and instructions that were complicated by State legal provisions on the issue of private school involvement.

It was therefore remarkable that 87 per cent of such school districts actually were able to submit instructional material orders under Title II by the end of May, 1966,[35] and that less than one per cent of all these Title II applications were denied or had to be revised.[36] To underline their intent that eligible public and private school children and teachers should have access to *all* the instructional resources added by Title II

32. The growth of interest of American business in an expanding educational market underwritten in part by Federal funds has been dramatic. See *Phi Delta Kappan,* January, 1967.

33. See Appendix C, Question #24. The Bureau of Social Science Research of Washington, D.C., sent a structured questionnaire that was developed for, and under the direction of senior author Stephen K. Bailey. The questionnaire was sent to a random sample of local school administrators in May, 1966, regarding their experiences with ESEA. For fuller explanation of the survey, see Chapter V, footnote 35.

34. See Appendix C, Question #16B.

35. See Appendix C, Question #19B.

36. See Appendix C, Question #30. One possible reason for the success of Title II applications is the fact that a substantial number of States simply copied or adapted the Title II proposal prepared by New York State's Department of Education. Frank Stevens of the New York department had been on a Title II advisory panel for USOE beginning in April, 1965. The fact that he was instrumental in developing the Title II Guidelines and that the New York State Department of Education was liberally staffed with specialists enabled New York to perform a "lighthouse" function for the rest of the States in the drafting of the Title II proposals. The State of Michigan, for example, took New York State's Title II proposal and used it verbatim except for substituting "Michigan" for "New York." Twenty-six other states borrowed heavily from the New York State submission. This lighthouse function was not confined to Title II or even to ESEA. States with well-financed and well-staffed departments of education perform an important function in setting the pace for the rest of the States in handling grant-in-aid programs. New York, California, and Texas are particularly influential.

funds, both Congressional education committees suggested in their 1965 *Reports* that local districts establish central depositories of the Title II materials, providing for their use under normal loan-library controls. The following year, the legislators registered their disappointment that the initial USOE *Guidelines* had not even mentioned this recommendation, and the House Committee Report stated emphatically that materials should be made widely available, with no permanent or "indefinite" loans made to private institutions. The evidence is that public-school-oriented educators were unimpressed by, and reluctant to implement, the proposed mode of sharing resources with a private school clientele especially when it was not mandated in law or state plan requirements. The revised USOE Title II *Guidelines* of February, 1966, contained a new section [Section 117.5 (c)] which underscored the policy of wide accessibility of loaned materials, with the creation of central depositories at the district level as an alternate method for its accomplishment. Local school administrators testifying before the Green subcommittee in the fall of 1966 termed the suggestion both impractical and prohibitively expensive, requiring funds for administration which could better be spent for books and instructional materials.[37]

Title III

The Division of Plans and Supplementary Centers of the Bureau of Elementary and Secondary Education was also assigned responsibility for the administration of Title III. The implementation of the provisions of Title III was distinguished by three conditions: first, grants were to be assigned on a competitive basis, depending upon the quality of local submissions; second, the U.S. Commissioner of Education, rather than the State departments of education, was to make the final allocative judgments; and, third, the very looseness of the concept of supplementary educational centers and services made the process of constructing *Regulations* and *Guidelines* inherently complex and indefinite. (Can one structure "creativity" in advance?)

These conditions had several consequences: (1) they led the DPSC and the USOE Advisory Council for Title III to emphasize planning grants rather than operational grants during the first year on the grounds

37. See *Senate Report No. 146,* 23–24; *House Report No. 143,* 13–14; and *House Report No. 1814,* 19, of the 89th Congress; and *House Document No. 193,* 277–78, of the 90th Congress, 1st Session. The issues are aired by George R. La Noue in "The Title II Trap", *Phi Delta Kappan,* June, 1966, 558–563. Responses to his comments by John M. Lunley and Msgr. James C. Donahue follow on 564–65.

that responsible innovations took considerable forethought and effort; (2) more than under any other title, they brought USOE into tension and conflict with SEA's and CSSO's; (3) they brought frustration to the understaffed, poorer, smaller school districts in the nation which lacked the human and financial resources to compete with larger wealthier districts in preparing Title III applications; (4) they involved the USOE staff, advisory panels, and outside consultants in a wider variety of interpretive and discretionary judgments than was the case under other ESEA titles; (5) they induced Congressmen to take more interest in the fate of individual submissions than was the case under any other ESEA title. This last was true, of course, because discretionary judgment under Title III was finally left to the Washington bureaucracy over which Congress was assumed to have some influence.

Title III *Regulations* and *Guidelines* were issued in October, 1965, and were distributed to LEA's through SEA's. The process of LEA preparation and USOE review of applications was inevitably time-consuming, and by June 1966, less than 12 per cent of the school districts surveyed had actually begun operations under Title III,[38] in spite of the fact that three separate, successive deadlines had been created by USOE during FY'66. This dismal showing was caused to some extent by a USOE decision to establish a "hold" category of applications pending further revisions and submissions. Even so, the quantity and quality of initial submissions was disappointing to USOE. Actually, most LEA's did not even apply.[39]

The Bureau of Social Science Research (hereafter BSSR) survey communicates clearly the difficulties faced by many smaller rural school districts in mounting the effort necessary to develop a viable Title III proposal.[40] The Department of Rural Education of NEA was so concerned about this inequity that it prepared a special brochure called *A Guide for Developing PACE*[41] which it distributed to rural school

38. See Appendix C, Question #22A.

39. By the end of the first fiscal year (July, 1966), only 2,700 proposals had been submitted by LEA's. Even though the final 839 approved projects affected 6,000 school districts, three-quarters of the nation's school districts were not represented. See *Notes and Working Papers . . . Title III of PL 89–10,* 90th Cong., 1st sess., Senate Subcommittee on Education, April, 1967, 27.

40. See Appendix C, Question #22B. In view of the hard data supplied in the Title III Notes and Working Papers (see fn. 38, above), little credence can be given to the total submission figures under Title III in the survey. But other evidence confirms the disproportionate number of submissions from wealthier suburban districts.

41. PACE (Projects to Advance Creativity in Education) was the USOE acronym for Title III.

superintendents throughout the nation. Their effort was justified in the introduction to their *Guide* in the following words:

> Within smaller school systems there is almost complete absence of either skill or experience in writing a project proposal of any kind for any purpose. Only a few have the ability to command specialized help. The danger is that the appropriations now available, the new approaches envisioned in the spirit of Title III, will be lost for large numbers of children by default.[42]

USOE also attempted to be helpful to understaffed or timid districts by compiling and summarizing reports on successful Title III applications and issuing periodic brochures called *Pace Setters in Innovation* for broad distribution. And some State departments of education assigned staff to assist the LEA's in Title III program development.

Because of the burdens of screening and evaluating hundreds of Title III submissions, the DPSC staff relied very heavily upon policies established by the Title III Advisory Council and upon the recommendations of outside consultants hired specifically to review Title III project proposals. This deference to external advice and guidance was administratively perhaps the most significant feature of Title III implementation, and procedurally marked it off most clearly from other ESEA titles.

Title IV

Administering the continuation and extension of the Cooperative Research Act of 1954 under Title IV logically fell to USOE's Bureau of Research under Acting Director Francis Ianni. Title IV was the only provision of ESEA administered outside of the Bureau of Elementary and Secondary Education. Although this assignment to the Bureau of Research caused some problems of internal communication and coordination, especially between Title III and Title IV activities, it was considered desirable to consolidate as many USOE research programs as possible under a single bureau.

The selection of nine university-connected Research and Development Centers under Title IV was carried out by the Bureau of Research with the help of a Research Advisory Council and a series of outside panels of experts who reviewed applications, conducted site visits, and made recommendations to the USOE staff. In some cases, previous research authorized under the Cooperative Research Act of 1954 was simply enlarged and extended in time. In other cases, R & D centers were

42. *A Guide for Developing PACE,* National Education Association, Department of Rural Education, 1966.

created *de novo* on the basis of new submissions by universities. But in both situations, the process of evaluation of project applications was generically identical. The emphasis of the USOE staff and of outside panels was placed upon basic research addressed to fundamental problems of educational method, organization, and practice. In most R & D centers, the USOE staff underscored the *R*.

The creation of a system of Regional Educational Laboratories was, however, quite a different matter. There were no precedents for the "labs"—as they came to be known. It was simply assumed, on the basis of the Gardner task force recommendations and subsequent in-house discussions within USOE, that laboratories would develop programs which went far beyond project research. It was assumed that these programs would be composed of a wide range of activities, including: basic or pure research; curriculum development and evaluation; development of promising innovations; demonstrations of noteworthy programs, practices, training and dissemination activities; and direct involvement with schools for the implementation of educational improvements. All programs, however, would be directed toward outcomes related to the improvement of the quality of educational practice.

The labs were not to be university-based. Each laboratory ". . . would be designed as an independent, non-profit corporation with its own governing board and management, . . . capable of making decisions regarding specific program objectives, attracting the resources—personnel, funds, and facilities—necessary to realize those objectives and directing the operations by which these objectives would be obtained." [43]

Because of the novelty and flexibility of the laboratory approach, the Bureau of Research in the fall of 1965 set up an ad hoc, advisory committee under the chairmanship of Professor Lawrence A. Cremin of Teachers College, Columbia University, to develop a series of recommendations as to how laboratories should be selected, how many there should be, and what activities they should pursue. Professor Cremin's report has not been made public, but it is known that the report pleaded caution in the number of laboratories to be initially funded. The Cremin Committee was obviously governed by a recognition that the kinds of talents needed to man highly innovative and experimental laboratory activities were in short supply throughout the nation, and that seven or eight pilot laboratories would probably absorb as many able educational innovators as then existed.

The Bureau of Research overrode the Cremin Committee recom-

43. *A Progress Report on the Twenty Educational Laboratories,* U.S. Office of Education, Division of Education Laboratories, Bureau of Research, July 1, 1967, 1.

mendations, however, and quickly covered the map of the continental United States with first 11 and then, by September 1966, 20 regional laboratories. This was done on the basis of project proposal evaluations by bureau staff, the Research Advisory Council, and by special panels of experts, and involved at times some fairly complex "horseback" judgments about appropriate area and functional jurisdictions.

The ignoring of some of the Cremin Committee recommendations lived to haunt the Bureau of Research. But even if the Cremin Committee recommendations had been followed, the inherent complexity of mounting an unprecedented program of quasi-autonomous educational laboratories would have amounted to one of the most difficult conceptual and administrative tasks undertaken in pursuit of ESEA objectives. The rapid turnover in the staff of the Bureau of Research, and key vacancies in its table of organization during the first month, only served to make the process of Title IV implementation excruciatingly difficult for all concerned.

Title V

In determining priorities of effort under ESEA, the Executive Group of USOE in April, 1965, had given a special green light to Title V. It was obvious that if Titles I and II were to be implemented effectively, State educational agencies would have to be strengthened in staff and in general administrative competence. Many of the SEA's had reputations of weakness and conservatism. Even the strongest of them would be faced with extraordinary extra burdens in helping USOE to carry out the provisions of ESEA and of other new Federal legislation.

Two major administrative assignments were made for implementing Title V: the first, to Dr. Robert Hopper who was to become chief of the Division of State Agency Cooperation in BESE; the second, to Wayne O. Reed, Associate Commissioner for Federal-State Relations.

Hopper's initial task was to design a system that would promote quality Title V applications from the SEA's. Once ESEA had been signed and the Executive Group had indicated its interest in having USOE give high priority to Title V implementation, Hopper, with the assistance of Dr. Edgar Fuller of the Council of Chief State School Officers, called in a half dozen CSSO's in May, 1965, to go over the provisions of the act and to get advice. This initial session was immediately followed by nine regional meetings, attended by USOE representatives, and organized for the purpose of explaining the nature of Title V to relevant state school officers and of discussing what would be expected of the SEA's. As was mentioned earlier, all CSSO's were brought to Washington in June, 1965, for a briefing and a general discussion of the act.

In the meantime, Hopper, his staff, and a couple of outside consultants, began putting together a long, involved questionnaire (60 pages). A draft of this was presented to the ESEA Planning Group which was in essence the operating arm of USOE's Executive Group for ESEA implementation purposes.

The need for the extensive questionnaire was justified by the fact that the reporting and accounting systems of the several States varied so considerably that without a fundamental data base and information bank, USOE could not make intelligent decisions about comparative State programs and needs. Actually, in developing the questionnaire, the CSSO's urged the Office of Education to err on the side of detailed instructions and questions.

A dozen states tried out the form as initially constructed. They reported their suggestions and criticisms back to Hopper who, in turn, incorporated them in the revised version. Perhaps the stickiest obstacle to circulating the final questionnaire was the hostility of the Director of the Division of Statistical Services in the U.S. Bureau of the Budget who is responsible for examining all agency questionnaires. He was personally opposed to the length and complexity of the 60-page Title V questionnaire. He would have stopped the questionnaire from being authorized if he had not been on leave when the questionnaire came up for approval. A junior Budget Bureau officer let it through.

Hopper took a number of the new recruits in his division and sent them on tour to work with each SEA in preparing answers to the questionnaire. For him this had a double advantage: it helped the States over a considerable hurdle of paper work, and it helped to train new, young USOE staff in the process of negotiating with State departments of education.

Title V was, of course, not the only source of Federal financial help for SEA administrative purposes. A number of previous education laws, as well as other titles of ESEA, provided administrative grants to state departments of education. In consequence, one of Hopper's jobs was to put in front of the States the whole range of Federal support available to them for purposes of administering specific Federal programs as well as for upgrading the quality of SEA performance generally.

Supplementing Hopper's official activities under Title V was the work of Wayne O. Reed, Associate Commissioner for Federal-State Relations. Reed was an old-timer in USOE. He had personal contacts with CSSO's across the land. Reed's job was to maintain informal contact with his friends and acquaintances in the several SEA's; to quiet their fears; to explain USOE policies; to reassure CSSO's and local school administrators of USOE's abiding commitment to local control of education; and to appear at various educational conferences and conventions as a symbol of USOE continuity and conservatism. This role he filled with great skill, and Hopper's way was smoothed more than once by Reed's quiet but effective efforts.

TITLE VI OF THE CIVIL RIGHTS ACT OF 1964 [44]

Any analysis of the first year of ESEA would be incomplete without at least a brief examination of the concurrent effort underway in USOE to implement Title VI of the 1964 Civil Rights Act. In its substantive relevance to Title I of ESEA, in its drain upon the energies of key OE officials, and in its creation of tensions and, more importantly, enmities at all levels of government and society, Title VI formed a large part of the context in which the Elementary and Secondary Education Act was effectuated.

The thrust of Title VI of the 1964 Civil Rights Act was simple and direct:

> No person . . . shall, on the ground of race, color, or national origin, be excluded from participation in, be denied the benefits of, or be subjected to discrimination under any program or activity receiving Federal financial assistance.
>
> Compliance . . . may be effectuated (1) by the termination of or refusal to grant or continue assistance . . . or (2) by any other means authorized by law.

The locus of primary responsibility was equally clear:

> Each Federal department and agency which is empowered to extend Federal financial assistance to any program or activity . . . is authorized and directed to effectuate the provisions of (this) section . . . by issuing rules, regulations, or orders of general applicability.[45]

In the light of a ten-year history of desegregation efforts, the sensitivity, magnitude, and potential of the provisions were unmistakable.

44. The authors are grateful to Joel S. Berke for the research and much of the language in the remaining sections of this chapter.

45. PL88–352, Title VI, Section 601, 2, 3.

Segregation in the Schools

In 1954, the U.S. Supreme Court had established in *Brown* v. *the Board of Education of Topeka, Kansas* [46] that enforced racial segregation of public education was unconstitutional as a denial of the equal protection of the laws guaranteed by the Fourteenth Amendment. This decision rendered unconstitutional the segregated school systems of 17 Southern and Border States. A year later, after having heard argument on how best to implement the 1954 decision, the Court made the following declaration on enforcement. Instead of ordering the immediate desegregation of all schools, the Court required "a prompt and reasonable start toward full compliance," and left to the lower Federal courts the responsibility for determining whether the local schools were in fact moving toward integration "with all deliberate speed." Factors to be taken into account in judging the rate and effectiveness of local efforts included location of physical plant, transportation, personnel, revision of district lines, and the attendant changes needed in local laws and regulations. But, the Court added, "it should go without saying that the vitality of the constitutional principles cannot be allowed to yield simply because of disagreement with them." [47]

Yet a full decade later it was undeniable that patterns of racial segregation in the South had not yielded to the vitality of constitutional principle, and the causes clearly lay in the habits, the folkways, and the politics of the region, not in the administrative problems of its school systems. This is not to deny that some cities, some districts, even some Border States had made the transition to integrated education. But the effective results of *Brown* v. *the Board* may be seen in these overall figures: in 1964 only 10.9 per cent of the Negro public school children in the 17 Southern and Border States were in biracial schools; in the 11 States of the old Confederacy, the percentage was 2.25.[48] As the Supreme Court said in *Griffin* v. *Prince Edward County School Board* that year, there had been "entirely too much deliberation and not enough speed." [49] Literally hundreds of desegregation cases had been brought throughout the South in the ten-year period, and a tortuous variety of plans and procedures had been sanctioned. In some instances the Supreme Court

46. 347 US 483.

47. *Brown* v. *Board of Education of Topeka, Kansas* 349 US 294, 300–301.

48. *Statistical Summary,* Southern Educational Reporting Service, December 1965, 29.

49. 377 US 218, 229.

had given guidance.[50] Precedents and approaches on other issues, however, varied between circuits and within them.[51] During the decade, pupil placement, freedom of choice, and grade-a-year plans coexisted, each with seemingly infinite variations as judges tailored their decrees to the conditions of individual communities. Years after a particular system was found wanting by the courts in one school district, it continued to be permitted in others.[52] Against this background Congress passed the Civil Rights Act of 1964.

Guidelines: Formulation. The task facing the Office of Education was staggering. It had to induce instant desegregation and to end programmatic discrimination in every school district slated for the award of Federal aid. The price of failure would be the sacrifice of the very programs, notably and prospectively ESEA, which could attack the conditions that had created, stimulated, and maintained segregation and discrimination. Compounding the dilemma was the fact that the Civil Rights Act provided no definitions of segregation and discrimination. Would the existence of a plan providing that students could select any school in the district be sufficient to show the absence of "discrimination" when not a single Negro had chosen to attend an all-white school? Would the desegregation of two, three, or four grades a year qualify? Might a school system maintain all-Negro faculties in some schools and all-white in others? Was *de facto* segregation a violation of the title? And most significant of the unanswered questions: on what precedents was the USOE to base its "rules, regulations, and orders of general applicability" in implementing the civil rights provision? These, and a host of similar problems confronted the Office of Education as it undertook its enforcement responsibilities.

In thinking through the substance of the guidelines, the USOE draftsmen had a variety of sources to consult. Congressional intent was of course a basic element, particularly since Title VI required that orders

50. See for example, *Cooper* v. *Aaron,* 358 US 1 (1958), making clear that community hostility was not an acceptable reason for delaying desegregation; *Watson* v. *City of Memphis,* 373 US 526 (1963), indicating that the time lapse since *Brown* might require more rapid pace and more stringent requirements than were permitted in earlier cases; and *Goss* v. *Board of Education of the City of Knoxville,* 373 US 683 (1963) striking down a "minority" transfer provision that operated as an escape route for white students geographically assigned to predominantly Negro schools.

51. See, for example, the discussion of free choice plans on pages 154–155.

52. For an excellent discussion of the legal background, implementation and results of Title VI, see *Survey of School Desegregation in the Southern and Border States, 1965–66,* U.S. Commission on Civil Rights.

of fund termination would have to be submitted to the Education Committees of both House and Senate thirty days prior to enforcement. However, little beyond exhortations of general purpose were yielded by the *Congressional Record* and the Committee Hearings and Reports. Departmental desegregation regulations covering all HEW programs had been issued three months prior to the USOE guidelines, and these, too, were taken into account. The President's Commission on Civil Rights, established by the Civil Rights Act of 1957, had eight valuable years of experience in problems attendant to desegregation, and commission reports and recommendations afforded background, suggestions, and a definite point of view. But the substance of USOE's *General Statement of Policies Under Title VI* for the desegregation of schools was based most heavily on the body of legal precedents that had been developed in the aftermath of the *Brown* decisions. As already indicated, these cases provided a variable body of doctrine. Guidelines writers, therefore, had considerable leeway in selecting procedures and lines of reasoning while still basing their policies in the bedrock of previously tested judicial decisions.

The USOE's *General Statement of Policies,*[53] the product of discussions among HEW, the Department of Justice, and White House staff, were issued in April, 1965. The resulting guidelines set forth the kinds of desegregation programs required to satisfy Title VI and the rates at which they had to be effected. Three basic alternate procedures were described for establishing eligibility for Federal assistance. First, districts with no vestiges of segregation in pupil and faculty assignment or in any other school activities and services could file an Assurance of Compliance (HEW form 441). Second, districts under court orders could qualify by filing a copy of the final order along with an Initial Compliance Report, which would describe the racial breakdown of school-age population, racial distribution of students and staff in the schools, and the procedures and activities utilized to accomplish desegregation. And third, formerly segregated districts could submit an Assurance of Compliance (HEW form 441-B), an Initial Compliance Reports and voluntary desegregation plans for either the establishment of non-racial attendance zones or student choice of schools, or a combination of both. The rate at which desegregation had to be achieved under voluntary desegregation plans was based on a target date of fall, 1967, for the desegregation of all grades in all schools. A "good-faith start" toward that

53. See *General Statement of Policies Under Title VI of the Civil Rights Act of 1964 Respecting Desegregation of Elementary and Secondary Schools,* U.S. Department of Health, Education, and Welfare, Office of Education: *Code of Federal Regulations,* Title 45, Sec. 181.

goal for newly desegregating systems would normally consist of at least four grades the first year. Detailed provisions in the guidelines elaborated on these major procedures, and covered faculty and staff, school services, notice to parents and the public, and transfer and reassignment policies. The guidelines explicitly reserved the Commissioner's flexibility to prescribe alternative procedures in particular situations where necessary.

Although the 1965 guidelines were carefully drawn to preclude evasion of their intent, in practice they exhibited some loopholes and weaknesses which had to be corrected in a revised statement of policies a year later. But when the initial guidelines were issued, most controversy centered not on the details of their many provisions, but on several key choices of substance and speed.

Geographic attendance zones had long been the favorite of proponents of rapid integration. The wording of the relevant guidelines provision, requiring a single, non-racial system of zones drawn on "natural boundaries or perimeters of compact areas surrounding particular schools," was taken directly from *Wheeler* v. *Durham*.[54] In that case a Federal District Court had struck down a gerrymandered zonal system. The guidelines also borrowed from another court-ordered requirement that all requests for transfers be treated on criteria other than race.[55] Clearly, the USOE rules provided an effective desegregation technique.

Freedom of choice plans, on the other hand, were far less popular with civil rights proponents. Unlike geographic plans, freedom of choice required an affirmative act on the part of Negro students who wanted to attend predominantly white schools. In the atmosphere of many deep South communities, such an act often required uncommon initiative and bravery on the part of students and self-sacrifice on the part of parents. Yet freedom of choice was a widely utilized method of desegregation. Although the Sixth Circuit in 1962 had held freedom of transfer unsatisfactory for Memphis,[56] most courts accepted the procedure on its face, subject to subsequent challenge for discriminatory operation. This was the approach adopted by the 1965 guidelines. However, the guidelines buttressed free choice with requirements intended to insure adequate notice to parents and children of the right to choose, and provided that students making no choice be assigned to the school nearest their home or on the basis of non-racial zones. The actual operation of the guidelines in permitting desegregation by the free choice method proved

54. Civil No. C–54–D–60, M.D.N.C. August 3, 1964.

55. See, for example, *Goss* v. *Board of Education of the City of Knoxville*, *op. cit.*

56. *Northcross* v. *Board of Education of the City of Memphis,* 302 F 2d 818, cert. denied 370 U.S. 944 (1962).

sufficiently unsatisfactory to become the subject of significant new requirements a year later. But, for the draftsmen to have forbidden it would have been to neglect a major, court-approved technique. Haunted by fears of white violence and an exodus to private schools in reaction to rapid desegregation, guidelines writers saw the freedom of choice procedure as a means of securing initial commitments to reform, commitments which could thereafter be strengthened without danger to public order and public institutions. As Commissioner Howe has since explained, "We are permitting a continuation of an arrangement [free choice] with which we are not 100 per cent sympathetic in principle, but the process of change demands some realism in what we require." [57]

Similarly, the provision that a district could satisfy Title VI by showing that it was complying with a court order for desegregation, regardless of the substance of that order, troubled those who favored speed. Many southern systems under court orders several years old were desegregating at rates which more recent decisions in other communities had made obsolete. Court decrees were often far less stringent than the USOE guidelines provisions. Yet, for the Office of Education to have declared that court orders were not a satisfactory measure of desegregation would have raised serious legal and political questions.[58]

Rates of desegregation, too, raised questions. Requiring only three school years for the desegregation of all 12 grades seemed unduly rapid to many stand-pat school boards that had not even begun the process; yet to many other educators, public officials, and civil rights activists, the legislative mandate of Title VI seemed a clear call for "desegregation now." Ever since *Brown* there had been considerable variation in mandated time schedules, but in 1964 the Supreme Court had made clear that grade-a-year plans were no longer adequate.[59] Rates were stepped up throughout the country on the theory that, according to the Fifth Circuit, "the later the start [toward desegregation], the shorter the time allowed for (full) transition." [60] Considering the variety of districts to which the guidelines applied, the three year transition was an attempt at a balanced solution.

The requirement for faculty integration posed an interesting problem. Section 604 of Title VI specifically exempted employment practices from its coverage. To the USOE, however, the maintenance by a school of an

57. Interview reported in the Syracuse *Herald-Journal,* August 18, 1966, 34.

58. See the analysis by Alexander Bickel in "Forcing Desegregation Through Title VI," *The New Republic,* April 9, 1966, 8–9.

59. *Calhoun* v. *Latimer,* 377 US 263 (1964).

60. *Lockett* v. *Board of Education of Muscogee County,* 342 F 2d 225, 118 (1964).

all-Negro faculty was incompatible with desegregation. Accordingly, the guidelines included a requirement for faculty and staff integration as a means of facilitating the achievement of student desegregation. And support for this position could be found in the *Congressional Record* and in numerous court decisions.[61] Provisions of the guidelines called for non-discriminatory initial staff assignments and a start at elimination of segregation resulting from previous assignments. Specific requirements for the first year were not overwhelming: desegregation of faculty meetings and in-service programs. But the principle was established, and the requirements were to be broadened the next year.

Guidelines: Implementation Implementation of Title VI turned out to be a Herculean labor for the Office of Education. Besides the burden of having to fend off the outflow of criticism from Congress and the South that greeted the newly issued guidelines, the sheer volume of work involved in processing the submissions of nearly 5,000 southern and border districts severely impeded other USOE efforts. As the end of FY'65 approached, the fear that sizable blocks of funds would not be distributed because the necessary Title VI assurances could not be negotiated and processed in time brought the problem to crisis proportions. In mid-April, 1965, just as ESEA was being passed and signed, the USOE Executive Group was told that all bureaus would have to contribute people and resources to help clear a backlog which was then holding up $170 million in funds and threatening to delay another $60 or $70 million. In May, Walter Mylecraine, assistant to the Deputy Commissioner, took responsibility for reorganizing the compliance processing and set up teams to move the operation into a two-shift pace. Later that month the staff of the Office of Equal Educational Opportunities began presenting weekly box scores showing in a detailed statistical report the precise status of compliance processing, and in June the USOE Commissioner and Deputy Commissioner began holding weekly meetings with the civil rights personnel to resolve problem cases. By the end of the fiscal year, it was possible to report that no FY'65 funds had been held up as a result of Federal-level processing problems.

The remainder of the summer saw no slackening of the Title VI effort. In August, 1965, Presidential Press Secretary Bill Moyers reported that the President had instructed HEW Secretary Gardner to have the USOE work "around the clock" to process more than 900 desegregation plans that were then pending, and to wire all school districts

61. *Congressional Record,* 1964, Vol. 110, 6545; e.g. *Board of Public Instruction of Duval County* v. *Braxton,* 326 F 2d 616, 620 (5th Circ. 1964) cert. denied 377 U.S. 924 (1964).

that had yet to submit plans that no Federal assistance would be available for the fall if compliance papers had not been filed and approved.

Responsibility for Title VI formulation and implementation had been assigned to the Office of Equal Educational Opportunities (hereafter OEEO) headed by David Seeley who was directly responsible to the USOE Commissioner. This assignment of civil rights responsibility to a top level staff office had several implications. For one thing, the arrangement freed the operating bureau personnel from a burdensome and politically sensitive overload. This was particularly fortunate because of the necessity to get the new ESEA programs underway. Further, separate status for civil rights assured that it would receive the attention of a staff who took it as their primary mission, with the importance of the task underlined by its placement in an office directly under the Commissioner.[62] A by-product of this arrangement, however, was a built-in tension within USOE between those in the operating bureaus anxious to get on with the job of education, and those in the OEEO who insisted that desegregation was a prior condition of educational program implementation. Inevitably, such conflicts required top level resolution. Along with the inherent emotional and political sensitivity of civil rights, then, the internal administrative arrangements within USOE contributed to making the issue the most pressing problem faced by Commissioners Keppel and Howe. Almost without exception, when Commissioner Keppel met with the Executive Group, civil rights was one, if not the chief, item of discussion. Commissioner Howe, in his first year and a half in office, spent more than two-thirds of his working time on civil rights questions.

The administrative dilemmas faced by USOE are exemplified by the conflict between the ESEA Title I mandate that funds be concentrated on educationally deprived children in "project areas" and that of Title VI of the Civil Rights Act that LEA's show progress in desegregating their schools on a district-wide basis. Because of the large overlap between low educational achievement and minority group status in school populations, it was possible that the targeting provisions of Title I might, by strict observance, be used to excuse or reinforce the isolation of Negro children in racially segregated classrooms. For example, school administrators reluctant to press for desegregation could point to the educational advantages which Title I could bring to minority group children in their target area schools. If Negro parents wished to exercise the transfer or freedom-of-choice options offered by school authorities to comply with

62. The reputation of the OE staff within the executive branch had been one of conservatism and foot-dragging on matters of reform. One of Commissioner Keppel's major concerns was to change the "inside" governmental image of the Office into that of an agency taking the lead in civil rights rather than being dragged into the movement.

Title VI regulations, their children might lose the benefits which their original target area school would enjoy under Title I.

Throughout FY'66 USOE remained officially silent on this policy dilemma, except for the inclusion in the Title I *Regulations* and *Guidelines* of a quotation from the Title VI statutory prohibitions on discrimination in federally-funded school programs. The SEA's and the LEA's were generally unwilling to raise any awkward questions, and if they did, they were referred by DPO to the Office of Equal Educational Opportunities or advised to consult their own lawyers. California, however, represents an exception to this generalization. There, State approval of LEA Title I proposals was made contingent on a satisfactory showing that they did not sanction or perpetuate school segregation. Title I funds could "follow the child" if an approvable project called for his transportation from a target school for activities elsewhere.[63]

As FY'66 drew to a close, the unresolved issues surfaced at the national level. When USOE learned that several southern school districts were cancelling summer Title I programs rather than offer them on a desegregated basis, Commissioner Howe issued the first memoranda linking the compliance requirements of the two statutes. Subsequently, more comprehensive, strongly worded policy statements were sent to the chief state school officers, and endorsement was given to the principle that Title I funds could "follow the child" out of racially segregated target areas.[64] Growing concern over the problems involved was reflected in the fact that school desegregation became a prominent item in discussion of Title I FY'67 programming at the National Conference on the Education of the Disadvantaged in July, 1966.

USOE's civil rights difficulties were compounded by the necessity to fight on several fronts at once. The most immediate battles were with southern school district officials. Almost a third of the southern school administrators responding to the BSSR Survey question on civil rights compliance indicated that they had had difficulties in satisfying USOE requirements.[65] This was a far higher percentage than for any other region. From the outset, the USOE had tried to make clear that its object was to achieve voluntary compliance, not to hold up funds. But in seeking to accomplish that end, USOE officials were faced with a variety of obstacles. Some southern officials refused to submit compliance forms;

63. Mike Milstein, "The Functions of the California State Department of Education as They Relate to Two Federally Funded Educational Programs" (unpublished Ph.D. dissertation, University of California, Berkeley, 1967), Chapter V.

64. See Commissioner Howe's memoranda dated April 25, 1966; July 1, 1966; August 18, 1966; and February 27, 1967.

65. See Appendix C, Question #27D.

others submitted plans with insufficient information; and still others submitted programs with desegregation rates too slow or procedures unsatisfactory under the guidelines. In all these instances USOE personnel attempted to persuade school districts to remedy defective compliance materials. Yet the U.S. Commissioner rapidly came to replace Earl Warren as the chief whipping-boy of southern politicians, and at least one State legislature passed a resolution calling for the impeachment of Commissioner Howe.

A second source of attack lay in the offices, on the floors, and in the committee rooms of Congress. Letters, telephone calls, and visits to the Commissioner on the part of southern Congressmen seeking leniency for districts in their constituencies were many. In floor debates over provisions to limit the fund deferral process, Commissioner Howe was described in colorful terms (and not only by southerners) as an "education commissar," "a commissioner of integration," and a "socialist quack." [66] House Special Education Subcommittee members seeking greater congressional participation in, and control of, guidelines formulation fenced with HEW and USOE officials. Throughout, in the face of charges that it was going too far too fast or that it was unfairly singling out the South, the USOE maintained that it was carrying out the intent of Congress as embodied in the 1964 Civil Rights Act.

During most of the criticism, the White House supported USOE civil rights activities, although occasionally conceding publicly that "some harassment and some mistakes" may have taken place.[67] But in one early and important instance, Commissioner Francis Keppel found himself out of line with Presidential intent, and the result of the affair had important consequences. As frequently pointed out by both southern and liberal critics, enforcement of prohibitions on discrimination was primarily restricted to the South. The problem of *de facto* segregation in the North remained largely untouched. Compliance submissions, for example, were required only in states that had formerly maintained legally segregated school systems. But in the summer of 1965, a militant civil rights organization, the Chicago Coordinating Council of Community Organizations, carried to the U.S. Office of Education its efforts to end *de facto* segregation in Chicago schools by seeking a fund cutoff under Title VI. The council's case was well enough documented and the

66. See for example, *New York Times,* Oct. 7, 1966, "Congress Votes School Aid Bill," 1, 25. One provision of the 1966 bill limited to 90 days the period during which the USOE could defer funds without calling a formal hearing on fund termination.

67. *New York Times,* October 7, 1966, "Johnson Concedes Errors on Rights," 25.

pending Chicago Title I plan sufficiently questionable that Keppel sent USOE investigators to that city. In late September Chicago School Superintendent Benjamin Willis indicated to the USOE that he could not supply requested compliance information for several more months. Commissioner Keppel then wrote to Willis that on the basis of the investigation so far, probable non-compliance with Title VI was indicated, and that the USOE was therefore deferring $30 million in ESEA funds until the matter could be satisfactorily settled. Keppel's letter was delivered on Friday, October 1. On the following Monday, Mayor Richard Daley, a power in national Democratic politics and a long time defender of Federal aid to education, was in New York on the occasion of the Papal visit to the United Nations. So was President Johnson. A discussion ensued in which the Mayor set forth his strong feelings on the fund delay. The next day, Keppel and top HEW officials were summoned to the White House, and after a meeting with the President, Under Secretary Wilbur Cohen flew to Chicago to work out an agreement that freed the ESEA funds.

For Keppel, the incident was deeply disturbing, even though Cohen had been able to wring some desegregation commitments out of the Chicago school system. For Title VI policy, the Chicago affair temporarily brought an effective end to attempts at northern enforcement since it graphically demonstrated the absence of a legislative mandate for dealing militantly with *de facto* segregation. Commissioner Howe subsequently stated that racial concentrations in schools resulting from housing patterns and other non-educational manifestations of discriminations, as well as from affirmative school board action in setting assignment patterns, are beyond the reach of Title VI "unless intent can be established." [68] Investigation of *de facto* segregation in several northern cities would continue, but the Commissioner made clear that the USOE would await a definitive legal decision before attempting enforcement.

But Title VI action is not the only means of attacking *de facto* segregation. In speeches Commissioner Howe delivered throughout the nation in an aggressive though indirect counterattack on USOE critics, he suggested alternative measures: programs under Title IV of the Civil Rights Act for teacher training in dealing with problems of integration; State and local efforts through open enrollment, paired schools, the bussing

68. Harold Howe II, *The Human Frontier: Remarks on Equality of Education* (Washington, D.C.: U.S. Government Printing Office, 1966), 5. For discussions of problems of northern desegregation see: Henry H. Hill, "School Desegregation North and South: It Will Take Time," and Harold Howe, II, "School Desegregation North and South: The Time is Now," *Saturday Review,* July 16, 1966. See also, Gerald Grant, "Desegregation in the North," *Saturday Review,* December 17, 1966, p. 75.

of students, and city and suburban exchanges of teachers and students. Howe urged the assignment of more experienced teachers and the utilization of more challenging programs in slum schools. He suggested school construction programs to break up patterns of segregation, and realistic in-depth curricula on racial problems. For a number of these approaches Howe pledged USOE support through planning funds, and called attention to the Kennedy and Powell bills to provide additional USOE authority in these areas. He called *de facto* segregation "education's most crucial" issue and took school administrators to task for their lack of leadership. "The load [schoolmen] must carry is that of irritating a fair percentage of our white constituents—of embarrassing some governors and mayors, of alarming some newspaper publishers, and of enraging suburban taxpayers who in proportion to their means are not paying as much for their good schools as paupers in the cities are paying for their bad ones." [69]

One place where the guidelines met an occasional happy reception was in the courts. In 1965 the Circuit Court of Appeals for the Eighth Circuit held that while administrative guidelines could not formally be binding upon courts, the USOE statement of policies should be "heavily relied upon" in settling school desegregation questions.[70] In the Fifth Circuit, which includes the deep South States of Alabama, Florida, Georgia, Louisiana, Mississippi and Texas, an even stronger decision indicated that courts of that circuit were to utilize the USOE guidelines as criteria in appropriate cases.[71]

Guidelines: Results Despite the intense effort and the grievous toll in political capital that Title VI took, its first year of operation yielded only moderate progress. The most widely accepted figures showed a tripling in the number of Negro children in biracial schools in the old Confederacy. Yet that increase, from 2 per cent to 6 per cent, still left 94 per cent of these Negro children in segregated schools in 1965–66. For the whole Southern and Border State region, the increase was from about 11 per cent to 16 per cent, again leaving the vast majority untouched. The number of districts beginning desegregation for the first time was an astounding 1,563—a one-year gain that exceeded the total number of districts that had desegregated in the ten year period following *Brown* v. *the Board*. But here, too, an assessment of achievement must take into account the vast extent of "tokenism" involved.

69. *Ibid.*, 40.

70. *Kemp* v. *Beasley* 352 F 2d 14, 21 (1965).

71. *Singleton* v. *Jackson Municipal Separate School District* 348 F 2d 729, 731 (1965).

Many of the cases of tokenism resulted from the free-choice procedures. A Civil Rights Commission survey based on site surveys of a carefully chosen cross-section of districts in five Southern and Border States, revealed 102 districts that had qualified for aid where not a single Negro was attending school with whites. The Southern Educational Reporting Service likewise identified districts with large numbers of Negro school children where the segregation wall remained unbroken despite USOE-approved desegregation plans. In most of these cases communities "desegregated" under freedom-of-choice procedures. In the deep South, the popularity of free-choice with school boards was almost overwhelming: all five of the USOE-approved plans in Louisiana were freedom-of-choice; 98 out of 100 in Mississippi; 85 of 88 in South Carolina; 87 of 93 in Alabama; and in Georgia, 164 of 179. After implementing their free-choice programs, these five states ranged from .43 per cent to 2.66 per cent in the percentage of Negroes in school with whites.[72]

Despite this widespread evidence of evasion, USOE had, as of January, 1966, conducted enforcement proceedings against only 65 districts. Fifty-two of these failed to comply voluntarily and therefore had funds terminated. Of these 52, 51 were districts that had not even submitted an assurance form and the 52nd had submitted an ineligible court order. No case involved failure to perform on desegregation promises. In fairness, none of these enforcement statistics count the hundreds of districts that received telephone calls, letters, and sometimes visits from USOE personnel, giving a preliminary warning that greater efforts were needed if the district was to avoid enforcement proceedings.

Two factors determined the character of USOE's efforts at enforcement. One was the explicit policy that sought to induce Title VI compliance through negotiation rather than punishment. Since a fund cutoff would necessarily entail a reduction in educational services to those needing them most, the OEEO staff considered the fiscal sanction as a kind of ultimate weapon whose threat was as important as its use. The second determinant of enforcement activity was the exceedingly limited size of the staff available for policing Title VI. At the height of 1965 processing activity, with people on loan to the OEEO from other sections of USOE and HEW as well as from the Justice Department, the professional OEEO staff numbered 75. After a reorganization in January, 1966, professional staff actually available for investigatory activity was

72. For sources of statistics and fuller discussion, see *Survey of School Desegregation in the Southern and Border States, 1965–66,* U.S. Commission on Civil Rights, *op. cit.,* 26–28, and Jim Leeson, "Desegregation in the South," *Saturday Review,* December 17, 1966, 74 ff.

set at less than 50. With responsibilities for performance under at least 1900 voluntary desegregation plans, not to mention the more than 2700 Assurances of Compliance and the 164 court orders whose promises had to be verified, the size of the available staff hardly suggests a rigorous enforcement capability. What Congress authorizes by law, Congress can make ineffective by failure to appropriate.

Guidelines: Revision. While the USOE was struggling with desegregation problems in 1965–66, OEEO went to work on a new *Statement of Policies* to cope with shortcomings revealed in the first year's operation.[73] In March, 1966, it issued a set of new requirements that clearly displayed a mood of impatience with the progress of the previous year. The major changes were aimed at free-choice plans and teacher integration, and sought to achieve performance rather than promise. For example, one new provision set out percentage figures that the USOE would use in judging how effectively free-choice was working. If 8 per cent or 9 per cent of Negro students were in integrated classes the previous year, double that number would be expected for 1966–67. If only 4 per cent or 5 per cent had been desegregated in the last year, triple that proportion would be expected for 1966–67. Smaller previous percentages required proportionately greater future increments, and districts where no integration had taken place under free-choice would generally be required to adopt a new method of integration. Other guidelines changes prescribed the actual mailing of information about the right to choose to affected students rather than permitting less effective forms of publicity. Changes were prescribed for plans utilizing geographic zones. The use of "feeder school" patterns to perpetuate segregation was prohibited; and districts were authorized to permit a student to transfer from a school where his race was in a majority. Faculty desegregation under all voluntary plans was revised to require "significant progress" over the previous year, and biracial staffing of some kind was required. Small, inadequate schools for Negroes had to be entirely closed down where they were inferior to other schools in the system. Reporting dates were adjusted to permit more adequate time for implementing changes prior to the start of school.

In general, the tone and the substance of the revised guidelines were tough, and the volume and intensity of southern and northern conservative reaction increased over 1965. USOE was charged with following a policy of "racial balancing" in violation of a prohibition on such meas-

73. *Revised Statement of Policies for School Desegregation Plans Under Title VI of the Civil Rights Act of 1964; Code of Federal Regulations,* Title 45, Part 181, U.S. Department of Health, Education, and Welfare.

ures in Title IV of the 1964 Civil Rights Act. In evidence, the conservatives pointed to the newly required percentages for incremental desegregation under free-choice plans. But the Commissioner insisted that the percentages were simply an effort "to give school officials some guidance as to a reasonable degree of progress. . ." [74] Secretary Gardner, in a letter to southern educational and political leaders, stressed that the new guidelines were reasonable and contained considerable flexibility. According to the *New York Times,* however, southern educators felt that the more stringent provisions of the 1966 *Statement of Policies* would constitute "the first real assault on the dual system." [75] A series of court decisions upholding and enforcing the revised guidelines has given support to this view.[76]

On May 10, 1967, at a time when southern and Republican opposition threatened the Elementary and Secondary Education Bill of 1967, Secretary Gardner announced consolidation of all civil rights enforcement responsibilities into a centralized staff unit attached to his own office. The shift in Title VI authority to this HEW Office for Civil Rights, headed by F. Peter Libassi, was attributed by Gardner to pressure from the House Appropriations Committee. The day after the announcement of the new arrangement, the House leadership, after previous delays, agreed to call up the 1967 education bill. The bill passed the House on May 22 with strategic southern support.[77]

De facto segregation has again come under legal and administrative attack. In June, 1967, U.S. District Court Judge J. Skelly Wright, in Hobson v. Hansen 265F. Supp. 902, held *de facto* segregation in Washington, D.C. schools unconstitutional *without* a finding of intent to discriminate. In April, 1968, the Department of Justice filed its first northern school desegregation case, charging racial bias in elementary school faculty and staff assignments in a suburban Chicago school district. (The United States v. School District 151 of Cook County.)

In March, 1968, the HEW Office for Civil Rights issued a revised set of school desegregation guidelines that placed new emphasis on ending denials of equal opportunities outside the South. For the first time, districts which had not formerly been legally segregated were required to provide detailed information on practices in their schools. Practices

74. "The 1966 Desegregation Guidelines: A Situation Report," speech reprinted in Howe, *op. cit.,* 27.

75. *New York Times,* April 12, 1966, 1, 18.

76. See, for example, *United States* v. *Jefferson County Board of Education,* 372 F 2d 836 (1966) 5th Circuit; rehearing *en banc* 380 F 1d 385 (1967).

77. See *Congressional Quarterly Weekly Edition,* May 19, 1967, 847; May 26, 1967, 859–60.

which may be considered denials of equal educational opportunity may include: overcrowded classes and activities; assigning less qualified teachers to schools attended largely by minority children, poorer facilities and instructional equipment at such schools; and higher pupil-teacher ratios or lower per pupil expenditures. The new policies also hold all local districts responsible for: planning the location of new schools in a way that does not segregate students on the ground of race, color, or national origin; and hiring and assigning teachers and other professional staff on a non-racial basis.

Whatever the results in terms of new directions, the implementation of Title VI by USOE was a halting and traumatic process. In terms of administrative strain and political controversy, the administration of Title VI overshadowed all of the titles of ESEA combined, and established a troubled environment within which ESEA itself had to be carried out.

The Coleman Report

In addition to Title VI responsibilities, the Civil Rights Act of 1964 mandated another significant activity upon the USOE. Section 402 of Title IV required that:

> The Commissioner shall conduct a survey and make a report to the President and the Congress, within two years of the enactment of this title, concerning the lack of availability of equal educational opportunities for individuals by reason of race, color, religion, or national origin in public educational institutions at all levels in the United States, its territories and possessions, and the District of Columbia.

Under the direction of Professor James Coleman of Johns Hopkins University, a mammoth nationwide study was undertaken that sampled 645,000 students, 60,000 teachers, and 4,000 schools. The racial composition, facilities and curriculum of the schools; the qualifications of teachers; and the family backgrounds and attitudes of students were among the variables carefully collected, collated and then correlated with student achievement. Issued in the summer of 1966 under the title of *Equality of Educational Opportunity,* the Coleman Report included hundreds of pages of statistics, graphs, sample questionnaires, and tests to explain, qualify, and document its conclusions.[78] Among its most important generalized findings were the following: [79]

78. Coleman, James S., *et al, Equality of Educational Opportunity* (Washington, D.C.: U.S. Government Printing Office, 1966).

79. *Ibid.,* 1–23.

1. *Segregation.* The great majority of American students throughout the nation attend schools where almost all of their fellow students are of the same racial background.

2. *School facilities and curriculum.* Minority group students on the whole have larger classes; less access to laboratories; fewer books in school libraries and fewer textbooks available; less access to college preparatory or accelerated curricula, and fewer extracurricular activities.

3. *Teachers.* Teachers of Negro students are more apt to have spent all their lives in a single community than are those of white students. In terms of types of colleges attended, scoring on a vocabulary test, educational background of mother, professional experience, and salary, teachers of Negro students are consistently of lower quality than those of white students.

4. *Student body.* "The average Negro has fewer classmates whose mothers graduated from high school; his classmates more frequently are members of large rather than small families; they are less often enrolled in a college preparatory curriculum; they have taken a smaller number of courses in English, mathematics, foreign language, and science." [80]

5. *Achievement.* Achievement tests, administered as part of the survey in grades 1, 3, 6, 9, and 12, revealed that, with the exception of oriental-Americans, minority group students scored lower at every level than the majority group and the gap increased with the number of years in school.

While this documentation of the extent of inequality in American education might in itself have adequately fulfilled the mandate of Title IV of the Civil Rights Act, the Coleman Report went significantly further in its analysis. Utilizing regression analysis to determine the differential effects of a variety of factors on student achievement, the study reached a series of causal conclusions that stirred intense interest and controversy in educational, social science, and governmental circles.

Coleman found that in comparison with family background and socioeconomic factors, "school factors" accounted for only a small fraction of the differences in student achievement. But this fraction varied significantly between majority and minority groups, with the achievement of the latter (again with the exception of oriental-Americans) being influenced to a much greater degree by the quality of the school they attended. For minority groups, higher performance was positively correlated (to a slight degree) with higher quality facilities and abler teachers. To a much greater degree, their achievement was related to school attendance with classmates of superior educational backgrounds and aspirations. On this latter point the report concluded:

80. *Ibid.*, 20.

> Thus, if a white pupil from a home that is strongly and effectively supportive of education is put in a school where most pupils do not come from such homes, his achievement will be little different than if he were in a school composed of others like himself. But if a minority pupil from a home without much educational strength is put with schoolmates with strong educational backgrounds, his achievement is likely to increase.[81]

Another of the major findings of the report identified an attitudinal factor that went further to explain achievement differences among students than any other: "the extent to which an individual feels that he has some control over his own destiny." [82] Minority group students, except for orientals, displayed far less conviction than whites that they can affect their own futures, but those who did had higher achievement scores than white students who lacked that conviction. The report went on to note that those Negroes who attended school with higher proportions of whites displayed a much greater sense of control over their own futures.

We shall return to the implications of these findings and to the controversy they aroused in the final chapters.

Overview

The process of implementing ESEA is not easily summarized. In essence, it involved an administrative dialectic—a series of promulgations from USOE which were preceded, accompanied, and followed by inputs and feedbacks from affected clientele. The process was cumbersome, and involved both under-prescriptions and over-prescriptions from Washington. Evidence shows, however, that USOE tried not to be arbitrary, and in many procedural and substantive areas it modified its practices and interpretations in order to take into account clientele problems and reactions. When USOE held firm, it did so in the considered belief that it was upholding congressional and constitutional mandates.

81. *Ibid.*, 22.
82. *Ibid.*, 23.

V. Results and Reactions

One of the hallmarks of the American political system is its emphasis on reviewing and evaluating public policies. This stock taking is both political and managerial. Politically, programs are scrutinized by presidential staff; by committees and subcommittees of Congress charged with considering the extensions and modifications of authorizations and appropriations; by the mass media; by cognate government agencies concerned with the politics of jurisdiction; by affected State and local public officials; by political parties and their leading candidates; by concerned interest groups; by public opinion pollsters; and by a scattering of individual essayists, academicians, letter-writers, and petition-signers who find meaning (and sometimes income) in life through persistent social criticism. The openness and diversity of such scrutiny does not, alas, guarantee detachment and rationality in the appraisal of public policies. Much scrutiny is tendentious, ill-informed, and self-serving. Miles Law ("where you stand depends upon where you sit") is persistently operable. The political calculus of a President may not be identical with that of a key Congressman, lobbyist, publisher, governor, priest, opposition candidate, or agency director. What pleases a northern school superintendent may horrify a southern chief State school officer. Policy success to one man may be policy disaster to another.

And yet, in the spirit of Milton's *Areopagitica* and John Stuart Mill's essay *On Liberty,* the American polity has for generations operated on the assumption that the marketplace of opinion and the clash and compromises of adversary proceedings are better guarantors of rational and responsible policy-making in the public interest than a system imposed by bureaucratic planners and enforced by authoritarian power.

It is one thing for political theorists to reify policy-making by muddle. It is quite another thing to expect the managers of large, complex, and increasingly technological systems (public or private) to relax in the face of (from their point of view) irrational gusts of political influence which can topple their best laid plans. A major compulsion of the public administrator is to achieve the presumed rational goals of law by rational techniques based upon a rational information system. In this compulsion, of course, he has the support of those who are politically oriented in the society and who at the same time accept the value premises of the law in question. Both wish to maximize the effectiveness of programs in which they have a common proprietary interest. And both assume (not without some empirical justification) that given certain value premises, administrative rationality can chasten and improve political decision-making. That "rationality" is sometimes a euphemism for self-serving advocacy on the part of public managers, and that "rational information systems" are sometimes little more than barrister-briefs before congressional juries, no one will question. But to leave the public manager as simply another sullen claimant in an intricate web of political tensions is to misunderstand the demands of his role and to deny man's capacity for intermittent nobility. The fact is that the socially accepted role of the public administrator is to achieve politically sanctioned goals by constitutionally mandated means. His terminal loyalty is to the public interest as defined and legitimized by the instruments of representative government. He is one of those instruments but he is also the servant of exogenous representatives (notably the President and the Congress) who are often closer to the electorate or whose independence from immediate popular control is hallowed by constitutional tradition (the courts). Once policy goals are legitimized, the assumption in our society is that the public administrator will attempt to develop the most rational possible means for accomplishing these goals.

The problem is that internally developed canons of administrative rationality may (almost inevitably will) produce effects which please some and alienate others, both inside and outside any particular administrative system. The fundamental dilemma of the managers of large-scale public programs is how to perfect and protect the increasingly intricate machinery needed for the rational accomplishment of complex goals, while remaining responsive to the variable winds of legitimate political influence.

The Modes and Purposes of ESEA Evaluation

All this needs saying, because throughout the first year, ESEA was subject to both political and administrative evaluations. These two types of evaluations overlapped, and in retrospect they are hard to disentangle. However, there are some ways in which they were quite distinct. In any case, they involved a multiplicity of participants with varying perspectives: public agencies at three levels of government; professionals in economics, psychology, and administration; advisory groups; congressmen, singly and in committees; interest groups; the press; research organizations; consultants; and independent scholars. The forms of evaluation were also various: fiscal and program audits; statistical and narrative reports and summaries; systems analyses relating program goals, costs, and benefits; contracted research reports; congressional testimony, reports, and floor debates; policy pronouncements by government offices and educational interest groups; opinion surveys; and ephemeral press comments. Most of the reviews and evaluations considered in this study emerged, of course, while ESEA was in its first weeks and months of implementation and at a time when the infrastructure of *systematic* program evaluation was either non-existent or woefully primitive. These facts must be borne in mind in what follows. That a bevy of progress reports were in fact issued during FY'66 and FY'67 was due not only to the traditional requirements of government accounting and of the congressional appropriations calendar, but also to a widespread interest in the new programs, and, especially, to unprecedented evaluation mandates in the law itself.

THE UNPRECEDENTED MANDATE

Perhaps no piece of social legislation in American history has placed a greater premium upon the reporting and evaluating of results than ESEA. Most laws, of course, call for or subsume annual reports and periodic financial statements. But these have tended in practice to be *pro forma*. They have been generally ignored by all except those in the General Accounting Office or in legislative or administrative staff positions whose melancholy but necessary function it is to monitor and file government paper. To the perceptive, of course, even the dreariest program reports and financial statements may be informative. Some observers have claimed, for example, that the success of Secretary McNamara's "whiz kids" in imposing a new rationality on Pentagon decisions in the early 1960's was due less to the computer and to fancy cost-benefit analyses than it was to the assiduousness with which bright young staff studied the routine reports of the several armed services. But even if this is so, it is the exception to prove the rule. Stacked in the archives and warehouses of the world's governments, or hidden away in legislative hearings and committee reports, are countless tons of now forgotten official statements and summaries which few have seen and even fewer have read and pondered. Each served its function at a particular time and place, for each symbolized someone's basic concern that the public business be conducted honestly and responsibly. And it can be argued that the essence of accountability is not the fact but the presumption and possibility of external audit. But, in practice, at least in the United States, formal reports have probably been of less moment as instruments of review and accountability than have been the less structured evaluations which find their way into congressional hearings or into trade journals and the mass media.

In the case of ESEA, however, the legislative mandate for formal reports and evaluations of programs was loud and clear, and unprecedented in scope. Each of the operating titles of the act provided either for the establishment of procedures for making continuing and periodic evaluations of the effectiveness of the programs; or for annual and other reports; or for both, including reports among various levels and branches of government (e.g., LEA to SEA; SEA to USOE; USOE to HEW; USOE to President and/or Congress).

The Official Accounts of First-Year Accomplishments

The most elaborate review of ESEA's first-year accomplishments came, of course, from the Office of Education itself. Struggling to establish a sophisticated apparatus for rigorous program evaluation through its own National Center for Educational Statistics, USOE was in fact reduced in the first year to traditional and conventional modes of compiling a history of program accomplishments. These inevitably fell shy of technical evaluations standards posited by devotees of cost-benefit analysis.[1] As Commissioner Howe pointed out in his first annual report on ESEA:

> Because of time limitations, lack of established evaluating procedures and technologies, failure to use achievement measuring systems, and the lack of trained evaluators, the report lacks some of the specifics of a technical evaluation report.[2]

But the record proves that within these limitations, USOE did everything within its power during the first year to lay the groundwork for a new inter-governmental system of reporting which would move toward fulfilling the unprecedented evaluation mandates of the act. A vast amount of information was in fact compiled from across the nation on the basis of reporting ground rules laid down by the Office of Education.

1. NCES has also been accused of falling short in providing traditional educational statistics. A statement submitted to a House Appropriations Subcommittee in the spring of 1968, by the American Council on Education and eleven other educational organizations, called for "increased support for the NCES . . . provided such support is used to bring about an urgently needed improvement in the U.S. Office of Education's ability to perform its basic historical function of gathering and disseminating statistical information . . ." The statement complained of "delayed or inaccessible information (in) many . . . vital survey areas."
See ACE Newsletter, "Higher Education and National Affairs," Vol. 27, No. 15, April 26, 1968, 2–3.

2. *First Annual Report, Title I, Elementary and Secondary Education Act of 1965*. U.S. Office of Education. 90th Cong., 1st Sess., Senate, Subcommittee on Education, *Notes and Working Papers . . . Title I of Public Law 89–10,* 914.

The following summaries of first-year accomplishments are based upon the information so gathered.

Title I

Commissioner Howe's *Annual Report* was the most comprehensive official statement of Title I activities. It was based upon data submitted by the States in response to the "Office of Education Guide for State Evaluation Reports"—USOE's attempt to elicit fairly standard and comparable responses from the 50 States, the District of Columbia, and the Territories of Guam, Puerto Rico, the Virgin Islands, and the Trust Territory of the Pacific.

The report showed that during the first year, 17,481 local educational agencies had participated in Title I—roughly three-quarters of all eligible LEA's.[3]

TABLE 7

SUMMARY OF FIRST-YEAR PARTICIPANTS IN TITLE I

Total LEA's (School districts), Fall 1965	26,983
Total LEA's eligible for Title I	24,926
Total LEA's participating in Title I	17,481
Total LEA's eligible, but not participating in Title I	7,445

Of the 7,445 LEA's eligible but not participating, 104 had not complied with Title VI of the Civil Rights Act of 1964. The rest had either failed to submit applications or their applications had been rejected at the State level as failing to meet Federal or State criteria for size, scope, and quality.

Five short paragraphs of the *Annual Report* give an overview of program results: [4]

> In all, during the first year of operation, 8.3 million children were served by Title I and some $987.6 million was expended, including almost $11 million for handicapped children under Public Law 89–313. Expenditures totalled 84 per cent of the allocations.
>
> The average Title I expenditure per pupil was $119, but the expenditures ranged from about $25 to $227. For many states, this represented a substantial increase over average current per

3. *Ibid.,* 915. The figures for total LEA's or school districts, Fall, 1965, "include non-operative taxing units."

4. *Ibid.*

pupil expenditures, the national average being about $532 for 1965–66.

Nearly 52 percent of the $987.6 million in Title I funds the first year was spent on instruction; about two-thirds of that amount was spent for language arts and remedial reading, which were identified as the top priority by the majority of local educational agencies.

Some 20 percent of the total was spent on educational equipment, and about 10 percent was spent for construction. Food and health services accounted for 4.5 percent of the total expenditures.

Nearly 65 percent of the participants in Title I programs were in pre-school through grade six. Ninety-two percent of the students were enrolled in public schools and 6 percent in non-public schools. About 2 percent of the students were not enrolled in school.

These statistical summaries suggest the overall scope of the program, but they are less dramatic than the *Annual Report's* recitation of program substance in specific and human terms. For example: [5]

In a Washington farm community, two nurses aides (one of whom spoke Spanish) treated children of migrant farm workers.

New York City assembled teams of specialists—reading experts, counselors, and psychiatrists—for intensive work with pre-schoolers.

A Tennessee project developed wireless auditory training units for deaf children.

A Louisiana school developed English as a foreign language for children of Cuban refugees and resident aliens from South America.

An Iowa school provided evening classes for high school dropouts.

A specially trained liaison worker was hired by a Texas project to visit families and children and evaluate needs.

The State reports, which were summarized in the Commissioner's *Annual Report,* stressed a variety of alleged achievements:

—educationally deprived children had been provided with more individual attention; (The Report quotes a boy in Iowa: "Happiness is two teachers so you can be helped when you need it.");

—exploratory and innovative educational projects had been encouraged;

—new interests and new confidence had been awakened among the educationally deprived—especially among potential dropouts;

—Title I money had resulted in higher student achievement, especially in reading, and especially with younger children;

5. *Ibid.,* 919.

—new equipment and material purchased with Title I funds had been ". . . of significant benefit to their disadvantaged children;"

—the program had intangible effects on general student attitudes. For example, the Texas Title I annual evaluation included the following illustration: "Consultants of the Division of Compensatory Education, through on-site visits to classrooms, frequently observed high levels of interest and application of pupils, increased feelings of self-worth as a result of new clothing or special attention, and a kind of blossoming of spirit in pupils, who, it appeared likely had previously been submissive and withdrawn." [6]

—teachers had ". . . learned to help culturally deprived disadvantaged children more effectively and with a greater depth of understanding than ever before;"

—those who plan and evaluate educational programs had been stimulated to further their efforts ". . . in planning, studying, and evaluating education in general and education for the disadvantaged in particular;"

—local districts had been stimulated ". . . to assess their school programs in terms of individual pupil needs, rather than school or system needs;"

—the program had ". . . given new vigor to the leadership capabilities of State departments of education;"

—a new spirit of cooperation and coordination had been fostered among school districts:

—new staff resources for education had been discovered in the communities; and in-service training of existing staff had been intensified;

—over a half million non-public school children had been aided, and ". . . lines of communication between public and non-public schools [had] been established and improved;"

—big city school systems had benefited; ("Title I programs in 32 of the largest school systems in the country involved about 1.5 million participants, 18 percent of the national total").[7]

These are impressive generalizations and claims, but they are almost entirely impressionistic. Some, undoubtedly, must be discounted as the inevitably rosy expressions of those who feel they must defend their status by emphasizing the positive side of performance. And there is something about the very nature of public accountability through processes of budgeting and legislative review which induces agencies to justify next year's appropriations by "show and tell" reports of an almost euphoric character.

Nevertheless, by the end of the first year, Title I was obviously having some kind of impact upon thousands of school districts and literally millions of children. The precise impact upon the educational achievement of affected youngsters, however, could not generally be measured.

6. *Ibid.*, 920.
7. *Ibid.*, 923.

This was not for want of USOE's trying. Chapter II of Commissioner Howe's first *Annual Report* is a fascinating account of the lengths to which USOE went in attempting to help SEA's and LEA's develop a valid evaluation procedure. Towards the end of the chapter, Commissioner Howe dolefully reports that "forty states presented incomplete test data and 11 presented none." He summarizes the reasons: [8]

> There was not enough uniformity in the objective tests to justify a compilation.
>
> Post testing was not attempted because the State was committed to obtain only baseline data in fiscal year 1966.
>
> Test data could not be compiled.
>
> There were no state-wide testing programs.
>
> Appropriate measuring instruments were not available.

One statistical table purporting to show *Examples of Achievement* was included in the *Annual Report,* but even this was qualified by the following caution:

> Since many unknown factors doubtless operated to influence the 19 groups represented in the exhibit, it is not possible to draw firm conclusions or make strong generalizations about improved academic achievement resulting from Title I programs.[9]

In the field of precise evaluation and measurement, what USOE lacked in terms of specific results, it compensated for in reportorial honesty.

Title II

In 1965, half the schools in the nation lacked a centralized library. At the elementary school level, the percentage figure jumped to two-thirds. Private elementary schools were slightly better off, but even here 56 per cent were without centralized library facilities. It was estimated that roughly 12 million school children did not even have access to classroom-help libraries. And schools with central libraries were woefully under-equipped with books and services. As Commissioner Howe reported in April, 1966,

> In the 56,000 schools with central libraries, there are approximately 192 million books. If those libraries were to meet minimum standards, they would have to acquire 233 million more volumes. Schools which have made valiant efforts to maintain adequate li-

8. *Ibid.,* 939.
9. *Ibid.,* 940.

> braries are falling behind because of rapidly growing enrollments and the increased cost of construction and library materials.[10]

In many schools the textbook situation was equally doleful. Again to quote Commissioner Howe:

> A survey of the needs of our schools for modern textbooks reveals that many children must use textbooks which are out of date and grossly inadequate for this era of expanding educational horizons. It is a sad fact that "modern history" books often have nothing to teach our children after WW I, and that physics texts frequently deal with the state of our knowledge in the forties and fifties—ignoring the atomic revolution and the space age.[11]

The lack in the loosely-defined field of "instructional materials" was more difficult to gauge, but no one doubted that the needs were substantial.

As a result of Title II, Commissioner Howe was able to point out in July, 1967,[12] that 3,600 new public school libraries had been opened; 1,545,000 public and non-public school children were being served by these new libraries; 89 per cent or 43 million school children were enrolled in the 91,000 schools participating in ESEA, Title II; and that 285 full-time staff had been assigned by State departments of education to administer the Title II program. How much of this progress had been made in FY'66 alone is unclear, but some of these dramatic results were unquestionably apparent by the end of the first year of ESEA's operation. In March, 1966, on the basis of 46 State plans submitted and 34 State plans approved, USOE had predicted that 40 million children and 1.5 million teachers would benefit from this first year of Title II expenditure.[13]

Title III

The first official report of projects approved for supplementary educational centers and services under Title III was issued in February 1966. Title III had been dubbed PACE, so the first report in the form

10. *Hearings on the Elementary and Secondary Education Amendments of 1966,* 89th Cong., 2d sess., Senate, Subcommittee on Education, April 1966, 477.

11. *Ibid.*

12. Statement by Harold Howe, II, U.S. Commissioner of Education, Department of Health, Education, and Welfare, before the Senate Subcommittee on Education, July 24, 1967 (mimeo.).

13. *Progress Under the Elementary and Secondary Education Act of 1965 (PL 89–10),* U.S. Department of Health, Education and Welfare (Offset sheet), March 1966, sheet 4.

of a brochure inevitably was entitled *Pace-setters in Innovation.* Two hundred and seventeen projects from 44 States were described. These had been approved by the Commissioner, ". . . upon the advice of an eight-member Advisory Committee, following review and recommendation by the State educational agencies. In addition, the projects had been evaluated by outside teams of consultants." [14] The 217 approved projects (most of them planning grants) had been winnowed from 746 proposals submitted by the first application deadline of November 10, 1965. Two additional deadlines were set for FY'66: February 9 and May 25. By the second deadline, 986 additional applications had been received. At the end of the fiscal year, 2706 project applications had been received,[15] requesting a total of over $250 million.

The individual projects would, of course, take months or years to become fully operational and to produce testable results. But the project proposals themselves were exciting reading, and gave evidence of the power of money to stimulate educational imagination and experimentation. The majority of projects approved during the first year were for planning ". . . to help schools lay the groundwork for action programs, perform research, and make analyses." [16] Both the planning and the operational projects gave evidence of substantial creativity. A few examples of approved Title III projects will suffice to suggest the range of diversity of submissions:

—Santa Ana, California planned to establish three service school centers for bringing dropouts back to school;

—Kennebunk, Maine proposed a mobile van to bring remedial reading assistance to children in a number of elementary and secondary schools that had no facilities for remedial reading;

—Hagerstown, Maryland, one of the nation's pioneers in educational television, wanted to establish an institute for writing and producing educational television lessons in order to improve its institutional television system;

—the submission from Binghamton, N. Y., included a center for teachers' in-service education in the arts, world affairs, and the sciences;

—Cleveland, Ohio wanted to take over a downtown factory and convert it into a science and technology educational museum;

—New York City proposed to bring to each of 50 selected New York

14. *Hearings, op. cit.,* 89th Cong., 2d sess., Senate, Subcommittee on Education, April 1966, 478.

15. As of September 30, 1966, 1,030 projects had been approved for requests of $75 million. In addition 64 projects requesting $13 million were in the "hold" category. A little less than half of the approved projects were for multi-purpose programs such as media and materials centers or cultural enrichment activities. About one-third were for special activities outside the regular curriculum, such as remedial and advanced instruction and programs for the handicapped.

16. *American Education,* U.S. Office of Education, August 1966, 15.

City schools a series of four live presentations by the Lincoln Center in the Performing Arts, including solo recitals, chamber music concerts, drama presentations, dance demonstrations and opera performances;

—Burlington, Vermont planned an instructional media center which would preview and produce new materials, and develop a central film and filmstrip library.

Wichita, Kansas proposed a regional program for educating the mentally, physically, and emotionally handicapped;

—Casper, Wyoming wanted to establish a planetarium which, in addition to offering instruction in astronomy and related sciences, would feature lectures on such topics as "the social implications of the space age," and "the skies of the ancient mariners."

Because of the limited resources available, USOE gave low priority to projects requesting funds to purchase equipment or to construct facilities. But it projected that the innovative and exemplary proposals approved in the first round would serve 20 million persons: children and teachers in public and private elementary and secondary schools, pre-schoolers, adults, handicapped children, and out-of-school youth.

These projections tell only part of the story, for one of the observable dividends of Title III was the promotion of conversations and contacts: among several schools or school districts intent on making a joint application; among public and private school teachers and administrators; and between schools and a variety of other cultural and educational agencies in the communities of the nation. Even where an application was finally disapproved in Washington, the very process of applying was a catalytic agent for innovative thinking and educational cooperation.

Title IV

Like Title III, *new* Title IV projects (i.e., those which were not simple extensions of activities under the Cooperative Research Act of 1954) could be measured during the first fiscal year only in terms of promise. Research and development centers and educational laboratories take time to organize and to produce effective results. Furthermore, USOE had given priority to implementing Titles I, II, and V. By the time *Regulations* and *Guidelines* had been established for Title IV, screening panels and site visits organized, and structures and staffs actually rendered operational, FY'66 was close to expiration.

Some forward motion was, however, observable. By the end of the first fiscal year, 12 regional educational laboratories had been approved (another seven had been given "developmental contracts"), and eight university-based research and development centers had either been created *de novo* or had had their original support under the Cooperative Research Act of 1954 increased and extended.

From the beginning, considerable ambiguity surrounded the related functions of educational laboratories and R & D centers. And in some cases, approved Title III projects looked curiously like laboratory or R & D center proposals. However, USOE saw these jurisdictional and definitional questions as an almost inevitable consequence of attempting to sponsor activities along a spectrum of educational innovation. The spectrum might be diagrammed as follows:

Basic Research/Development/Applied Research/Demonstration/Dissemination

---

R & D Centers   Educational Laboratories   Title III Centers

[Long-Hair]   [Short-Hair]

A review of the approved R & D Center projects on the one hand and those of the Educational Laboratories on the other reveals how difficult it is to separate pure from applied research in the field of education. Structurally, of course, the two types of research activities were quite distinct. R & D centers were university-based. Laboratories were regionally organized under an elaborate scheme of local representation (schools; universities; civic, cultural, ethnic, and religious groups; etc.). The *tendency* of the R & D centers was toward basic research; the *tendency* of the educational laboratories was toward fairly immediate problem-solving and pilot demonstrations. But, in fact, a lot of long-hair research found its way into laboratory plans; and some R & D centers became busily engaged in experimental applications of research findings. Any summary of R & D and laboratory projects is bound to be cryptic and inadequate, but Table 8, following, may give at least a sense of direction and assumed function.

The overlapping functions and the fuzzy program foci of many laboratories and a few of the R & D Centers should not hide the fact that Title IV of ESEA gave promise of attacking some of the most important and fundamental long-range issues in American education. The first year's accomplishments were meager. Only four or five of the Laboratories, for example, gave evidence of moving into high gear—organizationally and programmatically. But the ultimate promise was nonetheless encouraging.

Title V

In administrative terms, Title V was the keystone in the arch of ESEA. Unless the caliber and competence of State departments of education could be strengthened, the purposes of the act, especially of Titles I and II, could not be effectively realized, and the type of intergovernmental partnership in American education envisaged by the authors of ESEA would collapse. Previously, many Federal education laws had provided funds to States to cover the cost of program administration, but as Dr. Robert Hopper said, "no legislation had been passed designed specifically to strengthen State departments of education across the board." [17]

As noted earlier, Title V provided two different types of assistance to improve educational leadership in the States: (1) basic grants to develop, improve, and expand the professional leadership activities carried on by State education agencies; (2) special project grants to support experimental programs for developing State leadership, and special services designed to assist in solving problems common to educational agencies in several States.

Seventeen million dollars was appropriated for Title V in FY'66. Of this, 85 per cent was designated for basic grants. Each State was allowed a minimum of $100,000. The rest of the basic grant money was allocated on the basis of the relative number of public school pupils in the State. The remaining 15 per cent of Title V funds was reserved for the special grant program to help finance experimental projects. The special grants were to be issued by the Commissioner of Education upon his review of applications from the several States.

Understandably, the bulk of the basic grants was spent by the States on additional personnel. Over 1800 new positions were budgeted in the States and territories under Section 503 of Title V during the first year of its application. Over a thousand of those new positions were professional. In some cases, Title V money enabled SEA's to double the size of their professional staffs. The functions for which these new hirings were used can be grouped into five categories:

(1) Up-grading services to local school districts for the improvement of instruction;

(2) Improving general administration within the SEA—including coordinating machinery;

(3) Improving the capacity of the State to study, plan, develop, and evaluate the ESEA programs and to coordinate State and local research activities;

(4) Improving data processing and statistical services;

(5) Improving school accreditation, teacher education programs, certification, and licensing.

17. Robert L. Hopper, "Strength Where It Counts," *American Education,* June 1966, 20.

TABLE 8

PART I. THE FIRST EIGHT R & D CENTERS: [18]
A SUMMARY OF PROJECTS

Name	University Affiliation	Research Program
arning and ›search Center	University of Pittsburgh	Interaction between learning research in the behavioral sciences and instructional practices of the schools; using Learning Laboratories; computers; and field studies. Emphasis upon Individually Prescribed Instruction.
›nter for the lvanced Study of lucational lministration	University of Oregon	The social context within which educational institutions operate; special reference to innovative and organizational structures; educational administration and the value structure of American society; career processes of educational personnel; and the allocation of resources in higher education.
›search and evelopment Center r Cognitive ›arning	University of Wisconsin	Improvement of educational practice through better understanding of cognitive learning; special emphasis upon process of learning; conditions associated with efficient learning; instructional processes in the schools; program testing and evaluation; and work with other agencies in dissemination of results.
esearch and evelopment Center Early Stimulation	University of Georgia	Production of a series of comprehensive instructional programs for pre-primary, primary, and intermediate levels based upon research with structured segmental learning activities for children ages 3–12.
he Research and evelopment Center r Teacher Education	University of Texas	What kinds of teachers, teaching what kinds of children, using what kinds of control methods, produce what kinds of child learning?
enter for Research ıd Development Teaching	Stanford University	The effect of the teacher's acts on the pupil, desirable modification in teacher training, and the effect of administrative practices on the teacher.
enter for Research ıd Development in igher Education	University of California	To discover and to disseminate new perspectives on higher educational issues and new solutions to educational problems, by using theories and methodologies of the behavioral sciences.
enter for Study of valuation of ıstructional Progress	UCLA	Examination of the theory, methods, and operation of evaluation in both simple and complex educational settings and across a broad range of educational objectives.

18. *The Research and Development Centers Established under the Cooperative Research Pro-ram of USOE,* U.S. Department of Health, Education and Welfare, July 14, 1967.

PART II. THE FIRST 12 EDUCATIONAL LABORATORIES:[19]
A SUMMARY OF PROJECTS

Name	Region	Program Focus
Center for Urban Education	Metropolitan New York and Some Neighboring Cities	The reconstruction of educational services through the region with special reference to the social and c tural integration of students and school staffs and strengthening of instruction in the primary skills of re ing, mathematics, scientific thinking, social studies, a art.
Southwest Regional Laboratories	Southern California, Southern Nevada, and Western Arizona	To help schools insure that every child will master essential skills of reading and of generalized probl solving at pre-school and primary grade levels.
Research for Better Schools, Inc.	Delaware, N.J. and Eastern, Pa.	Field testing the Individually Prescribed Instruction P gram in Reading and Mathematics designed by the R & Center at Pittsburgh as an initial effort in designing, veloping, testing, and diffusing instructional syste which could help the schools to provide the conte scope, sequences, and variety of educational experien suitable to the total range of abilities and requireme of students.
Northwest Regional Educational Research Laboratory	Alaska, Idaho, Montana, Oregon, & Washington	(1) Encouraging the use of promising innovations; (lowering barriers to teacher effectiveness; (3) improv the education of ethnically different children; (4) i proving instruction in small isolated schools.
Appalachia Educational Laboratory	West Virginia and parts of Ohio, Pennsylvania, Virginia, Tennessee, and Kentucky	Improving the transition from school to work and i proving language and reading communication.
Far West Laboratory for Educational Research and Development	Northern California and all of Nexada except Clark County	(1) Insuring quality education for all students; (2) signing instructional programs that foster student dev opment over a wide range of individual differences; (making reasonable choices among the variety of curr ula innovations; (4) training school personnel for int ducing new methods and techniques into the school; (communicating the outcome of research to educatio agencies.

19. From: Memorandum from Norman J. Boyan, Director, Division of Educational Labora ries, U.S. Office of Education, to Participants in October Conference on Educational Laborator (mimeo.), September 29, 1967.

Name	Region	Program Focus
ntral Midwestern gional Educational boratory	Eastern Missouri, Southern Illinois, Western Tennessee, and Western Kentucky	Helping to bridge the gap between research and discovery on the one hand and deficiencies and improvements in the classroom on the other.
id-Continent gional Educational boratory	Western Missouri, Central Oklahoma, Eastern Nebraska, Eastern Kansas	Institutionalizing change and developing new ways to train professional personnel. Special emphasis upon reading, teacher training, and community service schools.
uthwest operative lucational boratory	Portions of Arizona, Oklahoma and Texas, and all of New Mexico	Improving education of the region's three major cultures: Indian, Spanish-American, and Anglo-migrant.
uthern Educational boratory	Georgia, Alabama, Florida	Reducing educational deprivation.
pper Midwest gional Educational boratory	South Dakota, North Dakota, Minnesota, Wisconsin, Iowa	Developing curriculum improvements aimed at solving pressing educational problems of the region and using available educational resources to the best advantage.
ocky Mountain lucational boratory	All or portions of Colorado, Utah, Wyoming, Arizona, Idaho, Montana, and Kansas	(1) developing methods of individualizing instruction; (2) improving pre-service teacher education; (3) utilizing educational television for in-service teacher education; (4) establishing educational media centers; (5) establishing centers on affective behavior.

The special grants during the first year were focused particularly on problem areas common to several States. Seventeen grants were made for interstate projects that involved in total 48 out of the 50 States. To quote from the Green Committee Hearings:

> These covered such subjects as the role of demonstration centers in educational change, school district reorganization, . . . the intermediate service unit, teacher preparation and certification, State educational information systems, educational television, pupil transportation services, the role of the State educational agency in providing services and leadership to educational programs for exceptional children, pre-school education, instructional media, statewide testing programs and . . . the education of migrant children.[20]

Some of the money inevitably found its way into SEA divisions concerned with implementing other titles of ESEA.

Once again, the precise effect of Title V during FY'66 is impossible to measure. As Robert L. Hopper has written,

> Progress has been made under Title V. . . . the progress is already being felt in classrooms across the nation, as for instance, more and new curricula specialists move out from State agencies to assist teachers in improving what they teach and how they teach it. Such progress, however, will remain difficult to measure in concrete terms.[21]

At the end of the first year, USOE could only rest its case on superficial evidence and a statement of faith:

> We can point to the number of professional and non-professional staff members who have been employed; we can point to conferences that have been held or materials that have been developed. We know that as time passes, the State education agencies will continue to assume the role in the Federal-State partnership that leads to better education: the role of the skilled, efficient, and responsible leaders in all phases and levels of American education.[22]

But this statement of faith raised an interesting and in some ways perverse issue. If one totals all of the Federal support available to strengthen the administrative and program capacity of state departments

20. *Hearings Before the Special Subcommittee on Education* (Green Committee), on the U.S. Office of Education, 89th Cong., 2d sess., House, 172.

21. Robert L. Hopper, *op. cit.*

22. *Ibid.*

of education (NDEA, Vocational Education, Title V of ESEA, etc.), it is clear that in many SEA's Federal funds exceed State funds. If one extrapolates this trend, at what point do SEA's become simply administrative appendages of USOE rather than autonomous and locally funded instruments of *state* law?

CONCURRENT MOVEMENTS FOR SYSTEMATIC EVALUATIONS OF EDUCATIONAL PERFORMANCE

The ambiguities and inadequacies of the official reviews of ESEA during its first year may not be evident to the casual observer. The reports and evaluations were on the whole no worse and in some respects were somewhat better than hundreds of similar reviews conducted over the years by other Washington agencies charged with administering new programs. But by 1965–66 there were efforts afoot in the nation's capital to develop new and more rational bases for judging the effectiveness of federally funded programs. Pushed by educational reformers, academic researchers, and avant-garde budgeteers, these new thrusts into systematic and quantifiable evaluations were affecting the whole climate of Washington decision-making and were to produce fears, insecurities, and discordant political overtones inside and outside of the government.

The Coleman Report and the Tyler Committee

In the field of education, the first major harbingers of the new movement were the so-called Coleman Report and the establishment under a Carnegie Corporation-Ford Foundation grant of an "Exploratory Committee on Assessing the Progress of Education" headed by Ralph W. Tyler.[23] Both of these were concerned with an assessment of student achievement. The Coleman study has already been alluded to. Commissioned by the Office of Education in early 1965 pursuant to Title IV of the Civil Rights Act, a team of behavioral scientists using a bevy of sampling, testing, and regression-analysis techniques produced a mammoth survey on *Equality of Educational Opportunity*.[24] The study was conducted before ESEA could be implemented, but its findings (published in 1966) are so pregnant with implications for programs targeting low-achievers in our society as to raise serious questions about the long-range validity of ESEA-type attacks on the basic problem of how to

23. For a description of the Tyler Committee project, see *Phi Delta Kappan*, September, 1965 and April, 1967.

24. Coleman, James S., *et al, Equality of Educational Opportunity* (Washington: U.S. Government Printing Office, 1966).

educate children of the poor. Since its publication, the methodology and the conclusions of the Coleman Report have been subject to spirited attacks by economists, psychologists, educators, HEW personnel and Congressmen.[25] But in the present context the validity and the implications of the study are of less importance than the fact of its having been undertaken at all. It was the first major attempt of USOE to use sophisticated social science analysis to evaluate educational performance across the nation.[26] Even while the study was in process, Coleman found that a substantial part of his time was consumed in quieting the fears of schoolmen whose schools and pupils were being tested.

The Tyler Committee faced even stiffer opposition. Undertaken in early 1965 with the encouragement of Commissioner Francis Keppel but with private foundation funding, the "Exploratory Committee" attempted to devise a national assessment program for education which would protect the anonymity of individual pupils and schools, but which would ultimately render a profile of national educational achievement. This seemingly innocuous and useful endeavor almost immediately ran into trouble. In July, 1965, the White House called a Conference on Education attended by schoolmen and educational reformers from across the nation. No issue was debated more heatedly than the projected national assessment.[27] The opponents stressed the dangers that a national

25. See, for instance:
Robert C. Nichols, "Schools and the Disadvantaged," *Science,* December 9, 1966, 1312–1314.
Samuel Bowles and Henry M. Levin, "The Determinants of Scholastic Achievement—An Appraisal of Some Recent Evidence," *Journal of Human Resources,* Winter 1968.
Joseph Alsop, "No More Nonsense About Ghetto Education!" *The New Republic,* July 22, 1967, 18–23.
Christopher Jenks, "Education: The Racial Gap," *The New Republic,* October 1, 1966, 21–26.
Floyd McKissick (Communication to the Editor) "Is Integration Necessary?" *The New Republic,* December 3, 1966, 33–36.
Charles S. Benson, "Coleman Report: Why the Schools Flunk Out," *The Nation,* April 10, 1967, 463–466.

26. USOE staff had used Coleman's talents earlier in drafting some sections of Title I.

27. *Contemporary Issues in American Education,* Consultants' Papers prepared for use at the White House Conference on Education, July 20–21, 1965, Washington, D.C., U.S. Department of Health, Education and Welfare; especially John L. Goodlad, "Assessment of Educational Performance," 33–41. Opposition to national assessment must be viewed as in part illogical, since a preponderance of schools across the nation have for years used various kinds of standardized tests in evaluating student ability and performance. The fact that schools were unwilling to use such test data in ESEA evaluation reports is further evidence of fear of federal evaluation generally.

assessment would lead to a federally dictated curriculum and to a monolithic Federal control of educational programs. They refused either to understand or to trust the protections built into the pilot study against invidious comparisons of pupils and schools. Supporters of the Tyler Study accused their opponents of anti-intellectualism and head-in-the-sand irrationality. As time went on, some of education's major professional associations developed policy statements attacking the Tyler Committee and urged their members not to cooperate in the assessment tests. Actually, as a result of the pressure of schoolmen, the Senate Appropriations Subcommittee extracted a promise from Commissioner Keppel that no FY'66 funds would be spent for any national testing program pending further consideration. This phalanx of professional educational associations did not in fact hold together, but even the tentative reactions of the professional associations was a clue to the insecurities and fears which may and do arise as more systematic attempts are made to assess educational performance, and, by implication, to evaluate the effectiveness of Federally funded educational programs.

Again, in the present context, the existence of the Tyler Committee as early as 1965 was a harbinger of new movements to develop systematic rather than casual evaluations of educational performance. When the mandated evaluation provisions were inserted into ESEA by Senator Robert Kennedy, both the Coleman and Tyler studies were underway and must surely have had an impact upon legislative drafting.

Program Planning and Budgeting System

Something else was happening in Washington that was even more formidable. The extraordinary concern of the drafters and amenders of ESEA with reporting and evaluating procedures cannot be understood apart from a general movement within the Federal government as a whole for a new and concerted emphasis upon program evaluation. President Johnson had been greatly impressed with the "cost-benefit" studies conducted under the leadership of Defense Secretary Robert McNamara in the early 1960's. A program planning and budgeting system (hereafter PPBS), based upon earlier work done by the Rand Corporation, had been developed by some of McNamara's key assistants (notably former Assistant Secretary of Defense Charles J. Hitch and his colleague Alan C. Enthoven). PPBS had enabled the Defense Department to create (some would add "the illusion of") a rational structure for making planning decisions by comparing projected costs and effectiveness of feasible program choices. The results of PPBS in terms of economy and operating effectiveness were believed by many to be dramatic. By 1964, PPBS had developed a sufficient number of devotees and converts—especially in the Bureau of the Budget—to lead the President to wonder why the system could not be generally applied to all programs and agencies of the Federal government. If, in Pentagon parlance, PPBS could create "a bigger bang for a buck," perhaps it could help Congress and the President to improve the rationality and effectiveness of government operations across the board. Ends and means had been articulated and quantified for purposes of decision-making about military hardware. Perhaps a similar system could be developed for the soft services of departments like HEW.

Although the presidential directive establishing a government-wide PPBS did not emerge formally until a cabinet meeting on August 25, 1965, Washington had been buzzing with the possibility for at least a year. PPBS had, in fact, become something of a Washington fad. One was "in" or "out" depending upon his knowledge of what the initials stood for. The nomenclature of the system crept increasingly into the jargon of the bureaucracy: "cost-benefit," "trade-offs," "resource impact," "functional budgets," "force structures," "programming."

It is little wonder, therefore, that the drafters of ESEA should have paid special attention to systems of program reporting and evaluation. This was true in spite of the fact that the wisest PPBS theorists and technicians knew that the application of systematic, cost-benefit analyses to an area like education was grotesque in its complexity, that program information even under the most ideal circumstances would still be partial, and that many State and most local educational officials would undoubtedly be hostile to budgetary innovations which would complicate the lives of both administrators and legislators. A few fadists tried to oversell the new system, but those closest to working out the presidential mandates knew its inherent difficulties and limitations. Nonetheless, PPBS was in the air at the time of ESEA's drafting and passage, and during 1965, both HEW and USOE attempted to upgrade themselves in terms of new staff and new concepts to carry PPBS as far as it could go.[28]

28. Concern for the issue of PPBS continued unabated throughout 1966. See for instance:
Special Analysis G, Supplement to U.S. Budget for FY'67, U.S. Bureau of the Budget.
Charles S. Benson, *Some Questions on Cost Effectiveness in Education* (mimeo. paper), February 28, 1966.
U.S. Department of Health, Education and Welfare, *Human Investment Programs, Elementary and Secondary Education, 1966–8,* September, 1966. (One of HEW's criticisms is that studies of compensatory education should examine the

At the HEW level, Secretary John Gardner appointed a new Assistant Secretary for Program Evaluation, William Gorham, and a new Deputy Assistant Secretary, Alice Rivlin, to develop program goals which might be stated, measured, and evaluated in cost-benefit terms.

Within USOE, in the Office of Planning and Evaluation; in the Bureau of Research; and in the National Center for Educational Statistics; new talent was brought in to develop information systems, analytic techniques, and computer hardware friendly to cost-benefit studies in several education program areas. At the same time, older, standard definitions of educational input data were being refined.

Simultaneously, the Bureau of the Budget, charged with the government-wide supervision of PPBS activities, attempted to provide a fiscal framework which would take account of the government-wide dispersal of educational programs.[29]

But during the first year of ESEA, most of the PPBS activity was a tooling-up operation and had little effect upon the actual conduct of ESEA evaluations. A few contracts were let by the Bureau of Research and by BESE to conduct systematic evaluations of Title I, and to explore the possible application to education of Program Evaluation Review Techniques (hereafter PERT) which had first been elaborated by the Navy Department in connection with the development of the Polaris submarine. A few State departments of education attempted to apply systematic testing procedures for evaluating Title I. The results and im-

---

effects of particular programs and that ESEA programs had been in progress for too short a time to show results.)

Memorandum on *Planning-Programming-Budgeting,* Supplement to Bulletin No. 66–3, to Heads of Executive Departments and Establishments, U.S. Bureau of the Budget, February 21, 1966.

William M. Capron, Assistant Director, Bureau of the Budget, *The Potential Role of Cost Effectiveness Analysis for Evaluation of Government Domestic Programs* (Address before the Symposium on Cost Effectiveness Analysis, Institute for Defense Analyses, Washington, D.C., June 15, 1965.

David Novick, *et al, Program Budgeting* (Cambridge: Harvard University Press, 1965).

Technomics, Inc., (Los Angeles, Calif.), *The Feasibility of Cost/Effectiveness Analysis for Title I, Public Law 89–10:* Final Report, prepared for Division of Operations Analysis, National Center for Educational Statistics, U.S. Office of Education, January 31, 1966.

"Planning-Programming-Budgeting System: A Symposium," *Public Administration Review,* December 1966.

Elaine Exton, "Here's How HEW Department Applies Planning-Programming-Budgeting System," *The American School Board Journal,* December 1966, 5.

29. *Special Analysis G,* Supplement to U.S. Budget for FY'67, U.S. Bureau of the Budget.

plications of some of these activities will be discussed in the final chapter. It is sufficient here to take note of the restless movements which were alive during ESEA's first year to develop staff, concepts, and electronic hardware aimed at imposing at least a "creeping rationality" upon the evaluation of new programs like ESEA. Both pressure group and congressional reaction to these more systematic attempts to assess the benefits and costs of Federal educational programs give little reason for either hope or fear that educational policy is about to be formed or substantially conditioned by economic wizards astride giant computers.

POLITICAL ACCOUNTING

If hard data on ESEA's first year was scarce, soft data in the form of various types of political accounting was not. And some of the soft data was perceptive and useful. Political accounting took place in at least three arenas: (1) advisory councils; (2) Congress; (3) interest groups. And, of course, all of the political accounting was informed by reactions from the grass-roots that will be examined in the final section of this chapter.

Advisory Councils

To make sure that USOE reports would not simply be in-house and self-serving, Congress mandated a series of statutory advisory councils or committees whose responsibilities included the filing of periodic summaries and evaluations of program performance.

Title I, for example, created a National Advisory Council on the Education of Disadvantaged Children. Composed of 12 persons appointed by the President, the Council was required to review by March 31 of each year ". . . the administration and operations of this Title, including its effectiveness in improving the educational attainment of educationally deprived children and making recommendations for the improvement of this title and its administration and operation."

Title III established an Advisory Committee on Supplementary Education Centers and Services consisting of the Commissioner as chairman and eight appointed members. Although the main function of the Title III Advisory Committee was to advise the Commissioner ". . . on the actions to be taken with regard to each application for a grant under this Title," and on "the preparation of general regulations," it was also to advise ". . . the Commissioner . . . with respect to policy matters arising in the administration of this title." This last clause obviously presumed a committee evaluation of Title III operations.

Title V provided for a 12-member Advisory Council on State departments of education to be appointed by the Secretary of HEW. This Council was to be concerned with ". . . reviewing and making recommendations with respect to (1) programs assisted under this title and their administration, and (2) other acts under which State educational agencies are assisted in administering Federal programs relating to education." The Council was to report annually to the Secretary ". . . who shall report to the President and the Congress."

Finally, Section 602 of Title VI authorized the Commissioner, subject to the approval of HEW, ". . . to appoint an advisory council of 10 members to advise and consult with him with respect to his functions" under ESEA generally.

Beyond mandated advisory councils and committees, the Commissioner of Education and his top subordinates created a number of advisory councils or committees by administrative order. Typical were the Research Advisory Council and the National Advisory Committee on Educational Laboratories for reviewing and evaluating programs and projects under Title IV.

The reports of these several advisory bodies were of various kinds. Some were in-house and have never been published. Others have been published and have received widespread attention by Congress, the Bureau of the Budget, the press, and the attentive educational public. The reports and memoranda of the National Advisory Committee on the Education of Disadvantaged Children (Title I) were especially significant.[30] Based upon independent surveys of Title I programs, the Advisory Committee reports were selective in their findings and mirrored the responsible unrest that emerged from States and localities. The Research Advisory Council and the National Advisory Committee on the Educational Laboratories have been equally significant in their impact upon Title IV programs, particularly in tightening up the plans and procedures of the Educational Laboratories. Other advisory councils and commissions under ESEA have performed similarly valuable functions.

Advisory councils, on the other hand, are not an unmixed blessing. Whatever their contribution to an objective and orderly review of programs, advisory councils and committees can be an administrative headache. The politics of appointment is complex and time-consuming, often involving elaborate regional or professional clearances. And the Commissioner must seek to insure adequate representation of a broader

30. See the first Annual Report of the National Advisory Council on the Education of Disadvantaged Children, dated March 31, 1966, and other reports dated November 25, 1966 and January 31, 1967.

public interest in order to keep the special interest groups, however well intentioned, from dominating committees. As a result, an unhealthy amount of his precious time is involved in making initial appointments or in filling vacancies. The missions of the several advisory councils often overlap. Their roles are often ambiguous, and members are constantly under the tension of attempting to be independent and helpful while not usurping the prerogatives of responsible line officials. If the councils attempt data-gathering functions of their own, for example, they may duplicate the work of the official staff. If they rely totally upon information provided by the agency staff, can they really exercise independent judgment? Advisory councils are a no-man's land of federal agency activity. They need far more analytic and normative attention than they have received from scholars and legislators.

But the fact that ESEA laid such a heavy emphasis upon advisory councils is a testament to the congressional desire for a careful and objective appraisal of agency performance in a field of unprecedented scope and complexity, and to HEW's desire to have a shield against congressional criticism. On balance, they have performed diligently and their constructively critical support of USOE programs has been of unquestioned value to USOE in its budget presentations and congressional hearings.

Presidential and Congressional Review

The President and the Congress have continuing responsibilities for reviewing and assessing the performance of executive branch agencies in carrying out legislative programs. In the presidential office this is done largely by the Bureau of the Budget. In Congress review is generally carried out at the level of subcommittees of the substantive committees and appropriations committees of both Houses. Occasionally, the Committee on Government Operations in each House gets into the act. In the case of ESEA, various reviews were carried out in 1966 by several congressional subcommittees.[31] In addition, the Special Subcommittee on

31. *Hearings,* 89th Cong., 2d sess., Senate, Subcommittee on Education, April 1966, *op. cit.*

Hearings on the Elementary and Secondary Education Amendments of 1966, 89th Cong., 2d sess., House, General Subcommittee on Education.

Hearings Before Subcommittee of the Committee on Appropriations, Second Supplemental Appropriation Bill, 1966, 89th Cong., 2d sess., House.

Hearings Before the Committee on Appropriations, Second Supplemental Appropriation Bill, 1966, 89th Cong., 2d sess., Senate.

Hearings Before a Subcommittee of the Committee on Appropriations, on Departments of Labor, and Health, Education and Welfare Appropriations for 1967, 89th Cong., 2d sess., House, Part 2.

Education in the House, chaired by Representative Edith Green, held extensive hearings on the U.S. Office of Education, and conducted questionnaire surveys among educational administrators, including non-public school administrators. In the course of these activities, substantial attention was given to the administration of ESEA.[32] The amendments to ESEA in 1966 [33] and the appropriations bill supporting it reflected, at least in part, what Congress felt it had learned from its extensive inquiries, and from direct contact with interested constituents, professional-association staffs, and USOE officials themselves. The net effect of these amendments was (1) to expand the Title I formula by including orphans and foster children and by using a more recent total of children assisted under the Aid to Families with Dependent Children Program; (2) to tack on a new program of aid to handicapped children; (3) to expand aid to school libraries and supplementary educational centers; (4) to provide for a program of assistance for adult basic education (transferred from OEO); and (5) to set procedures and conditions in cases where the Office of Education withholds funds from schools charged with practicing segregation.

Perhaps more important than formal amendments, however, congressional influence on administrative behavior is manifest in the nature of questions put to officials in hearings; in subcommittee requests for information; in press statements and in public speeches attacking or questioning existing practices within an agency; in letters or telephone calls to the Commissioner or to the Secretary of HEW. Agencies live by congressional favor, and congressional power is variable. For this reason, the views, opinions, and attitudes of key legislators (especially committee and subcommittee chairmen and their immediate staffs) are powerful influences on administrative behavior. Francis Keppel spent agonizing months trying to fill top level vacancies because Congressman Adam Clayton Powell insisted upon a number of Negro appointees. A great deal of time of top officials is taken up in the laborious and often harrowing processes of meeting both the legitimate and illegitimate calls of Congress for program review.

32. *Hearings Before the Special Subcommittee on Education,* 89th Cong., 2nd sess., House, *op. cit.* See also: *Study of the United States Office of Education,* Report of the Special Subcommittee on Education, 89th Cong., 2nd sess., House, 1967. The recommendations of the Green Committee will be considered as they relate to this text. In short compass, the Subcommittee report's major recommendations concerned: late funding, standardization of paperwork and procedures, fragmentation of the Federal educational effort, communication between the educational community and USOE on the one hand and Congress on the other, strengthening the regional offices, and the possibility of Federal control.

33. *Elementary and Secondary Education Amendments of 1966,* PL 89–750, 89th Cong., 2d sess.

The executive-branch counterparts to powerful and strategically placed legislators are the budgetary and program review officers at the departmental level and in the Bureau of the Budget, whose attitudes frequently shape important questions of resource allocation for agencies like USOE. The nature of these relationships is largely hidden from scholarly scrutiny, but even a cursory exposure to USOE officials conveys the impression that although the tone of discourse with key program and budget review officers in the executive branch is often more civilized than is the case with their counterparts in congress, the deferential patterns are in fact quite similar.

Interest Groups

Affected interest groups watch program implementation like hawks. The inevitably general character of law leaves much discretion to executive agencies. Administrative regulations, guidelines, and interpretive memoranda become in fact the cutting edge of the law. On the other hand, in grant-in-aid programs, lack of administrative precision or follow-through may allow state and local practices to develop which in fact contravene legislative intent, or which set precedents deemed dangerous by concerned professional interests. Under-prescription from Washington may be quite as upsetting as over-prescription.

In the case of ESEA, the most powerful of the attentive interests were the NEA and its affiliates: the American Federation of Teachers; the Council of Chief State School Officers; the National School Boards Association; the National Congress of Parents and Teachers; the National Catholic Welfare Conference (on behalf of the National Catholic Education Association); various civil rights organizations; and the congeries of Protestant, Jewish, and civil liberties groups concerned with the church-state aspects of the law. The headquarters staffs of these various groups collected information and reactions by formal surveys of their memberships; by commissioning special studies; by holding conferences and workshops; by listening to complaints of their membership submitted in writing, by phone, or in person; by attentive reading of newspapers, government reports, and legislative hearings. These bits and pieces of information were screened through the minds of staffs and professional-association officers who over the years had built up their own stereotypes of the interests of their clientele. Positions formed were relayed back to the membership through publications and conferences and were communicated to the congress and to Washington officialdom through both direct and indirect means: testimony before congressional committees, direct and grass-roots lobbying, press releases, trade journal articles,[34] and informal interfaces with the powerful. Washington policy-making is a search for friends and the isolation of enemies. It is quite impossible to separate public from private influences in the appraisal and modification of administrative and legislative activities concerned with either policy formulation or policy execution. Policy-making is more than the simple derivative of interest group pressures and clashes; on the other hand, it cannot be understood apart from such pressures and clashes.

ESEA Implementation: State and Local Problems and Reactions [35]

What then were the issues which troubled State and local educational agencies and related professional associations and interest groups affected by ESEA during the first year of its implementation?

The fact is that however welcome additional Federal money, schoolmen across the nation faced unprecedented strains in attempting to play their necessary role in helping to implement the act. All the titles except IV involved either SEA's or LEA's or both, and yet each of the other four operating titles mandated a different kind of inter-governmental partnership. As already noted, care had been taken by USOE to clear extensively with State and local clientele and with various professional associations in developing administrative ground rules, but misunderstandings, frictions, and frustrations haunted the new partnership

34. Interest-group publications serving such functions include, *inter alia: NEA Journal,* "Washington Monitor" in *Education USA* (National School Public Relations Association, NEA), *Special Report* of NEA's Division of Federal Relations, *The American School Board Journal* (National School Boards Association), *National Catholic Education Association Bulletin, NCEA NewsLetter, The Catholic Educational Review, The Hot Line* (American Association of School Administrators), *Fact Sheet* (National Committee for Support of the Public Schools), *School Management Magazine* (AASA), *Education Digest, Phi Delta Kappan,* and *Washington Outlook on Education.*

35. Data for the following section was acquired from a variety of published sources and personal interviews. These have been noted in footnotes and in the appendix. Particularly heavy reliance, however, has been placed upon (1) the responses of chief state school officers to an open-ended letter of inquiry submitted by the senior author in April and May, 1966. (See Appendix C.); and (2) the responses of a random sample of local school administrators to a structured questionnaire prepared by the senior author with the help of Dr. Eleanor Godfrey of the Bureau of Social Science Research, Washington, D.C. (see Appendix C). For a summary of the basic methodology used in this survey, see Appendix C. The full set of computer printouts are available in the Maxwell Library, Syracuse University. Responses to the most relevant questions are summarized in Appendix C.

throughout the first year. Some of the difficulties were the inevitable consequences of demanded hustle in negotiating the unfamiliar; but some were more deep-seated and cut to the core of political and philosophical differences about program and about the proper locus of power in American education. Not the least important strain, as we have already noted, was occasioned by the fact that ESEA had to be administered in the context of Title VI of the Civil Rights Act of 1964.

Although each one of the Titles of ESEA produced its own particular difficulties and problems, the major issues that developed in the partnership of implementation cut across most if not all of the titles. These issues were: (1) disagreements conditioned in part by a wishful hunger for general aid; (2) the timing of funding; (3) staffing; (4) paper work, red tape, and "federal control;" (5) inter-agency and church-state relations.

Congressional Intent

In spite of clear language in Title I's Section 205(a) (1) (A) and (B) which called upon LEA's to design programs of sufficient size, scope, and quality to give ". . . reasonable promise of substantial progress toward meeting . . . the special educational needs of educationally deprived children," a number of local educational agencies interpreted ESEA as a general aid-to-education bill. They submitted proposals for "the purchase of equipment and construction for the entire school system, rather than . . . [for] the provision of special activities and services for the disadvantaged." [36] How seriously were SEA's and LEA's to take Section 205? What if a new reading specialist were hired under Title I or Title III; could he be used to teach poor children only? What about the poor little rich kid who was a slow reader? Could a movie projector purchased to increase teaching effectiveness for the culturally deprived also be used to show films to the entire student body during convocations? Under Title III, did Congress mean that parochial schools could select and purchase books and simply bill a public educational agency, or must the public agency actually select and purchase books and other instructional materials desired by parochial schools? Under Title III, did a supplementary center have to concentrate primarily or exclusively on benefits to the culturally disadvantaged? Under Title IV, was a regional laboratory to work exclusively on problems peculiar to its region? Under Title V, could funds be used to cover the administrative costs of implementing the other titles of ESEA? How far could a school system

36. *Hearings, op. cit.*, Subcommittee on Education, 89th Cong., 2nd sess., Senate, April 1966, 738.

go in interpreting the will of Congress, or in bending that will to its own needs?

Some SEA's and LEA's were strict constructionists; others were loose constructionists. At one extreme, those with a callous conscience played around until they were caught; at the other extreme, some administrators proceeded with a cautious prudence which almost precluded forward motion of programs. But even with *Regulations* and *Guidelines* from USOE, a pervasive uncertainty existed about what really could or could not be done under the various titles. In some cases, congressional intent was clear and was misunderstood (e.g., Title I's mandate to focus attention on the disadvantaged). In other cases, there was real difficulty in understanding what the law meant and required, and genuine disagreements emerged as to whether specific provisions of the regulations and guidelines contravened or unnecessarily expanded upon legislative intent. USOE worked out many of these difficulties with SEA's and LEA's; but issues remained—perhaps most dramatically in the tangled judicial, legislative, and administrative jungle of desegregation policy under Title VI of the Civil Rights Act of 1964.

In any case, interpreting legislative intent involved USOE, SEA's, LEA's, professional associations, and the Congress in a cacaphonous colloquy and was a source of continuous unrest throughout the first year.

The Timing of Appropriations

No single issue caused greater concern to both SEA's and LEA's than the timing of Federal funding. When the Special Subcommittee on Education of the House (the Green Committee) undertook a study of the U.S. Office of Education in the fall and winter of 1966, they reported that ". . . of all the problem areas identified and discussed during the course of the subcommittee's study, late funding was perhaps brought up more frequently than any other matter, and the body of comments on it displayed the highest degree of uniformity." [37]

The issue was described by the Green Committee in the following words:

> Generally, the local school agency . . . conducts its planning for the academic year during the spring of the preceding academic year. Of course, sensible planning must be predicated on a firm knowledge of the fiscal resources that will be available in the following September. When Federal funds represented only a minis-

37. *Study of the United States Office of Education,* Report of the Special Subcommittee on Education, 1967, 89th Cong., 2nd sess., House, 439.

> cule portion of the agency's over-all budget, the agency could form its plans without any exact knowledge of the amount of the funds it would ultimately receive. But as the flow of Federal money has increased, the feasibility of this sort of planning has decreased. Today, many agencies and institutions simply cannot lay adequate plans for the coming academic year unless they have a firm idea of the amount of Federal support they will be granted.[38]

And the report continues:

> For the most part, however, the Congressional appropriations process does not mesh with the educational planning process. The former, unlike the latter, is not directed at all to the spring of the year; rather it is tied to the fiscal year running from July 1 to June 30. A firm commitment of Federal funds at the very beginning of this fiscal period would lead to difficulties for local agencies, since, by necessity, they must plan during the Spring months. In practice, however, actual appropriations, at least for educational assistance programs, are more likely to be made in August, September, or even October than in June. It may be said that if July commitments would lead to difficulties, commitments made in September or October—after the school year has already begun—can lead to something akin to chaos.[39]

The National Advisory Council on the Education of Disadvantaged Children added further comment. Referring to the experiences of the first year, the Council stated:

> There is no doubt that implementation of Title I was greatly hampered this year by the non-availability of funds until after the school year began. Most personnel in needed specialties were already under contract, and school administrators were forced to plan projects almost over night. The pressures of time gave State departments of education little opportunity to revise substantially many quickly conceived programs. We strongly urge the Congress to enact the next Title I appropriations bill as early as possible but not later than early summer 1966, to permit more careful program development and thus assure more effective use of the funds.[40]

These findings were corroborated both by the letters to the authors from virtually all of the CSSO's and by the Bureau of Social Science

38. *Ibid.*

39. *Ibid.* See also: *Report No. 726,* Kelly Task Force proposals addressed to the appropriations problem, 90th Cong., 1st sess., Senate, 45–46.

40. *Notes and Working Papers . . . Title I, op. cit.,* 90th Cong., 1st sess., 958.

Research survey (Appendix C). When the question was asked in the BSSR survey whether funds for the various titles had been received too late in the school year to spend properly, 48.6 per cent replied in the affirmative; only 36.1 per cent indicated that this was not a major issue. But the breakdown of these national percentages by size of school district is even more revealing.[41] Statistically significant is the fact that the large school districts of the nation found late funding particularly upsetting, whereas only a quarter of the districts with fewer than 300 pupils were troubled. This seems to suggest that the bureaucratic rigidities imposed by size place a premium on early and formal budget planning and execution. Variations in responses by region, median income, and population make-up were less dramatic, although urban school districts on the one hand and certain categories of rural districts on the other showed a sensitivity to late funding considerably above the national average.

Difficulty of Finding Specialized Staff

Tied closely to the problem of late funding, and to the mandated speed of implementation, was the trauma of finding qualified staff to man the newly-funded programs. This was true at the State level both in terms of administering Titles I and II and in terms of the effective use of Title V funds. But the real pinch was at the LEA level. Fifty-six per cent of all school districts surveyed in the nation identified the scarcity of qualified staff as a major problem. Here, again, the variation by size of school district is impressive. In the BSSR survey,[42] all of the largest school districts (more than 50,000 students) and 90 per cent of the next-to-largest category identified staffing as a major headache, whereas only 34.4 per cent of the smallest districts (300 students or less) were similarly troubled. The only other significant variable in determining responses on this issue seemed to be income. Almost three-quarters of the lowest income districts found staffing troublesome, whereas only a fifth of the districts with median incomes of $9,000-and-over had similar difficulties. Actually, there is almost a perfect negative correlation between school-district income and expressed difficulty in finding qualified staff for ESEA.

Putting factors of size and income together, it seems clear that large school districts with low median incomes had the greatest trouble in finding qualified staff—the very areas targeted by Title I. What is, of course, not clear is the definition of "qualified" applied by respective

41. See Appendix C, Question F.
42. See Appendix C, Question H.

districts. But a review of ESEA programs during the first year indicates that remedial-reading specialists, guidance counselors, health and nutrition experts, educational research scholars, and educational planners and evaluators were all in short supply—some critically so. What is clear from the evidence is that the strains upon school officials at all levels (including USOE itself) in finding qualified staff to mount the new programs under ESEA were substantial.

Paper Work, Red Tape, and "Federal Control"

A chorus of complaints arose during the first year on the issue of the amount of "unnecessary" paper work and red tape involved in complying with the provisions of the act. The hostility was not particularly related to initial delays in receiving regulations, guidelines and application forms. Here most SEA's and LEA's were quite charitable about the problems faced by USOE—the lateness of funding, the newness and scope of the programs. But the required reports, the complexity of the application forms, the duplicate information required under the various titles, the Washington bottleneck of clearance and approval, the ambiguities, and in some cases, the rigidities of regulations and guidelines, and the calls for complicated accounting and evaluation procedures caused frustration and anguish in every State capital and in thousands of LEA's.[43]

Some of the State education agencies were particularly incensed by the 60-page questionnaire developed by USOE's Title V staff. This was a forced self-evaluation and inventory of SEA resources. Its submission was the condition of receiving Title V funds. Dr. Robert L. Hopper, Director of USOE's Division of State Agency Cooperation, claims that the length and precision of the questionnaire was at the urging of the staff of the Council of Chief State School Officers who recommended detailed instruction and questions. It is true that some SEA's had participated in the initial examining of the questionnaire and were prepared for it, but most States were not. However valuable the information ultimately turned out to be—even to SEA's themselves—the chore of an-

43. The Green Committee report states that "nearly all of the witnesses heard by the subcommittee" questioned "the necessity for the huge amount of paperwork" involved in new Federal educational programs. The subcommittee recommended that the Office of Education "standardize rules, regulations, guidelines, applications, and reporting procedures, particularly as they relate to programs of a similar nature" and "establish realistic and regular application and reporting deadlines." The subcommittee deplored the "grantsmanship" that had developed as a result of technicalities and duplication in the new programs. *Study of the U.S. Office of Education, op. cit.*, 89th Cong., 2nd sess., House, 28–29, 401–420.

swering a complex, 60-page questionnaire as a condition of a Federal grant was bound to create temporary discomfort.

The local educational agencies, many of them limited in staff, were hard-pressed to find their way through unfamiliar thickets of paper compliance. When the BSSR survey asked the question of whether the complexity of the Title I application form had presented difficulties, over 55.3 per cent of the nation's school districts replied that it had, and only 31.2 per cent indicated that it had not.[44] If one assumes that at least a number of the 13.5 per cent of the respondents who did not answer this question were unhappy about answering questionnaires generally, the percentage of assumed malcontents is even higher. Some of the BSSR survey variables are of interest on this point. For example, almost 70 per cent of the lowest income districts were troubled by the complexity of the Title I application form, whereas only 31 per cent of districts with a median income of $9,000–$12,000 were upset. Heavily suburban districts had less trouble by and large than either urban districts or rural districts. Variations in response among regions of the nation turned out not to be statistically significant. But the three largest categories of districts were perceptively less bothered by the complexity of the Title I application form than were smaller sized districts.

Taken together, these figures suggest that the real strains of paper compliance were in the low income districts, urban and rural—the very districts targeted by the act as needing Federal assistance.

As implied earlier, the concerns of LEA's about red-tape were made manifest through a number of channels: professional associations, conferences with USOE officials, and directly to Congress. In the hearings before the Senate Subcommittee on Education in April 1966, Senator Yarborough commented:

> . . . we [the Congress] have had complaints from school superintendents that claim that the forms that they are required to fill out under Title I are the longest and most difficult they have ever seen, and so complicated in fact that in their opinion these forms act to the detriment of the act. . . . From all I hear this seems to be a pretty serious question with a lot of districts. They say they bog down in red-tape.[45]

Commissioner Howe responded with the following comment:

> We, too, have received this same kind of reaction. Of course, in endeavoring to collect detailed information, to carry out the will of

44. See Appendix C, Question I.

45. 89th Cong., 2nd sess., Senate, Subcommittee on Education, *Hearings, op. cit.,* April 1966, 738.

> Congress . . . we have had to have rather elaborate forms. They have had to go through the State to the local districts which in many cases have not been accustomed to providing this kind of information, organized this way and in this amount of detail. We have had to be sure that the aid is being handed out to local school districts by the State in accordance with the categorical nature of the aid, which must focus the projects in places where there are high concentrations of low-income children. This accounts in part for the complexity. . .
>
> We have tried to simplify the forms, and the package of forms, if you want to call it that, has been considerably slimmed as we have worked on this.[46]

Associate Commissioner Arthur Harris added that USOE had recently brought a group of local and State educational people to Washington to review the forms on the basis of the experience of the past 6–8 months. He concluded with a spirited defense of the information function of complex application forms:

> I would like to comment also that although we have had a number of criticisms of the length of the forms, more than 14,000 applications have been developed, submitted, and approved by State departments of education. We have had a few comments to the effect that 'these forms have required us for the first time to secure the kinds of information about our children and about our school system that we should have been securing for many years in order to make the educational judgments that are required of us in our position as local educational leaders. The information we have secured will permit us to develop, to plan, and to operate the kinds of programs which will truly meet the educational needs of our children.' [47]

Dr. Harris was doubtless sincere, but for most LEA's the process of paper compliance was bitter-sweet, and made both State and local educational officials painfully conscious of extra costs in time and personnel —costs incurred in the process of planning and applying for Federal funds, but not covered by USOE administrative grants. When the BSSR survey asked whether the provision in ESEA that planning costs would not be reimbursable had created difficulties, 56.7 per cent of the school districts indicated that it had.[48] On the related question of whether school districts had encountered difficulties because of the provision that indi-

46. *Ibid.*
47. *Ibid.*, 739.
48. See Appendix C, Question J.

rect cost of administering the program were not reimbursable, only 24 per cent replied in the negative. Again, the size of the school district turned out to be an important variable in the response.[49]

The burden of applying for Federal money under ESEA obviously was unequal across the nation. For the large school districts, many of them under-financed in terms of carrying out their continuing, local responsibilities, the task of organizing and staffing their several constituent units for a new and complex Federal program involved a significant additional strain on time and resources.

Many SEA's were equally concerned about the inadequacy of ESEA funds for planning and for indirect costs. Of the 32 responses to the authors' letter of inquiry to CSSO's, 13 pinpointed this issue as one that had created particular hardship. The problem was not only the hidden costs of time and staff involved in handling Titles I, II, and V which were directly administered by or through SEA's. Some States pointed to the additional burdens imposed upon SEA's by Titles III and IV of ESEA because of additional demands by LEA's for guidance and assistance in negotiating these complex legislative provisions. But there was little agreement as to what might constitute adequacy in Federal grants to SEA's for the administration of ESEA.

Two of the factors that caused SEA's and LEA's to give an inordinate amount of time to ESEA matters were the ambiguities and the shifts in USOE guidelines and other policy statements. This issue affected the administration of each title, especially Titles I and III. Seventeen CSSO's wrote that USOE changes in policy guidance or inconsistencies in or between written and oral instructions had caused considerable woe. The Deputy Commissioner of Education for the State of Maine claimed that this was "the greatest problem encountered in the area of administration . . . ," although he was generous enough to admit that "this . . . may be an unavoidable characteristic of the first year's operation of any program." [50] The boards and directors of the several educational laboratories created under Title IV found that, next to intermittent and unpredictable funding, policy shifts and ambiguities in guidelines were the most troublesome part of negotiating with USOE.

Guidelines for Title VI of the Civil Rights Act of 1964 was a matter of particular administrative and political confusion. The uncertainties in this tangled area of policy interpretation were exacerbated by the staff hiatuses and rotations in USOE during the first year of ESEA's implementation.

49. See Appendix C, Question K.

50. 89th Cong., 2nd Sess., House, *Hearings Before the Special Subcommittee on Education, op. cit.,* 414.

The absence of an effective field organization for USOE was also a contributing factor since most questions of interpretation had to be referred to the Washington headquarters for clearance. This was true for ESEA as well as for the Civil Rights Act of 1964.

However explainable, necessary, or tentative these evidences of bureaucratic confusion, they seemed to some an index of increasing "Federal control" over American education.[51] But this attitude varied by level of school government and by a number of other variables. Except for some unhappiness about the direct authority of the Commissioner of Education over Title III [52] and sections of Title V, most State education agencies were less concerned with the Federal control issue than were LEA's. In fact, one remarkable aspect of the CSSO response to the authors' letter of inquiry was their charitable understanding of USOE's problems, and their praise for the attitudes and actions of USOE officials in attempting to minimize Federal controls. Several replies indicated that after specific problems were discussed, USOE officials granted the SEA's enough leeway so that ESEA could be constructively applied to the various local situations. As Representative Edith Green said, "The educators of America are generally high in their praise of Office of Education personnel." [53] An illustration of this attitude is the comment of Dr. Wilson Riles, Title I State Coordinator for California: "In no small measure the success we have had in launching the Federal program in California has been due to the excellent services we have received from the U.S. Office of Education. We have had close and beneficial relationship with the Division of Compensatory Education headed by Mr. John F. Hughes. The U.S. Office of Education's administration of Title I has been one of extending services, rather than exerting control over the State and local district's operation of the program. The U.S. Office of Education's role has been to interpret the intent of Congress so that we at the State and local level may better carry out that intent." [54]

When, however, the BSSR survey asked *local* educational adminis-

51. The Green Committee's report documents these points. *Study of the U.S. Office of Education,* 89th Cong., 2nd sess., House, p. 31–32, 401–420.

52. Title III was amended in 1967. (See Chapter VI, footnote 1A.) However the fact is that almost from the beginning, strong state departments of education like New York and California were permitted by USOE to establish priority recommendations for approving Title III proposals. In such cases USOE virtually rubber-stamped SEA decisions.

53. *Study of the Office of Education,* speech by the Honorable Edith Green to Council of Chief State School Officers, Puerto Rico, November 16, 1967. (mimeo.), 2.

54. *Study of the United States Office of Education, op. cit.,* 89th Cong., 2nd sess., House, 250.

trators if ESEA presented a threat of Federal control over local education, over half the respondents believed that it did. Here the breakdown of the percentage figures by the survey's variables makes fascinating reading.[55] The concentration of fears was in the Southern States, the West North Central States, and the Mountain States, not in the more industrialized states of the Northeast and the Pacific Coast. The lowest income districts—those presumably targeted by ESEA—were those with the greatest fear of Federal control. Heavily urban and suburban districts feared Federal control far less than did mixed-rural and rural-farm districts.

Whatever else the tables mean, they suggest that there is in American society a philosophical split between what Alan K. Campbell has called the "cosmopolites" and the "provincials," and that the question of Federal control of education elicits answers which are a part of a more basic set of regional and class attitudes. The fact that the largest school districts (50,000 students and over) show the largest degree of fears of Federal control fits into this pattern, for 8 out of the 13 districts in this category (and responding to the BSSR survey) are located *outside* the populous Northeastern and Pacific industrial regions of the nation.

Interagency Relations

A fourth problem area—this almost entirely at the LEA level—stemmed from the legislative mandates for inter-agency clearances. This was particularly acute under Titles I and III. Section 205 of Title I, it will be remembered, insisted that where an area was served by a community action program under the Economic Opportunity Act of 1964, the programs and projects submitted under Title I of ESEA must be developed ". . . in cooperation with the public or private non-profit agency responsible for the community action program." Title III involved even more complex clearances. Section 304 provides that a Title III supplementary center, in addition to assuring ". . . representation of, or participation by, a local educational agency (if not itself the grantee), must relate to one or more of the following: institutions of higher education, the appropriate State educational agency or agencies and other public or non-profit private agencies, organizations, or institutions." Title III *Guidelines* had included among relevant participating agencies, organizations, and institutions, ". . . non-public schools, educational laboratories and research and development centers, libraries, museums, musical and artistic organizations, educational radio and television stations, private foundations, community youth organizations, technical

55. See Appendix C, Question 18 A.

institutes, private industry, professional associations, community action agencies, and other cultural and educational resources."

In spite of some marked successes in LEA-Community Action Agency (hereafter CAA) relations through the joint funding of projects and through formal and informal liaison devices in project planning, a variety of administrative problems remained. USOE guidelines had not made explicit the respective roles, responsibilities, and prerogatives of CAA's and LEA's. The ambiguities led to frequent and sometimes bitter controversies in about one out of every five school districts surveyed. Again, the large school districts faced the greatest problems.[56] In one revealing paragraph, USOE's first *Annual Report* on Title I stated what was probably the underlying issue:

> Joint planning of educational programs by educators and non-educators occasionally encountered difficulty because of a feeling among some local educators that CAA participation in developing projects constituted an interference. SEA's said this feeling produced reluctance on the part of some LEA's to involve the CAA's in preliminary plans and discussions. Some SEA's reported that CAA's lacked the qualifications and knowledge necessary for the development of educational projects and that their suggestions regarding curriculum, type of project and hiring of personnel were often in conflict with established educational policies and regulations and had to be rejected. Many states observed that a common misconception among both LEA's and CAA's was that the CAA could exercise veto power over the proposed Title I project.[57]

In spite of warm personal and official relations between Secretary Gardner and Commissioner Howe on the one hand and Sargent Shriver, Director of the Office of Economic Opportunity, on the other,[58] the mandated cooperation between local schools and local poverty agencies on programs like Operation Headstart and other experiments in pre-school or job training was inevitably fraught with conflicts over standards, control and personnel.

Interagency cooperation under Title III was more easily effected on paper, but often painfully difficult to achieve in any meaningful opera-

56. See Appendix C, Question 27 A.

57. See 90th Cong., 1st Sess., Senate, Subcommittee on Education, *Notes and Working Papers . . . Title I,* 958.

58. Shriver and Gardner, for example, had issued a joint letter to CAA's and LEA's on the need for close working relations between local schools and local poverty programs.

tional sense. With the carrot of Federal money, local school officials (if they had the time and the staff, which many did not),[59] could create or peddle proposals for supplementary centers in cooperation with a dozen cultural and educational institutions. But in some cases, once a grant had been received, the tendency in many states was either for the money to be scattered (almost indiscriminately) among the constituent agencies for a series of operationally unrelated activities, or for the local Title III director to go about spending the money for his own priorities without continuing reference to the partners who had collectively developed or signed the original proposal. In a number of areas, the administrative problem was made especially acute by the submission of applications from school district consortia. In the BSSR survey it became clear that three out of every four Title III applications involved more than a single school district.[60] Inter-school district clearances and cooperation often made eminent educational sense, but they were also time-consuming and fraught with delicacies of human and institutional interfaces. And, of course, Title III was subject to the continuing running fire of SEA's which resented the substantial independence of Title III programs from State control. Finally, a few jurisdictional tensions developed locally between Title III programs on the one hand and Title IV Educational Laboratories on the other, especially over questions of responsibility for demonstration centers and the dissemination of new educational techniques and materials.

For all of these reasons, the preparation, review, and implementation of Title III applications was an enormously complicated and time-consuming process.[61] There is little wonder that during the first year, half the school districts surveyed did not even initiate preliminary applications for Title III funds [62] and that as a result of the first year's experience 70 per cent of the LEA's surveyed indicated their belief that Title III funds should not be allocated on a competitive basis.[63] In this last connection, not the least important complaint was that Title III's emphasis upon "innovative" projects in fact penalized districts which had recently undertaken new programs on their own.[64]

59. See Appendix C, Question 22 B.

60. See Appendix C, Question 19b. Another source states that 63 per cent of the first 217 Title III projects involved two or more school districts. See Roald Campbell, "Federal impact on Boards' Decisions," in *School Boards in an Era of Conflict:* The Cubberley Conference, Stanford University, summer 1966, as reprinted in *The American School Board Journal,* March, 1967, 40.

61. See Appendix C, Question 23 B.

62. See Appendix C, Question 19 C.

63. See Appendix C, Question 18 E.

64. See Appendix C, Question 18 C.

Church-State

The administration of ESEA provisions relating to non-public schools created during the first year both administrative and constitutional issues. For example, could Title I money be spent for programs conducted on parochial school premises? Could Title II library or text books be ordered directly by parochial school principals provided that the list had been approved by public education agencies and that a public school name plate was attached to each book? What constituted a "fair share" of ESEA money for non-public school children?

The guidance which Federal officials gave SEA's and LEA's dealt with appropriate mechanics for maintaining the assumed, but by no means assured, constitutionality of the Act. The provisions of Section 205 (a) (3) explicitly gave to public school officials responsibility for program administration and title to all property for which Title I funds were used. But the ambiguous statutory language and conflicting viewpoints to be found in the legislative history made it difficult to interpret and develop criteria for judging compliance with the basic mandate of Section 205 (a) (2):

> that, to the extent consistent with the number of educationally deprived children in the school district of the local educational agency who are enrolled in private elementary and secondary schools, such agency has made provision for including special educational services and arrangements . . . in which such children can participate.

These uncertainties placed a substantial burden upon a number of public and non-public school officials, although according to the BSSR survey at no time and in no area of the nation was the burden excessive for the majority of school systems. In the BSSR survey, only 12.2 per cent of the respondents made an affirmative response to the question of whether coordinating projects with the non-public schools had *in fact* been a difficulty for them.[65] When a related question was raised, however, about general objections raised by educators to ESEA, half the school districts indicated their belief that "the administration of Title II funds for private schools places an undue burden on the local educational agency." But the regional response to this question indicates that in areas of the nation with the highest concentration of church-related schools (New England, Middle Atlantic, and Pacific), only a third of the responses were affirmative, whereas in the areas with the lowest concentration of church-related schools (West, North Central, South and

65. See Appendix C, Question 27 B.

Southwest), a substantial majority responded affirmatively.[66] In other words, where the relationships with public and private schools were in fact greatest, the concern with "undue burden" was lowest. This suggests that visceral attitudes and biases rather than direct experience governed many of the responses to the question asked.

The participation and involvement of parochial schools in Titles I, II, and III of ESEA was in fact substantial. In response to a questionnaire sent in the spring of 1966 by the National Catholic Welfare Conference to 100 local Catholic Dioceses across the nation, 84 indicated that they were participating under Title I; 80 indicated that they had been consulted prior to the submission of Title I; 88 were involved under Title II, and 66 were involved under Title III.[67] Some evidence of antipathy between parochial school leaders and the leadership of LEA's (School Boards and Superintendents) emerged,[68] but perhaps the most remark-

66. See Appendix C, Question 18 B.

67. National Catholic Welfare Conference, 1966. *Questionnaire on Participation of Catholic School Children under Title I, II, and III of Public Law 89–10.* The USOE analysis of a sample of 484 approved projects—forwarded by the SEA's to Washington by January 25, 1966—indicated that private school beneficiaries constituted slightly more than 5 per cent of the total and were concentrated mainly in the larger core cities. (See Hearings on *Elementary and Secondary Education Act of 1966,* 89th Cong., 2nd sess., Senate Subcommittee on Education, 617.) Some additional information on private school participation in ESEA can be found in Questionnaire #III in the Green Committee's report, *Study of the U.S. Office of Education, op. cit.,* 89th Cong., 2nd sess., House, 471–73, 614–23.

68. DPO issued a warning to State Title I coordinators that LEA failure to provide comparable and equitable services to parochial school children and adequate information concerning the project activities in which they were involved would "encourage complaints and criticism." (See Memorandum from John F. Hughes to Title I Coordinators, February 14, 1966.) Criticism was subsequently expressed in the first Annual Report of the National Council on the Education of Disadvantaged Children, and by Representative Carey on the failure of New York City schools to make sufficient provision for eligible parochial school children. (See U.S. Congress, 89th Cong., 2nd sess., House Subcommittee on Education, Hearings on *Elementary and Secondary Education Act Amendments of 1966,* 41–49.) Parochial school interests, though satisfied with first year Title I operations, stressed that the absence of "voluntary good will and consultation" on the part of public school educators prevented carrying out the intent of the legislation in certain cases. (See U.S. Congress, 89th Cong., 2nd sess., Senate Subcommittee on Education, Hearings on *Elementary and Secondary Education Act of 1966,* 1675.) For a full documentation of the conflict between public school and parochial school interests, see Vincent J. Nuccio and John J. Walsh, *A National Level Evaluation Study of the Impact of Title I of the Elementary and Secondary Education Act of 1965 on the Participation of Non-Public School Children: Phase I.* (Chestnut Hill, Mass.: Boston College, 1967) (mimeo.) For critical comment on alleged abuses of ESEA grants for parochial school children, see particularly the

able thing about the first year's experience under ESEA was the limited number of conflicts and tensions that marked the administration of non-public school benefits. The general tone of Catholic response was one of appreciation for the inducements offered by ESEA for public-private educational collaboration—often for the first time. If some Catholic leaders felt that parochial school children were not receiving all they were entitled to under the act, they were prudent in the tone of their concern—not wanting to upset by aggressiveness the delicate political balance which had produced the first major Federal assistance to parochial school children.

The positive Catholic response was the product of a continuing dialogue between USOE administrators and religious leaders. In developing Title I *Regulations* and *Guidelines,* USOE officials maintained the pre-enactment policy of conferring with official representatives of the principal religious groups concerned. Largely at the urging of the National Catholic Welfare Council, Section 116.19 of the *Regulations* incorporated some of the permissive wording to be found in the Congressional Committee reports concerning allowable Title I expenditures for non-public school students. Throughout the early stages of implementing the Federal instructions, the staff of DPO maintained regular contacts with the national Catholic educational leadership, and the relationship remained cordial. The chief spokesman for the latter, Msgr. Donohue, commended the efforts of the Federal officials to see that the Title I mandate became operative at state and local levels, and undertook to persuade parochial school officials throughout the country that they also should feel responsible for developing effective new forms of collaboration with the public schools in their communities.

But underneath this operational euphoria were deep constitutional rumbles. By the end of the first year a number of moves were afoot to challenge the constitutionality of the ESEA programs as they related to church-connected schools. These moves were encouraged by a split (5–4) decision by the Maryland Court of Appeals on June 2, 1966, on the constitutionality of state matching funds applied to church-related colleges. The Maryland ruling held that state matching grants (even for non-religious purposes) to Western Maryland, Notre Dame, and to St. Joseph Colleges were in violation of the First Amendment as applicable

---

writings and statements of Prof. George R. La Noue of Teachers College, Columbia University. Note especially: George R. La Noue "Church-State Problems in the Elementary and Secondary Education Act of 1965," "Public Funds for Parochial Schools," and John de J. Pemberton, Jr., "Guide to Community Action," in American Civil Liberties Union, *The Church State Problem Has been Handed to You: A Guide for Community Groups,* New York, American Civil Liberties Union, 1967.

to the States through the Fourteenth Amendment to the U.S. Constitution. Aid to a fourth institution of higher education in Maryland, Hood College, related to the United Church of Christ, was upheld on the grounds that Hood's "stated purposes in relation to religion are not of a fervent, intensive, or passionate nature, but seem to be based largely upon its historical background." [69] The Maryland case had been initiated by taxpayers who were allowed under State law to challenge State grants in Maryland Courts. But no such right was available to U.S. taxpayers in Federal Courts. In 1923, the U.S. Supreme Court decided in the case of *Frothingham* v. *Mellon* [70] that a Mrs. Frothingham, who had sought to enjoin the execution of an appropriation of Federal funds for grants to the State for maternal benefits, lacked substantial interest as an individual plaintiff. The Court said that a taxpayer's interest in the moneys of the Treasury ". . . is shared with millions of others; is comparatively minute and indeterminable; the effect upon future taxation . . . is so remote that no basis is afforded for an appeal to the preventive powers of the court."

The Maryland case had been initiated by the Horace Mann League—an organization of several hundreds, including some educators. The hope of the petitioners was presumably that the size of the organization would induce the U.S. Supreme Court to review the Maryland case if appealed, on the grounds that whereas a single taxpayer might not have a substantial interest in the nature of Federal spending, a large group of taxpayers might. In this they were to be disappointed, for on November 14, 1966 the U.S. Supreme Court refused to review the Maryland decision. But the hope was present in the summer of 1966, and a number of cases challenging the constitutionality of the church-school provisions of ESEA were prepared by organizations and groups in a number of States, including Ohio, Pennsylvania, and New York.

The New York suits, formally brought in early December, 1966, were submitted to both a Federal and a State court. As of this writing, no disposition has been made of any of the ESEA cases, although the Supreme Court agreed in October, 1967 to review the issue. The New York suits are of interest because they deal in part with questions of the administration of ESEA. The suits were brought by four organizations: The American Jewish Congress, The United Parents Association, The United Federation of Teachers, and The American Civil Liberties Union. These organizations charged, in part, that State and local officials ". . . had taken advantage of the ambiguities in the ESEA to discriminate in favor of the religious schools. . . ." They charged that the New York City

69. *Horace Mann League of the United States of America, et al.* v. *Board of Public Works of Maryland, et al.*, 220 A 2d 51, 67 (1966).

70. 262 U.S. 447.

Board of Education had ". . . followed a 'double standard' in determining the need for special assistance. . . ."

> The school board has decided that a parochial school qualifies for ESEA aid if 10 per cent of its pupils get federally-funded free lunches; a public school qualifies if 40 per cent of its pupils get free lunches.
>
> The school board has decided to assign one remedial or special teacher for every 157 eligible parochial school students. . . and one for every 230 public school students. In addition, certain remedial programs have been instituted in the parochial schools but not in the public schools. Such services drain off public funds that are urgently needed by the city's schools.[71]

It seems certain that State and Federal court tests of the church-state issue in Federal aid to education will someday take place. In the meantime, the issue lies in a limbo of uncertainty. In the absence of clear judicial guidelines, constitutional law is being affected by political combat and administrative precedent.

PARADOX AND CONTRADICTION

These then were the results of, and some of the reactions to, the first year of ESEA. Together they constituted a series of paradoxes and seeming contradictions. Overall, ESEA had been reported by USOE as successful, but the success could not be measured, and experiments with national assessment produced fears of a systematic evaluation of the program performance of individual schools. Federal money was welcomed; the timing of Federal funding was resented. USOE was praised for its restraint in constructing and working through a new partnership in American education; it was also condemned for instituting bureaucratic practices and for promoting "Federal control." The genius of the drafters of ESEA in finding a way through the tangled constitutional thicket of church-state relations was applauded; the constitutionality of the results was challenged. Finally, as noted in the previous chapters, USOE was condemned for going beyond congressional intent in enforcing racial desegregation; it was also pilloried for going too slowly and for failing to enforce the Civil Rights Act of 1964.

Can a balance sheet be drawn? Can any normative principles be established for the future? We turn to these difficult questions in the final chapter.

71. *Civil Liberties in New York,* New York Civil Liberties Union, Vol. XV, No. 1, January 1967, 1, 2.

VI. Conclusions and the Unfinished Agenda

A hundred years have passed since the creation by law of what was then called—and what may sometime again be called—the United States Department of Education. When Congressman James A. Garfield, in 1866, introduced the initial enabling legislation on behalf of the National Association of School Superintendents, he could not possibly have foreseen the explosive growth which would mark the activities of this agency during the next one hundred years. Nor could he have anticipated the continuity of opposition to the notion of a substantial involvement of the Federal government in the field of elementary and secondary education. Then, as now, there were cries against Federal control; then, as now, as Garfield bemoaned, "We are reminded of our debts and warned against increasing our expenditures." [1] Then, as now, idealists expected more of the Federal government than it could perform reasonably well in a short time; cynics expected less.

But 1968 has one advantage over 1867; the benefit of experience with significant and nation-wide Federal involvement in grass-roots education. The country is now in a position to take stock of its major Federal educational agency as an operating partner in the total educational enterprise. Citizens, officials, and representatives can begin to base their judgments upon performance rather than upon a spectre of possibilities. They can review the creation and implementation of a major Federal program like the Elementary and Secondary Education Act of 1965 and ask—even after brief experience—whether, in fact, the tendencies observed are in accord with various definitions of the public interest. They can begin to shape future policy on the basis of both the positive and negative lessons of Federal performance to date.

At least in theory, the nation is now in a position to do all of these things. Unfortunately, the actual task of assessment and prognosis is difficult and complex; for, as in 1867, the national concern with education is complicated by context and by competing philosophies and interpretations of reality. Then, the context was the trauma of post-civil war

1. Harry Kursh, *U.S. Office of Education* (Philadelphia: Chilton Press, 1965), 11.

reconstruction, the passions related to the final conquest and exploitation of the wilderness, and the love-hate syndrome created by flooding immigration. Today, the context is the fretfulness and sullen costs of international activity; the ghastly withdrawal symptoms from three centuries of addiction to the drug of prejudice; the neuroticism produced by complex technologies and urbanization interrupting and transforming traditional folkways and mores; the guilt complex of poverty amidst plenty. Questions of Federal resource allocation for education are inevitably conditioned by such contextual forces, by attendant fiscal constraints, and by the philosophical inertias of habit and tradition. To some, modern contextual forces suggest the imperative of massive increases in categorical Federal aid to education; to others, they suggest belt-tightening and the return of educational responsibility to traditional centers of State and local authority—either with or without general (no-strings-attached) Federal largess. Even if the evidence of recent USOE experience were clear, which it is not entirely, unanimity about the meaning of the evidence for future public policy would be obscured by competing public philosophies about fiscal policy and federalism. Furthermore, in the case of ESEA, generalizations and inferences from experiences to date are necessarily limited by the very newness of the program. Important changes and trends in American education may in fact be occurring as a result of the Act even though existing evidence is unavailable, unclear, or contradictory.

But if the search for the meaning of observed reality is complex and inevitably conditioned by context and by differing assumptions about political values, the search must continue. For the underlying premise of an open and democratic society is that free inquiry and a series of adversary proceedings based upon competing values can, together, create public policies which are increasingly responsive to social needs and increasingly refined, operationally, by rational criticisms.

THE KALEIDOSCOPE OF POLICY-MAKING

Whatever else the early experience of ESEA suggests, it reaffirms the kaleidoscopic nature of the policy-making process in the American society. The Act itself was not the product of any single dreamer or schemer. An accumulation of postwar tensions, competing group interests, legislative forerunners, academic colloquies, bureaucratic innovations, and personal political and administrative initiatives served to provide a multiple "authorship" for the bill. The Office of Education participated deeply in the interpretation of need, in the formulation of objectives, in political catalysis and brokerage. But its innovative and brokerage activities were a part of a complex, almost ineffable, series of interactions which involved scores of agencies—public and private—and hundreds of individual actors. The interactions followed no clear direction or directives. They reflected opportunity and fortuity modified by the perceptions and goals of political and educational leaders inside and outside of the Federal government. The ensuing compromises were not blind; but neither were they pre-ordained. The Act reflected a political logic hammered out in a vast number of confrontations and conversations. Bargains were struck, faces were saved, ambiguities were purposefully employed, credits were tactfully distributed, desirables were conditioned by possibles. The Act which emerged was politically tailored to unite traditional opponents without unduly blunting the edge of true innovation. But there was no master tailor—not Keppel, not Johnson, not Morse, not Gardner, not the NEA. The real tailor was the bargaining processes of a democratic polity informed and shaped here and there by the unusual skills of a few cutters and seamstresses sensitive to emerging fashion.

The Reciprocity of Implementation

Once the Act was signed, its implementation replicated its passage. The scene shifted from Congress to Fourth Street and Independence Ave., S.W., but the administrative process was generically similar to the legislative process. *Regulations, Guidelines* and other orders and protocols had to be drafted, but most of them were referred to key clientele for examination and response, and were subject to the unsolicited pressures of the offended. The early experience of implementing ESEA suggests that in spite of mistakes of bureaucratic commission and omission, USOE attempted to carry out its legislative mandate with dispatch, but with a deep concern for the feelings and problems of State and local educational agencies. Insofar as time and energy allowed, USOE officials attempted to gain the advice and assistance of affected clientele and of their professional-association representatives in developing and enforcing ESEA ground rules. Criticized for both overprescription and underprescription, the Office of Education staff struggled to discover administrative policies and practices which would carry out legislative intent while leaving a maximum of discretion and inventiveness to State and/or local education authorities. In the process, many SEA's and LEA's were in fact strengthened in staff size and competence. Aside from the peculiar field of civil rights enforcement, the most serious criticisms of ESEA from educational administrators across the country were not directed against USOE actions and attitudes; they were directed against the categorical nature of the Act with its attendant administrative problems, and the lateness and unpredictability of congressional funding. And insofar as criticisms of "Federal control" were levied directly at USOE, such criticisms, as we shall note below, frequently reflected an appalling naiveté on the part of the critics. Feedback, bargaining, and compromise are as much a part of administrative as of legislative activity, and reflect the attempt of civil servants and of political executives to be responsive to the endless winds of competition and the gusts of passion which swirl through the corridors of government office buildings.

People and Structures

In this atmosphere of harried reciprocities, counter-pressures, and adjustments, the role and fate of individual officials and of organization charts may seem almost incidental. But people and structures are important, even in their transiencies. Men like Keppel and Loomis interrupted the continuum of inertias which mark all large-scale organizations. They helped to set new directions of policy, structure, and procedures. In the process they inevitably used up reservoirs of good will both inside and outside the agency. In the evolution of institutions, as in the chronicle of individual lives, there is a time for men to live, a time to die. A year after the passage of ESEA, both Keppel and Loomis had left government service. But their incumbencies had helped to shape the mission and mode of USOE for years to come. And Keppel's successor, Harold Howe II, turned out to be a man of extraordinary courage and ability. With a rich background in public school administration and in educational research, and with the strong support of his long-time friend, Secretary John Gardner, Commissioner Howe gave an immediate and continuing impression of knowing what he was about, and of strength in holding fast to principle—especially in the tangled jungle of civil rights controversy.

And so part of the meaning of our story is that America can and does attract into the Federal bureaucracy able men capable of making hard choices; men who understand that power in Washington is the art of using, by-passing, and modifying complex machinery in a thoroughly political environment; men who, to change the idiom, know how to be midwives of the future. The successful ones know that accomplishment involves support from political superiors in the Executive and Legislative branches; from the press; from subordinate, tenured officials; and from powerful private interest groups on the outside. But they also know that all of these centers of power are preoccupied, and that for any specific cause they tend to remain inert unless constantly prodded and cultivated. In consequence, the ability of "able men" must be measured in terms less of command than of negotiating skills and the capacity to win support where and when it is needed. The story of ESEA is not a story of rampant autocracy.

The dramatic changes in structure and staff which marked USOE during the first year of ESEA produced temporary traumas and hiatuses. And some of the White House Task Force recommendations for agency reorganization were delayed in effective execution or were modified in practice. But few would question the importance of the reorganization of structures and procedures that was in fact accomplished in July, 1965. A creaking 19th century establishment had been shored up to enable it to carry 20th century loads. New boxes on the organization chart admitted new and younger faces; new information systems promoted more coherent planning and budgeting; new personnel procedures gradually narrowed what was once a frightening gap between positions available and positions filled; previously untapped skills among old-timers were discovered and utilized in Washington and in SEA's and LEA's across the country. And even if a reconstituted bureau and office structure left a number of jurisdictional ambiguities and unresolved tensions, clear gains were noticeable in the rational grouping of major functions reflecting a series of new priorities.

Again, the meaning is clear and hopeful. Bureaucracy is not inevitably sodden. Inertias can be overcome; dysfunctional structures can be modified or replaced; "iron-poor" blood can be reinvigorated; major shifts in policy can and do stimulate relevant shifts in an agency's way of doing business.

The Restiveness of the Traditional Educational Community

If these, then, are some of the hopeful tendencies illuminated by the first year's experience under ESEA, what can be said of the apparent restiveness of the traditional educational community with the implications of the new Federal involvement?

Obviously, some of the State and local discomfiture was a function of continuing needs which were not being met by the various titles of ESEA. Both capital and operating expenses of a general nature were mounting for school districts across the nation. Aside from "impacted area" funds, and a few spin-offs from NDEA, the hoped-for Federal relief for school construction and teachers' salaries had not in fact emerged. In its place were Federal laws like ESEA and the Civil Rights Act of 1964 which placed unprecedented administrative and political burdens on both SEA's and LEA's. Cognate developments like the poverty program, black power movements, and the emergence of teacher militancy forced many superintendents and school boards, especially in the big cities, to enter new arenas of conflict and negotiation that most school administrators found distasteful in the extreme. If many of the forces which were increasingly complicating the lives of schoolmen across the nation were not a direct result of Federal policy, the new Federal involvement became a convenient symbol of the multiple burdens which schoolmen were being forced to assume. Nostalgia for a simpler world was the inevitable result. At the State level, Federal programs which shifted power to Washington or to local school districts, or to both, exacerbated insecurities which many SEA's had suffered ever since big city school systems (often in desperation) had worked out *de facto* declarations of independence from weak and rurally-oriented State departments of education. *De facto* loss of power was painfully reinforced by a *de jure* loss of face implicit in Title III and IV of ESEA.[2] Title V helped to soften the blow but it did not quiet the restiveness.

It is difficult to appraise the extent and the meaning of the widespread restiveness attendant upon increased Federal influences in the field of education. It is clear, however, that schoolmen at the State and local levels are caught on the horns of a dilemma. Mounting educational costs are forcing claims upon local and State revenues that are less elastic politically and fiscally than Federal revenues. The need for general Federal relief for hard-pressed State and local educational budgets is increasingly manifest.[3] Schoolmen would like massively increased Federal aid for education. But they would like such aid without categorical strings—in their language without "Federal control."

On the other hand, certain kinds of "Federal control" are inevitable whenever and wherever Federal funds are granted. And there are reasons to believe that there are national interests in education which can be

2. Title III was amended on December 14, 1967, to give SEA's full control of allocations. Starting on July 1, 1968, 75 per cent of the Title III money will be allocated to the States for reallocation to LEA's. Starting on July 1, 1969, 100 per cent of the Title III money will be so allocated. See Elementary and Secondary Education Amendments of 1967 (Public Law 90–247).

3. Representative Edith Green, speaking to the Council of Chief State School Officers on her subcommittee's report, mentioned the inadequate funding for education by all three levels of government. One of her chief impressions resulting from the subcommittee's study was that the Office of Education was overloaded with work. "Throughout the study there appears to be too much for the Office to do with too few people and too little equipment. And surely not enough is being done when measured against the needs of education." See "Study of the Office of Education," speech by the Honorable Edith Green before the Council of Chief State School Officers, Puerto Rico, November 16, 1967, 9 pages (mimeo.).

served only if the national government imposes categorical restraints upon the use of at least some Federal money.

These issues are sufficiently important to warrant elucidation.

Federal Control

Whenever the Federal government (or any level of government for that matter) appropriates money for any purpose certain types of control are inevitable.

First, controls are necessary to insure that the money is spent according to legislative intent. If Congress appropriates money for education of the handicapped, for example, such money may not be spent for educating the non-handicapped.

Second, money spent must be accounted for according to prescribed fiduciary standards in order to protect against malfeasance and waste.

Third, granting the inevitable generality of law, money must be spent according to administrative ground rules established by the executive agency in charge of the program; and

Fourth, the donor government must establish standards of performance through evaluation and reporting requirements to insure that the desired results are being attained.

Without such direct controls, no effective public accountability could possibly be maintained. That these controls often involve elaborate paper work and accounting procedures is simply a manifestation of the necessary requirements for insuring responsible conduct in the spending of public funds. Bureaucratic red-tape may be modified and simplified; but it cannot be abolished.

Such controls are inevitable whether or not the Federal government is involved. State governments, municipal governments, and independent school systems must all establish similar controls at their respective levels. One may legitimately argue that the Federal government should not appropriate money to assist State and local educational enterprises, or that categorical programs should be grouped or liberalized. One can hardly argue that Federal money once appropriated should be spent by State or local authorities without strings of accountability attached.

In this sense, all Federal money spent for education involves Federal controls. The only way to avoid such Federal controls is to refuse to appropriate or to accept Federal money.

But Federal controls exist even where Federal money is not involved. If it is the national law, as it is, that segregated schools are unconstitutional because they deny certain citizens the equal protection of the laws,

State and local educational authorities are prohibited from practicing discrimination regardless of whether Federal funds are involved. This is not a nation of sovereign states. It is a nation of sovereign people. If the sovereign people, through their national representatives and through the Federal Courts, determine that certain practices in the States contravene the provisions of the United States Constitution, the Federal government has a mandate to regulate and to modify (i.e. to control) those practices. Local school officials are no more exempt from Federal laws than any other citizens. The history of the implementation and enforcement of the school desegregation cases and of the Civil Rights Act of 1964 can only make one conscious of the attenuated, intermittent and uneven character of Federal law enforcement where local mores are passionately involved. But in spite of such delays, law is social control. Federal laws necessarily involve Federal control.

What is true of civil rights is also true of the church-state issue. The "establishment of religion" clause in the First Amendment sets limits on the extent to which States and localities, as well as the national government, can provide support for private-parochial school systems. As noted earlier "shared-time" and "child benefit" formulae have been declared constitutional by the Supreme Court, but other forms of support for private-parochial education have not. State and local discretion in this general area is ultimately bound by decisions and dicta of the Federal judiciary. Again, issues of Federal money may not be involved, but Federal control is nonetheless real and present.

In sum, then, certain Federal controls over State and local educational policy are inevitable as long as Federal money is involved or as long as issues of constitutionality and national statutes are present.

Federal Influence

Some of the Federal impact upon American education in recent years has been criticized not because constitutional or statutory controls have been involved, but because legislative and administrative decisions have exerted a powerful influence on school programs and operations. The reasoning here has been that the carrot of Federal money has led schools into paths that otherwise would not have been followed. Hungry for additional financial support, local schools have been induced by Federal largess to undertake new curricula and new programs in conformance with national rather than locally-determined priorities. Vocational education; education for the handicapped; new experiments in science, math, and foreign languages; education for the culturally disadvantaged; supplementary educational centers; educational laboratories;—

these are samples of the new Federal influence. None of these theoretically involves Federal control, since State and local participation is voluntary. But in education, money is food, and education is hungry. And once the local school system accepts Federal money for matters of Federal priority, certain local autonomies may be curtailed. They may also, of course, be enhanced—especially when Federal money substitutes for local tax revenues, thereby releasing the latter for a larger support of locally determined priorities.

In short, while Federal money and influence may be welcomed on occasion, they are often resented. Most State and local educational authorities would far prefer to receive general aid in the form of tax credits or block grants that would allow them to determine educational priorities and would limit Federal controls to fairly routine matters of fiduciary accountability. In this pure form, such aid would involve no categorical inducement, no mandates, no guidelines, no red-tape, no federally sponsored systems of evaluation and reporting. Each school district, within limits set by State law, would simply have additional, unearmarked resources with which to work.

It is not inconceivable that Federal policy may move in this direction over the next several years. The need for general assistance to schools for teachers' salaries and for facilities has not abated. And enough has been said in recent months and years about the so-called Heller plan [4] and about tax credits, tax-sharing, and block grants to suggest that live political forces are agitating for policy shifts of this kind. On January 19, 1967, Representative Gerald R. Ford, minority leader of the House of Representatives, issued a "State of the Union" address which said in part:

> Republicans trust local school boards to formulate policy and set priorities far more than we trust bureaucrats in Washington.
>
> Congress should take the Federal handcuffs off our local educators. The best way to do this is by tax sharing and tax credits. If the Democrats, who control Congress, refuse to consider tax sharing legislation, Republicans will seek to substitute block education grants, without Federal ear-marking or controls.[5]

Similar suggestions have come from other legislators—Republican and Democratic—and the attempted Quie amendment to the Elementary and Secondary Education Act of 1967 may have been an important harbin-

4. Walter W. Heller, *New Dimensions of Political Economy* (New York: W. W. Norton & Company, Inc. 1967), 118.
5. *New York Times,* January 20, 1967, 16.

ger of new directions.[6] But the proposals for fiscal decentralization raise a series of difficult problems: philosophical, political, administrative, and economic.

The Philosophical Problem

Philosophically, a no-strings-attached approach to Federal aid to education raises the question of whether the sum of State and local interests does in fact add up to the best interests of the nation as a whole. This is a modern counterpart to the distinction made by Jean Jacques Rousseau between "the will of all" and the "general will." [7] Rousseau argued that the two are not the same: that the whole (the "general will") is greater than, and different from, the sum of its parts (the "will of all"). If educational policy, more elaborately funded, is set by a local school district in Mississippi, and some of the products of that school system migrate to Los Angeles and New York, is the adequacy of their education a matter of Mississippi's concern only? If national security does in fact involve the production of far greater numbers of scientists and engineers than are presently being trained by our school systems, can the nation allow State and local educational authorities to make program decisions which could make the "talented-manpower" gap even wider? If poverty, discrimination, and cultural deprivation in our major cities produce violence and hatred, and offend the moral sensitivity of the nation's representatives—legislative, executive, and judicial—should State legislatures and local school boards have the uninterrupted right to allocate educational resources in such a way as to perpetuate and increase these evils? If a revitalized international, civic, and humanistic education is the clue to international peace, domestic tranquility, and the pursuit of happiness, does not the national government have an obligation, in the words of the act creating the U.S. Office of Education in 1867, to ". . . promote the cause of education *throughout* the country"? [Emphasis supplied]

To argue, as Walter Heller has, that tax remissions for Federal purposes should go to the States (and, by "pass-through" devices, to local authorities) *on top of* categorical Federal grants, is one thing. Here a series of national interests might be preserved and promoted—including

6. Representative Albert Quie, Republican of Minnesota, proposed a "block grant" substitute for Titles I, II, III, and V of ESEA, amounting to a perpetual program at a $3 billion level for the fiscal year beginning on July 1, 1969.

7. Jean Jacques Rousseau, *The Social Contract and Discourses,* GDH Cole, trans., (New York: E. P. Dutton and Company, Inc., 1950) Book II, Section III, 26–27.

the national interest of increased public-sector spending at State and local levels. Federal block grants *added to* Federal categorical grants for education might accomplish similar results. Discretionary State and local money would be increased, but national inducements and influences would still be felt through the remaining or new categorical grants.

But to argue that all Federal money for education should be allocated to the States and localities with no strings attached whatsoever, is to argue that the national educational interest is identical with State and local interpretations of educational necessity. And it assumes that State and local educational agencies, unaided, have the staff, the talent pool, the imagination, and the freedom from irrational local pressures to use substantial increases in resources with creative wisdom in the national interest. Nothing in our past and present experience as a nation suggests that any of these postulates is valid.

The Political Problem

Even if it were clear philosophically that the nation's best interests would be served by making all Federal educational aid general rather than categorical, the political barriers to such a development are substantial if not prohibitive. First of all, it is not at all clear that in view of Supreme Court decisions parochial-school interests would settle for general aid to public education unless their interests were directly and explicitly protected. A number of States have constitutional prohibitions against aid—direct or indirect—to children of private or parochial schools. These prohibitions are far stronger than those in the first amendment to the United States Constitution. Some parochial systems might do far better working through State legislatures than through the Congress; but many would not. The Catholic hierarchy's attitude toward general aid bills in 1961 and 1963 may have been subsequently tempered by their experience under more recent legislation, but politically powerful doubts unquestionably remain about the desirability of strengthening the public education system at the expense of church-related schools.

Even if the church-state issue did not become deeply involved, however, congressional as well as bureaucratic political interests in categorical aid are substantial and vested. If congressional grants for education should become entirely faceless, Senators and Congressmen would have to face an inevitable loss in visibility. Committee and sub-committee chairmen derive substantial political and psychic income from their capacity to shape the direction of public policy. A simple tax-sharing or tax-credit arrangement would deny many powerfully situated Congressmen an important voice in shaping the future of educational policy.

The same is true—writ large—of the President, and of important officials in the executive departments and agencies. And these centers of power in the Federal government have influential private interest groups allied with them. It is not likely, for example, that civil rights organizations, councils of mayors, labor organizations, and even some urban school boards and superintendents would be happy about trusting State legislatures or State departments of education with the allocation of general Federal aid to the various educational claimants within a State. United States Senators are often at war with Governors of the same party for control of a State's political machinery. It is unlikely that Senators would wish to give these political rivals additional power and visibility in an area as important as education. Even if there were overwhelming political pressures to establish some block grants for education, the chances are substantial that national legislators and officials—upon sober second thought—would at the very minimum insist upon superimposing such grants upon, rather than substituting them for, categorical aid programs. There is still a healthy congressional fear that general aid would expose Congress to annual and ubiquitous grass-roots pressures (accompanied by threats of political retaliation) for additional aid for teachers' salaries.

The Administrative Problem

It seems clear that turning all Federal money for education into some form of general aid would exacerbate rather than lessen the administrative problems of intergovernmental and interagency relations. If anything has become obvious in recent years, it is that educational problems cannot be solved without reference to the ecology of the schools. Johnny's inability to read may have far more to do with instability, ill-health, or poverty in the family or with discrimination in the surrounding community than with the quality of pedagogy in the schools. If Federal programs in the fields of health, welfare, anti-discrimination, recreation, urban renewal, manpower training, and poverty were to continue unreinforced by categorical Federal programs in the education of the culturally and economically deprived, there would be no machinery available to induce administrative and programmatic coordination between education and these other related policy areas. Title I of ESEA, for example, mandates coordination between local school authorities and the community action programs of OEO. It is difficult to imagine how such coordination might be promoted under a tax-sharing or block-grant arrangement.

But interagency coordination is not the only issue. In many cases, the

State and local administration of education is in the hands of people who, however well-intentioned, lack the resources to establish, without the pressure of Federal standards and innovative requirements, efficient and effective administrative systems geared to educational improvement and evaluation. Without Titles III and IV of ESEA, for example, how many school districts would be moved to spend money on supplementary centers and regional laboratories to experiment with educational innovation and evaluation? How many State legislatures and local school boards would promote such experimentation in the face of clamorous pressures to use general Federal aid for improving teachers' salaries [8] or for building new junior colleges? Where is the evidence of prior concern with innovation, research, and experimentation on the part of SEA's and LEA's? It is slim indeed. Teachers' salaries need to be raised; junior colleges need to be built; but in the face of professional and local-government pressures, how can adequate funds be reserved by the State for improving the quality of educational research and practice? And how do states arrange for regional educational cooperation that cuts across State lines? Interstate compacts in the field of education, on the basis of initial experience, are cumbersome to administer and lack the flexibility and inducements of Federal programs and arrangements.

Economic Problems

Finally, tax-sharing and block-grant devices, if substituted totally for categorical aids to education, would have economic consequences of an uncertain, and possibly harmful, character. America's unprecedented national prosperity has been marred and marked by intractable pockets of poverty and unemployment. It would be in the national interest to wipe these pockets out as quickly as possible. They represent a moral blot; equally important they represent a serious economic drain. The unutilized or underutilized human resources in these pockets foster conditions of dependency, crime, delinquency, and disease. Instead of healthy tax and income producers, the poor become massive tax and income consumers. Unless Federal leverage exists to induce State and local authorities to arrange for compensatory formulae and programs to overcome the educational inadequacies in America's pockets of poverty,

8. See, for instance, the inaugural address delivered October 20, 1967 by Dr. Sam M. Lambert, new national secretary of the NEA. In it, Dr. Lambert emphasized the need for increasing teachers' salaries nearly 45 per cent, supported an effort for more general aid, and called for political action at the State, congressional district, and local levels. His remarks included a rousing call to action: "We can win when we are organized for political impact and this time we are going to be organized." Wash., D.C.: National Education Association.

there is no indication from past experience that State and local policies will emerge by themselves for such purposes. To the contrary, the studies of Alan K. Campbell and Seymour Sacks document a progressive shift of State and local resources away from the central city and towards schools in the wealthier suburbs.[9] If this trend continues, schools in the central cities will wallow in an economic morass that can only become more hopeless as the years go by.[10]

THE CONTINUING ROLE OF STATE AND LOCAL EDUCATIONAL AGENCIES

If there are reasons for continuing and expanding Federal categorical aid, there are also reasons for strengthening the educational roles of States and localities. Some of this strengthening may well come about through additional Federal revenues dispersed with a minimum of categorical restrictions. But for years to come the bulk of the revenue for education will come from State and local tax resources. And this is as it should be. Whatever weaknesses and inequities accrue from a decentralized educational system, such a system has enormous strengths—real and potential.[11] Pluralism is friendly to liberty. It also provides a wide variety of laboratories for carrying out educational experiments. It stimulates responses which are related to the needs of particular areas. At its best, it calls forth the interest and participation of local parents and citizens. It provides local instrumentalities for carrying out Federal programs. These are positive values. If they are to be realized as comple-

9. For data on central city—suburban disparities in educational expenditures and State aid, see Alan K. Campbell, "Educational Policy-Making Studied in Large Cities," a paper presented at the Cubberley Conference: School Boards in an Era of Conflict, at Stanford University in the summer of 1966, as reprinted in *The American School Board Journal,* March 1967, 18–19; and Seymour Sacks and David C. Ranney, "Suburban Education: A Fiscal Analysis," *Urban Affairs* (Fall 1966).
For a discussion of whether such disparities violate the "equal protection of the laws" clause of the Fourteenth Amendment see Arthur E. Wise, "Is Denial of Equal Educational Opportunity Constitutional?", *Administrator's Notebook* (University of Chicago, Midwest Administrative Center), Vol. XIII, February, 1965, No. 6.

10. The most recent studies of central city—suburban fiscal disparities in education conducted by the Advisory Commission on Intergovernmental Relations under the direction of Seymour Sacks demonstrate that the gap is widening. See ACIR, *The Fiscal Balance in the American Federal System* (Washington: U.S. Government Printing Office, 1968).

11. Nicholas A. Masters, "Partnership in Education: The Role of the States," *Contemporary Issues in American Education:* Consultants' Papers prepared for use at the White House Conference on Education July 20–21, 1965, Washington, D.C. (U.S. Department of Health, Education, and Welfare Office of Education, Bulletin 1966, No. 3).

mentary values to those achieved through Federal policy, however, State and local educational agencies need to pull up their socks. So do universities engaged in teacher education. Legitimate autonomies go to those who deserve them and who fight for them. State and local educational agencies and school systems suffer from a variety of diseases which no amount of Federal largess can cure.[12] School district consolidation is still desperately needed. Conversely and perversely, some school districts —especially in large cities—need to be decentralized and/or confederated. Community involvement in local school policy-making needs to be enhanced—especially in the ghettos of our large cities. In some metropolitan areas, school district boundaries need to be redrawn in order to achieve an appropriate student mix between suburban and central city children. State legislatures and State departments of education need to pay far more attention to the problems of low achievers—especially in urban schools. State aid formulae need to be readjusted to take account of urban educational needs. State constitutional and statutory limits upon the taxing and borrowing powers of local school districts need to be revised to provide LEA's greater fiscal flexibility. State and local educational agencies need to take a far greater interest in cooperating with universities and with private enterprise in upgrading teacher training and pedagogical techniques. Universities need to address themselves with a new sense of dedication to improving teacher education and State and local educational leadership.

Federal money can help in all this; so can new collaborative enterprises like the Educational Commission of the States. But responsibility rests ultimately upon State and local governments (general and educational) for upgrading their own capacities to fulfill their essential roles in the American educational system. If legislators, Governors, State Boards of Education, and Chief State School Officers, and their local counterparts, fail to assume the fiscal and programmatic burdens imposed by the contemporary educational needs and expectations of their respective publics, they have only themselves to blame if those publics turn increasingly to the Federal government for redress of educational grievances.

The Programmatic Shortfalls

The arguments against substituting general Federal aid totally for existing categorical aids, are not meant as an apologia for all existing

12. For discussions of the operation and potential of state and local boards of education, see papers presented at The Cubberley Conference, 1966, *op. cit.*, and Dean M. Schweickhard, *The Role and Policymaking Activities of State Boards of Education: Report on a Special Study Project*. (Denver, Colorado: National Association of State Boards of Education, 1967).

Federal policies and practices. Recent experience with the administration of ESEA and other Federal educational programs suggests that a number of things need correction. Some of the shortfalls are conceptual; some are administrative. Four areas of inadequacy warrant attention. The first three cut across many aspects of the American social system including, but not limited to, education. The fourth is a matter of particular concern to educators.

The Inadequacies of Social Policy

The first and most important issue has to do with the conceptual inadequacy of the Federal government's approach to the problems of low educational achievement among the nation's poor. It is possible that the learning problems of the children of the poor may have quite as much to do with the devastating effects of poverty, family insecurity, malnutrition, dependency, and discrimination upon the psyche of young people as they do with inadequacies of the formal educational system.[13] Although the logic for policy of the elaborate study conducted for the Office of Education by Dr. James Coleman on *Equality of Educational Opportunity* is uncertain, the study did show that low-achieving children were marked by a lack of self-confidence which appeared to be culturally determined. Schools may be able to help such children overcome these handicaps, especially if the exposure of the pupils to the school is made dramatically more intensive and extensive (pre-kindergarten classes, after-school remedial reading tutorials, summer schools, work and play identification with more secure peers). But it is unlikely that schools alone can overcome evils that are imbedded in the very fabric of our society.

This is not to argue that expenditures for compensatory education are unwarranted. It is to argue that unless the broader social and economic issues of poverty and discrimination are appropriately tackled, marginal Federal spending or upgrading of the school's capacity to help low achievers may bring only imperceptible educational results.

Church-State Relations

ESEA experience to date suggests that "child-benefit" and shared-time" doctrines promise little but a continuation of religious and admin-

13. See the testimony of Daniel P. Moynihan before the Senate Government Operations subcommittee on the Federal role in urban problems as reported in "The Case for a Family Allowance," *The New York Times Magazine,* February 5, 1967, 13.

istrative tensions and of judicial tightrope walking. The most promising escape from these dilemmas and ambiguities seems to rest in a notion that has only recently gained currency. Dr. James E. Russell, former Secretary of the Educational Policies Commission of the NEA, and Dr. James Michael Lee, Head of the Department of Education, Notre Dame University, have both proposed that parochial school interests should husband their resources by pulling totally out of elementary education.[14] Whether this is politically or philosophically possible or probable within the present limits of intra-Catholic church controversy is unclear. But Russell argues that the dire economic effect of such a move upon local public elementary schools, and the fact that this course of development would destroy one of the political barriers to general Federal aid, might induce the Federal government to undertake substantial grants for elementary public education throughout the nation. Russell has even suggested that Federal support start at the pre-school level—perhaps at age 4, and continue through age 10. Such an approach could be combined with some categorical aids for low achievers, but would be aimed at improving educational opportunity and services for all children in this age bracket. Limited Federal aid under "child-benefit" and "shared-time" formulae might be continued for secondary education. But pressure to operate on the margins of constitutionality would be tempered because the parochial systems would have more of their own money to spend on post-elementary education.

Developments of this kind, should they come, would not solve all of the thorny questions of church-state relations in education. But one substantial category of contemporary conflict and ambiguity would be eliminated, and a door would be opened to allow the Federal government to enhance equality of educational opportunity at the most formative stages of the learning process.

Injustice in Racially Segregated Schooling

In the area of school desegregation, the United States Office of Education and the Commissioner of Education have been attacked on the one hand for pushing too fast; on the other, for timidity. The direction of Federal policy has been irrevocably established by the Supreme Court and by the Civil Rights Act of 1964. The United States Office of Educa-

14. James Russell, *Universal Opportunity for Early Childhood Education,* (Wash., D.C.: Educational Policies Commission of The National Education Association, 1966).
James Michael Lee, ed., *Catholic Education in the Western World* (Notre Dame, Ind.: University of Notre Dame Press, 1967), 307–8.

tion is bound by the letter of the law to abolish *de jure* school segregation, and, under recent court orders, to move in this direction with increasing speed and decisiveness. It is bound by Title IV of the Civil Rights Act to do everything within its power to be helpful in relieving *de facto* segregation. The latter will have to be effected in large measure, however, by the carrot, not the stick. Title IV of the Civil Rights Act and Title III of ESEA are two of the inducements at the disposal of USOE; but more are needed—especially in the form of funds for experimental educational parks and supplementary centers, and in the form of operating subventions for transportation facilities which would make the concepts of neighborhood and community more elastic.[15] In the long run, however, school desegregation will be accomplished more effectively by broad economic, social, and attitudinal changes in the society as a whole, than by structural experimentation and educational gimmicks. Jobs, nondiscriminatory housing, and the general decline of prejudice are the ultimate pre-conditions of educational desegregation. Pressure and inducements from all levels and aspects of government can help speed the process of desegregation, and can become change agents for the larger community. But education cannot bear the entire burden of correcting America's deepest social malaise. In the meantime, continuing pressures for desegregation must be accompanied—perversely perhaps—by extraordinary efforts to improve the quality of education in the urban ghettos of the nation.

We Do Not Know How to Teach the Poor

Even if more rational and aggressive Federal policies were developed to change the ecology of learning for low status children, there is mounting evidence that American educators do not know how to teach the poor. Evaluations of the impact of ESEA to date are, as has been noted earlier, largely impressionistic and self-serving. But the limited, hard evidence that does exist on attempts to improve the educational performance of low status children by providing additional money and services is devastatingly pessimistic.[16] No State in the Union has con-

15. For a full and careful description of the experience of a medium-sized, northern city in taking steps toward desegregation in its schools, see Jerome Beker, *A Study of Integration in Racially Imbalanced Urban Public Schools: A Demonstration and Evaluation,* (Syracuse, N.Y.: Syracuse University Youth Development Center, 1967).

16. *Racial Isolation in the Public Schools,* U.S. Commission on Civil Rights, (Washington, D.C.: U.S. Commission on Civil Rights, 1967) esp. p. 205; Robert A. Dentler, "The Impact of Increasing Federal Aid to Education upon the Metropolitan Community," paper presented at the Session on Urban Sociology at the

ducted a more elaborate testing of pupil performance than New York. For the past three years, it has tested annually every first, third, sixth, and ninth grade child in the State in both public and private schools in terms of achieved skills in reading and arithmetic.[17] After two years of ESEA funding, there is no apparent change whatsoever in the performance of children attending Title I-aided schools in low status areas. Intensive and elaborate evaluations have been made of the 21 New York City schools which have now had over three full years of experience under what is known as the More Effective Schools Program (hereafter MES). Under this program, operating budgets for selected schools in low status areas were virtually doubled. Class sizes were cut in half. Remedial reading clinics were established. Teacher aides were hired. Guidance counsellors were added. New pedagogical experiments were carried out. Pre-school programs were conducted. To be sure, some progress has been demonstrated, if gross statistical averages are employed. But if those averages are broken down according to individual pupil backgrounds, the devastating fact is that dramatic improvements occurred largely among middle-class students. The hard core of low status children either made no perceptible progress at all, or they backslid after initial improvements, or they did worse than low status children in control schools which were used to check the MES experiment.[18]

It is possible (some would say probable) that existing tests are simply inadequate instruments of measurement. But existing tests provide the only hard data now available, and based upon such data the conclusion is inescapable that middle-class teachers, with middle-class backgrounds, using middle-class materials are obviously not getting through to the children of the subcultures of poverty and prejudice.[19] There is actually

---

Annual Convention of the American Sociological Association, San Francisco, August 29, 1967; *Evaluation of ESEA Title I Projects of California Schools, 1965–1966,* California State Department of Education; and *Report of Meetings With Big Cities,* U.S. Office of Education Memorandum From Division of Compensatory Education, Jan. 6, 1967.

17. For a description of the program and a discussion of findings see *Test Results of the 1965 Pupil Evaluation Program in New York State: Preliminary Overview,* and subsequent reports, Regents Examination and Scholarship Center, Division of Educational Testing (January, 1967), mimeo; and *The New York State Pupil Evaluation Program* (Albany: The State Education Department, 1966).

18. *Summary Report on Evaluation of the More Effective Schools Program,* Center for Urban Education (New York: August 1967).

19. A study which applied systems analysis to the high schools of Chicago and Atlanta concluded: "The most important finding of this study is that variations in educational outcomes in large-city high schools, measured in terms of test scores, are almost wholly conditioned by the socioeconomic environment of the neighborhood. The income class of the neighborhood, housing conditions, occupation of

some evidence that differences in class and caste between teachers and pupils set up subtle and self-fulfilling prophecies of failure. The teacher believes that the children are incapable of learning; this feeling is communicated by mood and grimace; these in turn reinforce the children's own sense of inadequacy; performance follows prediction.[20] Some experiments suggest that this phenomenon is exacerbated by dietary deficiencies among the children of the poor—deficiencies which hamper the development of brain cells for certain kinds of cognitive learning.

Whatever the explanation, the evidence is increasingly clear that our educational system is woefully unprepared to use marginal additions of money effectively for the redress of educational disadvantage.

The answer is surely not to cut back on financial investments for compensatory education, any more than years of failure in finding the causes and cures of cancer would have justified cutting back on cancer treatment and research. It is possible that massive infusions of resources for compensatory education might in fact work where limited funds have failed. In any case, the logic of the existing situation is that far greater resources must be plowed into basic educational research, laboratory testing, and controlled experiments. Title IV is the ultimate key—but "ultimate" may mean decades or even generations. Why should social cancer be any more amenable to quick solutions than human cancer? Because of the number and complexity of the variables, and society's present dearth of relevant skills for behavioral analysis, diagnosis, prognosis, and therapy, cures for social cancer may well take longer to unravel. But the need for a concerted attack is imperative. Congress, State

---

parents, ethnic status—these are the important determinants of variations in educational outcomes." Jesse Burkhead, with Thomas G. Fox and John W. Holland, *Input and Output in Large-City High Schools.* Education in Large Cities Series. (Syracuse: Syracuse University Press, 1967), 88.

20. Robert Rosenthal and Lenore Jacobson, *Pygmalion In The Classroom* (N.Y.: Holt, Rinehart & Winston, 1968).

A number of recent books and articles graphically describe these problems for a wide audience. See, for example, Nat Hentoff, *Our Children Are Dying,* (New York: Viking Press, 1967); Jonathan Kozol, *Death At An Early Age: The Destruction Of The Hearts And Minds Of Negro Children In The Boston Schools* (Boston: Houghton-Mifflin Co., 1967); Peter Shrag, *Village School Downtown: Politics and Education—A Boston Report* (Boston: Beacon Press, 1967); and Martin Mayer, "What's Wrong With Our Big City Schools," *The Saturday Evening Post,* September 9, 1967, 21.

Perversely there is some evidence that teacher attitudes make little or no difference. See Center for Urban Education, *Summary Report, op. cit.*

Current attempts at improving the abilities of middle class teachers in regard to the disadvantaged may be seen in NDEA Institutes, Title IV of the 1964 Civil Rights Act teacher training programs, and in the Teacher Corps.

legislatures, and local school authorities must face the reality that unless they patronize more effective educational research, clinical experimentation, and program evaluation for education as a whole, what they pour directly into compensatory education may bring indifferent and ineffable results. Research and development centers and regional educational laboratories must be sufficiently funded, over a long period of time. If they are so funded and if they are tied to supplementary education centers under Title III, to individual school programs under Title I, and above all, to teacher-training institutes and programs in American colleges and universities, then in time the educational intractabilities of low-status sub-cultures in our society can be cracked. Evidence to date suggests that nothing short of this will be permanently and dramatically effective.

The Administrative Agenda

If conceptual breakthroughs are needed in Washington—and in the society generally—to help the nation's schools move dramatically ahead in overcoming cultural deprivation, religious tensions over the church-state issues, and racial injustice, there is an equal and pressing need for administrative and structural reform.

Much of the confusion and red-tape which accompanied the first year of ESEA's implementation can be forgiven or discounted. The job was unprecedented in scope and magnitude, and it had to be accomplished by an agency undergoing the traumatic strains of massive internal re-organization and restaffing.

Lessons have been learned and changes in procedures and structures have been effected,[21] even though the troublesome problem of the timing and predictability of congressional appropriations has yet to be solved.[22] Administrative tensions will inevitably continue between USOE and its State, local, and professional clients. This is the price of maintaining

21. A pilot study completed in September, 1967, indicates that adoption of certain specific measures can reduce Federal grant-in-aid processing time by 50 per cent. See *Reducing Federal Grant-In-Aid Processing Time, An Interagency Report to the President, prepared by The Joint Administrative Task Force* (Dwight A. Ink of HUD, Chairman), September, 1967.

22. A step in the right direction was taken in December, 1967, when Congress passed the ESEA Amendments of 1967. Title IV, Section 403 says in part, "To the end of affording the responsible State, local and Federal officers concerned adequate notice of available Federal financial assistance for education, appropriations for grants, contracts, or other payments . . . are authorized to be included in the Appropriation Act for the fiscal year preceding the fiscal year for which they are available for obligation." See *Elementary and Secondary Education Amendments of 1967* (Public Law 90–247).

some counterpoise between necessary centripetal and inevitable centrifugal forces in the American educational enterprise. Many of these stresses and strains will lessen, however, as practice is gained in the reciprocities of partnership and as USOE succeeds in consolidating scores of discrete categorical programs into broader and more flexible mandates. Some of USOE's micro-administrative problems are serious and continuing—especially problems of inter-bureau planning, effective management controls, and attracting and holding able staff. But these are problems it shares with most of the other Federal agencies in Washington.

In terms of long-range political support, however, USOE has a special, almost desperate, need to succeed in the field of program evaluation. The volume of Federal money presently being spent in education is already substantial, and is growing year by year. Unless USOE can develop some valid indexes and proofs of accomplishment, it runs the risk of presidential, legislative, and public disillusionment.[23] But there are uncommon difficulties in the way of an effective evaluative effort. Evaluation techniques in the field of education are not well developed. The Tyler national assessment program has had rough sledding because of the totally unwarranted fears of schoolmen that the results of the tests would illuminate invidious distinctions among individual pupils and schools or would lead to the establishment of a national curriculum. No common agreement exists as to how evaluations should be conducted, at what level, and by whom. Unless Federal standards are set and enforced, evaluations by States and/or school districts will be disparate and non-additive. If Federal standards are set and enforced, the fear (and perhaps the reality) of Federal domination of America's pluralistic educational enterprise will increase.

Here is a realm for the closest possible collaboration of Federal and State educational agencies, devolving upon the latter the responsibilities for carrying out the intentions and mandates of the former.[24] Ultimately

23. The importance of evaluation was emphasized by the Green Committee Report. Among other things, the report suggests that OE submit a position paper to Congress on national educational assessment. See *Study of the United States Office of Education,* Report of the Special Subcommittee on Education, 1967; 89th Cong., 2nd sess., House, 421–37.

24. For a thoughtful and detailed discussion of the role of SEA's in evaluation and planning, see testimony of Commissioner Howe in support of a $15 million five-year program of support for State educational research. Testimony of Commissioner Howe before House Committee on Education and Labor, March 2, 1967, pp. 16–27. For materials on PPBS and educational evaluation, see *supra* fn. 24, Chapter 5.

all levels of education stand to benefit from more effective program evaluation. But who will be responsible and accountable is an issue of great administrative and political delicacy.

There are, however, three areas of macro-administration which need concentrated attention. These involve (1) intra-HEW and inter-agency relations in Washington; (2) Federal field offices for education; and (3) inter-governmental relations.

The Structure of Education in Washington

The recent emergence of education as a major national concern has raised insistent questions about the appropriate level and authority of USOE in the over-all structure of the Federal government. The essential issue is this: is bureau status for USOE commensurate with the importance of the functions it performs, and adequate to enable it to exert government-wide leadership in the field of education?

Three major doctrines have emerged. The first doctrine holds that there is virtue in maintaining the present arrangement. The argument here is that educational functions are presently scattered among a score of Federal agencies and departments; that there is little political possibility of corralling all of the educational functions into one agency or department; and that even if it were possible, it would be undesirable. There are values, it is contended, in intra- and inter-agency competition; the existing bureaucratic overlaps and hiatuses are in fact not serious; and anything that is done to raise the visibility of education in the Federal structure would increase both the fear and the possibility of Federal domination of the American educational enterprise. Furthermore, structural dispersal permits a healthy diffusion of political heat. Vested congressional and interest group pressures cannot be concentrated, and are consequently rendered relatively harmless.

A second doctrine holds that USOE is in fact at too low a level in the Federal structure; that it should be raised to a departmental status, but that it should remain subordinate to a super department which would continue to have jurisdiction over Health and Welfare as well as Education. The model here is the Department of Defense. HEW would be headed by a cabinet secretary who would have three subordinate non-cabinet secretaries (or under-secretaries) each in charge of a separate line department. The argument is that this arrangement would raise the status of the major operating functions of HEW while still promoting top-side coordination of programmatic areas which are in fact functionally interdependent.

This second doctrine has been attacked by thoughtful and eminent students of public administration—notably by Herbert Emmerich and Rufus Miles.[25] Both point out that the DOD analogue is specious and misleading; that departmental status for the major functions in HEW would tend to harden rather than dissolve existing parochialisms; that both the President and the Congress would find their legitimate authority subverted by the administrative ambiguities implicit in an added layer in the HEW hierarchy; and that no perceivable advantages would overcome the dangers of precedent in proliferating high-level titles. On this last issue, Emmerich quotes Gilbert and Sullivan, "When everyone is somebody then no one's anybody."

Both Emmerich and Miles advance a third doctrine: splitting HEW in two and creating separate cabinet-level departments for Health and Welfare on the one hand, and Education on the other. The proposed Department of Education would presumably encompass the present activities of USOE, and would have transferred to its jurisdiction some of the major educational grant activities of other agencies. Some of these agencies, such as the National Institutes of Health, are within HEW. Major educational grant programs are also found in the National Science Foundation, the National Humanities Foundation, the Department of Labor, and the Office of Economic Opportunity. This would still leave a substantial number of educational functions to be performed by other departments and agencies—notably the Veterans Administration, the Department of Defense, AID, NASA, AEC, and the Department of Agriculture. But education would have its symbolic home in the Federal structure, and the proposed department would have responsibilities and status commensurate with the emerging recognition of education as a national problem. Coordination with other agencies concerned with the ecology of education (e.g., Health and Welfare, Housing and Urban Development (hereafter HUD), Civil Rights Commission, Labor, Office of Economic Opportunity, and Agriculture) would still be needed; in this respect, however, all three doctrines are equally vulnerable. Certainly, a super-department of HEW would still face the necessity of relating its activities to other non-HEW agencies in Washington and in the field. Questions of relating Education to Welfare or Health are no more critical than questions of relating the three of these to the War on Poverty or to HUD's Model Cities Program.

On balance, which of the three doctrines makes the most sense? Prudentially, until USOE worked out the frictions of partnership with

25. Rufus E. Miles, Jr. "The Case For a Federal Department of Education" *Public Administration Review,* March 1967, 1; Herbert Emmerich, letter to the editor, *The Washington Post* (January 29, 1967).

its State, local, and professional clients, there was probably some virtue in keeping boat-rocking to a minimum. But sufficient experience has been gained since 1965 to suggest that Federal involvement in education is both necessary and relatively benign; that Federal control of education is in large measure a bogey-man; and that substantial Federal funding of educational activities is here to stay. The time has now come to confer departmental status upon USOE. The urgency in establishing a new Cabinet Department of Education stems not only from the unmanageable size and complexity of HEW, as presently constituted; America is the only major power on earth without a national educational ministry. The shifting fortunes of departmental and agency status over the years in the Federal government have reflected a shifting consensus about national priorities. Education has now become a national priority, supported by an increasingly sophisticated and energetic constituency. Acceptance of the Federal government's new role in education is bound to be hesitant and grudging among those who have strong interests in maintaining traditional State, local, and professional autonomies. The dilution of ancient sovereignties is always painful for some; but present trends are probably inexorable. Paradoxically, in spite of mistakes in judgment and execution, the Federal government's new role in education has surely had the effect of strengthening rather than weakening the authority and discretion of State and local educational agencies. Most new Federal money for education—categorical as it is—has actually induced new energies and new creativity at the State and local level. It is fair to say that the whole history of Federal grants-in-aid has been not to weaken lower levels of government, but to strengthen their capacities to deal with important areas of public policy. This appears to be the logic and experience of recent educational grants.

Myths, however, die hard. And creating a new department will not destroy these myths overnight; but it can symbolize the need to make the Federal presence in education both highly visible and increasingly responsible. And prestigious new political executive posts in a Cabinet Department should attract some of America's foremost educational leaders to the nation's service.

Equally important is the need, in the field of human resource development generally, for new administrative inventions to relate more effectively the programs presently carried on by USOE, HUD, OEO, Labor, Agriculture, the Veterans Administration, and the various health and welfare agencies within HEW, both in Washington and in the field. Ad hoc and statutory interdepartmental committees are patently inadequate; so are intermittent and casual clearances of an informal character. What is lacking is clear authority to accomplish coordinated program planning and execution. The Executive Office of the President needs new structures and staff to help the President plan, coordinate, and evaluate human resource development programs that cut across existing, or prospective, departmental lines and that are intergovernmental in character.

Federal Field Offices

Intra- and inter-agency coordination in Washington will have little effect if Federal agencies are still at loose ends in the field. Federal field establishments constitute one of the great uncharted jungles of American politics and government. Ninety per cent of all Federal employees work outside of the nation's capital. Federal offices and officers exist in every State in the Union, and are grouped kaleidoscopically into overlapping, historically fortuitous districts and regions. Some Federal departments and agencies have regional representatives of the department or agency as a whole; others permit regional or district representation of subordinate bureaus without an over-all department or agency representative. No mechanisms—except perhaps the Federal Executive Boards (hereafter FEB) established under President Kennedy by the U.S. Civil Service Commission and the provision for metropolitan expediters contained in the Model Cities Act—relate the field activities of the several Federal agencies to one another. Unfortunately, the FEB's are structurally and legally inadequate to do more than sort out fairly routine questions of inter-agency relations. And the concept of metropolitan expediters has not been effectively implemented.[26]

In consequence, Federal field activity is marked by a series of tensions, conflicts, hiatuses, and communication gaps. And these in turn are exacerbated by State, local, and private agency squabbles and jurisdictional struggles in related policy areas. Human resource conservation and development involves considerations of health, recreation, education, welfare, housing, employment opportunities, discrimination, delinquency, poverty, and crime. Every level of government and a variety of private agencies are presently in the act. But the stage is cluttered and the actors are unclear about their appropriate roles.

The United States Office of Education, viewing this mélange and desirous of decentralizing its operations in the name of efficiency and improved service to State and local educational clientele, has undertaken measures to strengthen the staff and the authority of its own field offices. Following the recommendations of the White House Task Force under Dwight Ink, USOE began in 1966 to take giant steps in the direction of administrative decentralization.

26. 1967 HUD appropriations legislation contains a specific prohibition against the funding of metropolitan expediters. *Congressional Quarterly Weekly Report* (Wash., D.C.: Congressional Quarterly Service, 1967), November 3, 1967, 9.

Ironically, these moves are being bitterly fought by some of education's major professional associations, which themselves are Washington-based. Ostensibly their opposition to decentralization is based upon their fear of "Federal tentacles" reaching out to all corners of the nation. The traditional bogey of "centralization in Washington" is giving way to a new bogey, the fear of Federal ubiquity. USOE views decentralization as a means of cutting red-tape, providing regional flexibility, and assuring closer contacts and a healthier dialogue with State and local educational agencies. Major divisions of NEA and the Council of State School Officers currently view decentralization as an attempt on the part of USOE to dominate State and local educational decision-making by establishing a system of powerful Federal pro-consuls—pro-consuls geographically distant from the watchful eyes of the Washington-based staffs of the professional associations themselves. In the thicket of group-interest politics there are even some signs that the national professional associations fear some consequent increase in power to their own regional, State, and local affiliates at the expense of the national association headquarters in Washington.

In any case, the concept of strengthened field offices for USOE raises extraordinarily complex questions—questions of how such field establishments can relate effectively to other Federal field offices concerned with human resource conservation and development; questions of political adjustment to the realities of pressure group politics in education's professional associations; questions of appropriate political and administrative relations to State, local, and private education authorities in each region; and questions of relations to non-educational agencies at the State and local level—private and public—which directly or indirectly affect educational interests.

No single precept or theory of organization can sort out matters of this complexity, but one guideline does seem clear. The evolution of USOE's regional offices should start with an initial emphasis upon heightened *service* to and *communication* with State and local educational agencies and interests. Field office *authority* will be accepted only as further confidence is established in the legitimacy of Federal educational infusions. This may take a few years; but during these years, a new Federal Department of Education and other organizational devices may evolve which can set a more appropriate framework than now exists for the exercise of enlarged discretion at the field office level.[27]

27. The Green Committee reported that "the educational community was apparently somewhat surprised" at USOE's move to decentralize and suggested that OE should improve communication with educators on decentralization plans. The subcommittee did recommend the strengthening of OE's regional offices, especially as related to "technical and informational services"; it endorsed decentralization

Inter-governmental Relations: The Matrix of Educational Policy-Making

The problem of Federal field agencies melds pervasively with the larger issue of intergovernmental relations. It is not enough to ask in the field of education how Federal, State, and local educational authorities should relate to each other in determining educational policy. One must also ask how various educational agencies should relate to each other at *each* level of government, and how they should relate to *general* government at each level of the Federal system. Patterns of potential interaction are almost too complex to be described, let alone negotiated. But a simplified grid, Table 9, may indicate some of the dimensions of the problem.

Cutting across the authority or involvement of the agencies listed in the rows and columns of the grid are the pervasive influences of various

---

on the condition that decision-making authority would also be decentralized and that sufficient trained staff would be assigned. See *Study of the U.S. Office of Education,* op. cit., 29–30, 377–400.

TABLE 9

INFLUENCES ON EDUCATIONAL POLICY-MAKING IN THE UNITED STATES

	National	State	Local
General Legislative	(1) Congress	(2) State Legislature	(3) Common Council
Educational Legislative	(4) Congressional Sub-Committee	(5) State School Board	(6) Local School Board
Executive	(7) President	(8) Governor	(9) Mayor
Administrative	(10) HEW-USOE	(11) State Department of Education	(12) School Superintendent
Judicial	(13) Supreme Court	(14) State Supreme Court	(15) Federal or State District Court
Professional Interests	(16) NEA	(17) State Teachers' Association	(18) Local PTA
Other Private Interests	(19) U.S. Catholic Conference	(20) State Chamber of Commerce	(21) John Birch Society Chapter

ideologues and journalists, and of the producers of textbooks and educational hardware.

The complexity of educational policy-making in the United States is a cause for concern; but it is hardly a cause for fear of Federal domination. Granted that appropriate weights for effective influence cannot be assigned to any one of the boxes or combination of boxes in the symbolic grid; all national government influences together add up to only 6 out of 24 boxes. In any single locality in the United States it is far more likely that, say, boxes 2, 5, 6, 12, and 21 are more influential in the making of educational policy than boxes 1, 7, 10, 16, and 19.

But regardless of relative influences at any point in time and space, educational policy increasingly is bound to reflect the extended interaction of all levels and types of government and of a wide variety of private and professional forces. The insistent need for the future is not to rationalize these various forces into neat packages of contending power—each army standing jealously on the bastions of its assumed prerogatives. The need is to assume and to value the pluralism of educational policy-making, and to develop attitudes and machinery which will permit and promote conflict resolution and cooperative planning in the larger educational interests of the nation and the world.

On balance, the experience of ESEA leads to the conclusion that colloquies and communications across this multiple partnership have been increased and enhanced. The need is for more rather than less interpenetration—with the clear understanding that in American education, as in the polity generally, "pluribus" is the condition of a viable "unum."

Coda

More than a half century ago in one of his now obscure novels, H. G. Wells wrote as follows:

> If humanity cannot develop an education far beyond anything that is now provided, if it cannot collectively invent devices and solve problems on a much richer, broader scale than it does at the present time, it cannot hope to achieve any very much finer order or any more general happiness than it now enjoys.[28]

In creating and implementing ESEA, the United States Office of Education demonstrated the continuing acceptance of this philosophy. Whatever its limitations in actual performance, and whatever the political and

28. H. G. Wells, *The New Machiavelli,* 2nd ed. (London: The Bodley-Head, 1911), 335.

administrative hazards of attempting to meld national and local educational activities, the new Federal involvement in education has demonstrated the capacity of the American society to develop new and viable programmatic and administrative experiments designed to serve the educational needs, claims, and values of the nation as a whole and of the nation's several constituent communities. A new, and on the whole an encouraging, chapter has been written in the ever evolving history of American federalism.

APPENDIX A

Public Law 89-10
89th Congress, H. R. 2362
April 11, 1965

An Act

79 STAT. 27.

To strengthen and improve educational quality and educational opportunities in the Nation's elementary and secondary schools.

Be it enacted by the Senate and House of Representatives of the United States of America in Congress assembled, That this Act may be cited as the "Elementary and Secondary Education Act of 1965". Elementary and Secondary Education Act of 1965.

TITLE I—FINANCIAL ASSISTANCE TO LOCAL EDUCATIONAL AGENCIES FOR THE EDUCATION OF CHILDREN OF LOW-INCOME FAMILIES AND EXTENSION OF PUBLIC LAW 874, EIGHTY-FIRST CONGRESS

SEC. 2. The Act of September 30, 1950, Public Law 874, Eighty-first Congress, as amended (20 U.S.C. 236–244), is amended by inserting: 64 Stat. 1100.

"TITLE I—FINANCIAL ASSISTANCE FOR LOCAL EDUCATIONAL AGENCIES IN AREAS AFFECTED BY FEDERAL ACTIVITY"

immediately above the heading of section 1, by striking out "this Act" wherever it appears in sections 1 through 6, inclusive (other than where it appears in clause (B) of section 4(a)), and inserting in lieu thereof "this title", and by adding immediately after section 6 the following new title: 67 Stat. 532. 20 USC 239.

"TITLE II—FINANCIAL ASSISTANCE TO LOCAL EDUCATIONAL AGENCIES FOR THE EDUCATION OF CHILDREN OF LOW-INCOME FAMILIES

"DECLARATION OF POLICY

"SEC. 201. In recognition of the special educational needs of children of low-income families and the impact that concentrations of low-income families have on the ability of local educational agencies to support adequate educational programs, the Congress hereby declares it to be the policy of the United States to provide financial assistance (as set forth in this title) to local educational agencies serving areas with concentrations of children from low-income families to expand and improve their educational programs by various means (including preschool programs) which contribute particularly to meeting the special educational needs of educationally deprived children.

"KINDS AND DURATION OF GRANTS

"SEC. 202. The Commissioner shall, in accordance with the provisions of this title, make payments to State educational agencies for basic grants to local educational agencies for the period beginning July 1, 1965, and ending June 30, 1968, and he shall make payments to State educational agencies for special incentive grants to local educational agencies for the period beginning July 1, 1966, and ending June 30, 1968.

"BASIC GRANTS—AMOUNT AND ELIGIBILITY

"SEC. 203. (a)(1) From the sums appropriated for making basic grants under this title for a fiscal year, the Commissioner shall reserve such amount, but not in excess of 2 per centum thereof, as he may determine and shall allot such amount among Puerto Rico, Guam, American Samoa, the Virgin Islands, and the Trust Territory of the Pacific Islands according to their respective need for such grants. The maximum basic grant which a local educational agency in Puerto Rico, Guam, American Samoa, the Virgin Islands, and the Trust Territory of the Pacific Islands shall be eligible to receive shall be determined pursuant to such criteria as the Commissioner determines will best carry out the purposes of this title.

"(2) In any case in which the Commissioner determines that satisfactory data for that purpose are available, the maximum basic grant which a local educational agency in a State shall be eligible to receive under this title for any fiscal year shall be (except as provided in paragraph (3)) an amount equal to the Federal percentage (established pursuant to subsection (c)) of the average per pupil expenditure in that State multiplied by the sum of (A) the number of children aged five to seventeen, inclusive, in the school district of such agency, of families having an annual income of less than the low-income factor (established pursuant to subsection (c)), and (B) the number of children of such ages in such school district of families receiving an annual income in excess of the low-income factor (as established pursuant to subsection (c)) from payments under the program of aid to families with dependent children under a State plan approved under title IV of the Social Security Act. In any other case, the maximum basic grant for any local educational agency in a State shall be determined on the basis of the aggregate maximum amount of such grants for all such agencies in the county or counties in which the school district of the particular agency is located, which aggregate maximum amount shall be equal to the Federal percentage of such per pupil expenditure multiplied by the number of children of such ages and families in such county or counties and shall be allocated among those agencies upon such equitable basis as may be determined by the State educational agency in accordance with basic criteria prescribed by the Commissioner. For purposes of this subsection the 'average per pupil expenditure' in a State shall be the aggregate current expenditures, during the second fiscal year preceding the fiscal year for which the computation is made, of all local educational agencies in the State (without regard to the sources of funds from which such expenditures are made), divided by the aggregate number of children in average daily attendance to whom such agencies provided free public education during such preceding year. In determining the maximum amount of a basic grant and the eligibility of a local educational agency for a basic grant for any fiscal year, the number of children determined under the first two sentences of this subsection or under subsection (b) shall be reduced by the number of children aged five to seventeen, inclusive, of families having an annual income of less than the low-income factor (as established pursuant to subsection (c)) for whom a payment was made under title I for the previous fiscal year.

49 Stat. 627.
42 USC 601-609.

"Average per pupil expenditure."

"(3) If the maximum amount of the basic grant determined pursuant to paragraph (1) or (2) for any local educational agency for the fiscal year ending June 30, 1966, is greater than 30 per centum of the sum budgeted by that agency for current expenditures for that year (as determined pursuant to regulations of the Commissioner), such maximum amount shall be reduced to 30 per centum of such budgeted sum.

"(4) For purposes of this subsection, the term 'State' does not include Puerto Rico, Guam, American Samoa, the Virgin Islands, and the Trust Territory of the Pacific Islands.

"(b) A local educational agency shall be eligible for a basic grant for a fiscal year under this title only if it meets the following requirements with respect to the number of children aged five to seventeen, inclusive, of families having an annual income of less than the low-income factor (as established pursuant to subsection (c)):

"(1) In any case (except as provided in paragraph (3)) in which the Commissioner determines that satisfactory data for the purpose of this subsection as to the number of such children of such families are available on a school district basis, the number of such children of such families in the school district of such local educational agency shall be—

"(A) at least one hundred, or

"(B) equal to 3 per centum or more of the total number of all children aged five to seventeen, inclusive, in such district,

whichever is less, except that it shall in no case be less than ten.

"(2) In any other case, except as provided in paragraph (3), the number of children of such ages of families with such income in the county which includes such local educational agency's school district shall be one hundred or more.

"(3) In any case in which a county includes a part of the school district of the local educational agency concerned and the Commissioner has not determined that satisfactory data for the purpose of this subsection are available on a school district basis for all the local educational agencies for all the counties into which the school district of the local educational agency concerned extends, the eligibility requirement with respect to the number of children of such ages of families of such income for such local educational agency shall be determined in accordance with regulations prescribed by the Commissioner for the purposes of this subsection.

"(c) For the purposes of this section, the 'Federal percentage' and the 'low-income factor' for the fiscal year ending June 30, 1966, shall be 50 per centum and $2,000, respectively. For each of the two succeeding fiscal years the Federal percentage and the low-income factor shall be established by the Congress by law. "Federal percentage." "Low-income factor."

"(d) For the purposes of this section, the Commissioner shall determine the number of children aged five to seventeen, inclusive, of families having an annual income of less than the low-income factor (as established pursuant to subsection (c)) on the basis of the most recent satisfactory data available from the Department of Commerce. At any time such data for a county are available in the Department of Commerce, such data shall be used in making calculations under this section. The Secretary of Health, Education, and Welfare shall determine the number of children of such ages from families receiving an annual income in excess of the low-income factor (established pursuant to subsection (c)) from payments under the program of aid to families with dependent children under a State plan approved under title IV of the Social Security Act on the basis of the best available data for the period most nearly comparable to those which are used by the Commissioner under the first two sentences of this subsection in making determinations for the purposes of subsections (a) and (b). When requested by the Commissioner, the Secretary of Commerce shall make a special estimate of the number of children of such ages who are from families having an annual income less than the low

49 Stat. 627.
42 USC 601-609.

income factor (established pursuant to subsection (c)) in each county or school district, and the Commissioner is authorized to pay (either in advance or by way of reimbursement) the Secretary of Commerce the cost of making this special estimate. The Secretary of Commerce shall give consideration to any request of the chief executive of a State for the collection of additional census information.

"SPECIAL INCENTIVE GRANTS

"SEC. 204. Each local educational agency which is eligible to receive a basic grant for the fiscal year ending June 30, 1967, shall be eligible to receive in addition a special incentive grant which does not exceed the product of (a) the aggregate number of children in average daily attendance to whom such agency provided free public education during the fiscal year ending June 30, 1965, and (b) the amount by which the average per pupil expenditure of that agency for the fiscal year ending June 30, 1965, exceeded 105 per centum of such expenditure for the fiscal year ending June 30, 1964. Each local educational agency which is eligible to receive a basic grant for the fiscal year ending June 30, 1968, shall be eligible to receive in addition a special incentive grant which does not exceed the product of (c) the aggregate number of children in average daily attendance to whom such agency provided free public education during the fiscal year ending June 30, 1966, and (d) the amount by which the average per pupil expenditure of that agency for the fiscal year ending June 30, 1966, exceeded 110 per centum of such expenditure for the fiscal year ending June 30, 1964. For the purpose of this section the 'average per pupil expenditure' of a local educational agency for any year shall be the aggregate expenditures (without regard to the sources of funds from which such expenditures are made, except that funds derived from Federal sources shall not be used in computing such expenditures) from current revenues made by that agency during that year for free public education, divided by the aggregate number of children in average daily attendance to whom such agency provided free public education during that year.

"Average per pupil expenditure."

"APPLICATION

"SEC. 205. (a) A local educational agency may receive a basic grant or a special incentive grant under this title for any fiscal year only upon application therefor approved by the appropriate State educational agency, upon its determination (consistent with such basic criteria as the Commissioner may establish)—

"(1) that payments under this title will be used for programs and projects (including the acquisition of equipment and where necessary the construction of school facilities) (A) which are designed to meet the special educational needs of educationally deprived children in school attendance areas having high concentrations of children from low-income families and (B) which are of sufficient size, scope, and quality to give reasonable promise of substantial progress toward meeting those needs, and nothing herein shall be deemed to preclude two or more local educational agencies from entering into agreements, at their option, for carrying out jointly operated programs and projects under this title;

"(2) that, to the extent consistent with the number of educationally deprived children in the school district of the local educational agency who are enrolled in private elementary and secondary schools, such agency has made provision for including special educational services and arrangements (such as dual enrollment, educational radio and television, and mobile educational services and equipment) in which such children can participate;

"(3) that the local educational agency has provided satisfactory assurance that the control of funds provided under this title, and title to property derived therefrom, shall be in a public agency for the uses and purposes provided in this title, and that a public agency will administer such funds and property;

"(4) in the case of any project for construction of school facilities, that the project is not inconsistent with overall State plans for the construction of school facilities and that the requirements of section 209 will be complied with on all such construction projects;

"(5) that effective procedures, including provision for appropriate objective measurements of educational achievement, will be adopted for evaluating at least annually the effectiveness of the programs in meeting the special educational needs of educationally deprived children;

"(6) that the local educational agency will make an annual report and such other reports to the State educational agency, in such form and containing such information, as may be reasonably necessary to enable the State educational agency to perform its duties under this title, including information relating to the educational achievement of students participating in programs carried out under this title, and will keep such records and afford such access thereto as the State educational agency may find necessary to assure the correctness and verification of such reports;

"(7) that wherever there is, in the area served by the local educational agency, a community action program approved pursuant to title II of the Economic Opportunity Act of 1964 (Public Law 88-452), the programs and projects have been developed in cooperation with the public or private nonprofit agency responsible for the community action program; and

78 Stat. 516.
42 USC 2781-2831.

"(8) that effective procedures will be adopted for acquiring and disseminating to teachers and administrators significant information derived from educational research, demonstration, and similar projects, and for adopting, where appropriate, promising educational practices developed through such projects.

"(b) The State educational agency shall not finally disapprove in whole or in part any application for funds under this title without first affording the local educational agency submitting the application reasonable notice and opportunity for a hearing.

"ASSURANCES FROM STATES

"SEC. 206. (a) Any State desiring to participate in the program of this title shall submit through its State educational agency to the Commissioner an application, in such detail as the Commissioner deems necessary, which provides satisfactory assurance—

"(1) that, except as provided in section 207(b), payments under this title will be used only for programs and projects which have been approved by the State educational agency pursuant to section 205(a) and which meet the requirements of that section, and that such agency will in all other respects comply with the provisions of this title, including the enforcement of any obligations imposed upon a local educational agency under section 205(a);

"(2) that such fiscal control and fund accounting procedures will be adopted as may be necessary to assure proper disbursement of, and accounting for, Federal funds paid to the State (including such funds paid by the State to local educational agencies) under this title; and

"(3) that the State educational agency will make to the Commissioner (A) periodic reports (including the results of objective measurements required by section 205(a)(5)) evaluating the effectiveness of payments under this title and of particular programs assisted under it in improving the educational attainment of educationally deprived children, and (B) such other reports as may be reasonably necessary to enable the Commissioner to perform his duties under this title (including such reports as he may require to determine the amounts which the local educational agencies of that State are eligible to receive for any fiscal year), and assurance that such agency will keep such records and afford such access thereto as the Commissioner may find necessary to assure the correctness and verification of such reports.

Records.

"(b) The Commissioner shall approve an application which meets the requirements specified in subsection (a), and he shall not finally disapprove an application except after reasonable notice and opportunity for a hearing to the State educational agency.

"PAYMENT

"Sec. 207. (a)(1) The Commissioner shall, subject to the provisions of section 208, from time to time pay to each State, in advance or otherwise, the amount which the local educational agencies of that State are eligible to receive under this title. Such payments shall take into account the extent (if any) to which any previous payment to such State educational agency under this title (whether or not in the same fiscal year) was greater or less than the amount which should have been paid to it.

"(2) From the funds paid to it pursuant to paragraph (1) each State educational agency shall distribute to each local educational agency of the State which is not ineligible by reason of section 203(b) and which has submitted an application approved pursuant to section 205(a) the amount for which such application has been approved, except that this amount shall not exceed an amount equal to the total of the maximum amount of the basic grant plus the maximum amount of the special incentive grant as determined for that agency pursuant to sections 203 and 204, respectively.

"(b) The Commissioner is authorized to pay to each State amounts equal to the amounts expended by it for the proper and efficient performance of its duties under this title (including technical assistance for the measurements and evaluations required by section 205(a)(5)), except that the total of such payments in any fiscal year shall not exceed 1 per centum of the total of the amount of the basic grants paid under this title for that year to the local educational agencies of the State.

"(c)(1) No payments shall be made under this title for any fiscal year to a State which has taken into consideration payments under this title in determining the eligibility of any local educational agency in that State for State aid, or the amount of that aid, with respect to the free public education of children during that year or the preceding fiscal year.

"(2) No payments shall be made under this title to any local educational agency for any fiscal year unless the State educational agency finds that the combined fiscal effort (as determined in accordance with regulations of the Commissioner) of that agency and the State with respect to the provision of free public education by that agency for the preceding fiscal year was not less than such combined fiscal effort for that purpose for the fiscal year ending June 30, 1964.

"ADJUSTMENTS WHERE NECESSITATED BY APPROPRIATIONS

"SEC. 208. If the sums appropriated for the fiscal year ending June 30, 1966, for making the payments provided in this title are not sufficient to pay in full the total amounts which all local and State educational agencies are eligible to receive under this title for such year, such amounts shall be reduced ratably. In case additional funds become available for making payments under this title for that year, such reduced amounts shall be increased on the same basis that they were reduced.

"LABOR STANDARDS

"SEC. 209. All laborers and mechanics employed by contractors or subcontractors on all construction projects assisted under this title shall be paid wages at rates not less than those prevailing on similar construction in the locality as determined by the Secretary of Labor in accordance with the Davis-Bacon Act, as amended (40 U.S.C. 276a—276a–5). The Secretary of Labor shall have with respect to the labor standards specified in this section the authority and functions set forth in Reorganization Plan Numbered 14 of 1950 (15 F.R. 3176; 5 U.S.C. 133z–15) and section 2 of the Act of June 13, 1934, as amended (40 U.S.C. 276c).

49 Stat. 1011; 78 Stat. 238.

64 Stat. 1267. 63 Stat. 108.

"WITHHOLDING

"SEC. 210. Whenever the Commissioner, after reasonable notice and opportunity for hearing to any State educational agency, finds that there has been a failure to comply substantially with any assurance set forth in the application of that State approved under section 206(b), the Commissioner shall notify the agency that further payments will not be made to the State under this title (or, in his discretion, that the State educational agency shall not make further payments under this title to specified local educational agencies affected by the failure) until he is satisfied that there is no longer any such failure to comply. Until he is so satisfied, no further payments shall be made to the State under this title, or payments by the State educational agency under this title shall be limited to local educational agencies not affected by the failure, as the case may be.

"JUDICIAL REVIEW

"SEC. 211. (a) If any State is dissatisfied with the Commissioner's final action with respect to the approval of its application submitted under section 206(a) or with his final action under section 210, such State may, within sixty days after notice of such action, file with the United States court of appeals for the circuit in which such State is located a petition for review of that action. A copy of the petition shall be forthwith transmitted by the clerk of the court to the Commissioner. The Commissioner thereupon shall file in the court the record of the proceedings on which he based his action, as provided in section 2112 of title 28, United States Code.

72 Stat. 941.

"(b) The findings of fact by the Commissioner, if supported by substantial evidence, shall be conclusive; but the court, for good cause shown, may remand the case to the Commissioner to take further evidence, and the Commissioner may thereupon make new or modified findings of fact and may modify his previous action, and shall file in the court the record of the further proceedings. Such new or modified findings of fact shall likewise be conclusive if supported by substantial evidence.

"(c) Upon the filing of such petition, the court shall have jurisdiction to affirm the action of the Commissioner or to set it aside, in whole or in part. The judgment of the court shall be subject to review by the Supreme Court of the United States upon certiorari or certification as provided in section 1254 of title 28, United States Code.

62 Stat. 928.

"NATIONAL ADVISORY COUNCIL

"SEC. 212. (a) The President shall, within ninety days after the enactment of this title, appoint a National Advisory Council on the Education of Disadvantaged Children for the purpose of reviewing the administration and operation of this title, including its effectiveness in improving the educational attainment of educationally deprived children, and making recommendations for the improvement of this title and its administration and operation. These recommendations shall take into consideration experience gained under this and other Federal educational programs for disadvantaged children and, to the extent appropriate, experience gained under other public and private educational programs for disadvantaged children.

"(b) The Council shall be appointed by the President without regard to the civil service laws and shall consist of twelve persons. When requested by the President, the Secretary of Health, Education, and Welfare shall engage such technical assistance as may be required to carry out the functions of the Council, and the Secretary shall make available to the Council such secretarial, clerical, and other assistance and such pertinent data prepared by the Department of Health, Education, and Welfare as it may require to carry out such functions.

Report to President and Congress.

"(c) The Council shall make an annual report of its findings and recommendations (including recommendations for changes in the provisions of this title) to the President not later than March 31 of each calendar year beginning after the enactment of this title. The President shall transmit each such report to the Congress together with his comments and recommendations.

"(d) Members of the Council who are not regular full-time employees of the United States shall, while serving on business of the Council, be entitled to receive compensation at rates fixed by the President, but not exceeding $100 per day, including travel time; and while so serving away from their homes or regular places of business, they may be allowed travel expenses, including per diem in lieu of subsistence, as authorized by section 5 of the Administrative Expenses Act of 1946 (5 U.S.C. 73b–2) for persons in Government service employed intermittently."

60 Stat. 808; 75 Stat. 339,340.

TECHNICAL AND CONFORMING AMENDMENTS

SEC. 3. (a) Clause (A) of section 3(c)(4) of the Act of September 30, 1950, Public Law 874, Eighty-first Congress, as amended (20 U.S.C. 238 (c)(4)(A)) is amended by striking out ") is," and inserting ", but excluding funds available under title II) is,".

67 Stat. 531; 70 Stat. 971.

(b) The sentence which immediately follows clause (B) of section 4(a) of such Act (20 U.S.C. 239(a)(B)) is amended by inserting "(exclusive of funds available under title II)" immediately after "Federal funds".

67 Stat. 532.

(c)(1) Such Act is further amended by inserting "TITLE III—GENERAL" above the heading for section 7, and by redesignating sections 7, 8, and 9, and references thereto, as sections 301, 302, and 303, respectively. 64 Stat. 1107. 20 USC 242-244.

(2) Subsections (b) and (c) of the section of such Act redesignated as section 302 are amended by striking out "this Act" wherever it appears and inserting in lieu thereof "title I".

DEFINITIONS

Sec. 4. (a) Paragraph (2) of the section of the Act of September 30, 1950, Public Law 874, Eighty-first Congress, as amended, redesignated by section 3 of this Act as section 303, is amended to read as follows:

"(2) The term 'child', except as used in title II, means any child who is within the age limits for which the applicable State provides free public education." "Child."

(b) Paragraph (4) of such section 303 is amended by inserting before the period at the end thereof ", except that for the purposes of title II such term does not include any education provided beyond grade 12".

(c) Paragraph (5) of such section 303 is amended by inserting immediately before the period at the end thereof the following: ", or any expenditures made from funds granted under title II of this Act or titles II or III of the Elementary and Secondary Education Act of 1965".

(d)(1) Paragraph (8) of such section 303 is amended by inserting "American Samoa," after "the District of Columbia,", and by inserting after "the Virgin Islands" the following: ", and for purposes of title II, such term includes the Trust Territory of the Pacific Islands".

(2) Sections 3(d) and 6(c) of such Act (20 U.S.C. 238(d), 241(c)) are each amended by inserting "American Samoa," after "Guam," each time that it appears. 64 Stat. 1102; 67 Stat. 530, 532, 535.

(e) Such section 303 is further amended by adding at the end thereof the following new paragraphs:

"(11) The term 'county' means those divisions of a State utilized by the Secretary of Commerce in compiling and reporting data regarding counties.

"(12) The term 'construction' includes the preparation of drawings and specifications for school facilities; erecting, building, acquiring, altering, remodeling, improving, or extending school facilities; and the inspection and supervision of the construction of school facilities.

"(13) The term 'school facilities' means classrooms and related facilities (including initial equipment) for free public education and interests in land (including site, grading, and improvements) on which such facilities are constructed, except that such term does not include those gymnasiums and similar facilities intended primarily for exhibitions for which admission is to be charged to the general public.

"(14) The term 'equipment' includes machinery, utilities, and built-in equipment and any necessary enclosures or structures to house them, and includes all other items necessary for the functioning of a particular facility as a facility for the provision of educational services, including items such as instructional equipment and necessary furniture, printed, published, and audio-visual instructional materials, and books, periodicals, documents, and other related materials.

"(15) For the purpose of title II, the term 'elementary school' means a day or residential school which provides elementary education, as determined under State law, and the term 'secondary school' means a day or residential school which provides secondary education, as determined under State law, except that it does not include any education provided beyond grade 12."

EXTENSION OF TITLE I OF PUBLIC LAW 874

EIGHTY-FIRST CONGRESS

SEC. 5. Sections 2(a), 3(b), and 4(a) of title I of the Act of September 30, 1950, Public Law 874, Eighty-first Congress, as amended (20 U.S.C. 237(a), 238(b), 239(a)), are each amended by striking out "1966" each place where it appears and inserting in lieu thereof "1968".

64 Stat. 1101; 67 Stat. 530, 532; 78 Stat. 1109.

TITLE II—SCHOOL LIBRARY RESOURCES, TEXTBOOKS, AND OTHER INSTRUCTIONAL MATERIALS

APPROPRIATIONS AUTHORIZED

SEC. 201. (a) The Commissioner shall carry out during the fiscal year ending June 30, 1966, and each of the four succeeding fiscal years, a program for making grants for the acquisition of school library resources, textbooks, and other printed and published instructional materials for the use of children and teachers in public and private elementary and secondary schools.

(b) For the purpose of making grants under this title, there is hereby authorized to be appropriated the sum of $100,000,000 for the fiscal year ending June 30, 1966; but for the fiscal year ending June 30, 1967, and the three succeeding fiscal years, only such sums may be appropriated as the Congress may hereafter authorize by law.

ALLOTMENT TO STATES

SEC. 202. (a) From the sums appropriated for carrying out this title for any fiscal year, the Commissioner shall reserve such amount, but not in excess of 2 per centum thereof, as he may determine and shall allot such amount among the Commonwealth of Puerto Rico, Guam, American Samoa, the Virgin Islands, and the Trust Territory of the Pacific Islands according to their respective needs for assistance under this title. From the remainder of such sums, the Commissioner shall allot to each State an amount which bears the same ratio to such remainder as the number of children enrolled in the public and private elementary and secondary schools of that State bears to the total number of children enrolled in such schools in all of the States. The number of children so enrolled shall be determined by the Commissioner on the basis of the most recent satisfactory data available to him. For purposes of this subsection, the term "State" shall not include the Commonwealth of Puerto Rico, Guam, American Samoa, the Virgin Islands, and the Trust Territory of the Pacific Islands.

(b) The amount of any State's allotment under subsection (a) for any fiscal year which the Commissioner determines will not be required for such fiscal year shall be available for reallotment from time to time, on such dates during such year as the Commissioner may fix, to other States in proportion to the original allotments to such States under subsection (a) for that year but with such proportionate amount for any of such other States being reduced to the extent it exceeds the sum the Commissioner estimates such State needs and will be able to use for such year; and the total of such reductions shall be similarly reallotted among the States whose proportionate amounts were not so reduced. Any amount reallotted to a State under this subsection during a year from funds appropriated pursuant to section 201 shall be deemed part of its allotment under section (a) for such year.

STATE PLANS

SEC. 203. (a) Any State which desires to receive grants under this title shall submit to the Commissioner a State plan, in such detail as the Commissioner deems necessary, which—

(1) designates a State agency which shall, either directly or through arrangements with other State or local public agencies, act as the sole agency for administration of the State plan;

(2) sets forth a program under which funds paid to the State from its allotment under section 202 will be expended solely for (A) acquisition of library resources (which for the purposes of this title means books, periodicals, documents, audio-visual materials, and other related library materials), textbooks, and other printed and published instructional materials for the use of children and teachers in public and private elementary and secondary schools in the State, and (B) administration of the State plan, including the development and revision of standards relating to library resources, textbooks, and other printed and published instructional materials furnished for the use of children and teachers in the public elementary and secondary schools of the State, except that the amount used for administration of the State plan shall not exceed for the fiscal year ending June 30, 1966, an amount equal to 5 per centum of the amount paid to the State under this title for that year, and for any fiscal year thereafter an amount equal to 3 per centum of the amount paid to the State under this title for that year;

(3) sets forth the criteria to be used in allocating library resources, textbooks, and other printed and published instructional materials provided under this title among the children and teachers of the State, which criteria shall—

(A) take into consideration the relative need of the children and teachers of the State for such library resources, textbooks, or other instructional materials, and

(B) provide assurance that to the extent consistent with law such library resources, textbooks, and other instructional materials will be provided on an equitable basis for the use of children and teachers in private elementary and secondary schools in the State which comply with the compulsory attendance laws of the State or are otherwise recognized by it through some procedure customarily used in the State;

(4) sets forth the criteria to be used in selecting the library resources, textbooks, and other instructional materials to be provided under this title and for determining the proportions of the State's allotment for each fiscal year which will be expended for library resources, textbooks, and other printed and published instructional materials, respectively, and the terms by which such library resources, textbooks, and other instructional materials will be made available for the use of children and teachers in the schools of the State;

(5) sets forth policies and procedures designed to assure that Federal funds made available under this title for any fiscal year will be so used as to supplement and, to the extent practical, increase the level of State, local, and private school funds that would in the absence of such Federal funds be made available for library resources, textbooks, and other printed and published instructional materials, and in no case supplant such State, local, and private school funds;

(6) sets forth such fiscal control and fund accounting procedures as may be necessary to assure proper disbursement of, and accounting for, Federal funds paid to the State (including any such funds paid by the State to any other public agency) under this title; and

(7) provides for making such reports, in such form and containing such information, as the Commissioner may reasonably require to carry out his functions under this title, and for keeping such records and for affording such access thereto as the Commissioner may find necessary to assure the correctness and verification of such reports.

(b) The Commissioner shall approve any State plan and any modification thereof which complies with the provisions of subsection (a).

PAYMENTS TO STATES

SEC. 204. (a) From the amounts allotted to each State under section 202 the Commissioner shall pay to that State an amount equal to the amount expended by the State in carrying out its State plan. Such payments may be made in installments, and in advance or by way of reimbursement, with necessary adjustments on account of overpayments or underpayments.

(b) In any State which has a State plan approved under section 203(b) and in which no State agency is authorized by law to provide library resources, textbooks, or other printed and published instructional materials for the use of children and teachers in any one or more elementary or secondary schools in such State, the Commissioner shall arrange for the provision on an equitable basis of such library resources, textbooks, or other instructional materials for such use and shall pay the cost thereof for any fiscal year ending prior to July 1, 1970, out of that State's allotment.

PUBLIC CONTROL OF LIBRARY RESOURCES, TEXTBOOKS, AND OTHER INSTRUCTIONAL MATERIAL AND TYPES WHICH MAY BE MADE AVAILABLE

SEC. 205. (a) Title to library resources, textbooks, and other printed and published instructional materials furnished pursuant to this title, and control and administration of their use, shall vest only in a public agency.

(b) The library resources, textbooks, and other printed and published instructional materials made available pursuant to this title for use of children and teachers in any school in any State shall be limited to those which have been approved by an appropriate State or local educational authority or agency for use, or are used, in a public elementary or secondary school of that State.

ADMINISTRATION OF STATE PLANS

SEC. 206. (a) The Commissioner shall not finally disapprove any State plan submitted under this title, or any modification thereof, without first affording the State agency administering the plan reasonable notice and opportunity for a hearing.

(b) Whenever the Commissioner, after reasonable notice and opportunity for hearing to such State agency, finds—

(1) that the State plan has been so changed that it no longer complies with the provisions of section 203(a), or

(2) that in the administration of the plan there is a failure to comply substantially with any such provisions,

the Commissioner shall notify such State agency that the State will not be regarded as eligible to participate in the program under this title until he is satisfied that there is no longer any such failure to comply.

JUDICIAL REVIEW

SEC. 207. (a) If any State is dissatisfied with the Commissioner's final action with respect to the approval of its State plan submitted under section 203(a) or with his final action under section 206(b), such State may, within sixty days after notice of such action, file with the United States court of appeals for the circuit in which such State is located a petition for review of that action. A copy of the petition shall be forthwith transmitted by the clerk of the court to the Commissioner. The Commissioner thereupon shall file in the court the record of the proceedings on which he based his action, as provided in section 2112 of title 28, United States Code. 72 Stat. 941.

(b) The findings of fact by the Commissioner, if supported by substantial evidence, shall be conclusive; but the court, for good cause shown, may remand the case to the Commissioner to take further evidence, and the Commissioner may thereupon make new or modified findings of fact and may modify his previous action, and shall certify to the court the record of the further proceedings. Such new or modified findings of fact shall likewise be conclusive if supported by substantial evidence.

(c) The court shall have jurisdiction to affirm the action of the Commissioner or to set it aside, in whole or in part. The judgment of the court shall be subject to review by the Supreme Court of the United States upon certiorari or certification as provided in section 1254 of title 28, United States Code. 62 Stat. 928.

TITLE III—SUPPLEMENTARY EDUCATIONAL CENTERS AND SERVICES

APPROPRIATIONS AUTHORIZED

SEC. 301. (a) The Commissioner shall carry out during the fiscal year ending June 30, 1966, and each of the four succeeding fiscal years, a program for making grants for supplementary educational centers and services, to stimulate and assist in the provision of vitally needed educational services not available in sufficient quantity or quality, and to stimulate and assist in the development and establishment of exemplary elementary and secondary school educational programs to serve as models for regular school programs.

(b) For the purpose of making grants under this title, there is hereby authorized to be appropriated the sum of $100,000,000, for the fiscal year ending June 30, 1966; but for the fiscal year ending June 30, 1967, and the 3 succeeding fiscal years, only such sums may be appropriated as the Congress may hereafter authorize by law.

APPORTIONMENT AMONG STATES

SEC. 302. (a) From the sums appropriated for carrying out this title for each fiscal year, the Commissioner shall reserve such amount, but not in excess of 2 per centum thereof, as he may determine and shall apportion such amount among the Commonwealth of Puerto Rico, Guam, American Samoa, the Virgin Islands, and the Trust Territory of the Pacific Islands, according to their respective needs for assistance under this title. From the remainder of such sums the Commissioner shall apportion $200,000 to each State and shall apportion the remainder of such sums among the States as follows:

(1) he shall apportion to each State an amount which bears the same ratio to 50 per centum of such remainder as the number of children aged five to seventeen, inclusive, in the State bears to the number of such children in all the States, and

(2) he shall apportion to each State an amount which bears the same ratio to 50 per centum of such remainder as the population of the State bears to the population of all the States.

For purposes of this subsection, the term "State" does not include the Commonwealth of Puerto Rico, Guam, American Samoa, the Virgin Islands, and the Trust Territory of the Pacific Islands.

(b) The number of children aged five to seventeen, inclusive, and the total population of a State and of all the States shall be determined by the Commissioner on the basis of the most recent satisfactory data available to him.

(c) The amount apportioned under this section to any State for the fiscal year ending June 30, 1966, shall be available for payments to applicants with approved applications in that State during that year and the next fiscal year.

(d) The amount apportioned to any State under subsection (a) for any fiscal year which the Commissioner determines will not be required for the period for which that amount is available shall be available for reapportionment from time to time, on such dates during that period as the Commissioner may fix, among other States in proportion to the amounts originally apportioned among those States under subsection (a) for that year, but with the proportionate amount for any of the other States being reduced to the extent it exceeds the sum the Commissioner estimates that State needs and will be able to use for that period; and the total of these reductions shall be similarly reapportioned among the States whose proportionate amounts were not so reduced. Any amount reapportioned to a State under this subsection from funds appropriated pursuant to section 301 for any fiscal year shall be deemed to be a part of the amount apportioned to it under subsection (a) for that year.

USES OF FEDERAL FUNDS

SEC. 303. Grants under this title may be used, in accordance with applications approved under section 304(b), for—

(a) planning for and taking other steps leading to the development of programs designed to provide supplementary educational activities and services described in paragraph (b), including pilot projects designed to test the effectiveness of plans so developed; and

(b) the establishment, maintenance, and operation of programs, including the lease or construction of necessary facilities and the acquisition of necessary equipment, designed to enrich the programs of local elementary and secondary schools and to offer a diverse range of educational experience to persons of varying talents and needs by providing supplementary educational services and activities such as—

(1) comprehensive guidance and counseling, remedial instruction, and school health, physical education, recreation, psychological, and social work services designed to enable and encourage persons to enter, remain in, or reenter educational programs, including the provision of special educational programs and study areas during periods when schools are not regularly in session;

(2) comprehensive academic services and, where appropriate, vocational guidance and counseling, for continuing adult education;

(3) developing and conducting exemplary educational programs, including dual-enrollment programs, for the purpose of stimulating the adoption of improved or new educational programs (including those programs described in section 503(a)(4)) in the schools of the State;

(4) specialized instruction and equipment for students interested in studying advanced scientific subjects, foreign languages, and other academic subjects which are not taught in the local schools or which can be provided more effectively on a centralized basis, or for persons who are handicapped or of preschool age;

(5) making available modern educational equipment and specially qualified personnel, including artists and musicians, on a temporary basis to public and other nonprofit schools, organizations, and institutions;

(6) developing, producing, and transmitting radio and television programs for classroom and other educational use;

(7) providing special educational and related services for persons who are in or from rural areas or who are or have been otherwise isolated from normal educational opportunities, including, where appropriate, the provision of mobile educational services and equipment, special home study courses, radio, television, and related forms of instruction, and visiting teachers' programs; and

(8) other specially designed educational programs which meet the purposes of this title.

APPLICATIONS FOR GRANTS AND CONDITIONS FOR APPROVAL

SEC. 304. (a) A grant under this title for a program of supplementary educational services may be made to a local educational agency or agencies, but only if there is satisfactory assurance that in the planning of that program there has been, and in the establishing and carrying out of that program there will be, participation of persons broadly representative of the cultural and educational resources of the area to be served. For the purposes of this section, the term "cultural and educational resources" includes State educational agen-

"Cultural and educational resources."

cies, institutions of higher education, nonprofit private schools, public and nonprofit private agencies such as libraries, museums, musical and artistic organizations, educational radio and television, and other cultural and educational resources. Such grants may be made only upon application to the Commissioner at such time or times, in such manner, and containing or accompanied by such information as the Commissioner deems necessary. Such applications shall—

(1) provide that the activities and services for which assistance under this title is sought will be administered by or under the supervision of the applicant;

(2) set forth a program for carrying out the purposes set forth in paragraph (a) or paragraph (b) of section 303 and provide for such methods of administration as are necessary for the proper and efficient operation of the program;

(3) set forth policies and procedures which assure that Federal funds made available under this title for any fiscal year will be so used as to supplement and, to the extent practical, increase the level of funds that would, in the absence of such Federal funds, be made available by the applicant for the purposes described in paragraphs (a) and (b) of section 303, and in no case supplant such funds;

(4) in the case of an application for assistance under this title which includes a project for construction of necessary facilities, provide satisfactory assurance (A) that reasonable provision has been made, consistent with the other uses to be made of the facilities, for areas in such facilities which are adaptable for artistic and cultural activities, (B) that upon completion of the construction title to the facilities will be in a State or local educational agency, and (C) that the requirements of section 308 will be complied with on all construction projects assisted under this title;

(5) provide for such fiscal control and fund accounting procedures as may be necessary to assure proper disbursement of and accounting for Federal funds paid to the applicant under this title; and

(6) provide for making an annual report and such other reports, in such form and containing such information, as the Commissioner may reasonably require to carry out his functions under this title and to determine the extent to which funds provided under this title have been effective in improving the educational opportunities of persons in the area served, and for keeping such records and for affording such access thereto as the Commissioner may find necessary to assure the correctness and verification of such reports.

Records.

(b) Applications for grants under this title may be approved by the Commissioner only if—

(1) the application meets the requirements set forth in subsection (a);

(2) the program set forth in the application is consistent with criteria established by the Commissioner for the purpose of achieving an equitable distribution of assistance under this title within each State, which criteria shall be developed by him on the basis of a consideration of (A) the size and population of the State, (B) the geographic distribution of the population within the State, (C) the relative need of persons in different geographic areas and in different population groups within the State for the kinds of services and activities described in paragraph (b) of

section 303, and their financial ability to provide those services and activities, and (D) the relative ability of particular local educational agencies within the State to provide those services and activities;

(3) in the case of an application for assistance for a program for carrying out the purposes described in paragraph (b) of section 303, the Commissioner determines (A) that the program will utilize the best available talents and resources and will substantially increase the educational opportunities in the area to be served by the applicant, and (B) that, to the extent consistent with the number of children enrolled in nonprofit private schools in the area to be served whose educational needs are of the type which the supplementary educational activities and services provided under the program are to meet, provision has been made for participation of such children; and

(4) the application has been submitted for review and recommendations to the State educational agency.

(c) Amendments of applications shall, except as the Commissioner may otherwise provide by or pursuant to regulations, be subject to approval in the same manner as original applications.

PAYMENTS

Sec. 305. (a) From the amounts apportioned to each State under section 302 the Commissioner shall pay to each applicant in that State which has an application approved under this title an amount equal to the total sums expended by the applicant under the application for the purposes set forth therein.

(b) Payments under this title may be made in installments and in advance or by way of reimbursement, with necessary adjustments on account of overpayments or underpayments.

ADVISORY COMMITTEE

Sec. 306. (a) The Commissioner shall establish in the Office of Education an Advisory Committee on Supplementary Educational Centers and Services, consisting of the Commissioner, who shall be Chairman, and eight members appointed, without regard to the civil service laws, by the Commissioner with the approval of the Secretary.

(b) The Advisory Committee shall advise the Commissioner (1) on the action to be taken with regard to each application for a grant under this title, and (2) in the preparation of general regulations and with respect to policy matters arising in the administration of this title, including the development of criteria for approval of applications thereunder. The Commissioner may appoint such special advisory and technical experts and consultants as may be useful in carrying out the functions of the Advisory Committee.

(c) Members of the Advisory Committee shall, while serving on the business of the Advisory Committee, be entitled to receive compensation at rates fixed by the Secretary, but not exceeding $100 per day, including travel time; and, while so serving away from their homes or regular places of business, they may be allowed travel expenses, including per diem in lieu of subsistence, as authorized by section 5 of the Administrative Expenses Act of 1946 (5 U.S.C. 73b-2) for persons in the Government service employed intermittently. 60 Stat. 808; 75 Stat. 339, 340.

RECOVERY OF PAYMENTS

SEC. 307. If within twenty years after completion of any construction for which Federal funds have been paid under this title—

(a) the owner of the facility shall cease to be a State or local educational agency, or

(b) the facility shall cease to be used for the educational and related purposes for which it was constructed, unless the Commissioner determines in accordance with regulations that there is good cause for releasing the applicant or other owner from the obligation to do so,

the United States shall be entitled to recover from the applicant or other owner of the facility an amount which bears to the then value of the facility (or so much thereof as constituted an approved project or projects) the same ratio as the amount of such Federal funds bore to the cost of the facility financed with the aid of such funds. Such value shall be determined by agreement of the parties or by action brought in the United States district court for the district in which the facility is situated.

LABOR STANDARDS

SEC. 308. All laborers and mechanics employed by contractors or subcontractors on all construction projects assisted under this title shall be paid wages at rates not less than those prevailing on similar construction in the locality as determined by the Secretary of Labor in accordance with the Davis-Bacon Act, as amended (40 U.S.C. 276a—
49 Stat. 1011; 276a-5). The Secretary of Labor shall have with respect to the labor
78 Stat. 238. standards specified in this section the authority and functions set forth in Reorganization Plan Numbered 14 of 1950 (15 F.R. 3176; 5 U.S.C.
64 Stat. 1267. 133z-15) and section 2 of the Act of June 13, 1934, as amended (40
63 Stat. 108. U.S.C. 276c).

TITLE IV—EDUCATIONAL RESEARCH AND TRAINING

SEC. 401. The second section of the Act of July 26, 1954 (20 U.S.C.
68 Stat. 533. 332), entitled "An Act to authorize cooperative research in education", is redesignated as section 3 and the material which precedes it is amended to read as follows:

"PURPOSE

"SEC. 1. The purpose of this Act is to enable the Office of Education more effectively to accomplish the purposes and to perform the duties for which it was originally established.

"EDUCATIONAL RESEARCH AND RESEARCH TRAINING

"SEC. 2. (a)(1) The Commissioner of Education (hereinafter in this Act referred to as the 'Commissioner') is authorized to make grants to universities and colleges and other public or private agencies, institutions, and organizations and to individuals, for research, surveys, and demonstrations in the field of education (including programs described in section 503(a)(4) of the Elementary and Secondary Education Act of 1965), and for the dissemination of information derived from educational research (including but not limited to information concerning promising educational practices developed under programs carried out under the Elementary and Secondary Education Act of 1965) and, without regard to sections 3648 and 3709 of the Revised Statutes (31 U.S.C. 529; 41 U.S.C. 5), to provide by contracts or jointly financed cooperative arrangements with them for the conduct of such activities; except that no such grant may be made to a private agency, organization, or institution other than a nonprofit one.

"(2) No grant shall be made or contract or jointly financed cooperative arrangement entered into under this subsection until the Commissioner has obtained the advice and recommendations of a panel of specialists who are not employees of the Federal Government and who are competent to evaluate the proposals as to the soundness of their design, the possibilities of securing productive results, the adequacy of resources to conduct the proposed research, surveys, or demonstrations, and their relationship to other similar educational research or dissemination programs already completed or in progress.

"(b) The Commissioner is authorized to make grants to public and other nonprofit universities and colleges and to other public or nonprofit agencies, institutions, and organizations to assist them in providing training in research in the field of education (including such research described in section 503(a)(4) of the Elementary and Secondary Education Act of 1965), including the development and strengthening of training staff and curricular capability for such training. Grants under this subsection may, when so authorized by the Commissioner, also be used by such grantees (1) in establishing and maintaining research traineeships, internships, personnel exchanges, and pre- and post-doctoral fellowships, and for stipends and allowances (including traveling and subsistence expenses) for fellows and others undergoing training and their dependents not in excess of such maximum amounts as may be prescribed by the Commissioner, or (2), where the grantee is a State educational agency, in providing for such traineeships, internships, personnel exchanges, and fellowships either directly or through arrangements with public or other nonprofit institutions or organizations. No grant shall be made under this subsection for training in sectarian instruction or, for work to be done in an institution, or a department or branch of an institution, whose program is specifically for the education of students to prepare them to become ministers of religion or to enter upon some other religious vocation or to prepare them to teach theological subjects.

"(c) In addition to the authority granted by section 603(b) of the Elementary and Secondary Education Act of 1965, funds available to the Commissioner for grants or contracts or jointly financed cooperative arrangements under this section shall, with the approval of the Secretary, be available for transfer to any other Federal agency for use (in accordance with an interagency agreement) by such agency (alone or in combination with funds of that agency) for purposes for which such transferred funds could be otherwise expended by the Commissioner under the foregoing provisions of this section, and the Commissioner is likewise authorized to accept and expend funds of any other Federal agency for use under this section.

Report to Congress.

"(d) The Commissioner shall transmit to the Congress annually a report concerning the research, surveys, and demonstrations, the information disseminating activities, and the training in research initiated under this Act, the recommendations made by research specialists pursuant to subsection (a)(2), and any action taken with respect to such recommendations."

CONFORMING AMENDMENTS

Ante, p. 44.

SEC. 402. The section of such Act redesignated as section 3 is amended by striking out "this Act" and inserting in lieu thereof "section 2".

CONSTRUCTION OF REGIONAL FACILITIES FOR RESEARCH AND RELATED PURPOSES

SEC. 403. Such Act is further amended by adding the following new sections at the end thereof:

"CONSTRUCTION OF REGIONAL FACILITIES FOR RESEARCH AND RELATED PURPOSES

"SEC. 4. (a) There is authorized to be appropriated over a period of five fiscal years beginning with the fiscal year ending June 30, 1966, $100,000,000 in the aggregate, to enable the Commissioner to carry out the purposes of this section. Sums so appropriated shall remain available until expended for payments with respect to projects for which applications have been filed under this section before July 1, 1970, and approved by the Commissioner before July 1, 1971.

"(b) Whenever the Commissioner finds that the purposes of this Act can best be achieved through the construction of a facility for research, or for research and related purposes (as defined in this section), and that such facility would be of particular value to the Nation or a region thereof as a national or regional resource for research or related purposes, he may make a grant for part or all of the cost of constructing such facility to a university, college, or other appropriate public or nonprofit private agency or institution competent to engage in the types of activity for which the facility is to constructed, or to a combination of such agencies or institutions, or may construct or make arrangements for constructing such facility through contracts for paying part or all of the cost of construction or otherwise. The Commissioner may, where he deems such action appropriate, make arrangements, by contract or otherwise, for the operation of such facilities or may make contributions toward the cost of such operation of facilities of this nature whether or not constructed pursuant to, or with the aid provided under, this section. Title to any facility constructed under this section, if vested in the United States, may be transferred by the Commissioner on behalf of the United States to any such college or university or other public or nonprofit private agency or institution, but such transfer shall be made subject to the condition that the facility will be operated for the purposes for which it was constructed and to such other conditions as the Commissioner deems necessary to carry out the objectives of this title and to protect the interests of the United States.

"(c) All laborers and mechanics employed by contractors or subcontractors in the performance of work on construction of any project under this section shall be paid wages at rates not less than those prevailing on similar construction in the locality as determined by the Secretary of Labor in accordance with the Davis-Bacon Act, as amended (40 U.S.C. 276a—276a-5). The Secretary of Labor shall have, with respect to the labor standards specified in this clause, the authority and functions set forth in Reorganization Plan Numbered 14 of 1950 (15 F.R. 3176; 5 U.S.C. 133z-15), and section 2 of the Act of June 13, 1934, as amended (40 U.S.C. 276c).

49 Stat. 1011;
78 Stat. 238.
64 Stat. 1267.
63 Stat. 108.

"(d) Payments under this section shall be made in advance or by way of reimbursement, in such installments consistent with construction progress, and on such conditions as the Commissioner may determine.

"(e) As used in this section, the term 'research and related purposes' means research, research training, surveys, or demonstrations in the field of education, or the dissemination of information derived therefrom, or all of such activities, including (but without limitation) experimental schools, except that such term does not include research, research training, surveys, or demonstrations in the field of sectarian instruction or the dissemination of information derived therefrom. "Research and related purposes."

"DEFINITIONS

"SEC. 5. As used in this Act—

"(1) The term 'State' includes, in addition to the several States of the Union, the Commonwealth of Puerto Rico, the District of Columbia, Guam, American Samoa, and the Virgin Islands.

"(2) The term 'State educational agency' means the State board of education or other agency or officer primarily responsible for the State supervision of public elementary and secondary schools, or, if there is no such officer or agency, an officer or agency designated by the Governor or by State law.

"(3) The term 'nonprofit' as applied to any agency, organization, or institution means an agency, organization, or institution owned and operated by one or more nonprofit corporations or associations no part of the net earnings of which inures, or may lawfully inure, to the benefit of any private shareholder or individual.

"(4) The terms 'construction' and 'cost of construction' include (A) the construction of new buildings and the expansion, remodeling, and alteration of existing buildings, including architects' fees, but not including the cost of acquisition of land or off-site improvements, and (B) equipping new buildings and existing buildings, whether or not expanded, remodeled, or altered.

"SHORT TITLE

"SEC. 6. This Act may be cited as the 'Cooperative Research Act'."

TITLE V—GRANTS TO STRENGTHEN STATE DEPARTMENTS OF EDUCATION

APPROPRIATIONS AUTHORIZED

SEC. 501. (a) The Commissioner shall carry out during the fiscal year ending June 30, 1966, and each of the four succeeding fiscal years, a program for making grants to stimulate and assist States in strengthening the leadership resources of their State educational agencies, and to assist those agencies in the establishment and improvement of programs to identify and meet the educational needs of States.

(b) For the purpose of making grants under this title, there is hereby authorized to be appropriated the sum of $25,000,000 for the fiscal year ending June 30, 1966; but for the fiscal year ending June 30, 1967, and the three succeeding fiscal years, only such sums may be appropriated as the Congress may hereafter authorize by law.

APPORTIONMENT AMONG STATES

SEC. 502. (a)(1) From 85 per centum of the sums appropriated for carrying out this title for each fiscal year, the Commissioner shall reserve such amount, but not in excess of 2 per centum of such 85 per centum of such sums, as he may determine and shall apportion such amount among the Commonwealth of Puerto Rico, Guam, American Samoa, and the Virgin Islands according to their respective needs for assistance under this title. From the remainder of such 85 per centum of such sums the Commissioner shall apportion $100,000 to each State, and shall apportion to each State such part of the remainder of such 85 per centum of such sums as the number of public school pupils in the State bears to the number of public school pupils in all the States, as determined by the Commissioner on the basis of the most recent satisfactory data available to him. For purposes of this paragraph, the term 'State' does not include the Commonwealth of Puerto Rico, Guam, American Samoa, and the Virgin Islands.

(2) Fifteen per centum of the sums appropriated pursuant to section 501 for each fiscal year shall be reserved by the Commissioner for grants for special projects pursuant to section 505.

(b)(1) The amount apportioned to any State under paragraph (1) of subsection (a) for any fiscal year which the Commissioner determines will not be required for that year shall be available for reapportionment from time to time, on such dates during that year as the Commissioner may fix, to other States in proportion to the amounts originally apportioned among those States under subsection (a)(1) for that year, but with the proportionate amount for any of the other States being reduced to the extent it exceeds the sum the Commissioner estimates that State needs and will be able to use for that year; and the total of these reductions shall be similarly reapportioned among the States whose proportionate amounts were not so reduced. Any amount reapportioned to a State under this subsection from funds appropriated pursuant to section 501 for any fiscal year shall be deemed part of the amount apportioned to it under subsection (a)(1) for that year.

(2) In accordance with regulations of the Commissioner any State may file with him a request that a specified portion of the amount apportioned to it under subsection (a)(1) be added to the amount apportioned to another State under that subsection for the purpose of meeting a portion of the Federal share (as defined in section 503 (b)) of the cost of carrying out one or more programs or activities under an approved application of that other State. If the Commissioner finds that the programs or activities with respect to which the request is made would meet needs of the State making the request and that use of the specified portion of the amount apportioned to that State, as requested by it, would assist in carrying out the purposes of this title, that portion shall be added to the amount apportioned to the other State under subsection (a)(1) to be used for the purpose referred to above. The Federal share of the total funds expended for such programs or activities shall be adjusted on the basis of the proportion of such total funds so expended by each participating State from the amounts originally apportioned to each such State.

GRANTS FROM APPORTIONED FUNDS

Sec. 503. (a) From the amount apportioned to any State for any fiscal year under section 502 the Commissioner may, upon approval of an application or applications therefor submitted to him by such State through the State educational agency, make a grant or grants to such agency equal to the Federal share of expenditures incurred by such agency for the planning of, and for programs for, the development, improvement, or expansion of activities promoting the purposes set forth in section 501(a) and more particularly described in such application and for which such application is approved, such as—

(1) educational planning on a statewide basis, including the identification of educational problems, issues, and needs in the State and the evaluation on a periodic or continuing basis of education programs in the State;

(2) providing support or services for the comprehensive and compatible recording, collecting, processing, analyzing, interpreting, storing, retrieving, and reporting of State and local educational data, including the use of automated data systems;

(3) dissemination or support for the dissemination of information relating to the condition, progress, and needs of education in the State;

(4) programs for conducting, sponsoring, or cooperating in educational research and demonstration programs and projects such as (A) establishing and maintaining curriculum research and innovation centers to assist in locating and evaluating curriculum research findings, (B) discovering and testing new educational ideas (including new uses of printed and audio-visual media) and more effective educational practices, and putting into use those which show promise of success, and (C) studying ways to improve the legal and organizational structure for education and the management and administration of education in the State;

(5) publication and distribution, or support for the publication and distribution, of curricular materials collected and developed at curriculum research centers and elsewhere;

(6) programs to improve the quality of teacher preparation, including student-teaching arrangements, in cooperation with institutions of higher education and local educational agencies;

(7) studies or support for studies concerning the financing of public education in the State;

(8) support for statewide programs designed to measure the educational achievement of pupils;

(9) training and otherwise developing the competency of individuals who serve State or local educational agencies and provide leadership, administrative, or specialist services throughout the State, or throughout the area served by a local educational agency, through the initiation, improvement, and expansion of activities such as (A) sabbatical leave programs, (B) fellowships and traineeships (including educational expenses and the cost of travel) for State educational agency personnel to pursue graduate studies, and (C) conducting institutes, workshops, and conferences (including related costs of operation and payment of the expenses of participants); and

(10) providing local educational agencies and the schools of those agencies with consultative and technical assistance and services relating to academic subjects and to particular aspects of edu-

cation such as the education of the handicapped, school building design and utilization, school social work, the utilization of modern instructional materials and equipment, transportation, educational administrative procedures, and school health, physical education, and recreation.

(b) (1) For the purposes of this section the Federal share for any State shall be 100 per centum for fiscal years ending prior to July 1, 1967. Thereafter the Federal share for any State shall be 100 per centum less the State percentage, except that (A) the Federal share shall in no case be more than 66 per centum or less than 50 per centum, and (B) the Federal share for the Commonwealth of Puerto Rico, Guam, American Samoa, and the Virgin Islands shall be 66 per centum. The "State percentage" for any State shall be that percentage which bears the same ratio to 50 per centum as the per capita income of that State bears to the per capita income of all the States (excluding the Commonwealth of Puerto Rico, Guam, American Samoa, and the Virgin Islands).

(2) The Federal share for each State for the fiscal years beginning July 1, 1967, and July 1, 1968, shall be promulgated by the Commissioner between July 1 and August 31, 1966, and the Federal share for each State for the fiscal year beginning July 1, 1969, shall be promulgated by the Commissioner between July 1 and August 31, 1968. Such Federal share shall be computed on the basis of the average of the per capita incomes of each State and of all the States (excluding the Commonwealth of Puerto Rico, Guam, American Samoa, and the Virgin Islands) for the three most recent consecutive years for which satisfactory data are available from the Department of Commerce.

APPROVAL OF APPLICATIONS FOR GRANTS FROM APPORTIONED FUNDS

SEC. 504. An application for a grant under section 503 may be approved by the Commissioner only upon his determination that—

(a) each of the proposed projects, programs, and activities for which it is approved meets the requirements of section 503(a) and will make a significant contribution to strengthening the leadership resources of the applicant or its ability to participate effectively in meeting the educational needs of the State;

(b) the application contains or is supported by adequate assurance that Federal funds made available under the approved application will be so used as to supplement, and to the extent practical, increase the amounts of State funds that would in the absence of such Federal funds be made available for projects and activities which meet the requirements of section 503(a);

(c) the application sets forth such fiscal control and fund accounting procedures as may be necessary to assure proper disbursement of, and accounting for, Federal funds paid to the State (including any such funds paid by the State to agencies, institutions, or organizations) under this title; and

Records.

(d) the application provides for making such reports, in such form and containing such information, as the Commissioner may require to carry out his functions under this title, and for keeping such records and for affording such access thereto as the Commissioner may find necessary to assure the correctness and verification of such reports.

SPECIAL PROJECT GRANTS

SEC. 505. Fifteen per centum of the sums appropriated pursuant to section 501 for each fiscal year shall be used by the Commissioner to make grants to State educational agencies to pay part of the cost of experimental projects for developing State leadership or for the establishment of special services which, in the judgment of the Commissioner, hold promise of making a substantial contribution to the solution of problems common to the State educational agencies of all or several States.

PAYMENTS

SEC. 506. Payments pursuant to grants under this title may be made in installments, and in advance or by way of reimbursement, with necessary adjustments on account of overpayments or underpayments, as the Commissioner may determine.

INTERCHANGE OF PERSONNEL WITH STATES

SEC. 507. (a) For the purposes of this section, the term "State" means a State or any agency of a State engaged in activities in the field of education, but it does not include a local educational agency; and the term "Office" means the Office of Education.

(b) The Commissioner is authorized, through agreements or otherwise, to arrange for assignment of officers and employees of States to the Office and assignment of officers and employees in the Office to States, for work which the Commissioner determines will aid the Office in more effective discharge of its responsibilities as authorized by law, including cooperation with States and the provision of technical or other assistance. The period of assignment of any officer or employee under an arrangement shall not exceed two years.

(c)(1) Officers and employees in the Office assigned to any State pursuant to this section shall be considered, during such assignment, to be (A) on detail to a regular work assignment in the Office, or (B) on leave without pay from their positions in the Office.

(2) Persons considered to be so detailed shall remain as officers or employees, as the case may be, in the Office for all purposes, except that the supervision of their duties during the period of detail may be governed by agreement between the Office and the State involved.

(3) In the case of persons so assigned and on leave without pay—

(A) if the rate of compensation (including allowances) for their employment by the State is less than the rate of compensation (including allowances) they would be receiving had they continued in their regular assignment in the Office, they may receive supplemental salary payments from the Office in the amount considered by the Commissioner to be justified, but not at a rate in excess of the difference between the State rate and the Office rate; and

(B) they may be granted annual leave and sick leave to the extent authorized by law, but only in circumstances considered by the Commissioner to justify approval of such leave.

Such officers and employees on leave without pay shall, notwithstanding any other provision of law, be entitled—

(C) to continuation of their insurance under the Federal Employees' Group Life Insurance Act of 1954, and coverage under the Federal Employees Health Benefits Act of 1959, so long

68 Stat. 736.
5 USC 2091 note.
73 Stat. 708.
5 USC 3001 note.

as the Office continues to collect the employee's contribution from the officer or employee involved and to transmit for timely deposit into the funds created under such Acts the amount of the employee's contributions and the Government's contribution from appropriations of the Office; and

(D) to credit the period of their assignment under the arrangement under this section toward periodic or longevity step increases and, upon payment into the civil service retirement and disability fund of the percentage of their State salary, and of their supplemental salary payments, if any, which would have been deducted from a like Federal salary for the period of such assignment and payment by the Commissioner into such fund of the amount which would have been payable by him during the period of such assignment with respect to a like Federal salary, to treat (notwithstanding the provisions of the Independent Offices Appropriation Act,
72 Stat. 1064. 1959, under the head "Civil Service Retirement and Disability
5 USC 2267 note. Fund") their service during such period as service within the
70 Stat. 743. meaning of the Civil Service Retirement Act;

5 USC 2251 note. except that no officer or employee or his beneficiary may receive any benefits under the Civil Service Retirement Act, the Federal Employees Health Benefits Act of 1959, or the Federal Employees' Group Life Insurance Act of 1954, based on service during an assignment hereunder for which the officer or employee or (if he dies without making such election) his beneficiary elects to receive benefits, under any State retirement or insurance law or program, which the Civil Service Commission determines to be similar. The Office shall deposit currently in the funds created under the Federal Employees' Group
68 Stat. 736. Life Insurance Act of 1954, the Federal Employees Health Benefits
5 USC 2091 note. Act of 1959, and the civil service retirement and disability fund,
73 Stat. 708. respectively, the amount of the Government's contribution under these
5 USC 3001 note. Acts on account of service with respect to which employee contributions are collected as provided in subparagraph (C) and the amount of the Government's contribution under the Civil Service Retirement Act on account of service with respect to which payments (of the amount which would have been deducted under that Act) referred to in subparagraph (D) are made to such civil service retirement and disability fund.

(4) Any such officer or employee on leave without pay who suffers disability or death as a result of personal injury sustained while in the performance of his duty during an assignment hereunder, shall be treated, for the purposes of the Federal Employees' Compensation
39 Stat. 742. Act, as though he were an employee, as defined in such Act, who had
5 USC 751 note. sustained such injury in the performance of duty. When such person (or his dependents, in case of death) entitled by reason of injury or death to benefits under that Act is also entitled to benefits from a State for the same injury or death, he (or his dependents in case of death) shall elect which benefits he will receive. Such election shall be made within one year after the injury or death, or such further time as the Secretary of Labor may for good cause allow, and when made shall be irrevocable unless otherwise provided by law.

(d) Assignment of any officer or employee in the Office to a State under this section may be made with or without reimbursement by the State for the compensation (or supplementary compensation), travel and transportation expenses (to or from the place of assignment), and allowances, or any part thereof, of such officer or employee during the period of assignment, and any such reimbursement shall be credited to the appropriation utilized for paying such compensation, travel or transportation expenses, or allowances.

(e) Appropriations to the Office shall be available, in accordance with the standardized Government travel regulations, for the expenses of travel of officers and employees assigned to States under an arrangement under this section on either a detail or leave-without-pay basis and, in accordance with applicable law, orders, and regulations, for expenses of transportation of their immediate families and expenses of transportation of their household goods and personal effects, in connection with the travel of such officers and employees to the location of their posts of assignment and their return to their official stations.

(f) Officers and employees of States who are assigned to the Office under an arrangement under this section may (1) be given appointments in the Office covering the periods of such assignments, or (2) be considered to be on detail to the Office. Appointments of persons so assigned may be made without regard to the civil service laws. Persons so appointed in the Office shall be paid at rates of compensation determined in accordance with the Classification Act of 1949, and shall not be considered to be officers or employees of the Office for the purposes of (1) the Civil Service Retirement Act, (2) the Federal Employees' Group Life Insurance Act of 1954, or (3) unless their appointments result in the loss of coverage in a group health benefits plan whose premium has been paid in whole or in part by a State contribution, the Federal Employees Health Benefits Act of 1959. State officers and employees who are assigned to the Office without appointment shall not be considered to be officers or employees of the Office, except as provided in subsection (g), nor shall they be paid a salary or wage by the Office during the period of their assignment. The supervision of the duties of such persons during the assignment may be governed by agreement between the Commissioner and the State involved.

63 Stat. 954; 78 Stat. 400. 5 USC 1071 note. 70 Stat. 743. 5 USC 2251 note. 68 Stat. 736. 5 USC 2091 note. 73 Stat. 708. 5 USC 3001 note.

Conflict-of-interest.

(g) (1) Any State officer or employee who is assigned to the Office without appointment shall nevertheless be subject to the provisions of sections 203, 205, 207, 208, and 209 of title 18 of the United States Code.

76 Stat. 1121.

(2) Any State officer or employee who is given an appointment while assigned to the Office, or who is assigned to the Office without appointment, under an arrangement under this section, and who suffers disability or death as a result of personal injury sustained while in the performance of his duty during such assignment shall be treated, for the purpose of the Federal Employees' Compensation Act, as though he were an employee, as defined in such Act, who had sustained such injury in the performance of duty. When such person (or his dependents, in case of death) entitled by reason of injury or death to benefits under that Act is also entitled to benefits from a State for the same injury or death, he (or his dependents, in case of death) shall elect which benefits he will receive. Such election shall be made within one year after the injury or death, or such further time as the Secretary of Labor may for good cause allow, and when made shall be irrevocable unless otherwise provided by law.

39 Stat. 742. 5 USC 751 note.

(h) The appropriations to the Office shall be available, in accordance with the standardized Government travel regulations, during the period of assignment and in the case of travel to and from their places of assignment or appointment, for the payment of expenses of travel of persons assigned to, or given appointments by, the Office under an arrangement under this section.

(i) All arrangements under this section for assignment of officers or employees in the Office to States or for assignments of officers or employees of States to the Office shall be made in accordance with regulations of the Commissioner.

ADMINISTRATION OF STATE PLANS

SEC. 508. (a) The Commissioner shall not finally disapprove any application submitted under section 504, or any modification thereof, without first affording the State educational agency submitting the application reasonable notice and opportunity for a hearing.

(b) Whenever the Commissioner, after reasonable notice and opportunity for hearing to the State educational agency administering a program under an application approved under this title, finds—

(1) that the application has been so changed that it no longer complies with the provisions of section 504(a), or

(2) that in the administration of the plan there is a failure to comply substantially with any such provision,

the Commissioner shall notify such State educational agency that the State will not be regarded as eligible to participate in the program under this title until he is satisfied that there is no longer any such failure to comply.

JUDICIAL REVIEW

SEC. 509. (a) If any State is dissatisfied with the Commissioner's final action with respect to the approval of an application submitted under section 504(a) or with his final action under section 508(b), such State may, within sixty days after notice of such action, file with the United States court of appeals for the circuit in which such State is located a petition for review of that action. A copy of the petition shall be forthwith transmitted by the clerk of the court to the Commissioner. The Commissioner thereupon shall file in the court the record of the proceedings on which he based his action as provided in
72 Stat. 941. section 2112 of title 28, United States Code.

(b) The findings of fact by the Commissioner, if supported by substantial evidence, shall be conclusive; but the court, for good cause shown, may remand the case to the Commissioner to take further evidence, and the Commissioner may thereupon make new or modified findings of fact and may modify his previous action, and shall certify to the court the record of the further proceedings. Such new or modified findings of fact shall likewise be conclusive if supported by substantial evidence.

(c) The court shall have jurisdiction to affirm the action of the Commissioner or to set it aside, in whole or in part. The judgment of the court shall be subject to review by the Supreme Court of the United States upon certiorari or certification as provided in section 1254 of
62 Stat. 928. title 28, United States Code.

PERIODIC REVIEW OF PROGRAM AND LAWS

SEC. 510. (a) The Secretary shall, within ninety days after the date of enactment of this title, appoint an Advisory Council on State Departments of Education for the purpose of reviewing the administration of the programs for which funds are appropriated pursuant to this title and making recommendations for improvement of such administration, and reviewing the status of and making recommendations with respect to such programs and this title and with respect to other Acts under which funds are appropriated to assist State educational agencies to administer Federal programs relating to education.

(b) The Council shall be appointed by the Secretary without regard to the civil service laws and shall consist of twelve persons who shall, to the extent possible, include persons familiar with the educational needs of the Nation, persons familiar with the administration of State and local educational programs, and persons representative of the general public.

(c) The Secretary is authorized to engage such technical assistance as may be required to carry out the functions of the Council, and the Secretary shall, in addition, make available to the Council such secretarial, clerical, and other assistance and such pertinent data prepared by the Department of Health, Education, and Welfare as it may require to carry out such functions.

(d) The Council shall make an annual report of its findings and recommendations (including recommendations for changes in the provisions of this title and of other education Acts) to the Secretary not later than March 31 of each calendar year beginning after the enactment of this title. The Secretary shall transmit each such report to the President and the Congress together with his comments and recommendations.

Report to President and Congress.

(e) Members of the Council who are not regular full-time employees of the United States shall, while serving on business of the Council, be entitled to receive compensation at rates fixed by the Secretary, but not exceeding $100 per day, including travel time; and while so serving away from their homes or regular places of business, they may be allowed travel expenses, including per diem in lieu of subsistence, as authorized by section 5 of the Administrative Expenses Act of 1946 (5 U.S.C. 73b-2) for persons in Government service employed intermittently.

60 Stat. 808; 75 Stat. 339, 340.

TITLE VI—GENERAL PROVISIONS

DEFINITIONS

SEC. 601. As used in titles II, III, and V of this Act—

(a) The term "Commissioner" means the Commissioner of Education.

(b) The term "construction" means (1) erection of new or expansion of existing structures, and the acquisition and installation of equipment therefor; or (2) acquisition of existing structures not owned by any agency or institution making application for assistance under this Act; or (3) remodeling or alteration (including the acquisition, installation, modernization, or replacement of equipment) of existing structures; or (4) a combination of any two or more of the foregoing.

(c) The term "elementary school" means a day or residential school which provides elementary education, as determined under State law.

(d) The term "equipment" includes machinery, utilities, and built-in equipment and any necessary enclosures or structures to house them, and includes all other items necessary for the functioning of a particular facility as a facility for the provision of educational services, including items such as instructional equipment and necessary furniture, printed, published, and audio-visual instructional materials, and books, periodicals, documents, and other related materials.

(e) The term "institution of higher education" means an educational institution in any State which—

(1) admits as regular students only individuals having a certificate of graduation from a high school, or the recognized equivalent of such a certificate;

(2) is legally authorized within such State to provide a program of education beyond high school;

(3) provides an educational program for which it awards a bachelor's degree, or provides not less than a two-year program which is acceptable for full credit toward such a degree, or offers a two-year program in engineering, mathematics, or the physical or biological sciences which is designed to prepare the student to work as a technician and at a semiprofessional level in engineering, scientific, or other technological fields which require the understanding and application of basic engineering, scientific, or mathematical principles or knowledge;

(4) is a public or other nonprofit institution; and

(5) is accredited by a nationally recognized accrediting agency or association listed by the Commissioner pursuant to this paragraph or, if not so accredited, is an institution whose credits are accepted, on transfer, by not less than three institutions which are so accredited, for credit on the same basis as if transferred from an institution so accredited: *Provided, however*, That in the case of an institution offering a two-year program in engineering, mathematics, or the physical or biological sciences which is designed to prepare the student to work as a technician and at a semiprofessional level in engineering, scientific, or technological fields which require the understanding and application of basic engineering, scientific, or mathematical principles or knowledge, if the Commissioner determines that there is no nationally recognized accrediting agency or association qualified to accredit such institutions, he shall appoint an advisory committee, composed of persons specially qualified to evaluate training provided by such institutions, which shall prescribe the standards of content, scope, and quality which must be met in order to qualify such institutions to participate under this Act and shall also determine whether particular institutions meet such standards. For the purposes of this paragraph the Commissioner shall publish a list of nationally recognized accrediting agencies or associations which he determines to be reliable authority as to the quality of education or training offered.

(f) The term "local educational agency" means a public board of education or other public authority legally constituted within a State for either administrative control or direction of, or to perform a service function for, public elementary or secondary schools in a city, county, township, school district, or other political subdivision of a State, or such combination of school districts or counties as are recognized in a State as an administrative agency for its public elementary or secondary schools. Such term also includes any other public institution or agency having administrative control and direction of a public elementary or secondary school.

(g) The term "nonprofit" as applied to a school, agency, organization, or institution means a school, agency, organization, or institution owned and operated by one or more nonprofit corporations or associations no part of the net earnings of which inures, or may lawfully inure, to the benefit of any private shareholder or individual.

(h) The term "secondary school" means a day or residential school which provides secondary education, as determined under State law, except that it does not include any education provided beyond grade 12.

(i) The term "Secretary" means the Secretary of Health, Education, and Welfare.

(j) The term "State" includes, in addition to the several States of the Union, the Commonwealth of Puerto Rico, the District of Columbia, Guam, American Samoa, and the Virgin Islands and for purposes of title II and title III, such term includes the Trust Territory of the Pacific Islands.

(k) The term "State educational agency" means the State board of education or other agency or officer primarily responsible for the State supervision of public elementary and secondary schools, or, if there is no such officer or agency, an officer or agency designated by the Governor or by State law.

ADVISORY COUNCILS

SEC. 602. (a) The Commissioner may, without regard to the civil service laws, and subject to the Secretary's approval in such cases as the Secretary may prescribe, from time to time appoint, in addition to the advisory councils and committees authorized in preceding titles, an advisory council of ten members to advise and consult with the Commissioner with respect to his functions under this law.

(b) Members of such an advisory council who are not regular full-time employees of the United States shall, while attending meetings or conferences of such council or otherwise engaged on business of such council, be entitled to receive compensation at a rate fixed by the Secretary, but not exceeding $100 per diem, including travel time, and, while so serving away from their homes or regular places of business, they may be allowed travel expenses, including per diem in lieu of subsistence, as authorized by section 5 of the Administrative Expenses Act of 1946 (5 U.S.C. 73b–2) for persons in the Government service employed intermittently.

60 Stat. 808; 75 Stat. 339, 340.

FEDERAL ADMINISTRATION

SEC. 603. (a) The Commissioner may delegate any of his functions under this Act or any Act amended by this Act, except the making of regulations, to any officer or employee of the Office of Education.

(b) In administering the provisions of this Act or any Act amended by this Act, the Commissioner is authorized to utilize the services and facilities of any agency of the Federal Government and of any other public or nonprofit agency or institution in accordance with appropriate agreements, and to pay for such services either in advance or by way of reimbursement, as may be agreed upon.

FEDERAL CONTROL OF EDUCATION PROHIBITED

SEC. 604. Nothing contained in this Act shall be construed to authorize any department, agency, officer, or employee of the United States to exercise any direction, supervision, or control over the curriculum, program of instruction, administration, or personnel of any educational institution or school system, or over the selection of library resources, textbooks, or other printed or published instructional materials by any educational institution or school system.

LIMITATION ON PAYMENTS UNDER THIS ACT

SEC. 605. Nothing contained in this Act shall be construed to authorize the making of any payment under this Act, or under any Act amended by this Act, for religious worship or instruction.

Approved April 11, 1965.

LEGISLATIVE HISTORY:

HOUSE REPORT No. 143 (Comm. on Education & Labor).
SENATE REPORT No. 146 (Comm. on Labor & Public Welfare).
CONGRESSIONAL RECORD, Vol. 111 (1965):
Mar. 24-25: Considered in House.
Mar. 26: Considered and passed House.
Apr. 6-8: Considered in Senate.
Apr. 9: Considered and passed Senate.

APPENDIX B
REGULATIONS AND GUIDELINES

INTRODUCTION

The following excerpts (the first four pages in each case) from the *Regulations* and the *Guidelines* governing the administration of Title I of ESEA are included in the appendix in order to give the reader a sample of their respective function and style. Similar *Regulations* and *Guidelines* exist, of course, for each operating title in ESEA.

Regulations are written in precise legal language. Substantial attention is given to the definition of terms and to specific powers, authorities, and discretions permitted under the Act. *Regulations* become in essence the legal bible for those applying for Federal funds under Title I. As a part of The Code of Federal Regulations, ESEA *Regulations* have the force of law.

In contrast, the *Guidelines* for Title I are written almost in narrative style, and are issued as an administrative service. Administrative responsibilities of the United States Commissioner, the State educational agencies, and local educational agencies are, for example, summarized but not elaborated with precision. Sections dealing with the substantive aspects of Title I provisions provide in a readable, summary fashion what is spelled out in far greater detail by the *Regulations*. In addition to what has been excerpted for this appendix, the *Guidelines* include exhibits of forms to be used in the Description of State Program Organization and Administration, Quarterly Report of Obligations, Annual Financial Report, Record of Project Transactions, and Quarterly Disbursement and Estimated Requirement of Federal Funds, as well as summary material on other sections of the title and instructions on how to develop project designs and evaluations.

The *Guidelines,* in short, map the forest; the *Regulations* describe and define the trees.

REGULATIONS

Title I of Public Law 89–10, the Elementary and Secondary Education Act of 1965. Title II, of Public Law 81–874 providing for Title 45, Part 116, as amended, of the CODE OF FEDERAL REGULATIONS Compiled from Federal Register (September 15, 1965) 30 F.R. 11817–11822 and (March 11, 1966) 30 F.R. 4299–4301. U.S. Department of Health, Education, and Welfare, Office of Education.)

TITLE 45—PUBLIC WELFARE

Chapter 1—Office of Education, Department of Health, Education, and Welfare

Part 116—Financial Assistance to Local Educational Agencies for the Education of Children of Low-Income Families

Grants made pursuant to the regulations set forth below are subject to the regulations in 45 CFR Part 80, issued by the Secretary of Health, Education, and Welfare and approved by the President, to effectuate the provisions of section 601 of the Civil Rights Act of 1964 (Public Law 88–352).

SUBPART A—DEFINITIONS

116.1 DEFINITIONS.

As used in this part—

(a) "Act" means Public Law 874, 81st Congress, as amended, Title II (20 U.S.C. 241A–241L) of which was added by Title I, Section 2, of the Elementary and Secondary Education Act of 1965 (Public Law 89–10).

(b) "Attendance area" means, in relation to a particular public school, the geographical area in which the children who are normally served by that school reside. An attendance area for an elementary school may not necessarily be coterminous with an attendance area for a secondary school.

(c) "Average daily attendance" means average daily attendance in elementary and secondary schools, not beyond grade 12, as determined in accordance with State Law, except that where the local educational agency of the school district in which a child resides makes or contracts to make a tuition payment for the free public education of that child in a school situated in another school district the attendance of that child shall be held and considered (1) to be in attendance at a school of the local educational agency so making or contracting to make such a tuition payment, and (2) not to be in attendance at a school of the local educational agency receiving such a tuition payment or entitled to receive such a tuition payment under the contract.

[Paragraph (d) amended March 11, 1966, 30 F.R.–4299]

(d) "Average per pupil expenditure in a State" means the aggregate of the current expenditures (as defined in paragraph (h) of this section but otherwise without regard to the sources of funds from which such expenditures are made) of all local educational agencies in the State, divided by the aggregate number of children in average daily attendance to whom such agencies provided free public education. For purposes of this paragraph the term "local educational agency" does not include a State agency which is directly responsible for providing, on a non-school-district basis, free public education for handicapped children who by reason of their handicap require special education.

(e) "Commissioner" means the United States Commissioner of Education.

(f) "Construction" means the erecting, building, acquiring, altering, remodeling, improving, or extending of school facilities, and includes the preparation of drawings and specifications for school facilities and the inspection and supervision of the construction of school facilities.

(g) "County" means a division of a State of the Union which is treated as a county by the Secretary of Commerce in compiling and reporting data regarding counties.

(h) "Current expenditures" means those expenditures for free public education to the extent that such expenditures are made from current revenues, except expenditures for the acquisition of land, the erection of facilities, interest, or debt service and except expenditures made from funds under Title II of the Act (Public Law 81–874, 81st Congress) or Titles II or III of the Elementary and Secondary Education Act of 1965 (Public Law 89–10).

[Paragraph (i) amended March 11, 1966, 30 F.R.–4299]

(i) "Educationally deprived children" means those children in a particular school district who have the greatest need for special educational assistance in order that their level of educational attainment may be raised to that appropriate for children of their age. The term includes children who are handicapped or whose needs for such special educational assistance is a result of poverty or cultural or linguistic isolation from the community at large.

(j) "Elementary school" means a day or residential school which provides elementary education as determined under State Law.

(k) "Equipment" includes machinery, utilities, and built-in equipment and any necessary enclosures or structures to house them, and includes all other items necessary for the functioning of a particular facility as a facility for providing educational services, including such items as instructional equipment and necessary furniture, printed, published, and audio-visual instructional materials, and books, periodicals, documents, and other related materials. Equipment does not include supplies which are consumed in use or which may not reasonably be expected to last longer than one year.

(l) "Federal percentage" means the percentage of the average per pupil expenditure in a State for a prior fiscal year which is used in computing maximum basic grants under Title II of the Act. For fiscal year 1966, the Federal percentage is fifty percent.

(m) "Fiscal year" means a period beginning on July 1 and ending on the following June 30. (A fiscal year is designated in accordance with the calendar year in which the ending date of the fiscal year occurs.)

(n) "Free public education" means education which is provided at public expense, under public supervision and direction, and without tuition charge, and which is provided as elementary or secondary education not above grade 12, in a State. Elementary education may, if so determined under State law, include education below grade 1 meeting the above criteria.

(o) "Handicapped children" means mentally retarded, hard of hearing, deaf, speech impaired, visually handicapped, seriously emotionally disturbed, crippled, or other health impaired children.

[Paragraph (p) amended March 11, 1966, 30 F.R.–4299]

(p) "Local educational agency" means a board of education or other legally constituted local school authority having administrative control and direction of free public education in a county, township, independent, or other school district located within a State, including a State agency which operates and maintains facilities for the providing of free public education in a county, township, independent, or other school district located within a State, but does not mean a public authority which merely provides a service function for public elementary or secondary schools. The term also includes any State agency which is by law, or in the absence of any such law by designation of the Governor of the State, directly responsible for providing, on a non-school-district basis, free public education for handicapped children who by reason of their handicap require special education.

(q) "Low-income factor" means the limit of family annual income which is used in determining families with low annual incomes for the purposes of Title II of the Act. For fiscal year 1966, the low-income factor is $2,000.

(r) "Program" means an overall plan with respect to funds made available under Title II of the Act during a fiscal year which is intended to be put into effect in a school district through individual projects of which it is the sum.

(s) "Project" means an activity, or a set of related activities, proposed by a local educational agency and designed to meet certain of the special educational needs of educationally deprived children in a designated geographical area.

[Paragraph (t) amended March 11, 1966, 30 F.R.–4299]

(t) "Project area" means the attendance area, or combination of attendance areas, having a high concentration of children from low-income families which is designated in an application by a local educational agency for a grant under Title II of the Act as the area to be served by the particular project. The term does not apply to a project to be carried out by a State agency at a school for handicapped children operated or supported by that State agency.

(u) "School facilities" means classrooms and related facilities (including initial equipment) for free public education and interests in land (including site grading and improvements) on which such facilities are constructed, but does not mean gymnasiums and similar facilities intended primarily for use for exhibitions for which admission is to be charged to the general public.

(v) "Secondary school" means a day or residential school which provides secondary education as determined under State law, except that it does not include any education provided beyond grade 12.

(w) "State" means a State of the Union, the District of Columbia, Wake Island, Puerto Rico, Guam, American Samoa, the Virgin Islands, or the Trust Territory of the Pacific Islands.

(x) "State educational agency" means the officer or agency primarily responsible for the State supervision of public elementary and secondary schools.

Subpart B—Eligibility for and Amount of Basic Grants

116.2 Eligibility of local educational agencies.

(a) In any case in which the Commissioner determines that satisfactory data are available on a school district basis, a local educational agency is eligible for a basic grant for a fiscal year if the number of children aged five to seventeen, inclusive, of families having an annual income of less than the low-income factor in the school district served by it is not less than ten and is (1) at least one hundred or (2) equal to three percent of the total number of children aged five to seventeen, inclusive, in such district, whichever is less.

(b) In any case in which a school district of a local educational agency is located within a single county and its boundaries are not coterminous with those of the county, and the Commissioner determines that satisfactory data are not available on a school district basis, such a local educational agency shall be eligible for a basic grant for a fiscal year if that county has at least one hundred children aged five to seventeen, inclusive, of families having an annual income of less than the low-income factor.

(c) In any case in which the school district of a local educational agency is located in more than one county and the Commissioner determines that satisfactory data are not available on a school district basis, the eligibility of such a local educational agency for a basic grant for a fiscal year shall be determined separately with respect to (1) such part of the school district as comprises a whole county or combination of counties and (2) such parts of the school districts as are located in a single county but comprise only a part of that county. Such a local educational agency shall be eligible for a basic grant if it meets either the criteria prescribed in paragraph (a) where clause (1) of this paragraph applies or the criterion prescribed in paragraph (b) where clause (2) of this paragraph applies.

(d) The eligibility of local educational agencies will be determined by the Commissioner on the basis of the most recent census data available for counties or minor civil divisions and places as adjusted to the extent necessary to reflect changes in boundaries of such counties or minor civil divisions and places which may have occurred subsequent to the date of the census. [Paragraph (e) added March 11, 1966, 30 F.R.–4299]

(e) The provisions of this section shall not apply to a State agency which qualifies as a local educational agency by virtue of being directly responsible for providing, on a non-school-district basis, free public education for handicapped children who by reason of their handicap require special education.

116.3 Determination of maximum basic grants.

(a) In any case in which the Commissioner determines that satisfactory data are available, the maximum basic grant for which a local educational agency in a State (other than Puerto Rico, Guam, American Samoa, the

Virgin Islands, and the Trust Territory of the Pacific Islands) shall be eligible for any fiscal year shall be an amount equal to the Federal percentage of the average per pupil expenditure in that State multiplied by the sum of (1) the number of children aged five to seventeen, inclusive, in the school district of that agency of families having an annual income of less than the low-income factor and (2) the number of children of those ages in the school district of families receiving payments in excess of the low-income factor under a program of aid to families with dependent children under a State plan approved pursuant to Title IV of the Social Security Act.

(b) In any case in which the Commissioner determines that satisfactory data are not available to enable him to determine maximum basic grants for which a local educational agency in a State (other than Puerto Rico, Guam, American Samoa, the Virgin Islands, and the Trust Territory of the Pacific Islands) shall be eligible, he will determine county aggregate maximum basic grants. A county aggregate maximum basic grant is an amount equal to the Federal percentage of the average per pupil expenditure of that State multiplied by the number of children in that county who meet the criteria of paragraph (a).

[Paragraph (d) added March 11, 1966, 30 F.R.–4299]

(c) The maximum basic grant for which Puerto Rico, Guam, American Samoa, the Virgin Islands, and the Trust Territory of the Pacific Islands shall be eligible for a fiscal year is the amount allotted by the Commissioner to each such State, respectively, from the two percent of the sums appropriated for making basic grants which the Commissioner reserves for such States.

(d) The maximum basic grant for which a State agency which qualifies as a local educational agency by virtue of being directly responsible for providing, on a non-school-district basis, free public education for handicapped children who by reason of their handicap require special education, is eligible for any fiscal year shall be an amount equal to the Federal percentage of the average per pupil expenditure in that State multiplied by the number of handicapped children for whose education public funds were provided by that State agency in average daily attendance, in the most recent year for which satisfactory data are available, in schools for handicapped children operated or supported by that State agency. The provisions of this paragraph (d) do not apply to Puerto Rico, Guam, American Samoa, the Virgin Islands, or the Trust Territory of the Pacific Islands.

116.4 ALLOCATION OF COUNTY AGGREGATE MAXIMUM BASIC GRANTS BY STATE EDUCATIONAL AGENCY.

(a) The State educational agency shall allocate a county aggregate maximum basic grant among the several local educational agencies within the county on the basis of the number of children aged five to seventeen, inclusive, who are from families having an annual income of less than the low-income factor (as derived by compiling for such school districts the data from the Eighteenth (1960) Decennial Census for minor civil divisions and places and, in the case of the school districts which now include only a part of a minor civil division or place as used in the Eighteenth (1960) Decennial Census, by estimating such number) plus the number of children who are from families receiving during calendar year 1962 payments in excess of the low-income factor under a program of aid to families with dependent children under a State approved pursuant to Title IV of the Social Security Act, if such numbers can be extracted or readily derived from available data.

(b) If the method of allocation prescribed in paragraph (a) cannot readily be applied in certain instances, the State educational agency shall allocate county aggregate maximum basic grants among local educational agencies in a county on the basis of the distribution percentage-wise among the school districts of the several local educational agencies in a county of the total number of children aged five to seventeen, inclusive, in one of the following categories, which basis shall be uniformly applied in all such instances:

(1) The number of children aged five to seventeen, inclusive, who are from families having an annual income of less than the low-income factor (compiled or estimated in the manner prescribed in paragraph (a)) or

(2) The number of such children who are from families receiving, during the most recent year for which such data are available, payments under a program of aid to families with dependent children under a State plan approved pursuant to Title IV of the Social Security Act, regardless of the amount of such payments.

(c) If a State is able to demonstrate to the satisfaction of the Commissioner that it is not feasible to allocate county aggregate maximum basic grants on any of the bases described in paragraph (a) or paragraph (b), the Commissioner may approve such alternative basis as the State educational agency may propose taking into consideration comparable factors.

GUIDELINES

Special Programs for Educationally Deprived Children

(Elementary and Secondary Education Act of 1965/Title I. Bureau of Elementary and Secondary Education/Division of Program Operations, U.S. Department of Health, Education, and Welfare, Office of Education.)

SECTION I—ADMINISTRATION AND FINANCE

Part A. Administration and Reporting

GENERAL INFORMATION

Title I of the Elementary and Secondary Education Act of 1965 is the major thrust of the national effort to "bring better education to millions of disadvantaged youth who need it most." [1] The Congress has made available more than $1 billion for 1965–66, the first year of this title.

ADMINISTRATIVE RESPONSIBILITIES

The act places responsibilities for administering programs supported by Federal funds under Title I on the U.S. Commissioner of Education, State educational agencies, and local educational agencies. It is incumbent upon all concerned to use such funds in accordance with the spirit and intent of the act and regulations.

U.S. COMMISSIONER OF EDUCATION

The U.S. Commissioner of Education is responsible not only for the overall conduct of the program at the national level but also for the determination of the maximum amounts to be allocated to eligible districts or counties and to State agencies that operate or support schools for handicapped children. Federal control of any aspect of education at any level, however, is prohibited.

In the performance of its responsibilities, the Office of Education—

- Approves applications submitted by State educational agencies for participation in the program.
- Makes funds available for the program.
- Develops regulations, guidelines, and other materials relating to the administration of the program.
- Provides consultative services to State educational agencies in carrying out their responsibilities.
- Reviews and assesses programs and progress made under Title I throughout the Nation.
- Compiles from reports submitted by the State agencies various fiscal and program reports to the Congress and to the public.

STATE EDUCATIONAL AGENCIES

In its formal application to the Commissioner of Education to participate in the Title I program, a State educational agency includes assurances that it will administer the program and submit reports in accordance with the provisions of the law and the regulations. Following the approval of its application, it furnishes to the Office of Education a description of its plans for staffing, organizing, and administering the program (see p. 13, exhibit No. 1, OE-4315). In the administration of the program, its major responsibilities are to—

- Suballocate basic grant funds, where necessary, to eligible local educational agencies.
- Assist local educational agencies in the development of projects.
- Approve proposed projects in accordance with the provisions of section 205 (a) of Title I and make payment of funds to local educational agencies.

[1] Message from the President of the United States transmitting the education program, Jan. 12, 1965.

Maintain fiscal records of all grant funds.

Prepare and submit fiscal and evaluative reports to the Office of Education.

LOCAL EDUCATIONAL AGENCIES

The local educational agency is responsible for developing and implementing approved projects to fulfill the intent of Title I. It is therefore responsible for identifying the educationally deprived children in areas where there are high concentrations of children from low-income families, for determining their special needs, for designing projects to carry out the purposes of the legislation with regard to such children, and for submitting applications to the appropriate State educational agency for grants to fund proposed projects. The local educational agency is also responsible for—

Using grant funds in accordance with approved project budgets and for the purposes for which the projects have been approved.

Making available for inspection by the public the terms and provisions of each approved project.

Maintaining adequate fiscal records on all project funds and reporting to the State educational agency on the use of such funds.

Maintaining fiscal effort with respect to total current expenditures for education and also with respect to such expenditures in the project areas.

EMPHASIS ON EVALUATION

In view of the pioneering nature of this national program and of the amount of new ground that will be broken under it, Title I emphasizes and contains special provisions for the evaluation of the extent to which projects and programs conducted under it are effective in improving the educational attainment of educationally deprived children and for periodic reports on the results of this evaluation. It also creates a National Advisory Council on the Education of Disadvantaged Children which will review the effectiveness of the Title I program in improving the educational attainment of educationally deprived children and make recommendations for the improvement of its provisions, administration, and operation. The Council will make its first annual report to the President not later than March 31, 1966; the President will transmit this report, with his comments and recommendations, to the Congress.

RELATED STATUTES

CIVIL RIGHTS ACT OF 1964

Title VI of the Civil Rights Act of 1964 states: "No person in the United States shall, on the grounds of race, color, or national origin, be excluded from participation in, be denied the benefits of, or be subjected to discrimination under any program or activity receiving Federal financial assistance." Programs under Title I of the Elementary and Secondary Education Act of 1965 must be operated in compliance with this law, and State and local educational agencies must provide satisfactory assurance of compliance.

ECONOMIC OPPORTUNITY ACT OF 1964

In an area where a community action program under Title II of the Economic Opportunity Act of 1964 is in effect, any project under Title I of the Elementary and Secondary Education Act must be developed in cooperation with the public or nonprofit agency responsible for the community action program.

FINANCIAL ASSISTANCE FOR LOCAL EDUCATIONAL AGENCIES IN AREAS AFFECTED BY FEDERAL ACTIVITY (TITLE I OF PUBLIC LAW 81–874)

Title I of the Elementary and Secondary Education Act of 1965 amends Public Law 81–874 by adding Title II "Financial Assistance to Local Educational Agencies for the Education of Children of Low-Income Families." Title III "General" of Public Law 81–874, as amended, contains various definitions which, with minor exceptions, are applicable to both the program for federally affected areas and the program for children of low-income families.

OTHERS

A number of other statutes, including the Manpower Development and Training Act, the Vocational Education Act of 1963 (programs for potential school dropouts and unemployed youth), and the National Defense Education Act (institutes for training teachers of the disadvantaged), as well as other titles of the Elementary and Secondary Education Act itself provide educational programs designed to benefit the educationally deprived. Public Law 89–313 amended Title I to provide for grants to State agencies operating or supporting schools for handicapped children.

ELIGIBILITY AND MAXIMUM GRANTS

DETERMINATION OF ELIGIBILITY OF LOCAL EDUCATIONAL AGENCIES

A local educational agency is defined as an agency which has administrative control and direction of free public education up to and including, but not beyond, grade 12 in a county, township, independent, or other school district. To be eligible to participate in the Title I program in 1965–66, such an agency must serve a school district in which the concentration of children aged 5 through 17 from families with an annual income of less than $2,000, as shown in the 1960 census, meets the minimum statutory requirements. The bases on which the Commissioner of Education determines whether an agency meets these requirements are outlined below.

SCHOOL DISTRICT BASIS

The Commissioner determines the eligibility of local educational agencies on a school district basis, if satisfactory census data are available by school district. The 1960 census data, which are the most recent available, are in most cases not satisfactory for making such determinations. Where, however, the 1960 census data are satisfactory for this purpose, these data are used, and the eligibility of school districts is determined in accordance with the following criteria:

- All school districts in which the total number of children aged 5 through 17 from families with an annual income of less than $2,000 represents at least 3 percent of all children aged 5 through 17 in the district and totals not less than 10 are eligible to receive grants under Title I.
- All districts containing 100 or more children aged 5 through 17 from families with an annual income of less than $2,000 are automatically eligible, regardless of the percentage of such children.

County Basis

When satisfactory census data are not available on a school district basis—as was the case for most districts in fiscal year 1966—the Commissioner determines eligibility on a county basis. If a county, according to the 1960 census, contained 100 or more children aged 5 through 17 from families with an annual income of less than $2,000, the county is eligible and all local educational agencies within that county are also eligible. It should be noted, however, that if the county is coterminous with the district of a local educational agency, that is, if the boundaries of the county conform substantially to the boundaries of the school district, the eligibility of that agency is determined in accordance with the criteria given above for determining eligibility on a school district basis.

Individual School District Basis Within an Ineligible County

Even when a county is ineligible on a county basis, it is still possible that an individual school district within that county might be determined to be eligible to receive grants. To obtain such a determination, the State educational agency should provide the Commissioner with sufficient information concerning the boundaries of the school districts within the county to enable him to determine from available census data that, in the district in question, the number of children aged 5 through 17 from families with an annual income of less than $2,000 was at least 10 and was equal to at least 3 percent of the total number of children in this age bracket in the district.

Determination of Maximum Basic Grants to Local Educational Agencies

Title I provides that the U.S. Commissioner of Education shall make payments to the States, in amounts to be determined in accordance with the act, for grants to local educational agencies. These grants are to be of two kinds: Basic grants for each of the 3 years beginning July 1, 1965, and incentive grants for each of the 2 years beginning July 1, 1966. These guidelines deal only with basic grants.

Determination by the U.S. Commissioner of Education

The computations of the amounts of maximum basic grants follow a pattern similar to that just outlined regarding eligibility. The law provides that the Commissioner determine maximum basic grants for each eligible district for which the requisite census data are available. When they are not —as was the case in most instances for the year ending June 30, 1966—the Commissioner determines the aggregate maximum basic grant for each eligible county.

FORMULA USED IN COMPUTATION, 1965–66

In all cases the formula used in the computation of maximum basic grants for the year ending June 30, 1966, was the same. It was based on an impartial count of children aged 5 through 17 of low-income families without regard to whether these children were in public school, in private school, or out of school. It involved the following three factors:

A. The number of children aged 5 through 17 from families with an annual income of less than $2,000.
B. The number of children aged 5 through 17 from families with incomes exceeding $2,000 in the form of aid to families with dependent children under Title IV of the Social Security Act.
C. One-half the average per pupil expenditure in the State for the second preceeding year.

Substituting the symbols used above for the factors themselves, the formula applied was:

$(A + B) \times C =$ the number of dollars of the maximum basic grant.

DETERMINATION BY STATE EDUCATIONAL AGENCIES

Where the boundaries of an eligible county do not conform substantially with the boundaries of a single school district, the State educational agency determines suballocations to individual local educational agencies within that county in accordance with criteria set forth in the regulations. The regulations require that the State educational agency inform the Commissioner of the bases used in determining these suballocations and of the maximum amount allocated to each local educational agency.

LIMITATION ON AMOUNT OF BASIC GRANTS, 1965–66

During fiscal year 1966 (but not during subsequent years) the amount of a maximum basic grant may not exceed 30 percent of the amount budgeted by the local educational agency for current expenditures. Current expenditures are expenditures from current revenues with the exception of expenditures for the acquisition of land, erection of facilities, interest, and debt services, and expenditures from Federal funds received under this title or other titles of the Elementary and Secondary Education Act of 1965.

GRANTS TO STATE AGENCIES OPERATING OR SUPPORTING PROGRAMS FOR HANDICAPPED CHILDREN

Separate allocations of maximum basic grants are made to State agencies directly responsible for providing free public education, not beyond grade 12, for handicapped children on a nondistrict basis. Their free public education may be provided in State-operated or State-supported schools. A State agency's maximum grant under this portion of the program is based on the average daily attendances of all of the handicapped children for whom it provides free public education, multiplied by one-half the average per pupil expenditure in the State for the second preceeding year. The allocations for 1965–66 to State agencies do not in any way affect allocations to local educational agencies. . . .

APPENDIX C

The Sampling of Opinion of Chief State School Officers and of Local School Superintendents on the Administration of Public Law 89–10

One aspect of the administration of ESEA that could not be adequately illuminated through research and interviews in Washington, D.C., was the attitudes, opinions, and experiences of State and local school administrators who participated in the implementation of the Act.

Obviously it was impossible to visit the more than 50 State and territorial governments and 23,000 separate school districts in the nation. So some kind of questionnaire schedule and sampling technique had to be devised.

In the case of State administrators, author Bailey designed a fairly open-ended letter which was sent to all the chief State school officers. One part of the letter read as follows:

> (A) The efficiency and dispatch of USOE in giving you information about provisions of the Act, your responsibility under it, and assisting you in providing adequate guidelines and instructions for filing applications.
>
> (B) The adequacy of Federal funds to support both the direct and indirect costs incurred by your department in planning for and in carrying out the various provisions of the Act.
>
> (C) Requirements imposed by the Act and by the Office of Education which you consider needlessly bureaucratic.
>
> (D) The promptness of the U.S. Office of Education in handling your application and in sending you grant money.
>
> (E) Positive or negative evidence of undue Federal control over State and Local decision-making—including your sense of the attitudes and behavior of the top staff of USOE in relationship to this issue.
>
> (F) Problems of assisting local school districts in understanding and reacting to requirements of the Act.
>
> (G) The impact of the internal reorganization of the USOE (July 1965) on your dealings with that agency in Washington and in the field.
>
> (H) Your judgment about ways in which the administration of the Act could be improved from the Washington end.

Thirty-four of the CSSO's responded. Most of the replies were extensive and extremely thoughtful. These replies served to buttress evidence found in Congressional hearings, in-house documents in USOE, and the reports of Advisory Committees concerned with the several titles of ESEA. Some of the conclusions in Chapters IV and V reflect these mutually reinforced findings. Since the preservation of the anonymity of respondents was guaranteed, the individual CSSO replies are not publicly available.

The sampling of opinion of local school administrators involved a far more elaborate undertaking. Author Bailey, with the help of a special supplementary grant from the Carnegie Corporation, worked with Dr. Eleanor P. Godfrey of the Bureau of Social Science Research in constructing a structured and coded questionnaire involving more than 60 individual items. This questionnaire was mailed to a sample of school superintendents across the nation.

The sample was drawn from the list of members of the American Association of School Administrators; only persons identified as public school *superintendents in charge of operating school districts* were considered qualified. This means that the following persons were eliminated before selection: (1) assistant superintendents, (2) parochial school administrators, and (3) county superintendents in States where the county is not the lowest level legally operating school district but an intermediate administrative office between the local district and the state education agency.

The selection from the qualified universe was based on a 1:5 sampling ratio; a random start was used, followed by the selection of every fifth name. In this manner names and addresses of superintendents of 1467 school districts were chosen. The sample may well represent the "universe of qualified AASA members"; but data obtained from this sample may not be generalized to the population of the U.S. public school superintendents, since it is not known to what extent this totality is represented by the AASA membership.[1]

A seven-page questionnaire and a covering letter from Dr. Forrest Conner, Executive Secretary of the AASA, was sent to each of the 1467 sample school superintendents the second week in May, 1966. The mailing time was planned so that district administrators would have completed their final Title I applications by the early May deadline required for consideration of a project for operation in fiscal year 1966. By June 1, approximately 570, or 39 per cent, of the sample had replied. A general follow-up letter was sent to the remaining 900 cases the first week in June and an additional follow-up reminder was sent to all nonresponding districts in states where fewer than 50 per cent of the sample had replied by June 15. Tabulation was begun on July 20; hence, any completed questionnaires received after that date were not included in the tabular reports.

By August 10, 964, or 66 per cent, of the superintendents addressed had replied to our invitation to participate in the study; 937 of those replying, or 64 per cent of the total sample, returned completed questionnaires in

[1] For a description of the characteristics of the AASA membership in 1964 see *Operation Check-up, A Profile of the AASA Membership,* American Association of School Administrators, Washington, D.C.

time for tabulation. The remaining 27 replies were excluded because of lateness or incompleteness (17 cases), because the district was not operating as an independent school system in 1965–66 (4 cases), or because the district superintendent declined to participate in the study (6 cases).

Considering the demands on the time of the respondents, the fact that the survey was launched toward the end of the school year, and that limitations of time and budget precluded elaborate follow-up procedures, the response rate may be considered satisfactory.

The coded returns were run through a computer and were programmed for four variables: size of district (in terms of student population in average daily attendance); median family income in the district; region; and make-up (various subclassifications of urban, suburban, and rural).

The data from the computer printouts most relevant to the text have been included in this appendix. The complete tabulation is available for inspection and scholarly inquiry through the Maxwell Library, Syracuse University.

Since this data is unique, interested scholars of educational administration and public policy may find in this tabulated material a source of data whose utility goes far beyond this present study. They are encouraged to use the basic material themselves and to urge their graduate students to use this appendix for exercises and for heuristic research designs.

BSSR Survey of 937 School Administrators on ESEA——Responses in Percentages

Question No. 14

Question: When did you first learn of the general provisions of ESEA?

KEY *	SAMPLE	U.S. Total	BY SIZE OF STUDENT POPULATION									BY MEDIAN FAMILY INCOME							
			More Than 50,000 Students	25,000 to 49,999 Students	12,000 to 24,999 Students	6,000 to 11,999 Students	3,000 to 5,999 Students	1,200 to 2,999 Students	600 to 1,199 Students	300 to 599 Students	Less Than 300 Students	Less Than $3,000.	$3,000. to $4,999.	$5,000. to $6,999.	$7,000. to $8,999.	$9,000. to $11,999.	$12,000. and Over	Can't Evaluate Income	No Answer On Income
Y	No answer	1.6	7.7	.0	.0	.0	0.7	1.7	2.9	1.8	3.1	1.7	1.2	.6	1.7	2.4	.0	.0	9.4
1	Before 4/65	32.0	77.0	54.8	45.7	41.5	33.6	30.6	28.1	21.9	15.6	35.6	27.4	28.9	37.9	50.0	47.0	30.0	37.5
2	Between 4/65 & 9/65	40.2	15.4	27.4	34.8	38.7	44.6	42.0	36.8	42.1	40.6	42.4	43.3	40.5	38.8	23.8	35.3	40.0	37.5
3	Between 9/65 & 11/65	20.3	.0	18.2	17.4	18.9	15.8	18.5	25.1	25.4	31.3	18.6	24.0	22.5	13.8	14.3	11.8	25.0	10.9
4	After 11/65	6.1	.0	.0	2.2	0.9	5.5	4.1	7.0	8.8	9.4	1.7	4.2	7.5	7.8	9.5	5.9	5.0	4.7

*Deviations from totals of 100 percent in each column are due to additional BSSR Keys judged by the senior author to be statistically insignificant.

BSSR Survey of 937 School Administrators on ESEA——Responses in Percentages

Question No. 14

Question: When did you first learn of the general provisions of ESEA?

		BY POPULATION MAKEUP												BY REGION							
KEY *	SAMPLE	90-100% Urban	60-89% Urban	90-100% Suburban	60-89% Suburban	Mixed Rural and Urban	Mixed Rural Urban and Suburban	Mixed Rural and Suburban	60-89% Rural Non-Farm	60-89% Rural Farm	90-100% Rural Non-Farm	100% Mixed Rural	90-100% Rural Farm	New England	Middle Atlantic	East North Central	West North Central	Southern	Southwest	Mountain	Pacific
Y	No answer	1.2	.9	1.4	2.8	4.5	1.4	1.7	1.3	.8	.0	2.7	.0	1.5	.0	2.4	2.9	1.0	1.3	.0	1.3
1	Before 4/65	40.7	35.2	40.0	32.7	31.8	33.8	27.1	36.8	17.8	23.8	32.5	19.0	35.8	33.9	25.2	24.7	44.2	40.4	32.3	36.9
2	Between 4/65 & 9/65	39.5	41.7	34.3	38.5	31.8	43.6	49.1	36.8	48.3	47.6	27.0	45.2	35.8	42.4	39.4	44.2	43.2	36.4	32.3	35.5
3	Between 9/65 & 11/65	15.1	19.5	19.3	21.4	21.6	18.3	16.9	13.2	27.1	23.8	27.0	23.8	25.4	16.4	23.2	24.7	8.8	18.2	29.4	18.4
4	After 11/65	3.5	2.8	5.0	4.3	1.0	2.8	5.1	11.8	5.9	4.8	10.8	11.9	1.5	7.3	9.8	3.5	2.9	3.9	5.9	7.9

*Deviations from totals of 100 percent in each column are due to additional BSSR Keys judged by the senior author to be statistically insignificant.

BSSR Survey of 937 School Administrators on ESEA——Responses in Percentages   Question No. 15

Question: How did you first learn of ESEA?

KEY*	SAMPLE	U.S. Total	BY SIZE OF STUDENT POPULATION									BY MEDIAN FAMILY INCOME							
			More Than 50,000 Students	25,000 to 49,999 Students	12,000 to 24,999 Students	6,000 to 11,999 Students	3,000 to 5,999 Students	1,200 to 2,999 Students	600 to 1,199 Students	300 to 599 Students	Less Than 300 Students	Less Than $3,000.	$3,000. to $4,999.	$5,000. to $6,999.	$7,000. to $8,999.	$9,000. to $11,999.	$12,000. and Over	Can't Evaluate Income	No Answer On Income
Y	No answer	2.3	7.7	.0	2.2	.9	2.7	2.0	3.5	1.8	3.1	.0	1.5	1.9	3.4	2.4	.0	10.0	2.4
1	Professional conference	31.1	23.1	45.5	15.2	34.9	29.4	32.9	30.4	33.3	25.0	20.4	34.0	32.8	29.3	23.8	35.3	15.0	31.0
2	Professional newsletter	23.5	30.8	18.2	34.8	31.1	24.0	25.5	15.8	19.3	15.6	22.0	21.2	23.4	23.2	21.4	29.4	20.0	23.5
3	State education agency	39.8	.0	36.4	32.6	35.9	34.9	41.6	41.5	43.9	62.4	47.5	46.4	40.5	33.6	28.6	5.9	60.0	39.8
4	U. S. Office of Education	8.3	30.8	18.2	17.4	15.1	5.5	7.7	4.7	6.1	6.2	11.9	8.5	7.0	9.5	11.9	.0	20.0	8.4
5	Newspaper Reports	36.7	30.8	27.3	45.7	48.1	43.8	30.9	38.6	29.0	31.2	39.0	39.8	34.4	37.1	31.0	47.1	25.0	36.7
6	Professional colleague	5.2	7.7	9.1	8.7	8.5	6.8	3.0	2.9	7.0	6.2	1.7	4.2	5.6	6.0	7.1	.0	10.0	5.2
7	Other	2.7	15.4	.0	.0	2.8	2.7	1.7	2.9	3.5	6.2	6.8	1.9	2.2	3.4	2.4	.0	.0	2.7

*Deviations from totals of 100 percent in each column are due to additional BSSR Keys judged by the senior author to be statistically insignificant.

BSSR Survey of 937 School Administrators on ESEA——Responses in Percentages

Question No. 15

Question: How did you first learn of ESEA?

		BY POPULATION MAKEUP												BY REGION							
KEY *	SAMPLE	90-100% Urban	60-89% Urban	90-100% Suburban	60-89% Suburban	Mixed Rural and Urban	Mixed Rural Urban and Suburban	Mixed Rural and Suburban	60-89% Rural Non-Farm	60-89% Rural Farm	90-100% Rural Non-Farm	100% Mixed Rural	90-100% Rural Farm	New England	Middle Atlantic	East North Central	West North Central	Southern	Southwest	Mountain	Pacific
Y	No answer	2.3	2.8	2.9	4.3	2.3	2.8	1.7	2.6	.8	4.8	.0	.0	4.5	1.2	2.4	1.8	.1	5.2	.0	4.0
1	Professional conference	37.2	27.8	35.0	22.9	26.1	29.6	23.7	26.3	39.8	28.6	40.5	28.6	25.4	32.8	30.5	30.0	30.4	42.8	32.3	25.0
2	Professional newsletter	30.2	26.9	22.1	27.2	28.4	32.4	25.4	19.7	14.4	19.0	13.5	16.7	28.4	18.2	25.2	22.9	29.5	16.9	14.7	29.0
3	State education agency	26.7	46.3	33.6	32.9	45.5	43.7	33.9	36.9	49.2	40.5	37.9	52.2	52.2	33.9	32.5	47.1	39.3	41.6	.0	38.2
4	U. S. Office of Education	16.3	15.7	7.1	14.3	8.0	2.8	.0	3.9	6.8	2.4	8.1	7.1	7.5	6.1	9.4	65.0	13.7	11.7	.0	7.9
5	Newspaper reports	36.0	34.3	35.7	38.6	40.9	31.0	45.7	35.5	38.1	23.8	35.1	45.2	29.9	35.2	38.6	38.3	53.0	22.1	26.5	34.2
6	Professional colleague	9.3	4.6	5.0	5.7	5.7	7.0	3.4	1.3	5.1	2.4	2.7	9.5	1.5	4.8	7.3	4.7	6.9	3.9	.0	5.3
7	Other	3.5	2.8	2.9	.0	1.1	5.6	.0	5.3	1.7	4.8	.0	4.8	3.0	.6	2.4	1.2	4.9	3.9	2.9	6.6

*Deviations from totals of 100 percent in each column are due to additional BSSR Keys judged by the senior author to be statistically insignificant.

BSSR Survey of 937 School Administrators on ESEA——Responses in Percentages

Question No. 16-A

Question: When approximately did you receive guidelines and instructions for preparing project plans for Titles I, II and III?

Sub-Question: Title I

KEY *	SAMPLE	U.S. Total	BY SIZE OF STUDENT POPULATION									BY MEDIAN FAMILY INCOME							
			More Than 50,000 Students	25,000 to 49,999 Students	12,000 to 24,999 Students	6,000 to 11,999 Students	3,000 to 5,999 Students	1,200 to 2,999 Students	600 to 1,199 Students	300 to 599 Students	Less Than 300 Students	Less Than $3,000.	$3,000. to $4,999.	$5,000. to $6,999.	$7,000. to $8,999.	$9,000. to $11,999.	$12,000. and Over	Can't Evaluate Income	No Answer On Income
Y	No answer	8.3	.0	9.1	2.2	2.8	4.1	9.7	11.7	10.5	18.8	3.4	7.3	6.7	10.3	14.3	17.6	.0	18.8
0	Sept. 1965	16.2	15.4	36.4	23.9	15.1	17.8	15.8	13.5	14.0	21.9	18.6	18.5	16.7	13.8	16.7	11.8	15.0	7.8
1	Oct. 1965	17.7	15.4	36.4	26.1	23.6	16.4	17.1	14.0	17.5	12.5	16.9	17.8	16.4	25.0	14.3	5.9	15.0	18.8
2	Nov. 1965	22.5	23.1	9.1	26.1	23.6	28.8	21.1	20.5	20.2	21.9	16.9	23.6	25.0	14.7	16.7	23.5	20.0	28.1
3	Dec. 1965	15.7	30.8	9.1	6.5	17.0	15.1	15.8	17.0	18.4	6.3	22.0	12.4	15.8	16.4	21.4	11.8	30.0	14.1
4	Jan. 1966	8.9	.0	.0	6.5	9.4	6.8	8.7	10.5	12.3	6.3	10.2	9.7	8.1	10.3	7.1	17.6	15.0	3.1
5	Feb. 1966	5.7	15.4	.0	4.3	7.5	5.5	6.4	4.7	3.5	6.3	3.4	5.8	6.4	6.0	7.1	5.9	5.0	1.6
6	Mar. 1966	2.6	.0	.0	.0	.9	3.4	2.3	4.1	3.5	.0	6.8	1.9	3.1	1.7	.0	5.9	.0	1.6
7	Apr. 1966	1.6	.0	.0	2.2	.0	2.1	2.0	1.8	.0	6.3	1.7	1.9	1.4	.9	2.4	.0	.0	3.1
8	May or June 1966	.5	.0	.0	.0	.0	.0	.7	1.8	.0	.0	.0	.8	.6	.9	.0	.0	.0	.0

*Deviations from totals of 100 percent in each column are due to additional BSSR Keys judged by the senior author to be statistically insignificant.

BSSR Survey of 937 School Administrators on ESEA——Responses in Percentages

Question No. 16-A

Question: When approximately did you receive guidelines and instructions for preparing project plans for Titles I, II and III?

Sub-Question: Title I

		BY POPULATION MAKEUP												BY REGION							
KEY*	SAMPLE	90-100% Urban	60-89% Urban	90-100% Suburban	60-89% Suburban	Mixed Rural and Urban	Mixed Rural Urban and Suburban	Mixed Rural and Suburban	60-89% Rural Non-Farm	60-89% Rural Farm	90-100% Rural Non-Farm	100% Mixed Rural	90-100% Rural Farm	New England	Middle Atlantic	East North Central	West North Central	Southern	Southwest	Mountain	Pacific
Y	No answer	8.1	4.6	9.3	14.3	11.4	4.2	10.2	2.6	8.5	7.1	13.5	9.5	10.4	6.1	11.8	8.2	4.9	10.4	2.9	5.3
0	Sept. 1965	17.4	23.1	13.6	11.4	14.8	25.4	16.9	14.5	15.3	16.7	8.1	11.9	25.4	15.2	11.0	10.0	15.7	39.0	20.6	17.1
1	Oct. 1965	20.9	22.2	17.1	20.0	21.6	9.9	15.3	21.1	15.3	16.7	13.5	11.9	28.4	18.2	13.8	14.7	15.7	22.1	11.8	27.6
2	Nov. 1965	18.6	25.0	22.9	18.6	18.2	28.2	20.3	27.6	20.3	21.4	21.6	31.0	20.9	21.8	18.7	22.4	33.3	15.6	23.5	30.3
3	Dec. 1965	15.1	11.1	18.6	15.7	14.8	14.1	16.9	18.4	17.8	9.5	18.9	14.3	6.0	15.2	17.1	20.6	14.7	7.8	32.4	11.8
4	Jan. 1966	9.3	4.6	10.0	8.6	8.0	2.8	8.5	9.2	14.4	7.1	18.9	4.8	3.0	11.5	12.2	11.8	8.8	.0	2.9	2.6
5	Feb. 1966	4.7	4.6	6.4	2.9	9.1	8.5	5.1	3.9	5.9	4.8	2.7	7.1	1.5	5.5	8.1	8.8	5.9	.0	.0	2.6
6	Mar. 1966	2.3	2.8	1.4	5.7	1.1	2.8	3.4	1.3	1.7	9.5	.0	2.4	.0	4.2	3.7	2.4	1.0	1.3	2.9	1.3
7	Apr. 1966	1.2	1.9	.7	2.9	.0	2.8	3.4	.0	.8	7.1	.0	2.4	4.5	1.8	2.4	.6	.0	1.3	2.9	.0
8	May or June 1966	1.2	.0	.0	.0	1.1	1.4	.0	1.3	.0	.0	2.7	.0	.0	.6	.0	.6	.0	2.6	.0	1.3

*Deviations from totals of 100 percent in each column are due to additional BSSR Keys judged by the senior author to be statistically insignificant.

BSSR Survey of 937 School Administrators on ESEA——Responses in Percentages

Question No. 16-B

Question: When approximately did you receive guidelines for preparing project plans for Titles I, II and III?

Sub-Question: Title II

KEY *	SAMPLE	U.S. Total	BY SIZE OF STUDENT POPULATION									BY MEDIAN FAMILY INCOME							
			More Than 50,000 Students	25,000 to 49,999 Students	12,000 to 24,999 Students	6,000 to 11,999 Students	3,000 to 5,999 Students	1,200 to 2,999 Students	600 to 1,199 Students	300 to 599 Students	Less Than 300 Students	Less Than $3,000.	$3,000. to $4,999.	$5,000. to $6,999.	$7,000. to $8,999.	$9,000. to $11,999.	$12,000. and Over	Can't Evaluate Income	No Answer On Income
Y	No answer	11.5	7.7	18.2	6.5	4.7	4.8	13.1	15.2	16.7	18.8	6.8	11.2	11.7	12.1	11.9	5.9	.0	20.3
0	Sept. 1965	6.3	.0	9.1	6.5	7.5	7.5	4.7	6.4	6.1	12.5	8.5	8.9	6.1	2.6	9.5	5.9	5.0	.0
1	Oct. 1965	4.5	15.4	18.2	10.9	4.7	4.1	3.4	3.5	2.6	9.4	8.5	3.1	3.3	7.8	2.4	.0	5.0	9.4
2	Nov. 1965	4.8	.0	9.1	4.3	5.7	6.8	4.4	2.9	3.5	12.5	3.4	3.9	6.7	5.2	2.4	5.9	.0	1.6
3	Dec. 1965	7.6	7.7	18.2	13.0	7.5	8.9	7.4	5.8	7.9	.0	5.1	6.6	8.1	8.6	9.5	23.5	10.0	3.1
4	Jan. 1966	11.3	30.8	.0	17.4	16.0	16.4	10.7	7.6	5.3	6.3	16.9	8.1	11.1	12.9	9.5	11.8	25.0	14.1
5	Feb. 1966	18.0	7.7	9.1	10.9	19.8	15.1	21.5	19.3	15.8	12.5	18.6	18.9	18.1	19.8	16.7	11.8	5.0	17.2
6	Mar. 1966	19.7	7.7	.0	23.9	20.8	19.2	19.8	22.2	19.3	12.5	15.3	17.4	21.4	15.5	28.6	29.4	35.0	18.8
7	Apr. 1966	12.1	15.4	18.2	6.5	8.5	13.0	11.1	12.3	17.5	12.5	13.6	16.2	10.8	10.3	4.8	5.9	5.0	12.5
8	May or June 1966	2.6	7.7	.0	.0	3.8	3.4	2.7	1.8	1.8	3.1	3.4	3.9	1.7	2.6	4.8	.0	.0	1.6

*Deviations from totals of 100 percent in each column are due to additional BSSR Keys judged by the senior author to be statistically insignificant.

BSSR Survey of 937 School Administrators on ESEA——Responses in Percentages

Question No. 16-B

Question: When approximately did you receive guidelines and instructions for preparing project plans for Titles I, II and III?

Sub-Question: Title II

		BY POPULATION MAKEUP												BY REGION							
KEY*	SAMPLE	90-100% Urban	60-89% Urban	90-100% Suburban	60-89% Suburban	Mixed Rural and Urban	Mixed Rural Urban and Suburban	Mixed Rural and Suburban	60-89% Rural Non-Farm	60-89% Rural Farm	90-100% Rural Non-Farm	100% Mixed Rural	90-100% Rural Farm	New England	Middle Atlantic	East North Central	West North Central	Southern	Southwest	Mountain	Pacific
Y	No answer	9.3	9.3	12.1	14.3	11.4	7.0	11.9	5.3	16.9	11.9	18.9	11.9	13.4	8.5	13.8	16.5	8.8	10.4	2.9	6.6
0	Sept. 1965	9.3	8.3	3.6	4.3	3.4	11.3	5.1	2.6	6.8	16.7	5.4	2.4	7.5	6.1	2.8	2.4	2.9	29.9	8.8	5.3
1	Oct. 1965	8.1	6.5	2.9	5.7	3.4	5.6	3.4	5.3	2.5	4.8	2.7	2.4	6.0	4.2	2.0	3.5	2.9	13.0	11.8	3.9
2	Nov. 1965	2.3	8.3	5.0	5.7	2.3	7.0	3.4	5.3	5.9	2.4	2.7	2.4	7.5	4.2	2.8	3.5	3.9	9.1	14.7	5.3
3	Dec. 1965	5.8	8.3	12.1	8.6	4.5	4.2	16.9	7.9	5.9	7.1	.0	2.4	6.0	9.7	4.5	6.5	6.9	2.6	23.5	15.8
4	Jan. 1966	14.0	8.3	17.1	15.7	11.4	15.5	5.1	10.5	8.5	7.1	8.1	4.8	3.0	15.2	11.0	4.1	19.6	6.5	14.7	19.7
5	Feb. 1966	22.1	16.7	12.9	18.6	23.9	15.5	20.3	17.1	15.3	11.9	29.7	23.8	13.4	17.6	23.2	16.5	14.7	20.8	14.7	13.2
6	Mar. 1966	15.1	22.2	24.3	11.4	25.0	16.9	13.6	26.3	17.8	16.7	21.6	19.0	16.4	23.0	23.2	24.1	15.7	6.5	2.9	21.1
7	Apr. 1966	10.5	10.2	8.6	12.9	10.2	12.7	13.6	13.2	12.7	19.0	10.8	21.4	25.4	6.7	14.6	13.5	17.6	.0	5.9	7.9
8	May or June 1966	3.5	1.9	1.4	.0	2.3	2.8	5.1	6.6	3.4	2.4	.0	.0	1.5	4.8	1.2	1.8	6.9	1.3	.0	1.3

*Deviations from totals of 100 percent in each column are due to additional BSSR Keys judged by the senior author to be statistically insignificant.

BSSR Survey of 937 School Administrators on ESEA——Responses in Percentages

Question No. 16-C

Question: When approximately did you receive guidelines and instructions for preparing project plans for Titles I, II and III?

Sub-Question: Title III

KEY *	SAMPLE	U.S. Total	BY SIZE OF STUDENT POPULATION: More Than 50,000 Students	25,000 to 49,999 Students	12,000 to 24,999 Students	6,000 to 11,999 Students	3,000 to 5,999 Students	1,200 to 2,999 Students	600 to 1,199 Students	300 to 599 Students	Less Than 300 Students	BY MEDIAN FAMILY INCOME: Less Than $3,000.	$3,000. to $4,999.	$5,000. to $6,999.	$7,000. to $8,999.	$9,000. to $11,999.	$12,000. and Over	Can't Evaluate Income	No Answer On Income
Y	No answer	36.5	.0	27.3	23.9	26.4	26.0	38.6	45.6	50.0	37.5	30.5	38.2	35.3	37.9	38.1	5.9	15.0	53.1
0	Sept. 1965	7.2	15.4	9.1	10.9	6.6	6.2	7.7	4.7	5.3	18.8	10.2	8.9	6.9	5.2	7.1	11.8	5.0	1.6
1	Oct. 1965	9.7	46.2	27.3	17.4	17.0	11.6	7.0	5.6	3.5	12.5	10.2	6.6	8.9	12.9	9.5	23.5	5.0	18.8
2	Nov. 1965	11.0	15.4	18.2	17.4	17.0	16.4	9.7	7.0	4.4	9.4	6.8	8.5	13.6	6.9	16.7	17.6	20.0	9.4
3	Dec. 1965	8.0	.0	9.1	13.0	11.3	8.2	7.4	4.7	11.4	3.1	11.9	6.2	8.6	9.5	7.1	29.4	5.0	1.6
4	Jan. 1966	7.4	7.7	9.1	6.5	7.5	8.9	7.7	8.8	4.4	.0	8.5	7.2	6.1	8.6	9.5	11.8	5.0	9.4
5	Feb. 1966	5.2	15.4	.0	4.3	3.8	5.5	4.7	7.6	4.4	3.1	8.5	6.6	4.4	6.9	7.1	.0	.0	.0
6	Mar. 1966	3.4	.0	.0	.0	1.9	4.1	5.4	2.9	1.8	3.1	1.7	4.2	4.2	2.6	2.4	.0	.0	1.6
7	Apr. 1966	2.5	.0	.0	4.3	3.8	2.7	1.7	2.9	.0	9.4	6.8	1.5	2.5	4.3	.0	.0	5.0	.0
8	May or June 1966	1.7	.0	.0	.0	.0	3.4	1.0	2.3	3.5	.0	3.4	3.1	1.4	.9	.0	.0	.0	.0

*Deviations from totals of 100 percent in each column are due to additional BSSR Keys judged by the senior author to be statistically insignificant.

BSSR Survey of 937 School Administrators on ESEA——Responses in Percentages

Question No. 16-C

Question: When approximately did you receive guidelines and instructions for preparing project plans for Titles I, II and III?

Sub-Question: Title III

		BY POPULATION MAKEUP												BY REGION							
KEY*	SAMPLE	90-100% Urban	60-89% Urban	90-100% Suburban	60-89% Suburban	Mixed Rural and Urban	Mixed Rural Urban and Suburban	Mixed Rural and Suburban	60-89% Rural Non-Farm	60-89% Rural Farm	90-100% Rural Non-Farm	100% Mixed Rural	90-100% Rural Farm	New England	Middle Atlantic	East North Central	West North Central	Southern	Southwest	Mountain	Pacific
Y	No answer	31.4	31.5	31.4	28.6	43.2	29.6	45.8	31.6	42.4	35.7	56.8	50.0	28.4	30.9	42.7	41.2	36.3	36.4	23.5	31.6
0	Sept. 1965	9.3	9.3	5.0	10.0	8.0	11.3	3.4	3.9	5.1	14.3	5.4	2.4	10.4	6.7	4.1	4.1	7.8	18.2	11.8	7.9
1	Oct. 1965	15.1	12.0	12.1	7.1	10.2	11.3	8.5	5.3	5.9	11.9	10.8	2.4	14.9	10.3	8.1	6.5	11.8	10.4	5.9	14.5
2	Nov. 1965	10.5	13.9	11.4	22.9	4.5	12.7	11.9	13.2	7.6	9.5	2.7	7.1	19.4	12.7	7.7	7.6	12.7	11.7	17.6	11.8
3	Dec. 1965	10.5	6.5	12.1	5.7	4.5	2.8	10.2	10.5	8.5	11.9	5.4	2.4	6.0	10.3	6.5	10.0	4.9	1.3	23.5	9.2
4	Jan. 1966	8.1	8.3	10.0	10.0	6.8	9.9	1.7	5.3	6.8	4.8	5.4	4.8	6.0	9.1	8.5	8.2	4.9	5.2	8.8	3.9
5	Feb. 1966	2.3	3.7	7.9	8.6	4.5	5.6	3.4	2.6	5.1	4.8	.0	14.3	3.0	7.9	5.7	5.3	5.9	5.2	.0	1.3
6	Mar. 1966	3.5	4.6	2.9	.0	5.7	4.2	3.4	5.3	2.5	.0	5.4	2.4	4.5	3.0	4.1	3.5	2.9	1.3	5.9	2.6
7	Apr. 1966	1.2	1.9	2.1	1.4	2.3	2.8	1.7	3.9	4.2	.0	2.7	4.8	1.5	1.8	2.8	2.4	4.9	.0	2.9	2.6
8	May or June 1966	.0	.9	.0	1.4	.0	4.2	1.7	3.9	5.1	.0	.0	2.4	.0	.6	2.0	1.8	2.9	3.9	.0	1.3

*Deviations from totals of 100 percent in each column are due to additional BSSR Keys judged by the senior author to be statistically insignificant.

BSSR Survey of 937 School Administrators on ESEA——Responses in Percentages

Question No. 17-A

Question: What was the reaction of your School Board toward participation in Titles I, II and III of ESEA? <u>Please check the most appropriate statement for EACH title</u>.

Sub-Question: Title I

KEY *	SAMPLE	U.S. Total	BY SIZE OF STUDENT POPULATION: More Than 50,000 Students	25,000 to 49,999 Students	12,000 to 24,999 Students	6,000 to 11,999 Students	3,000 to 5,999 Students	1,200 to 2,999 Students	600 to 1,199 Students	300 to 599 Students	Less Than 300 Students	BY MEDIAN FAMILY INCOME: Less Than $3,000.	$3,000. to $4,999.	$5,000. to $6,999.	$7,000. to $8,999.	$9,000. to $11,999.	$12,000. and Over	Can't Evaluate Income	No Answer On Income
Y	No answer	1.7	.0	.0	.0	.9	3.4	1.0	1.2	3.5	3.1	.0	1.2	1.4	1.7	2.4	17.6	.0	3.1
1	Participation necessary	52.3	84.6	63.6	58.7	59.4	56.8	51.3	47.4	43.9	46.9	69.5	63.7	48.6	48.3	26.2	5.9	35.0	53.1
2	Participation desirable	35.1	7.7	27.3	28.3	34.9	28.1	36.2	39.8	43.0	28.1	22.0	24.3	42.5	39.7	42.9	52.9	35.0	31.3
3	Participation undesirable	8.6	7.7	.0	10.9	2.8	9.6	9.1	9.4	7.0	21.9	5.1	6.6	6.9	9.5	26.2	23.5	25.0	7.8

*Deviations from totals of 100 percent in each column are due to additional BSSR Keys judged by the senior author to be statistically insignificant.

BSSR Survey of 937 School Administrators on ESEA——Responses in Percentages

Question No. 17-A

Question: What was the reaction of your School Board toward participation in Titles I, II and III of ESEA? Please check the most appropriate statement for EACH title.

Sub-Question: Title I

KEY*	SAMPLE	BY POPULATION MAKEUP												BY REGION							
		90-100% Urban	60-89% Urban	90-100% Suburban	60-89% Suburban	Mixed Rural and Urban	Mixed Rural Urban and Suburban	Mixed Rural and Suburban	60-89% Rural Non-Farm	60-89% Rural Farm	90-100% Rural Non-Farm	100% Mixed Rural	90-100% Rural Farm	New England	Middle Atlantic	East North Central	West North Central	Southern	Southwest	Mountain	Pacific
Y	No answer	.0	1.9	3.6	2.9	2.3	1.4	1.7	1.3	.0	2.4	2.7	.0	3.0	1.2	2.8	.6	1.0	1.3	2.9	1.3
1	Participation necessary	60.5	54.6	40.0	54.3	56.8	54.9	42.4	53.9	52.5	61.9	37.8	66.7	52.2	43.6	49.6	47.1	67.6	71.4	44.1	55.3
2	Participation desirable	31.4	31.5	42.9	31.4	33.0	33.8	40.7	38.2	34.7	31.0	43.2	23.8	34.3	43.6	35.4	41.8	21.6	22.1	44.1	28.9
3	Participation undesirable	7.0	7.4	12.9	10.0	5.7	9.9	11.9	5.3	9.3	2.4	13.5	4.8	7.5	7.9	11.0	8.2	7.8	3.9	5.9	11.8

*Deviations from totals of 100 percent in each column are due to additional BSSR Keys judged by the senior author to be statistically insignificant.

BSSR Survey of 937 School Administrators on ESEA——Responses in Percentages

Question No. 17-B

Question: What was the reaction of your School Board toward participation in Titles I, II and III of ESEA? Please check the most appropriate statement for EACH title.

Sub-Question: Title II

KEY *	SAMPLE	U.S. Total	BY SIZE OF STUDENT POPULATION									BY MEDIAN FAMILY INCOME							
			More Than 50,000 Students	25,000 to 49,999 Students	12,000 to 24,999 Students	6,000 to 11,999 Students	3,000 to 5,999 Students	1,200 to 2,999 Students	600 to 1,199 Students	300 to 599 Students	Less Than 300 Students	Less Than $3,000.	$3,000. to $4,999.	$5,000. to $6,999.	$7,000. to $8,999.	$9,000. to $11,999.	$12,000. and Over	Can't Evaluate Income	No Answer On Income
Y	No answer	5.2	.0	.0	.0	3.8	4.1	5.7	4.7	7.9	15.6	1.7	6.6	5.3	5.2	2.4	5.9	5.0	4.7
1	Participation necessary	53.5	76.9	63.6	63.0	63.2	56.2	53.7	48.0	43.9	43.8	64.4	65.6	50.3	49.1	31.0	11.8	30.0	53.1
2	Participation desirable	34.2	23.1	27.3	28.3	30.2	35.6	33.9	39.2	37.7	28.1	28.8	20.8	40.3	36.2	54.8	76.5	45.0	31.3
3	Participation undesirable	5.8	.0	.0	6.5	2.8	2.7	5.4	8.2	8.8	12.5	5.1	5.0	3.9	8.6	9.5	5.9	15.0	9.4

*Deviations from totals of 100 percent in each column are due to additional BSSR Keys judged by the senior author to be statistically insignificant.

BSSR Survey of 937 School Administrators on ESEA——Responses in Percentages

Question No. 17-B

Question: What was the reaction of your School Board toward participation in Titles I, II and III of ESEA? Please check the most appropriate statement for EACH title.

Sub-Question: Title II

		BY POPULATION MAKEUP												BY REGION							
KEY*	SAMPLE	90-100% Urban	60-89% Urban	90-100% Suburban	60-89% Suburban	Mixed Rural and Urban	Mixed Rural Urban and Suburban	Mixed Rural and Suburban	60-89% Rural Non-Farm	60-89% Rural Farm	90-100% Rural Non-Farm	100% Mixed Rural	90-100% Rural Farm	New England	Middle Atlantic	East North Central	West North Central	Southern	Southwest	Mountain	Pacific
Y	No answer	1.2	4.6	2.9	4.3	8.0	5.6	5.1	5.3	9.3	4.8	5.4	7.1	4.5	2.4	5.3	11.8	2.9	2.6	8.8	1.3
1	Participation necessary	61.6	55.6	47.1	55.7	56.8	63.4	45.8	47.4	50.8	54.8	43.2	61.9	59.7	46.7	54.5	38.8	66.7	76.6	38.2	57.9
2	Participation desirable	33.7	31.5	42.9	32.9	30.7	26.8	35.6	43.4	33.9	38.1	37.8	16.7	29.9	45.5	32.9	38.2	27.5	18.2	44.1	32.9
3	Participation undesirable	3.5	5.6	6.4	4.3	3.4	4.2	13.6	2.6	5.9	.0	13.5	11.9	3.0	3.6	6.5	10.0	2.9	2.6	8.8	6.6

*Deviations from totals of 100 percent in each column are due to additional BSSR Keys judged by the senior author to be statistically insignificant.

BSSR Survey of 937 School Administrators on ESEA——Responses in Percentages

Question No. 17-C

Question: What was the reaction of your School Board toward participation in Titles I, II and III of ESEA? Please check the most appropriate statement for EACH title.

Sub-Question: Title III

KEY *	SAMPLE	U.S. Total	BY SIZE OF STUDENT POPULATION									BY MEDIAN FAMILY INCOME							
			More Than 50,000 Students	25,000 to 49,999 Students	12,000 to 24,999 Students	6,000 to 11,999 Students	3,000 to 5,999 Students	1,200 to 2,999 Students	600 to 1,199 Students	300 to 599 Students	Less Than 300 Students	Less Than $3,000.	$3,000. to $4,999.	$5,000. to $6,999.	$7,000. to $8,999.	$9,000. to $11,999.	$12,000. and Over	Can't Evaluate Income	No Answer On Income
Y	No answer	25.2	.0	9.1	10.9	17.9	22.6	29.5	26.3	36.0	12.5	23.7	25.9	25.3	24.1	29.0	5.9	30.0	32.8
1	Participation necessary	24.8	61.5	63.6	39.1	24.5	25.3	22.8	19.9	18.4	40.6	35.6	30.9	21.7	24.1	16.7	5.9	10.0	23.4
2	Participation desirable	31.3	38.5	18.2	37.0	46.2	34.2	27.2	29.8	25.4	28.1	27.1	23.9	36.1	36.2	35.7	64.7	25.0	18.8
3	Participation undesirable	17.6	.0	.0	8.7	11.3	16.4	29.5	23.4	19.3	15.6	13.6	17.4	16.4	14.7	26.2	23.5	30.0	23.4

*Deviations from totals of 100 percent in each column are due to additional BSSR Keys judged by the senior author to be statistically insignificant.

BSSR Survey of 937 School Administrators on ESEA——Responses in Percentages

Question No. 17-C

Question: What was the reaction of your School Board toward participation in Titles I, II and III of ESEA? Please check the most appropriate statement for EACH Title.

Sub-Question: Title III

KEY*	SAMPLE	BY POPULATION MAKEUP												BY REGION							
		90-100% Urban	60-89% Urban	90-100% Suburban	60-89% Suburban	Mixed Rural and Urban	Mixed Rural Urban and Suburban	Mixed Rural and Suburban	60-89% Rural Non-Farm	60-89% Rural Farm	90-100% Rural Non-Farm	100% Mixed Rural	90-100% Rural Farm	New England	Middle Atlantic	East North Central	West North Central	Southern	Southwest	Mountain	Pacific
Y	No answer	17.4	27.8	20.0	14.3	34.1	23.9	33.9	27.6	28.8	9.5	27.0	40.5	13.4	19.4	28.5	31.2	29.4	22.1	17.6	25.0
1	Participation necessary	37.2	22.2	19.3	30.0	25.0	26.8	20.3	14.5	22.9	31.0	27.0	33.3	32.8	24.2	22.0	22.4	29.4	33.8	26.5	17.1
2	Participation desirable	33.7	36.1	37.1	35.7	27.3	31.0	27.1	38.2	23.7	38.1	21.6	11.9	34.3	33.9	28.0	26.5	31.4	31.2	35.3	42.1
3	Participation undesirable	9.3	12.0	22.9	17.1	12.5	18.3	16.9	19.7	24.6	16.7	24.3	14.3	14.9	21.8	21.1	18.2	9.8	11.7	20.6	13.2

*Deviations from totals of 100 percent in each column are due to additional BSSR Keys judged by the senior author to be statistically insignificant.

BSSR Survey of 937 School Administrators on ESEA——Responses in Percentages

Question No. 18-A

Question: Below are some of the major objections educators have raised about the Provisions of the ESEA. Please indicate whether you agree or disagree with EACH statement.

Sub-Question: The ESEA presents a threat of federal control over local education.

KEY *	SAMPLE	U.S. Total	BY SIZE OF STUDENT POPULATION									BY MEDIAN FAMILY INCOME							
			More Than 50,000 Students	25,000 to 49,999 Students	12,000 to 24,999 Students	6,000 to 11,999 Students	3,000 to 5,999 Students	1,200 to 2,999 Students	600 to 1,199 Students	300 to 599 Students	Less Than 300 Students	Less Than $3,000.	$3,000. to $4,999.	$5,000. to $6,999.	$7,000. to $8,999.	$9,000. to $11,999.	$12,000. and Over	Can't Evaluate Income	No Answer On Income
Y	No answer	1.8	.0	9.1	2.2	.9	1.4	1.3	2.3	2.6	3.1	.0	.8	1.9	2.6	.0	11.8	.0	4.7
1	Agree	52.6	84.6	63.6	39.1	46.2	50.0	51.3	52.6	61.4	68.8	67.8	54.1	51.7	43.1	47.6	23.5	60.0	64.1
2	Disagree	45.5	15.4	27.3	58.7	52.8	48.6	47.3	44.4	36.0	28.1	32.2	45.2	46.4	53.4	52.4	64.7	40.0	31.3

*Deviations from totals of 100 percent in each column are due to additional BSSR Keys judged by the senior author to be statistically insignificant.

BSSR Survey of 937 School Administrators on ESEA——Responses in Percentages

Question No. 18-A

Question: Below are some of the major objections educators have raised about the Provisions of the ESEA. Please indicate whether you agree or disagree with EACH statement.

Sub-Question: The ESEA presents a threat of federal control over local education.

		BY POPULATION MAKEUP												BY REGION							
KEY*	SAMPLE	90-100% Urban	60-89% Urban	90-100% Suburban	60-89% Suburban	Mixed Rural and Urban	Mixed Rural Urban and Suburban	Mixed Rural and Suburban	60-89% Rural Non-Farm	60-89% Rural Farm	90-100% Rural Non-Farm	100% Mixed Rural	90-100% Rural Farm	New England	Middle Atlantic	East North Central	West North Central	Southern	Southwest	Mountain	Pacific
Y	No answer	3.5	1.9	.7	7.1	1.1	2.8	.0	1.3	.8	.0	2.7	.0	1.5	2.4	1.2	.6	1.0	2.6	.0	6.6
1	Agree	43.0	54.6	40.0	58.6	59.1	56.3	52.5	43.4	61.0	52.4	62.2	64.3	40.3	45.5	50.8	61.8	76.5	42.9	61.8	38.2
2	Disagree	53.5	43.5	59.3	34.3	39.8	39.4	47.5	55.3	38.1	47.6	35.1	35.7	58.2	52.1	48.0	37.6	22.5	54.5	35.3	55.3

*Deviations from totals of 100 percent in each column are due to additional BSSR Keys judged by the senior author to be statistically insignificant.

BSSR Survey of 937 School Administrators on ESEA——Responses in Percentages

Question No. 18-B

Question: Below are some of the major objections educators have raised about the Provisions of the ESEA. Please indicate whether you agree or disagree with EACH statement.

Sub-Question: The administration of Title II funds for private schools places an undue burden on the local education agency.

KEY *	SAMPLE	U.S. Total	BY SIZE OF STUDENT POPULATION									BY MEDIAN FAMILY INCOME							
			More Than 50,000 Students	25,000 to 49,999 Students	12,000 to 24,999 Students	6,000 to 11,999 Students	3,000 to 5,999 Students	1,200 to 2,999 Students	600 to 1,199 Students	300 to 599 Students	Less Than 300 Students	Less Than $3,000.	$3,000. to $4,999.	$5,000. to $6,999.	$7,000. to $8,999.	$9,000. to $11,999.	$12,000. and Over	Can't Evaluate Income	No Answer On Income
Y	No answer	7.8	.0	.0	2.2	6.6	4.1	10.1	8.8	9.6	9.4	13.6	6.2	7.8	5.2	9.5	11.8	.0	14.1
1	Agree	45.5	38.5	45.5	34.8	32.1	41.8	43.0	55.0	57.9	53.1	52.5	47.9	53.6	36.2	42.9	47.1	65.0	51.6
2	Disagree	46.2	61.5	54.5	60.9	60.4	54.1	47.0	36.3	30.7	34.4	33.9	45.2	47.8	58.6	47.6	41.2	35.0	34.4

*Deviations from totals of 100 percent in each column are due to additional BSSR Keys judged by the senior author to be statistically insignificant.

BSSR Survey of 937 School Administrators on ESEA——Responses in Percentages

Question No. 18-B

Question: Below are some of the major objections educators have raised about the Provisions of the ESEA. Please indicate whether you agree or disagree with EACH statement.

Sub-Question: The administration of Title II funds for private schools places an undue burden on the local education agency.

		BY POPULATION MAKEUP												BY REGION							
KEY*	SAMPLE	90-100% Urban	60-89% Urban	90-100% Suburban	60-89% Suburban	Mixed Rural and Urban	Mixed Rural Urban and Suburban	Mixed Rural and Suburban	60-89% Rural Non-Farm	60-89% Rural Farm	90-100% Rural Non-Farm	100% Mixed Rural	90-100% Rural Farm	New England	Middle Atlantic	East North Central	West North Central	Southern	Southwest	Mountain	Pacific
Y	No answer	3.5	6.5	7.1	7.1	10.2	2.8	8.5	9.2	6.8	11.9	16.2	14.3	10.4	7.9	4.5	8.2	8.8	13.0	5.9	9.2
1	Agree	39.5	40.7	35.7	55.7	48.9	45.1	40.7	46.1	58.5	52.4	40.5	45.2	34.3	38.2	45.5	55.3	50.0	50.6	47.1	36.8
2	Disagree	57.0	51.9	57.1	37.1	40.9	52.1	47.5	43.4	33.9	35.7	43.2	40.5	55.2	53.9	49.6	35.3	40.2	35.1	47.1	53.9

*Deviations from totals of 100 percent in each column are due to additional BSSR Keys judged by the senior author to be statistically insignificant.

BSSR Survey of 937 School Administrators on ESEA——Responses in Percentages

Question No. 18-C

Question: Below are some of the major objections educators have raised about the Provisions of the ESEA. Please indicate whether you agree or disagree with EACH statement.

Sub-Question: The emphasis on "Innovative" projects (particularly in Title III) penalizes districts which have undertaken new programs of their own.

			BY SIZE OF STUDENT POPULATION									BY MEDIAN FAMILY INCOME							
KEY *	SAMPLE	U.S. Total	More Than 50,000 Students	25,000 to 49,999 Students	12,000 to 24,999 Students	6,000 to 11,999 Students	3,000 to 5,999 Students	1,200 to 2,999 Students	600 to 1,199 Students	300 to 599 Students	Less Than 300 Students	Less Than $3,000.	$3,000. to $4,999.	$5,000. to $6,999.	$7,000. to $8,999.	$9,000. to $11,999.	$12,000. and Over	Can't Evaluate Income	No Answer On Income
Y	No answer	7.7	.0	.0	.0	.9	5.5	10.1	10.5	11.4	6.3	6.8	8.1	8.3	2.6	4.8	.0	10.0	15.6
1	Agree	56.6	46.2	45.5	47.8	50.0	55.5	57.4	58.5	60.5	71.9	45.8	55.6	59.2	61.2	52.4	52.9	50.0	53.1
2	Disagree	35.3	53.8	54.5	52.2	49.1	39.0	31.5	31.0	27.2	21.9	47.5	35.5	32.2	36.2	42.9	47.1	40.0	29.7

*Deviations from totals of 100 percent in each column are due to additional BSSR Keys judged by the senior author to be statistically insignificant.

BSSR Survey of 937 School Administrators on ESEA——Responses in Percentages

Question No. 18-C

Question: Below are some of the major objections educators have raised about the Provisions of the ESEA. Please indicate whether you agree or disagree with EACH statement.

Sub-Question: The emphasis on "Innovative" projects (particularly in Title III) penalizes districts which have undertaken new programs of their own.

		BY POPULATION MAKEUP												BY REGION							
KEY*	SAMPLE	90-100% Urban	60-89% Urban	90-100% Suburban	60-89% Suburban	Mixed Rural and Urban	Mixed Rural Urban and Suburban	Mixed Rural and Suburban	60-89% Rural Non-Farm	60-89% Rural Farm	90-100% Rural Non-Farm	100% Mixed Rural	90-100% Rural Farm	New England	Middle Atlantic	East North Central	West North Central	Southern	Southwest	Mountain	Pacific
Y	No answer	9.3	13.9	5.0	2.9	9.1	4.2	3.4	6.6	7.6	9.5	10.8	11.9	7.5	4.8	8.1	8.8	6.9	10.4	5.9	9.2
1	Agree	48.8	51.9	60.0	61.4	71.6	49.3	55.9	53.9	54.2	61.9	56.8	52.4	52.2	55.2	59.3	64.7	46.1	41.6	67.6	60.5
2	Disagree	41.9	33.3	34.3	35.7	19.3	46.5	40.7	39.5	37.3	28.6	32.4	33.3	38.8	40.0	32.1	25.3	47.1	48.1	26.5	30.3

*Deviations from totals of 100 percent in each column are due to additional BSSR Keys judged by the senior author to be statistically insignificant.

BSSR Survey of 937 School Administrators on ESEA——Responses in Percentages

Question No. 18-D

Question: Below are some of the major objections educators have raised about the Provisions of the ESEA. <u>Please indicate whether you agree or disagree with EACH statement</u>.

Sub-Question: Title I funds should not be allocated on a poverty basis.

KEY *	SAMPLE	U.S. Total	BY SIZE OF STUDENT POPULATION									BY MEDIAN FAMILY INCOME							
			More Than 50,000 Students	25,000 to 49,999 Students	12,000 to 24,999 Students	6,000 to 11,999 Students	3,000 to 5,999 Students	1,200 to 2,999 Students	600 to 1,199 Students	300 to 599 Students	Less Than 300 Students	Less Than $3,000.	$3,000. to $4,999.	$5,000. to $6,999.	$7,000. to $8,999.	$9,000. to $11,999.	$12,000. and Over	Can't Evaluate Income	No Answer On Income
Y	No answer	2.6	.0	9.1	6.5	1.9	3.4	2.0	3.5	.0	3.1	1.7	1.2	2.2	1.7	2.4	5.9	.0	12.5
1	Agree	69.6	61.5	54.5	60.9	71.7	69.2	72.1	69.0	67.5	71.9	67.8	70.7	72.2	64.7	66.7	41.2	75.0	68.8
2	Disagree	27.9	38.5	36.4	32.6	26.4	27.4	25.8	27.5	32.5	25.0	30.5	28.2	25.6	33.6	31.0	52.9	25.0	18.8

*Deviations from totals of 100 percent in each column are due to additional BSSR Keys judged by the senior author to be statistically insignificant.

BSSR Survey of 937 School Administrators on ESEA——Responses in Percentages

Question No. 18-D

Question: Below are some of the major objections educators have raised about the Provisions of the ESEA. Please indicate whether you agree or disagree with EACH statement.

Sub-Question: Title I funds should not be allocated on a poverty basis.

		BY POPULATION MAKEUP												BY REGION							
KEY *	SAMPLE	90-100% Urban	60-89% Urban	90-100% Suburban	60-89% Suburban	Mixed Rural and Urban	Mixed Rural Urban and Suburban	Mixed Rural and Suburban	60-89% Rural Non-Farm	60-89% Rural Farm	90-100% Rural Non-Farm	100% Mixed Rural	90-100% Rural Farm	New England	Middle Atlantic	East North Central	West North Central	Southern	Southwest	Mountain	Pacific
Y	No answer	5.8	2.8	2.1	2.9	2.3	2.8	1.7	2.6	1.7	4.8	.0	.0	3.0	1.8	2.8	1.8	1.0	3.9	5.9	3.9
1	Agree	55.8	71.3	65.0	67.1	80.7	76.1	74.6	67.1	73.7	71.4	56.8	73.8	65.7	69.1	69.1	70.6	79.4	62.3	64.7	69.7
2	Disagree	38.4	25.9	32.9	30.0	17.0	21.1	23.7	30.3	24.6	23.8	43.2	26.2	31.3	29.1	28.0	27.6	19.6	33.8	29.4	26.3

*Deviations from totals of 100 percent in each column are due to additional BSSR Keys judged by the senior author to be statistically insignificant.

BSSR Survey of 937 School Administrators on ESEA——Responses in Percentages

Question No. 18-E

Question: Below are some of the major objections educators have raised about the Provisions of the ESEA. Please indicate whether you agree or disagree with EACH statement.

Sub-Question: Title III funds should not be allocated on a competitive basis.

KEY *	SAMPLE	U.S. Total	BY SIZE OF STUDENT POPULATION									BY MEDIAN FAMILY INCOME							
			More Than 50,000 Students	25,000 to 49,999 Students	12,000 to 24,999 Students	6,000 to 11,999 Students	3,000 to 5,999 Students	1,200 to 2,999 Students	600 to 1,199 Students	300 to 599 Students	Less Than 300 Students	Less Than $3,000.	$3,000. to $4,999.	$5,000. to $6,999.	$7,000. to $8,999.	$9,000. to $11,999.	$12,000. and Over	Can't Evaluate Income	No Answer On Income
Y	No answer	9.6	7.7	.0	2.2	4.7	7.5	11.1	11.1	16.7	3.1	13.6	8.1	10.3	5.2	9.5	.0	5.0	20.3
1	Agree	70.0	46.2	63.6	67.4	76.4	68.5	69.5	68.4	71.1	81.3	66.1	73.0	70.0	70.7	76.2	58.8	85.0	54.7
2	Disagree	19.9	46.2	36.4	30.4	18.9	23.3	19.1	19.9	11.4	12.5	18.6	18.5	18.9	24.1	14.3	41.2	10.0	25.0

*Deviations from totals of 100 percent in each column are due to additional BSSR Keys judged by the senior author to be statistically insignificant.

BSSR Survey of 937 School Administrators on ESEA——Responses in Percentages

Question No. 18-E

Question: Below are some of the major objections educators have raised about the Provisions of the ESEA. Please indicate whether you agree or disagree with EACH statement.

Sub-Question: Title III funds should not be allocated on a competitive basis.

KEY*	SAMPLE	BY POPULATION MAKEUP												BY REGION							
		90-100% Urban	60-89% Urban	90-100% Suburban	60-89% Suburban	Mixed Rural and Urban	Mixed Rural Urban and Suburban	Mixed Rural and Suburban	60-89% Rural Non-Farm	60-89% Rural Farm	90-100% Rural Non-Farm	100% Mixed Rural	90-100% Rural Farm	New England	Middle Atlantic	East North Central	West North Central	Southern	Southwest	Mountain	Pacific
Y	No answer	11.6	13.0	7.1	10.0	11.4	4.2	5.1	9.2	12.7	4.8	10.8	11.9	6.0	8.5	7.7	12.9	13.7	7.8	11.8	9.2
1	Agree	67.4	65.7	70.0	68.6	73.9	73.2	78.0	68.4	66.9	76.2	73.0	66.7	77.6	67.3	70.7	68.8	70.6	71.4	64.7	69.7
2	Disagree	20.9	21.3	22.9	21.4	14.8	21.1	15.3	21.1	20.3	19.0	16.2	16.7	16.4	24.2	19.9	17.6	15.7	20.8	23.5	21.1

*Deviation from totals of 100 percent in each column are due to additional BSSR Keys judged by the senior author to be statistically insignificant.

BSSR Survey of 937 School Administrators on ESEA——Responses in Percentages

Question No. 19-A

Question: Have you done any of the following?
<u>Please check YES or NO for EACH statement</u>.

Sub-Question: Submitted one or more project plans under Title I.

KEY *	SAMPLE	U.S. Total	BY SIZE OF STUDENT POPULATION: More Than 50,000 Students	25,000 to 49,999 Students	12,000 to 24,999 Students	6,000 to 11,999 Students	3,000 to 5,999 Students	1,200 to 2,999 Students	600 to 1,199 Students	300 to 599 Students	Less Than 300 Students	BY MEDIAN FAMILY INCOME: Less Than $3,000.	$3,000. to $4,999.	$5,000. to $6,999.	$7,000. to $8,999.	$9,000. to $11,999.	$12,000. and Over	Can't Evaluate Income	No Answer On Income
1	Yes	92.7	100.0	100.0	100.0	96.2	93.2	93.6	91.2	89.5	75.0	98.3	95.0	95.6	92.2	64.3	58.8	85.0	93.8
2	No	7.3	.0	.0	.0	3.8	6.8	6.4	8.8	10.5	25.0	1.7	5.0	4.4	7.8	35.7	41.2	15.0	6.3

*Deviations from totals of 100 percent in each column are due to additional BSSR Keys judged by the senior author to be statistically insignificant.

BSSR Survey of 937 School Administrators on ESEA——Responses in Percentages

Question No. 19-A

Question: Have you done any of the following? Please check YES or NO for EACH statement.

Sub-Question: Submitted one or more project plans under Title I.

		BY POPULATION MAKEUP												BY REGION							
KEY *	SAMPLE	90-100% Urban	60-89% Urban	90-100% Suburban	60-89% Suburban	Mixed Rural and Urban	Mixed Rural Urban and Suburban	Mixed Rural and Suburban	60-89% Rural Non-Farm	60-89% Rural Farm	90-100% Rural Non-Farm	100% Mixed Rural	90-100% Rural Farm	New England	Middle Atlantic	East North Central	West North Central	Southern	Southwest	Mountain	Pacific
1	YES	95.3	96.3	83.6	90.0	97.7	95.8	88.1	97.4	95.8	90.5	94.6	88.1	86.6	93.9	89.8	95.9	98.0	94.8	88.2	90.8
2	NO	4.7	3.7	16.4	10.0	2.3	4.2	11.9	2.6	4.2	9.5	5.4	11.9	13.4	6.1	10.2	4.1	2.0	5.2	11.8	9.2

*Deviations from totals of 100 percent in each column are due to additional BSSR Keys judged by the senior author to be statistically insignificant.

BSSR Survey of 937 School Administrators on ESEA——Responses in Percentages

Question No. 19-B

Question: Have you done any of the following?
Please check YES or NO for EACH statement.

Sub-Question: Submitted an instructional materials order under Title II.

KEY *	SAMPLE	U.S. Total	BY SIZE OF STUDENT POPULATION									BY MEDIAN FAMILY INCOME							
			More Than 50,000 Students	25,000 to 49,999 Students	12,000 to 24,999 Students	6,000 to 11,999 Students	3,000 to 5,999 Students	1,200 to 2,999 Students	600 to 1,199 Students	300 to 599 Students	Less Than 300 Students	Less Than $3,000.	$3,000. to $4,999.	$5,000. to $6,999.	$7,000. to $8,999.	$9,000. to $11,999.	$12,000. and Over	Can't Evaluate Income	No Answer On Income
1	Yes	86.8	100.0	100.0	93.5	96.2	89.0	88.9	85.4	72.8	62.5	86.4	87.3	88.6	83.6	90.5	88.2	85.0	78.1
2	No	13.2	.0	.0	6.5	3.8	11.0	11.1	14.6	27.2	37.5	13.6	12.7	11.4	16.4	9.5	11.8	15.0	21.9

*Deviations from totals of 100 percent in each column are due to additional BSSR Keys judged by the senior author to be statistically insignificant.

BSSR Survey of 937 School Administrators on ESEA——Responses in Percentages

Question No. 19-B

Question: Have you done any of the following? Please check YES or NO for EACH statement.

Sub-Question: Submitted an instructional materials order under Title II.

KEY *	SAMPLE	BY POPULATION MAKEUP												BY REGION							
		90-100% Urban	60-89% Urban	90-100% Suburban	60-89% Suburban	Mixed Rural and Urban	Mixed Rural Urban and Suburban	Mixed Rural and Suburban	60-89% Rural Non-Farm	60-89% Rural Farm	90-100% Rural Non-Farm	100% Mixed Rural	90-100% Rural Farm	New England	Middle Atlantic	East North Central	West North Central	Southern	Southwest	Mountain	Pacific
1	YES	94.2	89.8	90.7	80.0	84.1	90.1	88.1	92.1	80.5	90.5	89.2	61.9	91.0	86.7	89.4	72.9	93.1	92.2	82.4	93.4
2	NO	5.8	10.2	9.3	20.0	15.9	9.9	11.9	7.9	19.5	9.5	10.8	38.1	9.0	13.3	10.6	27.1	6.9	7.8	17.6	6.6

*Deviations from totals of 100 percent in each column are due to additional BSSR Keys judged by the senior author to be statistically insignificant.

BSSR Survey of 937 School Administrators on ESEA——Responses in Percentages

Question No. 19-C

Question: Have you done any of the following?
<u>Please check YES or NO for EACH statement</u>.

Sub-Question: Submitted an application for a grant under Title III, either alone or in cooperation with one or more districts.

KEY *	SAMPLE	U.S. Total	BY SIZE OF STUDENT POPULATION									BY MEDIAN FAMILY INCOME							
			More Than 50,000 Students	25,000 to 49,999 Students	12,000 to 24,999 Students	6,000 to 11,999 Students	3,000 to 5,999 Students	1,200 to 2,999 Students	600 to 1,199 Students	300 to 599 Students	Less Than 300 Students	Less Than $3,000.	$3,000. to $4,999.	$5,000. to $6,999.	$7,000. to $8,999.	$9,000. to $11,999.	$12,000. and Over	Can't Evaluate Income	No Answer On Income
1	Yes	50.9	92.3	90.9	71.7	61.3	56.2	49.0	39.2	37.7	59.4	54.2	50.2	39.7	57.8	50.0	76.5	40.0	42.2
2	No	49.1	7.7	9.1	28.3	38.7	43.8	51.0	60.8	62.3	40.6	45.8	49.8	50.3	42.2	50.0	23.5	60.0	57.8

*Deviations from totals of 100 percent in each column are due to additional BSSR Keys judged by the senior author to be statistically insignificant.

BSSR Survey of 937 School Administrators on ESEA——Responses in Percentages

Question No. 19-C

Question: Have you done any of the following? Please check YES or NO for EACH statement.

Sub-Question: Submitted an application for a grant under Title III, either alone or in cooperation with one or more districts.

		BY POPULATION MAKEUP												BY REGION							
KEY *	SAMPLE	90-100% Urban	60-89% Urban	90-100% Suburban	60-89% Suburban	Mixed Rural and Urban	Mixed Rural Urban and Suburban	Mixed Rural and Suburban	60-89% Rural Non-Farm	60-89% Rural Farm	90-100% Rural Non-Farm	100% Mixed Rural	90-100% Rural Farm	New England	Middle Atlantic	East North Central	West North Central	Southern	Southwest	Mountain	Pacific
1	YES	61.6	56.5	55.0	62.9	45.5	54.9	40.7	48.7	40.7	66.7	35.1	31.0	70.1	52.7	43.9	39.4	56.9	53.2	61.8	63.2
2	NO	38.4	43.5	45.0	37.1	54.5	45.1	59.3	51.3	59.3	33.3	64.9	69.0	29.9	47.3	56.1	60.6	43.1	46.8	38.2	36.8

*Deviations from totals of 100 percent in each column are due to additional BSSR Keys judged by the senior author to be statistically insignificant.

BSSR Survey of 937 School Administrators on ESEA——Responses in Percentages

Question No. 19-C (b)

Question:

Sub-Question: If you have participated in a cooperative Title III application, please indicate with whom.

KEY *	SAMPLE	U.S. Total	BY SIZE OF STUDENT POPULATION									BY MEDIAN FAMILY INCOME							
			More Than 50,000 Students	25,000 to 49,999 Students	12,000 to 24,999 Students	6,000 to 11,999 Students	3,000 to 5,999 Students	1,200 to 2,999 Students	600 to 1,199 Students	300 to 599 Students	Less Than 300 Students	Less Than $3,000.	$3,000. to $4,999.	$5,000. to $6,999.	$7,000. to $8,999.	$9,000. to $11,999.	$12,000. and Over	Can't Evaluate Income	No Answer On Income
Y	No answer	1.7	.0	.0	.0	1.9	3.4	2.0	1.2	.9	.0	3.4	1.2	1.7	1.7	.0	5.9	.0	3.1
X	Didn't apply for Title	49.1	7.7	9.1	28.3	38.7	43.8	51.0	60.8	62.3	40.6	45.8	49.8	50.3	42.2	50.0	23.5	60.0	57.8
O	Respondent district only	11.3	30.8	36.4	17.4	17.9	15.8	7.7	5.8	6.1	25.0	11.9	11.6	11.1	11.2	7.1	11.8	5.0	15.6
1	One other school district	2.9	.0	.0	.0	3.8	1.4	3.7	2.3	4.4	3.1	1.7	1.9	3.6	1.9	4.8	5.9	5.0	3.1
2	More than one district (but not #3)	6.4	7.7	9.1	17.4	4.7	5.5	8.7	2.9	4.4	3.1	6.8	5.8	5.6	10.3	11.9	5.9	10.0	1.6
3	Countywide Intermediate district	10.5	.0	36.4	15.2	14.2	13.0	9.4	9.9	5.3	6.3	1.7	8.5	10.0	16.4	9.5	35.3	10.0	7.8
4	Regional District intrastate	14.6	15.4	9.1	19.6	14.2	14.4	14.1	15.2	13.2	18.8	25.4	18.1	13.9	11.2	11.9	5.9	5.0	7.8
5	College or university	2.1	.0	.0	.0	1.9	2.7	2.7	1.2	2.6	3.1	3.4	2.3	1.4	2.6	2.4	5.9	5.0	1.6
6	Other	1.4	38.5	.0	2.2	2.8	.0	.7	.6	.9	.0	.0	.8	1.7	2.6	2.4	.0	.0	1.6

*Deviations from totals of 100 percent in each column are due to additional BSSR Keys judged by the senior author to be statistically insignificant.

BSSR Survey of 937 School Administrators on ESEA——Responses in Percentages

Question No. 19-C (b)

Question:

Sub-Question: If you have participated in a cooperative Title III application, please indicate with whom.

		BY POPULATION MAKEUP												BY REGION							
KEY	SAMPLE	90-100% Urban	60-89% Urban	90-100% Suburban	60-89% Suburban	Mixed Rural and Urban	Mixed Rural Urban and Suburban	Mixed Rural and Suburban	60-89% Rural Non-Farm	60-89% Rural Farm	90-100% Rural Non-Farm	100% Mixed Rural	90-100% Rural Farm	New England	Middle Atlantic	East North Central	West North Central	Southern	Southwest	Mountain	Pacific
Y	No answer	1.2	.9	2.1	2.9	2.3	2.8	.0	.0	.8	4.8	2.7	2.4	3.0	1.2	2.4	1.2	2.9	1.3	.0	.0
X	Didn't apply for Title	38.4	43.5	45.0	37.1	54.5	45.1	59.3	51.3	59.3	33.3	64.9	69.0	29.9	47.3	56.1	60.6	43.1	46.8	38.2	36.8
0	Respondent district only	17.4	14.8	10.7	15.7	6.8	12.7	5.1	5.3	8.5	14.3	10.8	16.7	16.4	7.9	8.5	10.0	13.7	18.2	20.6	11.8
1	One other school district	4.7	1.9	3.6	4.3	.0	2.8	.0	5.3	4.2	2.4	2.7	.0	1.5	1.8	3.7	1.8	2.9	2.6	11.8	2.6
2	More than one district(but not#3)	8.1	7.4	10.0	15.7	3.4	2.8	6.8	3.9	3.4	7.1	2.7	.0	23.9	6.7	4.9	7.1	4.9	3.9	2.9	.0
3	Countywide inter-med. district	14.0	11.1	15.7	11.4	6.8	9.9	15.3	15.8	3.4	7.1	8.1	.0	7.5	14.5	10.2	2.9	9.8	6.5	2.9	30.3
4	Regional district intrastate	11.6	15.7	8.6	10.0	19.3	21.1	10.2	18.4	18.6	23.8	8.1	9.5	14.9	15.2	11.0	13.5	20.6	11.7	23.5	18.4
5	College or university	.0	2.8	2.1	1.4	4.5	2.8	3.4	.0	1.7	4.8	.0	2.4	1.5	3.0	2.0	1.2	1.0	7.8	.0	.0
6	Other	4.7	1.9	2.1	1.4	2.3	.0	.0	.0	.0	2.4	.0	.0	1.5	2.4	1.2	1.8	1.0	1.3	.0	.0

*Deviations from totals of 100 percent in each column are due to additional BSSR Keys judged by the senior author to be statistically insignificant.

BSSR Survey of 937 School Administrators on ESEA——Responses in Percentages

Question No. 20-A

Question: If you have not submitted a project plan under one or more of the titles, please indicate why by checking the most appropriate statement for EACH Title.

Sub-Question: Title I

KEY *	SAMPLE	U.S. Total	BY SIZE OF STUDENT POPULATION: More Than 50,000 Students	25,000 to 49,999 Students	12,000 to 24,999 Students	6,000 to 11,999 Students	3,000 to 5,999 Students	1,200 to 2,999 Students	600 to 1,199 Students	300 to 599 Students	Less Than 300 Students	BY MEDIAN FAMILY INCOME: Less Than $3,000.	$3,000. to $4,999.	$5,000. to $6,999.	$7,000. to $8,999.	$9,000. to $11,999.	$12,000. and Over	Can't Evaluate Income	No Answer On Income
Y	No answer	.2	.0	.0	.0	.0	.0	0.3	0.6	0.0	.0	.0	.4	.0	.0	.0	5.9	.0	.0
X	Not applicable	92.8	100.0	100.0	100.0	96.3	93.4	93.6	91.3	89.5	75.0	98.3	95.0	95.6	92.3	64.3	58.9	85.0	94.0
1	Guidelines received too late	1.7	.0	.0	.0	2.8	2.7	.7	1.8	2.6	3.1	1.7	.0	1.9	.9	11.9	.0	10.0	.0
2	Not eligible	1.8	.0	.0	.0	.0	1.4	1.0	2.3	3.5	12.5	.0	1.2	1.1	2.6	4.8	17.6	.0	3.1
3	District policy opposed	1.3	.0	.0	.0	.0	2.7	1.3	1.2	1.8	.0	.0	.4	.3	2.6	7.1	11.7	5.0	1.7
4	Insufficient staff	2.7	.0	.0	.0	2.8	1.4	3.0	3.5	3.5	6.3	1.7	1.5	1.9	3.5	11.9	5.9	10.0	1.7
5	Not worth the time	2.4	.0	.0	.0	2.8	2.1	2.0	2.9	3.5	6.3	.0	.8	1.7	3.5	16.7	5.9	10.0	.0
6	Lack of capital	.5	.0	.0	.0	.0	.7	.3	1.2	.9	.0	1.7	.8	.3	.0	.0	.0	5.0	.0

*Deviations from totals of 100 percent in each column are due to additional BSSR Keys judged by the senior author to be statistically insignificant.

BSSR Survey of 937 School Administrators on ESEA——Responses in Percentages

Question No. 20-A

Question: If you have not submitted a project plan under one or more of the titles, please indicate why by checking the most appropriate statement for EACH Title.

Sub-Question: Title I

		BY POPULATION MAKEUP												BY REGION							
KEY*	SAMPLE	90-100% Urban	60-89% Urban	90-100% Suburban	60-89% Suburban	Mixed Rural and Urban	Mixed Rural Urban and Suburban	Mixed Rural and Suburban	60-89% Rural Non-Farm	60-89% Rural Farm	90-100% Rural Non-Farm	100% Mixed Rural	90-100% Rural Farm	New England	Middle Atlantic	East North Central	West North Central	Southern	Southwest	Mountain	Pacific
Y	No answer	.0	.0	.7	.0	.0	.0	.0	.0	.0	.0	.0	2.4	.0	.0	.0	.6	.0	.0	.0	1.3
X	Not applicable	95.3	95.3	83.6	90.0	97.7	95.6	88.1	97.4	95.8	90.4	94.6	88.1	86.5	94.0	90.2	95.9	98.2	94.8	88.2	90.8
1	Guidelines received too late	1.2	.9	2.1	2.9	1.1	2.8	5.1	.0	1.7	.0	.0	2.4	3.0	1.2	3.7	1.2	1.0	.0	.0	.0
2	Not eligible	1.2	1.9	4.3	1.4	1.1	1.4	.0	.0	1.7	4.8	.0	2.4	3.0	2.4	.4	.6	1.0	2.6	8.8	4.0
3	District policy opposed	1.2	.9	4.3	1.4	.0	.0	1.7	1.3	.8	.0	.0	.0	.0	1.8	2.0	.6	.0	1.3	.0	2.6
4	Insufficient staff	1.2	.9	6.4	2.9	1.1	.0	3.4	2.6	1.7	4.8	2.7	4.8	6.0	2.4	4.5	1.8	1.0	1.3	.0	1.3
5	Not worth the time	1.2	1.9	5.7	2.9	1.1	1.4	5.1	1.3	.8	.0	2.7	2.4	1.5	1.8	4.9	1.8	.0	.0	.0	4.0
6	Lack of capital	.0	.0	.0	.0	.0	.0	3.4	1.3	.8	.0	2.7	.0	1.5	.6	.4	.6	1.0	.0	.0	.0

*Deviations from totals of 100 percent in each column are due to additional BSSR Keys judged by the senior author to be statistically insignificant.

BSSR Survey of 937 School Administrators on ESEA——Responses in Percentages

Question No. 20-B

Question: If you have not submitted a project plan under one or more of the titles, please indicate why by checking the most appropriate statement for EACH title.

Sub-Question: Title II

KEY *	SAMPLE	U.S. Total	BY SIZE OF STUDENT POPULATION: More Than 50,000 Students	25,000 to 49,999 Students	12,000 to 24,999 Students	6,000 to 11,999 Students	3,000 to 5,999 Students	1,200 to 2,999 Students	600 to 1,199 Students	300 to 599 Students	Less Than 300 Students	BY MEDIAN FAMILY INCOME: Less Than $3,000.	$3,000. to $4,999.	$5,000. to $6,999.	$7,000. to $8,999.	$9,000. to $11,999.	$12,000. and Over	Can't Evaluate Income	No Answer On Income
Y	no answer	5.6	.0	.0	4.3	0.9	6.8	5.0	5.3	10.5	9.4	8.5	7.0	4.4	5.2	.0	.0	5.0	9.4
X	Not applicable.	86.8	100.0	100.0	93.5	96.3	89.0	89.0	85.4	72.8	62.5	86.5	87.3	88.6	83.6	90.5	88.2	85.0	78.6
1	Guidelines received too late.	1.7	.0	.0	.0	0.9	1.4	1.7	1.2	3.5	6.2	1.7	.4	2.2	2.6	2.4	.0	.0	3.1
2	Not eligible.	9.6	.0	.0	.0	.0	0.7	0.7	1.2	1.8	6.2	.0	1.5	.6	.0	.0	5.9	.0	3.1
3	District policy opposed.	.7	.0	.0	.0	.0	0.7	1.0	.0	1.8	3.1	.0	.4	.0	3.5	2.4	.0	.0	1.7
4	Insufficient staff.	2.4	.0	.0	2.2	0.9	.0	1.3	2.9	5.3	15.6	3.4	1.9	1.7	3.5	4.8	5.9	.0	3.1
5	Not worth the time.	2.0	.0	.0	2.2	.0	.0	1.0	1.8	6.1	15.6	1.7	.8	1.9	4.3	2.4	5.9	.0	3.1
6	Lack of capital.	.1	.0	.0	.0	.0	.0	.0	.0	0.9	.0	.0	.0	.3	.0	.0	.0	.0	.0

* Deviations from totals of 100% in each column are due to additional BSSR Keys judged by the senior author to be statistically insignificant.

BSSR Survey of 937 School Administrators on ESEA——Responses in Percentages — Question No. 20-B

Question: If you have not submitted a project plan under one or more of the titles, please indicate why by checking the most appropriate statement for EACH title.

Sub-Question: Title II

KEY*	SAMPLE	BY POPULATION MAKEUP												BY REGION							
		90-100% Urban	60-89% Urban	90-100% Suburban	60-89% Suburban	Mixed Rural and Urban	Mixed Rural Urban and Suburban	Mixed Rural and Suburban	60-89% Rural Non-Farm	60-89% Rural Farm	90-100% Rural Non-Farm	100% Mixed Rural	90-100% Rural Farm	New England	Middle Atlantic	East North Central	West North Central	Southern	Southwest	Mountain	Pacific
Y	no answer.	3.5	4.6	3.6	7.1	6.8	5.6	3.4	3.9	5.9	7.1	.0	21.4	4.5	9.7	2.8	9.4	2.9	3.9	8.8	1.3
X	Not applicable.	94.2	89.9	90.8	80.0	84.1	90.1	88.1	92.1	80.5	90.4	89.1	61.9	91.0	86.6	89.4	7.3	93.3	92.3	82.4	93.5
1	Guidelines received too late.	1.2	.9	.0	4.3	3.4	1.4	3.4	2.6	1.7	.0	.0	2.4	.0	1.2	2.4	1.8	2.0	2.6	.0	1.3
2	Not eligible.	.0	.0	.7	.0	.0	.0	.0	1.3	3.4	2.4	2.7	2.4	1.5	.0	.0	4.1	.0	.0	2.9	.0
3	District policy opposed.	.0	.9	2.9	1.4	.0	.0	1.7	.0	.0	.0	.0	.0	.0	1.2	1.2	.6	.0	1.3	.0	.0
4	Insufficient staff.	.0	1.9	1.4	4.3	5.7	.0	1.7	1.3	2.5	.0	2.7	9.5	.0	.6	4.1	2.3	2.9	.0	2.9	1.3
5	Not worth the time.	1.2	2.8	2.1	1.4	2.3	.0	5.1	1.3	1.7	.0	.0	7.1	3.0	.6	4.1	1.2	1.0	.0	2.9	5.3
6	Lack of capital.	.0	.9	.0	.0	.0	.0	.0	.0	.0	.0	.0	.0	.0	.0	.0	.0	.0	.0	.0	1.3

* Deviations from totals of 100% in each column are due to additional BSSR Keys judged by the senior author to be statistically insignificant.

BSSR Survey of 937 School Administrators on ESEA——Responses in Percentages

Question No. 20-C

Question: If you have not submitted a project plan under one or more of the titles, please indicate why by checking the most appropriate statement for EACH title.

Sub-Question: Title III

KEY *	SAMPLE	U.S. Total	BY SIZE OF STUDENT POPULATION: More Than 50,000 Students	25,000 to 49,999 Students	12,000 to 24,999 Students	6,000 to 11,999 Students	3,000 to 5,999 Students	1,200 to 2,999 Students	600 to 1,199 Students	300 to 599 Students	Less Than 300 Students	BY MEDIAN FAMILY INCOME: Less Than $3,000.	$3,000. to $4,999.	$5,000. to $6,999.	$7,000. to $8,999.	$9,000. to $11,999.	$12,000. and Over	Can't Evaluate Income	No Answer On Income
Y	no answer	18.6	.0	.0	13.0	8.5	15.1	22.7	19.9	29.8	9.4	16.9	19.7	18.6	17.3	9.5	11.8	15.0	26.7
X	Not applicable.	50.9	92.3	91.0	71.7	61.4	56.2	49.0	39.2	37.7	59.4	54.2	50.2	49.8	57.7	50.0	76.5	40.0	42.5
1	Guidelines received too late.	6.3	.0	9.1	.0	12.3	3.4	5.7	3.5	8.8	3.1	3.4	7.3	7.8	2.6	7.1	.0	10.0	3.1
2	Not eligible.	3.1	.0	.0	.0	.9	.7	2.0	4.1	5.3	12.5	.0	3.5	3.9	3.5	2.4	.0	5.0	.0
3	District policy opposed.	1.6	.0	.0	.0	1.9	.7	1.7	2.3	1.8	3.1	1.7	.8	1.1	3.5	7.1	.0	.0	1.7
4	Insufficient staff.	19.5	7.7	.0	13.0	17.9	19.9	19.8	27.5	15.8	12.5	22.1	21.2	18.6	13.8	21.4	11.8	30.0	23.6
5	Not worth the time.	5.6	.0	9.1	2.2	3.8	4.5	4.0	7.6	10.5	9.4	5.1	4.6	5.6	5.2	7.1	11.8	15.0	6.3
6	Lack of capital.	2.2	.0	9.1	.0	.0	2.1	2.7	4.7	.8	.0	5.1	2.7	2.2	.9	.0	.0	5.0	1.6

*Deviations from totals of 100% in each column are due to additional BSSR Keys judged by the senior author to be statistically insignificant.

BSSR Survey of 937 School Administrators on ESEA——Responses in Percentages

Question No. 20-C

Question: If you have not submitted a project plan under one or more of the titles, please indicate why by checking the most appropriate statement for EACH title.

Sub-Question: Title III

KEY *	SAMPLE	BY POPULATION MAKEUP												BY REGION							
		90-100% Urban	60-89% Urban	90-100% Suburban	60-89% Suburban	Mixed Rural and Urban	Mixed Rural Urban and Suburban	Mixed Rural and Suburban	60-89% Rural Non-Farm	60-89% Rural Farm	90-100% Rural Non-Farm	100% Mixed Rural	90-100% Rural Farm	New England	Middle Atlantic	East North Central	West North Central	Southern	Southwest	Mountain	Pacific
Y	no answer	11.6	16.7	17.1	8.6	23.9	15.5	20.3	22.4	22.0	7.1	29.7	35.7	9.6	13.9	24.4	22.4	19.6	13.0	14.7	14.5
X	Not applicable	61.6	56.5	55.0	62.9	45.4	54.9	40.7	48.7	40.7	66.7	35.1	31.0	70.2	52.8	43.9	39.4	56.9	53.1	61.8	63.2
1	Guidelines received too late	7.0	9.3	1.4	8.6	11.4	5.1	6.8	3.9	7.6	2.4	2.7	7.1	1.5	3.0	7.3	9.4	9.8	9.1	.0	2.6
2	Not eligible	1.2	3.7	1.4	1.4	5.7	1.4	3.4	5.3	5.9	2.4	2.7	.0	.0	3.6	2.4	5.3	.0	1.3	2.9	7.9
3	District policy opposed	1.2	.9	3.6	2.9	.0	1.4	1.7	1.3	1.7	.0	.0	2.4	.0	1.8	2.8	1.8	.0	2.6	.0	.0
4	Insufficient staff	17.4	13.0	14.3	21.4	18.2	25.3	25.4	21.0	22.9	21.4	27.0	19.0	19.4	20.6	20.7	21.2	18.6	23.4	17.6	7.9
5	Not worth the time	5.8	7.4	4.3	2.9	4.5	2.8	3.4	5.3	8.5	7.1	10.8	7.1	.0	4.9	8.1	6.5	3.9	3.9	5.9	6.6
6	Lack of capital	2.3	2.8	.7	2.9	1.1	4.2	3.4	2.6	3.4	2.4	.0	.0	.0	1.2	3.3	1.2	2.9	5.2	2.9	1.3

* Deviations from totals of 100% in each column are due to additional BSSR Keys judged by the senior author to be statistically insignificant.

BSSR Survey of 937 School Administrators on ESEA——Responses in Percentages

Question No. 22-A

Question: What is the present status of your application(s)? Please check appropriate status for each Title.

Sub-Question: Date began operation Title III.

KEY	SAMPLE	U.S. Total	BY SIZE OF STUDENT POPULATION: More Than 50,000 Students	25,000 to 49,999 Students	12,000 to 24,999 Students	6,000 to 11,999 Students	3,000 to 5,999 Students	1,200 to 2,999 Students	600 to 1,199 Students	300 to 599 Students	Less Than 300 Students	BY MEDIAN FAMILY INCOME: Less Than $3,000.	$3,000. to $4,999.	$5,000. to $6,999.	$7,000. to $8,999.	$9,000. to $11,999.	$12,000. and Over	Can't Evaluate Income	No Answer On Income
Y	no answer	17.2	.0	9.1	23.9	9.4	17.8	19.1	19.9	14.0	18.8	18.6	18.5	13.9	21.6	16.7	35.3	15.0	17.2
X	Non applicable	71.1	38.5	63.6	63.0	70.8	67.8	74.2	70.2	78.1	65.6	57.6	68.0	76.1	69.8	71.4	35.3	85.0	75.0
0	Nov. 1965	1.0	.0	.0	.0	.0	1.4	.7	.0	2.6	6.3	3.4	1.2	.8	.0	.0	.0	.0	1.6
1	Dec. 1965	.2	.0	.0	.0	.0	.7	.0	.0	.9	.0	.0	.4	.3	.0	.0	.0	.0	.0
2	Jan. 1966	1.4	15.4	9.1	2.2	.9	1.4	1.7	.6	.0	.0	3.4	.8	1.9	1.7	.0	.0	.0	.0
3	Feb. 1966	1.5	15.4	9.1	.0	3.8	.7	.3	2.3	.9	.0	.0	2.3	1.1	1.7	2.4	.0	.0	1.6
4	Mar. 1966	1.4	15.4	.0	.0	4.7	1.4	.7	.6	.0	3.1	3.4	1.2	.8	.0	4.8	11.8	.0	1.6
5	April 1966	2.2	7.7	.0	6.5	2.8	1.4	1.3	4.1	.9	.0	5.1	2.7	2.2	.9	.0	5.9	.0	1.6
6	May 1966	2.3	.0	9.1	.0	6.6	3.4	.7	2.3	1.8	3.1	6.8	2.3	2.2	1.7	2.4	5.9	.0	.0
7	June 1966	1.7	7.7	.0	4.3	.9	4.1	1.3	.0	.9	3.1	1.7	2.7	.6	2.6	2.4	5.9	.0	1.6

BSSR Survey of 937 School Administrators on ESEA——Responses in Percentages

Question No. 22-A

Question: What is the present status of your application(s)? Please check appropriate status for each Title.

Sub-Question: Date began operation Title III.

KEY	SAMPLE	BY POPULATION MAKEUP												BY REGION							
		90-100% Urban	60-89% Urban	90-100% Suburban	60-89% Suburban	Mixed Rural and Urban	Mixed Rural Urban and Suburban	Mixed Rural and Suburban	60-89% Rural Non-Farm	60-89% Rural Farm	90-100% Rural Non-Farm	100% Mixed Rural	90-100% Rural Farm	New England	Middle Atlantic	East North Central	West North Central	Southern	Southwest	Mountain	Pacific
Y	no answer	11.6	13.9	17.9	28.6	19.3	12.7	13.6	21.1	16.9	31.0	13.5	7.1	17.9	22.4	16.3	11.2	15.7	15.6	32.4	18.4
X	Nonapplicable	68.6	68.5	72.9	61.4	73.9	73.2	81.4	67.1	72.9	54.8	75.7	83.3	68.7	66.1	76.8	77.6	69.6	64.9	52.9	67.1
0	November 1965	.0	.9	.7	.0	1.1	.0	.0	3.9	.0	.0	5.4	2.4	.0	1.2	.4	.0	.0	7.8	.0	.0
1	December 1965	.0	.0	.0	.0	.0	.0	.0	1.3	.0	.0	.0	2.4	.0	.0	.0	.6	.0	.0	.0	1.3
2	January 1966	4.7	1.9	.7	.0	1.1	1.4	.0	.0	.8	2.4	2.7	2.4	.0	.6	1.2	1.2	3.9	1.3	.0	2.6
3	February 1966	3.5	1.9	.7	1.4	3.4	.0	1.7	1.3	.8	2.4	.0	.0	3.0	2.4	.8	1.2	1.0	1.3	2.9	1.3
4	March 1966	1.2	2.8	2.1	1.4	.0	2.8	.0	.0	2.5	.0	.0	.0	1.5	1.2	.8	.6	2.9	2.6	2.9	1.3
5	April 1966	5.8	2.8	2.1	4.3	.0	1.4	1.7	2.6	1.7	2.4	.0	.0	3.0	1.2	2.8	2.4	2.0	3.9	2.9	.0
6	May 1966	1.2	2.8	1.4	2.9	.0	7.0	1.7	1.3	2.5	4.8	2.7	2.4	3.0	4.2	.4	2.4	2.9	1.3	.0	5.3
7	June 1966	3.5	4.6	1.4	.0	1.1	1.4	.0	1.3	1.7	2.4	.0	.0	3.0	.6	.4	2.9	2.0	1.3	5.9	2.6

BSSR Survey of 937 School Administrators on ESEA——Responses in Percentages

Question No. 22-B

Question: What is the present status of your application(s)? Please check appropriate status for each Title.

Sub-Question: What is the present status of your Title III application(s)?

KEY	SAMPLE	U.S. Total	BY SIZE OF STUDENT POPULATION: More Than 50,000 Students	25,000 to 49,999 Students	12,000 to 24,999 Students	6,000 to 11,999 Students	3,000 to 5,999 Students	1,200 to 2,999 Students	600 to 1,199 Students	300 to 599 Students	Less Than 300 Students	BY MEDIAN FAMILY INCOME: Less Than $3,000.	$3,000. to $4,999.	$5,000. to $6,999.	$7,000. to $8,999.	$9,000. to $11,999.	$12,000. and Over	Can't Evaluate Income	No Answer On Income
Y	no answer	17.0	.0	9.1	23.9	9.4	16.4	17.3	19.3	14.0	8.7	16.9	18.1	14.2	2.2	16.7	29.4	15.0	17.2
X	Nonapplicable.	9.1	53.9	18.2	8.7	12.3	12.3	5.4	8.2	7.0	9.4	22.0	10.0	7.5	6.9	7.1	29.4	.0	4.7
1	Approved. Project starts summer.	2.9	7.7	18.2	2.2	7.6	1.4	2.7	1.8	.9	3.1	.0	1.5	3.6	5.2	2.4	11.8	5.0	.0
2	Approved. Project starts September.	2.3	.0	.0	4.3	1.9	2.7	2.0	2.3	1.8	6.2	1.7	2.3	2.2	1.7	7.1	.0	.0	.0
3	Approved pending revisions.	2.0	.0	9.1	2.2	.9	1.4	2.7	2.3	.9	3.1	.0	3.5	1.7	3.5	.0	.0	.0	.0
4	Not yet approved.	11.6	30.8	27.3	21.7	18.9	13.0	11.1	5.3	7.9	6.2	11.9	10.0	12.2	1.6	9.5	5.9	10.0	10.9
5	Denied. Will resubmit.	4.9	.0	36.4	4.3	9.4	5.5	4.4	.6	4.4	9.6	1.7	4.2	6.7	4.3	7.1	.0	10.0	.0
6	Denied. Will not resubmit.	2.6	.0	9.1	8.7	2.8	3.4	2.7	.6	.9	3.1	1.7	2.7	2.5	2.6	.0	.0	.0	6.3
7	Did not apply for Title.	49.0	7.7	9.1	28.3	38.7	43.9	50.7	60.8	62.3	40.6	45.8	49.8	50.0	42.3	50.0	23.5	60.0	57.8

BSSR Survey of 937 School Administrators on ESEA——Responses in Percentages

Question No. 22-B

Question: What is the present status of your application(s)?
Please check appropriate status for each Title.

Sub-Question: What is the present status fo your Title III application(s)?

		BY POPULATION MAKEUP												BY REGION							
KEY	SAMPLE	90-100% Urban	60-89% Urban	90-100% Suburban	60-89% Suburban	Mixed Rural and Urban	Mixed Rural Urban and Suburban	Mixed Rural and Suburban	60-89% Rural Non-Farm	60-89% Rural Farm	90-100% Rural Non-Farm	100% Mixed Rural	90-100% Rural Farm	New England	Middle Atlantic	East North Central	West North Central	Southern	Southwest	Mountain	Pacific
Y	no answer	11.6	13.0	17.2	30.0	19.3	12.7	15.3	21.1	16.1	28.6	13.5	7.1	17.9	22.4	15.9	11.2	15.7	14.3	29.4	19.7
X	Nonapplicable.	12.8	12.0	7.1	10.0	5.7	11.3	3.4	11.8	7.6	7.1	10.8	9.5	4.5	9.1	5.7	8.8	13.7	15.6	11.8	10.5
1	Approved. Project starts summer.	3.5	2.8	2.9	5.7	3.4	5.6	3.4	2.6	.0	2.4	.0	2.4	9.0	1.8	2.0	2.4	2.9	.0	2.9	6.6
2	Approved. Project starts September.	3.5	.9	5.0	.0	.0	2.8	3.4	.0	4.2	4.8	.0	.0	3.0	4.9	2.0	1.2	.0	1.3	2.9	3.9
3	Approved pending revisions.	3.5	1.9	2.1	2.9	3.4	.0	.0	2.6	.8	2.4	5.4	.0	9.0	.6	1.2	1.8	2.9	2.6	2.9	.0
4	Not yet approved.	18.6	13.9	13.6	14.3	6.8	15.5	8.5	6.6	9.3	11.9	5.4	9.5	20.9	8.5	10.2	11.8	14.7	13.0	8.8	10.5
5	Denied, will resubmit.	9.3	7.4	5.0	2.9	3.4	7.0	6.8	3.9	3.4	4.8	.0	.0	9.0	3.6	6.1	2.4	3.9	6.5	.0	7.9
6	Denied, will not resubmit.	4.7	5.6	2.9	.0	3.4	2.8	.0	1.3	.0	7.1	.0	2.4	6.0	2.4	1.2	1.8	2.9	1.3	5.9	5.3
7	Did not apply for Title.	38.7	43.5	45.0	35.7	54.8	45.1	59.4	51.3	59.3	33.3	64.9	69.0	29.8	47.6	56.1	60.0	43.2	46.7	38.3	36.8

BSSR Survey of 937 School Administrators on ESEA——Responses in Percentages

Question No. 23-A

Question: Approximately how long did it take your state education agency or the USOE to review your proposal?

Sub-Question: Review of Title I.

KEY *	SAMPLE	U.S. Total	BY SIZE OF STUDENT POPULATION: More Than 50,000 Students	25,000 to 49,999 Students	12,000 to 24,999 Students	6,000 to 11,999 Students	3,000 to 5,999 Students	1,200 to 2,999 Students	600 to 1,199 Students	300 to 599 Students	Less Than 300 Students	BY MEDIAN FAMILY INCOME: Less Than $3,000.	$3,000. to $4,999.	$5,000. to $6,999.	$7,000. to $8,999.	$9,000. to $11,999.	$12,000. and Over	Can't Evaluate Income	No Answer On Income
Y	No answer	5.2	.0	.0	2.2	1.9	4.1	7.4	5.3	3.5	15.6	1.7	5.8	5.0	5.2	2.4	5.9	5.0	9.4
X	No Title I project.	7.3	.0	.0	.0	3.8	6.8	6.4	8.8	10.5	25.0	1.7	5.0	4.4	7.8	35.7	41.2	15.0	6.3
1	1 week	10.5	23.1	.0	21.7	16.0	11.6	7.0	8.8	10.5	9.4	20.3	13.1	8.6	10.3	2.4	5.9	5.0	9.4
2	2 weeks	21.7	46.2	9.1	23.9	24.5	18.5	25.5	18.7	17.5	12.5	23.7	17.0	25.8	26.7	16.7	.0	10.0	18.8
3	3 weeks	16.8	23.1	9.1	15.2	18.9	19.2	14.8	21.6	11.4	12.5	18.6	20.8	13.3	19.8	11.9	29.4	5.0	15.6
4	4 weeks	13.7	7.7	27.3	15.2	9.4	15.8	14.4	11.7	15.8	9.4	13.6	12.0	16.4	11.2	9.5	5.9	10.0	15.6
5	5 weeks	3.2	.0	18.2	.0	4.7	2.7	4.7	1.8	1.8	.0	1.7	2.3	3.6	2.6	2.4	.0	.0	9.4
6	6 weeks	7.3	.0	.0	10.9	2.8	8.2	5.7	8.8	11.4	9.4	5.1	7.3	7.8	7.8	4.8	.0	20.0	4.7
7	7-10 weeks	7.6	.0	18.2	8.7	13.2	8.2	6.0	6.4	8.8	.0	5.1	7.7	8.3	1.7	9.5	11.8	20.0	9.4
8	More than 10 weeks	5.1	.0	18.2	2.2	2.8	3.4	5.7	7.6	5.3	3.1	5.1	6.9	4.4	5.2	4.8	.0	10.0	1.6
9	Still pending	1.5	.0	.0	.0	.9	1.4	1.7	.6	3.5	3.1	3.4	1.2	2.2	.9	.0	.0	.0	.0

* Deviations from totals of 100% in each column are due to additional BSSR Keys judged by the senior author to be statistically in significant.

BSSR Survey of 937 School Administrators on ESEA——Responses in Percentages

Question No. 23-A

Question: Approximately how long did it take your state education agency or the USOE to review your proposal?

Sub-Question: Review of Title I.

KEY *	SAMPLE	BY POPULATION MAKEUP												BY REGION							
		90-100% Urban	60-89% Urban	90-100% Suburban	60-89% Suburban	Mixed Rural and Urban	Mixed Rural Urban and Suburban	Mixed Rural and Suburban	60-89% Rural Non-Farm	60-89% Rural Farm	90-100% Rural Non-Farm	100% Mixed Rural	90-100% Rural Farm	New England	Middle Atlantic	East North Central	West North Central	Southern	Southwest	Mountain	Pacific
Y	No answer	3.5	3.7	5.7	1.4	8.0	9.9	1.7	5.3	4.2	11.9	8.1	2.4	4.5	5.5	7.7	1.8	2.0	9.1	11.8	2.6
X	No Title I project.	4.7	3.7	16.4	10.0	2.3	4.2	11.9	2.6	4.2	9.5	5.4	11.9	13.4	6.1	10.2	4.1	2.0	5.2	11.8	9.2
1	1 week	5.8	16.7	3.6	12.9	13.6	16.9	10.2	9.2	6.8	16.7	10.8	11.9	16.4	3.0	11.4	10.6	17.6	14.3	17.6	1.3
2	2 weeks	32.6	20.4	17.9	20.0	18.2	23.9	28.8	17.1	20.3	16.7	27.0	23.8	26.9	12.1	23.2	18.8	30.4	36.4	23.5	11.8
3	3 weeks	12.8	16.7	22.1	14.3	15.9	18.3	15.3	17.1	16.9	14.3	16.2	14.3	9.0	18.8	15.0	21.8	21.6	13.0	8.8	14.5
4	4 weeks	19.8	13.0	10.7	14.3	12.5	9.9	10.2	21.1	13.6	14.3	8.1	16.7	14.9	15.8	11.4	11.8	12.7	11.7	8.8	25.0
5	5 weeks	5.8	4.6	2.1	4.3	1.1	4.2	1.7	3.9	2.5	.0	.0	7.1	4.5	2.4	2.8	2.4	2.9	1.3	5.9	7.9
6	6 weeks	5.8	8.3	4.3	7.1	9.1	7.0	6.8	7.9	11.0	4.8	8.1	4.8	.0	10.9	6.9	9.4	2.0	5.2	8.8	10.5
7	7-10 weeks	7.0	6.5	12.9	7.1	3.4	2.8	6.8	9.2	11.9	2.4	10.8	.0	1.5	15.8	5.7	6.5	3.9	2.6	2.9	15.8
8	More than 10 weeks	1.2	4.6	2.9	8.6	11.4	.0	6.8	5.3	7.6	7.1	5.4	.0	6.0	5.5	4.5	10.0	4.9	1.3	.0	1.3
9	Still pending	1.2	.9	.7	.0	4.5	2.8	.0	1.3	.8	2.4	.0	4.8	3.0	3.0	1.2	2.4	.0	.0	.0	.0

* Deviations from totals of 100% in each column are due to additional BSSR Keys judged by the senior author to be statistically insignificant.

BSSR Survey of 937 School Administrators on ESEA——Responses in Percentages

Question No. 23-B

Question: Approximately how long did it take your state education agency or the USOE to review your proposal?

Sub-Question: Review of Title III

KEY *	SAMPLE	U.S. Total	BY SIZE OF STUDENT POPULATION: More Than 50,000 Students	25,000 to 49,999 Students	12,000 to 24,999 Students	6,000 to 11,999 Students	3,000 to 5,999 Students	1,200 to 2,999 Students	600 to 1,199 Students	300 to 599 Students	Less Than 300 Students	BY MEDIAN FAMILY INCOME: Less Than $3,000.	$3,000. to $4,999.	$5,000. to $6,999.	$7,000. to $8,999.	$9,000. to $11,999.	$12,000. and Over	Can't Evaluate Income	No Answer On Income
Y	No answer	19.4	.0	18.2	28.3	9.4	21.2	20.8	16.4	21.9	34.4	15.3	21.6	1]	22.4	21.4	23.5	20.0	17.2
X	No Title I Project.	49.1	7.7	9.1	28.3	38.7	43.8	51.0	60.8	62.3	40.6	45.8	49.8	1]	42.2	50.0	23.5	60.0	57.8
1	1 week	1.2	.0	.0	.0	1.9	3.4	.7	1.2	.0	.0	6.8	.8	.8	.9	2.4	.0	.0	.0
2	2 weeks	2.0	.0	.0	2.2	1.9	4.1	1.3	1.2	.9	9.4	3.4	2.3	1.1	2.6	.0	11.8	.0	3.1
3	3 weeks	1.8	.0	.0	.0	3.8	2.1	1.3	1.2	2.6	3.1	.0	3.1	.6	3.4	2.4	.0	.0	3.1
4	4 weeks	2.7	7.7	.0	2.2	3.8	2.7	2.3	3.5	1.8	.0	3.4	3.5	1.9	4.3	2.4	5.9	.0	.0
5	5 weeks	1.1	15.4	.0	4.3	.9	.7	1.0	.6	.0	.0	.0	.4	1.9	1.7	.0	.0	.0	.0
6	6 weeks	4.1	.0	27.3	6.5	7.5	4.1	4.4	2.3	.9	.0	1.7	2.7	5.3	6.0	2.4	5.9	.0	3.1
7	7-10 weeks	5.2	23.1	36.4	10.9	10.4	5.5	3.4	2.9	2.6	.0	5.1	5.0	4.2	2.6	9.5	23.5	10.0	7.8
8	More than 10 weeks	3.4	7.7	.0	8.7	4.7	3.4	3.0	3.5	.9	3.1	6.8	4.2	3.3	2.6	.0	.0	.0	3.1
9	Still pending	6.4	30.8	9.1	2.2	12.3	6.2	7.4	2.9	2.6	6.3	5.1	4.6	8.3	6.0	4.8	5.9	10.0	4.7

* Deviations from totals of 100% in each column are due to additional BSSR Keys judged by the senior author to be statistically insignificant.

1] Items omitted from survey.

BSSR Survey of 937 School Administrators on ESEA——Responses in Percentages

Question No. 23-B

Question: Approximately how long did it take your state education agency or the USOE to review your proposal?

Sub-Question: Review of Title III

KEY *	SAMPLE	BY POPULATION MAKEUP												BY REGION							
		90-100% Urban	60-89% Urban	90-100% Suburban	60-89% Suburban	Mixed Rural and Urban	Mixed Rural Urban and Suburban	Mixed Rural and Suburban	60-89% Rural Non-Farm	60-89% Rural Farm	90-100% Rural Non-Farm	100% Mixed Rural	90-100% Rural Farm	New England	Middle Atlantic	East North Central	West North Central	Southern	Southwest	Mountain	Pacific
Y	No answer	17.4	15.7	20.7	25.7	20.5	14.1	15.3	18.4	21.2	40.5	16.2	9.5	22.4	20.6	20.3	13.5	17.6	20.8	26.5	22.4
X	No Title I Project.	38.4	43.5	45.0	37.1	54.5	45.1	59.3	51.3	59.3	33.3	64.9	69.0	29.9	47.3	56.1	60.6	43.1	46.8	38.2	36.8
1	1 week	1.2	3.7	.7	1.4	.0	2.8	.0	.0	.0	2.4	.0	2.4	1.5	1.2	.4	.6	2.9	2.6	2.9	.0
2	2 weeks	2.3	2.8	1.4	1.4	4.5	2.8	.0	.0	2.5	.0	2.7	2.4	1.5	.6	1.6	2.4	2.0	5.2	.0	3.9
3	3 weeks	.0	1.9	1.4	2.9	1.1	.0	1.7	3.9	1.7	7.1	.0	2.4	6.0	1.8	.4	1.2	2.0	2.6	2.9	2.6
4	4 weeks	2.3	2.8	5.0	.0	2.3	2.8	1.7	3.9	.8	2.4	5.4	2.4	3.0	3.6	1.6	2.4	3.9	3.9	2.9	1.3
5	5 weeks	1.2	2.8	1.4	1.4	1.1	1.4	1.7	.0	.0	.0	.0	.0	.0	.6	2.0	1.8	.0	.0	.0	1.3
6	6 weeks	3.5	4.6	7.1	4.3	4.5	5.6	1.7	5.3	1.7	2.4	.0	2.4	9.0	4.8	4.9	2.9	2.0	.0	2.9	5.3
7	7-10 weeks	14.0	5.6	5.7	7.1	3.4	5.6	5.1	5.3	.8	4.8	2.7	.0	6.0	6.1	4.1	4.1	5.9	2.6	5.9	10.5
8	More than 10 weeks.	3.5	4.6	.7	2.9	3.4	11.3	3.4	3.9	2.5	2.4	2.7	.0	10.4	.6	2.4	2.4	6.9	2.6	2.9	5.3
9	Still pending	10.5	10.2	5.7	10.0	4.5	2.8	5.1	2.6	5.9	4.8	5.4	7.1	7.5	6.7	3.3	7.1	9.8	9.1	11.8	3.9

* Deviations from totals of 100% in each column are due to additional BSSR Keys judged by the senior author to be statistically insignificant.

BSSR Survey of 937 School Administrators on ESEA——Responses in Percentages

Question No. 24

Question: In preparing the application(s) did you depend upon or receive help from any of the following? Please check all that apply.

KEY *	SAMPLE	U.S. Total	BY SIZE OF STUDENT POPULATION									BY MEDIAN FAMILY INCOME							
			More Than 50,000 Students	25,000 to 49,999 Students	12,000 to 24,999 Students	6,000 to 11,999 Students	3,000 to 5,999 Students	1,200 to 2,999 Students	600 to 1,199 Students	300 to 599 Students	Less Than 300 Students	Less Than $3,000.	$3,000. to $4,999.	$5,000. to $6,999.	$7,000. to $8,999.	$9,000. to $11,999.	$12,000. and Over	Can't Evaluate Income	No Answer On Income
Y	No answer	4.9	.0	.0	1.2	1.9	4.8	6.0	3.5	3.5	25.0	1.7	6.9	3.9	5.2	2.4	11.8	10.0	3.1
X	Did not apply for Titles.	4.9	.0	.0	.0	3.8	4.1	3.7	6.4	8.8	12.5	1.7	3.5	3.1	5.2	26.2	11.8	10.0	6.2
1	Professional Associations.	18.5	30.8	9.1	21.7	20.8	19.2	16.4	20.5	17.5	12.5	15.3	20.5	20.0	19.0	16.7	5.9	.0	14.1
2	Nearby Universities.	17.8	30.8	36.4	19.7	33.0	22.6	15.8	14.6	7.9	3.1	16.9	19.7	16.7	20.7	19.0	11.8	5.0	17.2
3	State Education Agency.	72.1	77.0	10.0	74.0	83.0	76.7	72.5	75.7	66.7	50.0	81.4	94.1	72.5	75.1	50.0	58.8	70.0	65.6
4	Regional HEW Office.	4.4	15.4	9.1	6.5	6.6	6.2	4.0	2.3	2.6	.0	5.1	5.4	5.0	.0	4.8	11.8	.0	3.1
5	USOE staff.	5.4	46.2	18.2	4.3	13.2	6.2	4.0	1.2	3.5	.0	8.5	3.5	6.7	5.2	7.1	5.9	.0	4.7
6	Special Consultants.	10.6	15.4	9.1	8.7	14.2	9.6	11.1	12.9	5.3	3.1	5.1	13.1	10.0	10.4	7.1	23.5	15.0	4.7
7	Other Superintendents.	33.7	70.7	18.2	21.7	23.6	23.3	36.2	43.4	44.8	34.4	39.0	37.1	35.0	28.5	28.6	35.3	25.0	23.4
8	School supplies.	18.5	7.7	9.1	10.9	17.8	17.8	18.1	21.6	21.0	18.7	2.3	20.5	22.2	5.2	11.9	17.6	10.0	18.7

* Deviations from totals of 100% in each column are due to additional BSSR Keys judged by the senior author to be statistically insignificant.

BSSR Survey of 937 School Administrators on ESEA——Responses in Percentages

Question No. 24

Question: In preparing the application(s) did you depend upon or receive help from any of the following? Please check all that apply.

KEY*	SAMPLE	BY POPULATION MAKEUP												BY REGION							
		90-100% Urban	60-89% Urban	90-100% Suburban	60-89% Suburban	Mixed Rural and Urban	Mixed Rural Urban and Suburban	Mixed Rural and Suburban	60-89% Rural Non-Farm	60-89% Rural Farm	90-100% Rural Non-Farm	100% Mixed Rural	90-100% Rural Farm	New England	Middle Atlantic	East North Central	West North Central	Southern	Southwest	Mountain	Pacific
Y	No answer	2.3	4.6	5.7	.0	5.7	7.0	6.8	5.3	4.2	11.9	5.4	2.4	7.5	1.8	7.3	2.4	1.0	6.5	21.1	3.9
X	Did not apply for Titles.	2.3	3.7	11.4	7.1	2.3	1.4	5.1	2.6	3.4	4.8	5.4	7.1	6.0	4.9	7.7	3.5	1.0	3.9	5.9	3.9
1	Professional associations.	18.6	20.4	15.7	22.9	15.9	22.5	13.6	22.4	17.8	16.7	18.9	16.7	22.4	17.6	22.4	15.9	17.6	18.2	17.7	11.8
2	Nearby Universities.	18.6	24.1	17.2	14.3	25.0	25.4	18.6	21.1	9.3	9.5	10.8	11.9	19.4	15.8	22.8	9.4	26.5	19.5	21.1	9.2
3	State Education Agency	78.0	76.0	63.6	80.0	75.2	73.3	67.8	76.3	68.7	62.0	73.0	71.5	74.6	70.3	65.4	76.5	84.2	75.3	73.6	64.5
4	Regional HEW Office.	9.3	3.7	4.3	1.4	5.7	8.5	3.4	2.9	2.5	.0	2.7	4.8	4.5	3.0	4.5	1.2	8.8	10.4	5.9	1.3
5	USOE staff.	12.8	7.4	4.3	5.7	5.7	5.6	5.1	5.3	1.7	2.4	5.4	2.4	6.0	66.7	4.1	2.9	10.8	5.2	11.8	2.6
6	Special consultants.	9.3	9.3	10.7	12.9	15.9	5.6	10.2	10.5	11.9	11.9	5.4	7.1	10.4	14.6	11.8	5.3	9.8	11.7	11.8	7.9
7	Other Superintendents.	26.7	25.0	26.4	34.3	39.8	32.4	40.7	38.2	37.3	35.7	45.9	42.9	29.8	30.3	30.9	47.1	29.4	36.4	14.7	35.5
8	School suppliers.	16.3	12.0	14.3	11.4	27.3	21.1	20.3	19.7	27.1	11.9	24.3	14.3	10.4	16.4	18.3	28.2	27.5	23.4	8.8	9.2

* Deviations from totals of 100% in each column are due to additional BSSR Keys judged by the senior author to be statistically insignificant.

BSSR Survey of 937 School Administrators on ESEA——Responses in Percentages

Question No. 24-a

Question: In preparing the application(s) did you depend on or receive help from any of the following? Please check all that apply.

Sub-Question: Which of the above sources was most helpful?

KEY *	SAMPLE	U.S. Total	BY SIZE OF STUDENT POPULATION									BY MEDIAN FAMILY INCOME							
			More Than 50,000 Students	25,000 to 49,999 Students	12,000 to 24,999 Students	6,000 to 11,999 Students	3,000 to 5,999 Students	1,200 to 2,999 Students	600 to 1,199 Students	300 to 599 Students	Less Than 300 Students	Less Than $3,000.	$3,000. to $4,999.	$5,000. to $6,999.	$7,000. to $8,999.	$9,000. to $11,999.	$12,000. and Over	Can't Evaluate Income	No Answer On Income
Y	No answer	10.2	7.7	.0	8.7	8.5	8.9	11.4	9.4	8.8	28.1	5.1	13.1	10.0	7.8	4.8	17.6	15.0	9.4
X	Did not apply for Titles.	4.9	.0	.0	.0	3.8	4.1	3.7	6.5	8.8	12.5	1.7	3.5	3.1	5.2	16.2	11.8	10.0	6.2
0	None.	15.2	15.4	9.1	30.4	15.1	15.8	13.4	12.3	19.3	9.4	18.7	13.5	16.1	11.2	16.7	11.8	20.2	18.8
1	Professional associations.	1.5	.0	.0	2.2	.9	2.1	1.0	2.9	.9	.0	.0	1.2	1.9	3.5	.0	.0	.0	.0
2	Nearby universities.	3.4	.0	.0	6.5	8.5	3.4	2.7	1.8	2.6	3.1	.0	4.6	1.4	6.9	4.8	5.9	.0	6.2
3	State education agency.	52.1	61.6	91.0	56.5	58.5	54.1	57.4	42.7	42.1	34.4	69.5	49.8	52.8	57.0	35.7	47.1	45.0	46.9
4	Regional HEW Office.	0.4	.0	.0	.0	.9	.7	.7	.0	.0	.0	.0	.4	.8	.0	.0	.0	.0	.0
5	USOE staff.	1.1	15.4	9.1	.0	2.8	1.4	.7	.0	.0	.0	.0	.4	1.4	2.6	2.4	.0	.0	.0
6	Special consultants.	5.0	7.7	.0	2.2	4.7	5.5	4.4	8.8	3.5	.0	.0	5.4	5.6	6.0	2.4	.0	10.0	4.7
7	Other Superintendents.	7.7	.0	.0	.0	2.8	4.8	6.4	12.9	14.9	12.5	5.1	10.0	7.8	6.0	7.1	5.9	.0	6.2
8	School suppliers.	2.2	.0	.0	.0	1.9	3.4	1.0	4.7	1.8	3.1	3.4	2.7	2.5	.9	.0	.0	.0	3.1

* Deviations from totals of 100% in each column are due to additional BSSR Keys judged by the senior author to be statistically insignificant.

BSSR Survey of 937 School Administrators on ESEA——Responses in Percentages

Question No. 24-a

Question: In preparing the application(s) did you depend on or receive help from any of the following? Please check all that apply.

Sub-Question: Which of the above sources was most helpful?

KEY*	SAMPLE	BY POPULATION MAKEUP												BY REGION							
		90-100% Urban	60-89% Urban	90-100% Suburban	60-89% Suburban	Mixed Rural and Urban	Mixed Rural Urban and Suburban	Mixed Rural and Suburban	60-89% Rural Non-Farm	60-89% Rural Farm	90-100% Rural Non-Farm	100% Mixed Rural	90-100% Rural Farm	New England	Middle Atlantic	East North Central	West North Central	Southern	Southwest	Mountain	Pacific
Y	No answer	9.3	9.3	10.0	2.9	15.9	11.3	11.9	11.8	9.3	16.7	10.8	4.8	9.0	4.9	13.8	8.2	7.8	9.1	26.5	13.2
X	Did not apply for Titles.	2.3	3.7	11.4	7.1	2.3	1.4	5.1	2.6	3.4	4.8	5.4	7.1	6.0	4.9	7.7	3.5	1.0	3.9	5.9	3.9
O	None.	16.3	18.5	16.4	10.0	10.2	14.1	18.6	14.5	17.8	11.9	16.2	11.9	14.9	22.4	11.4	14.7	19.6	7.8	.0	21.0
1	Professional associations.	2.3	1.9	2.9	1.4	1.1	1.4	.0	.0	.8	4.8	.0	.0	.0	2.4	2.4	1.2	.0	2.6	.0	.0
2	Nearby universities.	4.7	5.6	4.3	1.4	5.7	5.6	.0	2.6	.8	2.4	2.7	2.4	3.0	4.2	3.3	2.9	1.0	9.1	5.9	.0
3	State education agency.	59.3	51.9	47.2	62.9	47.8	57.8	50.8	52.6	50.0	47.6	43.2	54.8	58.2	5.1	42.3	54.7	63.7	57.2	64.7	48.7
4	Regional HEW office.	.0	.9	.7	.0	.0	1.4	.0	.0	.8	.0	.0	.0	.0	.0	.8	.0	2.0	.0	.0	.0
5	USOE staff.	3.5	3.7	.7	1.4	.0	1.4	.0	.0	.0	.0	.0	.0	3.0	.6	1.6	.6	1.0	.0	.0	1.3
6	Special consultants.	3.5	2.8	4.3	5.7	8.0	2.8	5.1	5.3	6.8	7.1	2.7	7.1	7.5	6.7	8.5	1.2	2.9	5.2	2.9	.0
7	Other superintendents.	9.3	3.7	5.7	5.7	12.5	2.8	6.8	7.9	10.2	4.8	13.5	14.3	1.5	5.5	8.1	12.4	2.0	9.1	.0	15.8
8	School suppliers.	1.2	2.8	.7	1.4	1.1	7.0	.0	1.3	3.4	4.8	5.4	.0	3.0	.0	2.8	4.1	2.9	2.6	.0	.0

* Deviations from totals of 100% in each column are due to additional BSSR Keys judged by the senior author to be statistically insignificant.

BSSR Survey of 937 School Administrators on ESEA——Responses in Percentages

Question No. 25-A

Question: Please estimate the number of man weeks spent by your staff in preparing your proposal(s). <u>Please check the appropriate statement for EACH title</u>.

Sub-Question: Title I

KEY	SAMPLE	U.S. Total	BY SIZE OF STUDENT POPULATION									BY MEDIAN FAMILY INCOME							
			More Than 50,000 Students	25,000 to 49,999 Students	12,000 to 24,999 Students	6,000 to 11,999 Students	3,000 to 5,999 Students	1,200 to 2,999 Students	600 to 1,199 Students	300 to 599 Students	Less Than 300 Students	Less Than $3,000.	$3,000. to $4,999.	$5,000. to $6,999.	$7,000. to $8,999.	$9,000. to $11,999.	$12,000. and Over	Can't Evaluate Income	No Answer On Income
Y	No answer	4.8	.0	9.1	6.5	5.7	4.1	4.4	4.1	3.5	15.6	3.4	5.4	4.7	4.3	2.4	5.9	10.0	4.7
1	1 week or less.	5.4	.0	.0	2.2	2.8	4.8	5.0	7.6	7.9	9.4	5.1	3.9	6.1	7.8	2.4	11.8	10.0	3.1
2	2 weeks	17.1	.0	.0	6.5	10.4	11.6	19.8	22.2	23.7	15.6	16.9	14.7	19.2	19.8	19.0	11.8	5.0	14.1
3	3 weeks	16.9	7.7	9.1	13.0	11.3	11.6	19.8	21.1	19.3	12.5	16.9	15.1	19.2	16.4	21.4	5.9	15.0	12.5
4	4 weeks	31.2	15.4	18.2	32.6	34.0	41.1	33.6	27.5	23.7	9.4	36.6	38.6	29.4	25.0	14.3	17.6	30.0	32.8
5	Other.	17.4	76.9	63.6	39.1	32.1	19.9	11.1	8.8	11.4	12.5	20.3	17.4	16.9	19.0	4.8	5.9	15.0	26.6
6	Did not apply under this Title.	7.3	.0	.0	.0	3.8	6.8	6.4	8.8	10.5	25.0	1.7	5.0	4.4	7.8	35.7	41.2	15.0	6.3

BSSR Survey of 937 School Administrators on ESEA——Responses in Percentages

Question No. 25-A

Question: Please estimate the number of man weeks spent by your staff in preparing your proposal(s). Please check the appropriate statement for EACH title.

Sub-Question: Title I

KEY	SAMPLE	BY POPULATION MAKEUP: 90-100% Urban	60-89% Urban	90-100% Suburban	60-89% Suburban	Mixed Rural and Urban	Mixed Rural Urban and Suburban	Mixed Rural and Suburban	60-89% Rural Non-Farm	60-89% Rural Farm	90-100% Rural Non-Farm	100% Mixed Rural	90-100% Rural Farm	BY REGION: New England	Middle Atlantic	East North Central	West North Central	Southern	Southwest	Mountain	Pacific
Y	No answer	4.7	5.6	5.0	1.4	5.7	9.9	1.7	3.9	2.5	9.5	5.4	4.8	7.5	2.4	6.5	2.9	2.9	9.1	8.8	2.6
1	1 week or less.	4.7	4.6	6.4	5.7	1.1	7.0	6.8	5.3	6.8	7.1	2.7	7.1	9.0	3.6	6.9	5.3	.0	7.8	14.7	2.6
2	2 weeks	10.5	8.3	17.9	15.7	14.8	16.9	23.7	26.3	19.5	16.7	32.4	11.9	13.4	17.6	18.3	22.9	7.8	10.4	17,6	21.1
3	3 weeks	11.6	17.6	11.4	24.3	14.8	15.5	22.0	17.1	21.2	11.9	16.2	23.8	9.0	17.0	14.6	21.8	11.8	20.8	23.5	19.7
4	4 weeks	27.9	34.3	27.9	30.0	44.3	28.2	20.3	32.9	33.9	35.7	27.0	23.8	32.8	33.9	26.4	28.8	40.2	35.1	20.6	32.9
5	Other.	36.0	25.9	15.0	12.9	17.0	18.3	13.6	11.8	11.9	9.5	10.8	16.7	14.9	19.4	17.1	14.1	35.3	11.7	2.9	11.8
6	Did not apply under this Title.	4.7	3.7	16.9	10.0	2.3	4.2	11.9	2.6	4.2	9.5	5.4	11.9	13.4	6.1	10.2	4.1	2.0	5.2	11.8	9.2

BSSR Survey of 937 School Administrators on ESEA——Responses in Percentages

Question No. 25-B

Question: Please estimate the number of man weeks spent by your staff in preparing your proposal(s). Please check the appropriate statement for EACH title.

Sub-Question: Title III

KEY	SAMPLE	U.S. Total	BY SIZE OF STUDENT POPULATION: More Than 50,000 Students	25,000 to 49,999 Students	12,000 to 24,999 Students	6,000 to 11,999 Students	3,000 to 5,999 Students	1,200 to 2,999 Students	600 to 1,199 Students	300 to 599 Students	Less Than 300 Students	BY MEDIAN FAMILY INCOME: Less Than $3,000.	$3,000. to $4,999.	$5,000. to $6,999.	$7,000. to $8,999.	$9,000. to $11,999.	$12,000. and Over	Can't Evaluate Income	No Answer On Income
Y	No answer	21.8	.0	18.2	26.1	19.8	20.5	23.5	22.2	17.5	34.4	18.6	23.2	22.5	24.1	16.7	29.4	20.0	12.5
1	1 week or less.	6.3	.0	.0	4.3	3.8	6.2	7.0	5.3	8.8	12.5	15.3	6.2	4.2	8.6	4.8	11.8	10.0	4.7
2	2 weeks	5.1	7.7	9.1	6.5	6.6	8.2	4.7	1.2	5.3	6.3	5.1	4.2	4.7	5.2	4.8	5.9	5.0	10.9
3	3 weeks	4.9	15.4	.0	10.9	9.4	4.8	4.7	2.9	2.6	.0	5.1	3.5	6.7	4.3	4.8	11.8	.0	1.6
4	4 weeks	6.5	30.8	27.3	17.4	11.3	10.3	4.4	2.9	.9	.0	8.5	5.0	6.4	6.9	9.5	11.8	5.0	7.8
5	Other.	6.3	38.5	36.4	6.5	10.4	6.2	4.7	4.7	2.6	6.3	1.7	8.1	5.3	8.6	9.5	5.9	.0	4.7
6	Did not apply under this Title.	49.1	7.7	9.1	28.3	38.7	43.8	51.0	60.8	62.3	40.6	45.8	49.8	50.3	42.2	50.0	23.5	60.0	57.8

BSSR Survey of 937 School Administrators on ESEA——Responses in Percentages

Question No. 25-B

Question: Please estimate the number of man weeks spent by your staff in preparing your proposal(s). Please check the appropriate statement for EACH title.

Sub-Question: Title III

KEY	SAMPLE	BY POPULATION MAKEUP												BY REGION							
		90-100% Urban	60-89% Urban	90-100% Suburban	60-89% Suburban	Mixed Rural and Urban	Mixed Rural Urban and Suburban	Mixed Rural and Suburban	60-89% Rural Non-Farm	60-89% Rural Farm	90-100% Rural Non-Farm	100% Mixed Rural	90-100% Rural Farm	New England	Middle Atlantic	East North Central	West North Central	Southern	Southwest	Mountain	Pacific
Y	No answer	22.1	19.4	21.4	30.0	22.7	18.3	18.6	27.6	22.0	35.7	13.5	4.8	22.4	26.7	19.9	12.9	20.6	24.7	32.4	30.3
1	one week or less.	3.5	4.6	7.1	8.6	4.5	2.8	8.5	7.9	5.9	7.1	10.8	9.5	10.4	4.2	4.9	8.2	5.9	7.8	11.8	3.9
2	2 weeks	3.5	6.5	4.3	2.9	5.7	12.7	5.1	2.6	2.5	7.1	5.4	7.1	9.0	4.8	4.1	3.5	7.8	3.9	.0	9.2
3	3 weeks	4.7	9.3	7.9	5.7	4.5	4.2	3.4	1.3	2.5	7.1	.0	2.4	4.5	3.0	4.5	6.5	3.9	3.9	5.9	9.2
4	4 weeks	12.8	9.3	7.9	8.6	4.5	14.1	1.7	3.9	4.2	.0	.0	.0	11.9	8.5	5.3	2.9	11.8	5.2	2.9	5.3
5	Other.	15.1	7.4	6.4	7.1	3.4	2.8	3.4	5.3	3.4	9.5	5.4	7.1	11.9	5.5	5.3	5.3	6.9	7.8	8.8	5.3
6	Did not apply under this Title.	38.4	43.5	45.0	37.1	54.5	45.1	59.3	51.3	59.3	33.3	64.9	69.0	29.9	47.3	56.1	60.0	43.1	46.8	38.2	36.8

BSSR Survey of 937 School Administrators on ESEA——Responses in Percentages

Question No. 27A

Question: Below are some of the difficulties school districts have encountered with ESEA. Please indicate which have been problems for your district by checking either YES or NO for EACH statement.

Sub-Question: Coordinating projects with those of the local community action agency

KEY	SAMPLE	U.S. Total	BY SIZE OF STUDENT POPULATION									BY MEDIAN FAMILY INCOME							
			More Than 50,000 Students	25,000 to 49,999 Students	12,000 to 24,999 Students	6,000 to 11,999 Students	3,000 to 5,999 Students	1,200 to 2,999 Students	600 to 1,199 Students	300 to 599 Students	Less Than 300 Students	Less Than $3,000.	$3,000. to $4,999.	$5,000. to $6,999.	$7,000. to $8,999.	$9,000. to $11,999.	$12,000. and Over	Can't Evaluate Income	No Answer On Income
Y	No answer	13.6	.0	.0	10.9	7.5	12.3	14.1	12.9	18.4	34.4	11.9	15.4	11.1	12.9	11.9	17.6	15.0	21.9
X	Did not apply for Titles.	4.8	.0	.0	.0	3.8	4.1	3.7	6.4	8.8	9.4	1.7	3.1	3.1	5.2	26.2	10.8	10.0	6.3
1	Yes	12.8	30.8	27.3	26.1	20.8	11.6	11.7	9.4	7.0	9.4	16.6	11.6	13.9	17.2	7.1	11.8	.0	7.8
2	No	68.8	69.2	72.7	63.0	67.9	71.9	70.5	71.3	65.8	46.9	69.5	69.9	71.9	64.7	54.8	58.8	75.0	64.1

BSSR Survey of 937 School Administrators on ESEA——Responses in Percentages

Question No. 27A

Question: Below are some of the difficulties school districts have encountered with ESEA. Please indicate which have been problems for your district by checking either YES or NO for EACH statement.

Sub-Question: Coordinating projects with those of the local community action agency

		BY POPULATION MAKEUP												BY REGION							
KEY	SAMPLE	90-100% Urban	60-89% Urban	90-100% Suburban	60-89% Suburban	Mixed Rural and Urban	Mixed Rural Urban and Suburban	Mixed Rural and Suburban	60-89% Rural Non-Farm	60-89% Rural Farm	90-100% Rural Non-Farm	100% Mixed Rural	90-100% Rural Farm	New England	Middle Atlantic	East North Central	West North Central	Southern	Southwest	Mountain	Pacific
Y	No answer	7.0	13.9	15.7	5.7	15.9	14.1	13.6	11.8	11.9	21.4	24.3	16.7	13.4	11.5	14.2	12.4	12.7	22.1	17.6	9.2
X	Did not apply for Titles	2.3	3.7	11.4	7.1	2.3	1.4	5.1	2.6	3.4	4.8	5.4	4.8	6.0	4.8	7.7	3.5	1.0	2.6	5.9	3.9
1	Yes	18.6	18.5	10.0	20.0	9.1	11.3	15.3	9.2	11.9	9.5	2.7	11.9	14.9	15.8	12.6	10.0	16.7	11.7	5.9	10.5
2	No	72.1	63.9	62.9	67.1	72.7	73.2	66.1	76.3	72.9	64.3	67.6	66.7	65.7	67.9	65.4	74.1	69.6	63.6	70.6	76.3

BSSR Survey of 937 School Administrators on ESEA——Responses in Percentages

Question No. 27B

Question: Below are some of the difficulties school districts have encountered with ESEA. Please indicate which have been problems for your district by <u>checking either YES or NO for EACH statement</u>.

Sub-Question: Coordinating projects with the nonpublic schools

KEY	SAMPLE	U.S. Total	BY SIZE OF STUDENT POPULATION									BY MEDIAN FAMILY INCOME							
			More Than 50,000 Students	25,000 to 49,999 Students	12,000 to 24,999 Students	6,000 to 11,999 Students	3,000 to 5,999 Students	1,200 to 2,999 Students	600 to 1,199 Students	300 to 599 Students	Less Than 300 Students	Less Than $3,000.	$3,000. to $4,999.	$5,000. to $6,999.	$7,000. to $8,999.	$9,000. to $11,999.	$12,000. and Over	Can't Evaluate Income	No Answer On Income
Y	No answer.	13.2	.0	.0	13.0	5.7	10.3	14.1	12.9	19.3	34.4	11.9	14.7	11.9	12.1	11.9	17.6	15.0	17.2
X	Did not apply for Titles.	4.8	.0	.0	.0	3.8	4.1	3.7	6.4	8.8	9.4	1.7	3.1	3.1	5.2	26.2	11.8	10.0	6.3
1	Yes	12.2	53.8	18.2	13.0	23.6	11.6	11.1	8.8	6.1	6.3	11.9	10.0	13.6	18.1	4.8	11.8	10.0	7.8
2	No	69.8	46.2	81.8	73.9	67.0	74.0	71.1	71.9	65.8	50.0	74.6	72.2	71.4	64.7	57.1	58.8	65.0	68.8

BSSR Survey of 937 School Administrators on ESEA——Responses in Percentages

Question No. 27B

Question: Below are some of the difficulties school districts have encountered with ESEA. Please indicate which have been problems for your district by <u>checking either YES or NO for EACH statement</u>.

Sub-Question: Coordinating projects with the nonpublic schools

		BY POPULATION MAKEUP												BY REGION							
KEY	SAMPLE	90-100% Urban	60-89% Urban	90-100% Suburban	60-89% Suburban	Mixed Rural and Urban	Mixed Rural Urban and Suburban	Mixed Rural and Suburban	60-89% Rural Non-Farm	60-89% Rural Farm	90-100% Rural Non-Farm	100% Mixed Rural	90-100% Rural Farm	New England	Middle Atlantic	East North Central	West North Central	Southern	Southwest	Mountain	Pacific
Y	No answer	4.7	13.0	14.3	4.3	18.2	18.3	13.6	11.8	13.6	19.0	16.2	16.7	14.9	10.9	14.2	12.9	12.7	18.2	17.6	7.9
X	Did not apply for Titles.	2.3	3.7	11.4	7.4	2.3	1.4	5.1	2.6	3.4	4.8	5.4	4.8	6.0	4.8	7.7	3.5	1.0	2.6	5.9	3.9
1	Yes	22.1	11.1	12.9	18.6	13.6	11.3	8.5	9.2	5.9	11.9	10.8	9.5	11.9	15.8	13.8	11.2	11.8	7.8	.0	11.8
2	No	70.9	72.2	61.4	70.0	65.9	69.0	72.9	76.3	77.1	64.3	67.6	69.0	67.2	68.5	64.2	72.4	74.5	71.4	76.5	76.3

BSSR Survey of 937 School Administrators on ESEA——Responses in Percentages

Question No. 27C

Question: Below are some of the difficulties school districts have encountered with ESEA. Please indicate which have been problems for your district by checking either YES or NO for EACH statement.

Sub-Question: Identification of target schools for Title I projects

KEY	SAMPLE	U.S. Total	BY SIZE OF STUDENT POPULATION: More Than 50,000 Students	25,000 to 49,999 Students	12,000 to 24,999 Students	6,000 to 11,999 Students	3,000 to 5,999 Students	1,200 to 2,999 Students	600 to 1,199 Students	300 to 599 Students	Less Than 300 Students	BY MEDIAN FAMILY INCOME: Less Than $3,000.	$3,000. to $4,999.	$5,000. to $6,999.	$7,000. to $8,999.	$9,000. to $11,999.	$12,000. and Over	Can't Evaluate Income	No Answer On Income
Y	No answer	11.0	.0	.0	4.3	4.7	8.2	12.1	10.5	16.7	34.4	6.8	13.5	9.4	9.5	7.1	17.6	15.0	15.6
X	Did not apply for Titles.	4.8	.0	.0	.0	3.8	4.1	3.7	6.4	8.8	9.4	1.7	.0	3.1	5.2	46.2	11.8	10.0	6.3
1	Yes	27.3	46.2	54.5	30.4	36.8	36.3	31.5	17.0	9.6	12.5	23.7	22.0	30.8	32.8	21.4	11.8	40.0	26.2
2	No	56.9	53.8	45.5	65.2	54.7	51.4	52.6	66.1	64.9	43.8	67.8	64.5	56.7	52.6	45.2	58.6	35.0	51.6

BSSR Survey of 937 School Administrators on ESEA——Responses in Percentages

Question No. 27C

Question: Below are some of the difficulties school districts have encountered with ESEA. Please indicate which have been problems for your district by checking either YES or NO for EACH statement.

Sub-Question: Identification of target schools for Title I projects

KEY	SAMPLE	BY POPULATION MAKEUP												BY REGION							
		90-100% Urban	60-89% Urban	90-100% Suburban	60-89% Suburban	Mixed Rural and Urban	Mixed Rural Urban and Suburban	Mixed Rural and Suburban	60-89% Rural Non-Farm	60-89% Rural Farm	90-100% Rural Non-Farm	100% Mixed Rural	90-100% Rural Farm	New England	Middle Atlantic	East North Central	West North Central	Southern	Southwest	Mountain	Pacific
Y	No answer	3.5	9.3	12.9	2.9	17.0	12.7	11.9	9.2	9.3	19.0	16.2	16.7	10.4	9.1	12.2	12.4	8.8	13.0	14.7	7.9
X	Did not apply for Titles.	2.3	3.7	11.4	7.1	2.3	1.4	5.1	2.6	3.4	4.8	5.4	4.8	6.0	4.8	7.7	3.5	1.0	2.6	5.9	3.9
1	Yes	30.2	38.0	22.1	35.7	28.4	31.0	23.7	27.6	24.6	16.7	18.9	19.0	32.8	24.2	29.3	17.6	35.3	24.7	23.5	38.2
2	No	64.0	49.1	53.5	54.3	52.3	54.9	59.3	60.5	62.7	59.5	59.5	59.5	50.7	61.8	50.8	66.5	54.9	59.7	55.9	50.0

BSSR Survey of 937 School Administrators on ESEA——Responses in Percentages

Question No. 27D

Question: Below are some of the difficulties school districts have encountered with ESEA. Please indicate which have been problems for your district by <u>checking</u> <u>either</u> <u>YES</u> <u>or</u> <u>NO</u> <u>for</u> <u>EACH</u> <u>statement</u>.

Sub-Question: Compliance with the Civil Rights provisions of the Act

KEY	SAMPLE	U.S. Total	BY SIZE OF STUDENT POPULATION									BY MEDIAN FAMILY INCOME							
			More Than 50,000 Students	25,000 to 49,999 Students	12,000 to 24,999 Students	6,000 to 11,999 Students	3,000 to 5,999 Students	1,200 to 2,999 Students	600 to 1,199 Students	300 to 599 Students	Less Than 300 Students	Less Than $3,000.	$3,000. to $4,999.	$5,000. to $6,999.	$7,000. to $8,999.	$9,000. to $11,999.	$12,000. and Over	Can't Evaluate Income	No Answer On Income
Y	No answer	13.1	.0	.0	8.7	7.5	11.0	15.1	11.1	18.4	31.3	11.9	15.8	10.6	12.1	9.5	17.6	15.0	20.3
X	Did not apply for Titles.	4.8	.0	.0	.0	3.8	4.1	3.7	6.4	8.8	9.4	1.7	3.1	3.1	5.2	26.2	11.8	10.0	6.3
1	Yes	4.3	7.7	9.1	10.9	5.7	6.8	3.7	2.3	.9	3.1	11.9	5.0	3.3	1.7	2.4	.0	10.0	4.7
2	No	77.8	92.3	90.9	80.4	83.0	78.1	77.5	80.1	71.9	56.3	74.6	76.1	83.1	81.0	61.9	70.6	65.0	68.8

BSSR Survey of 937 School Administrators on ESEA——Responses in Percentages

Question No. 27D

Question: Below are some of the difficulties school districts have encountered with ESEA. Please indicate which have been problems for your district by checking either YES or NO for EACH statement.

Sub-Question: Compliance with the Civil Rights provisions of the Act

KEY	SAMPLE	BY POPULATION MAKEUP												BY REGION							
		90-100% Urban	60-89% Urban	90-100% Suburban	60-89% Suburban	Mixed Rural and Urban	Mixed Rural Urban and Suburban	Mixed Rural and Suburban	60-89% Rural Non-Farm	60-89% Rural Farm	90-100% Rural Non-Farm	100% Mixed Rural	90-100% Rural Farm	New England	Middle Atlantic	East North Central	West North Central	Southern	Southwest	Mountain	Pacific
Y	No answer	2.3	13.0	15.7	5.7	15.9	15.5	16.9	10.5	11.9	21.4	21.6	16.7	11.9	12.1	13.4	12.4	15.7	16.9	14.7	9.2
X	Did not apply for Titles.	2.3	3.7	11.4	7.1	2.3	1.4	5.1	2.6	3.4	4.8	5.4	4.8	6.0	4.8	7.7	3.5	1.0	2.6	5.9	3.9
1	Yes	3.5	3.7	1.4	1.4	4.5	7.0	3.4	9.2	5.9	2.4	5.4	4.8	1.5	.6	1.2	.6	28.4	5.2	2.9	.0
2	No	91.9	79.6	71.4	85.7	77.3	76.1	74.6	77.6	78.8	71.4	67.6	73.8	80.6	82.4	77.6	83.5	54.9	75.3	76.5	86.8

BSSR Survey of 937 School Administrators on ESEA——Responses in Percentages

Question No. 27E

Question: Below are some of the difficulties school districts have encountered with ESEA. Please indicate which have been problems for your district by <u>checking either YES or NO for EACH statement</u>.

Sub-Question: Establishing acceptable evaluation procedures

KEY	SAMPLE	U.S. Total	BY SIZE OF STUDENT POPULATION									BY MEDIAN FAMILY INCOME							
			More Than 50,000 Students	25,000 to 49,999 Students	12,000 to 24,999 Students	6,000 to 11,999 Students	3,000 to 5,999 Students	1,200 to 2,999 Students	600 to 1,199 Students	300 to 599 Students	Less Than 300 Students	Less Than $3,000.	$3,000. to $4,999.	$5,000. to $6,999.	$7,000. to $8,999.	$9,000. to $11,999.	$12,000. and Over	Can't Evaluate Income	No Answer On Income
Y	No answer	9.7	.0	.0	8.7	6.6	7.5	11.7	7.6	11.4	25.0	5.1	11.2	7.2	11.2	11.9	17.6	10.0	15.6
X	Did not apply for Titles.	4.8	.0	.0	.0	3.8	4.1	3.7	6.4	8.8	9.4	1.7	3.1	3.1	5.2	26.2	11.8	10.0	6.3
1	Yes	49.1	38.5	63.6	34.8	44.3	50.7	50.0	52.6	47.4	56.3	57.6	51.4	51.4	37.1	26.2	29.4	50.0	60.9
2	No	36.4	61.5	36.4	56.5	45.3	37.7	34.6	33.3	32.5	9.4	35.6	34.4	38.3	46.6	35.7	41.2	30.0	17.2

BSSR Survey of 937 School Administrators on ESEA——Responses in Percentages

Question No. 27E

Question: Below are some of the difficulties school districts have encountered with ESEA. Please indicate which have been problems for your district by <u>checking either YES or NO for EACH statement</u>.

Sub-Question: Establishing acceptable evaluation procedures

KEY	SAMPLE	BY POPULATION MAKEUP												BY REGION							
		90-100% Urban	60-89% Urban	90-100% Suburban	60-89% Suburban	Mixed Rural and Urban	Mixed Rural Urban and Suburban	Mixed Rural and Suburban	60-89% Rural Non-Farm	60-89% Rural Farm	90-100% Rural Non-Farm	100% Mixed Rural	90-100% Rural Farm	New England	Middle Atlantic	East North Central	West North Central	Southern	Southwest	Mountain	Pacific
Y	No answer	7.0	6.5	14.3	2.9	15.9	12.7	10.2	6.6	5.9	14.3	18.9	4.8	10.4	10.3	12.2	5.3	10.8	13.0	11.8	3.9
X	Did not apply for Titles.	2.3	3.7	11.4	7.1	2.3	1.4	5.1	2.6	3.4	4.8	5.4	4.8	6.0	4.8	7.7	3.5	1.0	2.6	5.9	3.9
1	Yes	39.5	57.4	35.7	45.7	52.3	43.7	39.0	59.2	61.9	50.0	56.8	52.4	40.3	42.4	41.1	60.6	55.9	51.9	55.9	56.6
2	No	51.2	32.4	38.6	44.3	29.5	42.3	45.8	31.6	28.8	31.0	18.9	38.1	43.3	42.4	39.0	30.6	32.4	32.5	26.5	35.5

BSSR Survey of 937 School Administrators on ESEA——Responses in Percentages

Question No. 27F

Question: Below are some of the difficulties school districts have encountered with ESEA. Please indicate which have been problems for your district by checking either YES or NO for EACH statement.

Sub-Question: Receipt of funds too late in school year to spend properly.

KEY	SAMPLE	U.S. Total	BY SIZE OF STUDENT POPULATION									BY MEDIAN FAMILY INCOME							
			More Than 50,000 Students	25,000 to 49,999 Students	12,000 to 24,999 Students	6,000 to 11,999 Students	3,000 to 5,999 Students	1,200 to 2,999 Students	600 to 1,199 Students	300 to 599 Students	Less Than 300 Students	Less Than $3,000.	$3,000. to $4,999.	$5,000. to $6,999.	$7,000. to $8,999.	$9,000. to $11,999.	$12,000. and Over	Can't Evaluate Income	No Answer On Income
Y	No answer	10.6	.0	.0	8.7	4.7	8.2	12.8	8.2	14.0	31.3	8.5	12.0	9.2	10.3	11.9	11.8	10.0	14.1
X	Did not apply for Titles.	4.8	.0	.0	.0	3.8	4.1	3.7	6.4	8.8	9.4	1.7	3.1	3.1	5.2	26.2	11.8	10.0	6.3
1	Yes	48.6	76.9	90.9	47.8	49.1	51.4	45.0	53.2	46.5	25.0	49.2	50.2	51.9	39.7	26.2	35.3	55.0	54.7
2	No	36.1	23.1	9.1	43.5	42.5	36.3	38.6	32.2	30.7	34.4	40.7	34.7	35.8	44.8	35.7	41.2	25.0	25.0

BSSR Survey of 937 School Administrators on ESEA——Responses in Percentages

Question No. 27F

Question: Below are some of the difficulties school districts have encountered with ESEA. Please indicate which have been problems for your district by checking either YES or NO for EACH statement.

Sub-Question: Receipt of funds too late in school year to spend properly.

KEY	SAMPLE	BY POPULATION MAKEUP												BY REGION							
		90-100% Urban	60-89% Urban	90-100% Suburban	60-89% Suburban	Mixed Rural and Urban	Mixed Rural Urban and Suburban	Mixed Rural and Suburban	60-89% Rural Non-Farm	60-89% Rural Farm	90-100% Rural Non-Farm	100% Mixed Rural	90-100% Rural Farm	New England	Middle Atlantic	East North Central	West North Central	Southern	Southwest	Mountain	Pacific
Y	No answer	3.5	8.3	12.9	8.6	11.4	9.9	13.6	11.8	7.6	16.7	13.5	19.0	11.9	9.7	13.8	6.5	10.8	10.4	17.6	6.6
X	Did not apply for Titles.	2.3	3.7	11.4	7.1	2.3	1.4	5.1	2.6	3.4	4.8	5.4	4.8	6.0	4.8	7.7	3.5	1.0	2.6	5.9	3.9
1	Yes	55.8	55.6	35.0	48.6	47.7	39.4	49.2	48.7	61.0	38.1	62.2	40.5	31.3	54.5	40.7	54.1	55.9	59.7	35.3	48.7
2	No	38.4	32.4	40.7	35.7	38.6	49.3	32.2	36.8	28.0	40.5	18.9	35.7	50.7	30.9	37.8	35.9	32.4	27.3	41.2	40.8

BSSR Survey of 937 School Administrators on ESEA——Responses in Percentages

Question No. 27G

Question: Below are some of the difficulties school districts have encountered with ESEA. Please indicate which have been problems for your district by checking either YES or NO for EACH statement

Sub-Question: Lack of building space in which to carry out planned program.

KEY*	SAMPLE	U.S. Total	BY SIZE OF STUDENT POPULATION: More Than 50,000 Students	25,000 to 49,999 Students	12,000 to 24,999 Students	6,000 to 11,999 Students	3,000 to 5,999 Students	1,200 to 2,999 Students	600 to 1,199 Students	300 to 599 Students	Less Than 300 Students	BY MEDIAN FAMILY INCOME: Less Than $3,000.	$3,000. to $4,999.	$5,000. to $6,999.	$7,000. to $8,999.	$9,000. to $11,999.	$12,000. and Over	Can't Evaluate Income	No Answer On Income
Y	No answer	10.6	.0	.0	8.7	4.7	9.6	11.4	9.9	14.0	28.1	5.1	12.0	8.6	13.8	11.9	17.6	15.0	10.9
X	Did not apply for Titles.	4.8	.0	.0	.0	3.8	4.1	3.7	6.4	8.8	9.4	1.7	3.1	3.1	5.2	26.2	11.8	10.0	6.3
1	Yes	48.1	92.3	72.7	67.4	53.8	54.1	45.3	40.9	42.1	34.4	62.7	53.3	46.1	39.7	31.0	35.3	50.0	54.7
2	No	36.5	7.7	27.3	23.9	37.7	32.2	39.6	42.7	35.1	28.1	30.5	31.7	42.2	41.4	31.0	35.3	25.0	28.1

* Deviations from totals of 100% in each column are due to additional BSSR Keys judged by the senior author to be statistically insignificant.

BSSR Survey of 937 School Administrators on ESEA——Responses in Percentages

Question No. 27G

Question: Below are some of the difficulties school districts have encountered with ESEA. Please indicate which have been problems for your district by <u>checking either YES or NO for EACH statement</u>

Sub-Question: Lack of building space in which to carry out planned program.

KEY *	SAMPLE	BY POPULATION MAKEUP												BY REGION							
		90-100% Urban	60-89% Urban	90-100% Suburban	60-89% Suburban	Mixed Rural and Urban	Mixed Rural Urban and Suburban	Mixed Rural and Suburban	60-89% Rural Non-Farm	60-89% Rural Farm	90-100% Rural Non-Farm	100% Mixed Rural	90-100% Rural Farm	New England	Middle Atlantic	East North Central	West North Central	Southern	Southwest	Mountain	Pacific
Y	No answer	2.3	6.5	16.4	8.6	11.4	8.5	11.9	10.5	10.2	16.7	18.9	9.5	9.0	10.9	13.0	7.6	9.8	11.7	14.7	7.9
X	Did not apply for Titles.	2.3	3.7	11.4	7.1	2.3	1.4	5.1	2.6	3.4	4.8	5.4	4.8	6.0	4.8	7.7	3.5	1.0	2.6	5.9	3.9
1	Yes	57.0	56.5	31.4	48.6	54.5	63.4	37.3	44.7	50.8	35.7	54.1	45.2	47.8	37.0	41.9	53.5	69.6	50.6	32.4	56.6
2	No	38.4	33.3	40.7	35.7	31.8	26.8	45.8	42.1	35.6	42.9	21.6	40.5	37.3	47.3	37.4	35.3	19.6	35.1	47.1	31.6

* Deviations from totals of 100% in each column are due to additional BSSR Keys judged by the senior author to be statistically insignificant.

BSSR Survey of 937 School Administrators on ESEA——Responses in Percentages

Question No. 27-H

Question: Below are some of the difficulties school districts have encountered with ESEA. Please indicate which have been problems for your district by checking YES or NO for EACH statement.

Sub-Question: Inability to hire qualified personnel for the planned program.

KEY	* SAMPLE	U.S. Total	BY SIZE OF STUDENT POPULATION									BY MEDIAN FAMILY INCOME							
			More Than 50,000 Students	25,000 to 49,999 Students	12,000 to 24,999 Students	6,000 to 11,999 Students	3,000 to 5,999 Students	1,200 to 2,999 Students	600 to 1,199 Students	300 to 599 Students	Less Than 300 Students	Less Than $3,000.	$3,000. to $4,999.	$5,000. to $6,999.	$7,000. to $8,999.	$9,000. to $11,999.	$12,000. and Over	Can't Evaluate Income	No Answer On Income
Y	No answer	8.8	.0	.0	6.5	3.8	8.9	10.1	6.4	10.5	28.1	3.4	10.8	7.2	8.6	11.9	17.6	10.0	9.4
X	Did not apply for Titles.	4.8	.0	.0	.0	3.8	4.1	3.7	6.4	8.8	9.4	1.7	3.1	3.1	5.2	26.2	11.8	10.0	6.3
1	Yes	56.0	100.0	90.9	67.4	59.4	54.1	55.4	56.7	49.1	34.4	72.9	58.3	60.0	45.7	21.4	23.5	45.0	62.5
2	No	30.3	.0	9.1	26.1	33.0	32.2	30.9	30.4	31.6	28.1	22.0	27.8	29.7	40.5	40.5	47.1	30.0	21.9

* Deviations from totals of 100% in each column are due to additional BSSR Keys judged by the senior author to be statistically insignificant.

BSSR Survey of 937 School Administrators on ESEA——Responses in Percentages

Question No. 27-H

Question: Below are some of the difficulties school districts have encountered with ESEA. Please indicate which have been problems for your district by checking YES or NO for EACH statement.

Sub-Question: Inability to hire qualified personnel for the planned program.

KEY*	SAMPLE	BY POPULATION MAKEUP												BY REGION							
		90-100% Urban	60-89% Urban	90-100% Suburban	60-89% Suburban	Mixed Rural and Urban	Mixed Rural Urban and Suburban	Mixed Rural and Suburban	60-89% Rural Non-Farm	60-89% Rural Farm	90-100% Rural Non-Farm	100% Mixed Rural	90-100% Rural Farm	New England	Middle Atlantic	East North Central	West North Central	Southern	Southwest	Mountain	Pacific
Y	No answer	2.3	7.4	13.6	4.3	10.2	8.5	10.2	6.6	6.8	14.3	13.5	11.9	11.9	9.1	11.0	4.7	7.8	9.1	14.7	5.3
X	Did not apply for Titles.	2.3	3.7	11.4	7.1	2.3	1.4	5.1	2.6	3.4	4.8	5.4	4.8	6.0	4.8	7.7	3.5	1.0	2.6	5.9	3.9
1	Yes	67.4	65.7	37.1	50.0	62.5	60.6	49.2	60.5	57.6	64.3	45.9	57.1	41.8	53.3	50.0	62.9	74.5	61.0	47.1	52.6
2	No	27.9	22.2	37.9	38.6	25.0	29.6	35.6	30.3	32.2	16.7	35.1	26.2	40.3	32.1	31.3	28.8	16.7	27.3	32.4	38.2

* Deviations from totals of 100% in each column are due to additional BSSR Keys judged by the senior author to be statistically insignificant.

BSSR Survey of 937 School Administrators on ESEA——Responses in Percentages

Question No. 27-I

Question: Below are some of the difficulties school districts have encountered with ESEA. Please indicate which have been problems for your district by checking either YES or NO for EACH statement.

Sub-Question: Complexity of Title I application form.

		BY SIZE OF STUDENT POPULATION									BY MEDIAN FAMILY INCOME							
KEY * SAMPLE	U.S. Total	More Than 50,000 Students	25,000 to 49,999 Students	12,000 to 24,999 Students	6,000 to 11,999 Students	3,000 to 5,999 Students	1,200 to 2,999 Students	600 to 1,199 Students	300 to 599 Students	Less Than 300 Students	Less Than $3,000.	$3,000. to $4,999.	$5,000. to $6,999.	$7,000. to $8,999.	$9,000. to $11,999.	$12,000. and Over	Can't Evaluate Income	No Answer On Income
Y No Answer	8.6	.0	.0	6.5	3.8	8.2	9.7	7.0	10.5	28.1	6.8	10.4	5.6	10.3	9.5	17.6	10.0	14.1
X Didn't Apply for Titles.	4.8	.0	.0	.0	3.8	4.1	3.7	6.4	8.8	9.4	1.7	3.1	3.1	5.2	26.2	11.8	10.0	6.3
1 Yes	55.3	46.2	54.5	34.8	57.5	57.5	58.4	58.5	49.1	46.9	69.5	53.3	60.3	44.8	31.0	52.9	65.0	54.7
2 No	31.2	53.8	45.5	58.7	34.9	29.5	28.2	28.1	31.6	15.6	22.0	33.2	31.1	39.7	33.3	17.6	10.0	25.0

*Deviations from totals of 100% in each column are due to additional BSSR Keys judged by the senior author to be statistically insignificant.

BSSR Survey of 937 School Administrators on ESEA——Responses in Percentages

Question No. 27-I

Question: Below are some of the difficulties school districts have encountered with ESEA. Please indicate which have been problems for your district by <u>checking</u> <u>either</u> <u>YES</u> <u>or</u> <u>NO</u> <u>for</u> <u>EACH</u> <u>statement</u>.

Sub-Question: Complexity of Title I application form.

KEY*	SAMPLE	BY POPULATION MAKEUP												BY REGION							
		90-100% Urban	60-89% Urban	90-100% Suburban	60-89% Suburban	Mixed Rural and Urban	Mixed Rural Urban and Suburban	Mixed Rural and Suburban	60-89% Rural Non-Farm	60-89% Rural Farm	90-100% Rural Non-Farm	100% Mixed Rural	90-100% Rural Farm	New England	Middle Atlantic	East North Central	West North Central	Southern	Southwest	Mountain	Pacific
Y	No answer	4.7	7.4	12.1	2.9	8.0	9.9	6.8	9.2	9.3	16.7	13.5	4.8	9.0	7.3	9.8	5.3	10.8	11.7	14.7	6.6
X	Didn't apply for Titles.	2.3	3.7	11.4	7.1	2.3	1.4	5.1	2.6	3.4	4.8	5.4	4.8	6.0	4.8	7.7	3.5	1.0	2.6	5.9	3.9
1	YES	55.8	62.0	45.0	55.7	61.4	60.6	54.2	53.9	53.4	45.2	62.2	61.9	50.7	59.4	50.0	58.2	57.8	62.3	50.0	52.6
2	NO	37.2	25.9	31.4	34.3	28.4	28.2	33.9	34.2	33.9	33.3	18.9	28.6	34.3	27.9	32.5	32.9	30.4	23.4	29.4	36.8

*Deviations from totals of 100% in each column are due to additional BSSR Keys judged by the senior author to be statistically insignificant.

BSSR Survey of 937 School Administrators on ESEA——Responses in Percentages

Question No. 27-J

Question: Below are some of the difficulties school districts have encountered with ESEA. Please indicate which have been problems for your district by checking either YES or NO for EACH statement.

Sub-Question: Provision that planning costs are not reimbursable.

KEY *	SAMPLE	U.S. Total	BY SIZE OF STUDENT POPULATION									BY MEDIAN FAMILY INCOME							
			More Than 50,000 Students	25,000 to 49,999 Students	12,000 to 24,999 Students	6,000 to 11,999 Students	3,000 to 5,999 Students	1,200 to 2,999 Students	600 to 1,199 Students	300 to 599 Students	Less Than 300 Students	Less Than $3,000.	$3,000. to $4,999.	$5,000. to $6,999.	$7,000. to $8,999.	$9,000. to $11,999.	$12,000. and Over	Can't Evaluate Income	No Answer On Income
Y	No answer	10.5	.0	.0	6.5	3.8	8.2	12.4	8.8	13.2	37.5	16.9	12.0	7.5	11.2	9.5	17.6	15.0	10.9
X	Didn't apply for Titles	4.8	.0	.0	.0	3.8	4.1	3.7	6.4	8.8	9.4	1.7	3.1	3.1	5.2	26.2	11.8	10.0	6.3
1	YES	56.7	76.9	81.8	69.6	70.8	62.3	56.7	50.9	42.1	31.3	50.8	56.4	58.6	55.2	47.6	47.1	55.0	64.1
2	NO	28.0	23.1	18.2	23.9	21.7	24.7	27.2	33.9	36.0	21.9	30.5	28.2	30.8	28.4	16.7	23.5	20.0	18.8

*Deviations from totals of 100% in each column are due to additional BSSR Keys judged by the senior author to be statistically insignificant.

BSSR Survey of 937 School Administrators on ESEA——Responses in Percentages

Question No. 27-J

Question: Below are some of the difficulties school districts have encountered with ESEA. Please indicate which have been problems for your district by checking either YES or NO for EACH statement.

Sub-Question: Provision that planning costs are not reimbursable.

		BY POPULATION MAKEUP												BY REGION							
KEY*	SAMPLE	90-100% Urban	60-89% Urban	90-100% Suburban	60-89% Suburban	Mixed Rural and Urban	Mixed Rural Urban and Suburban	Mixed Rural and Suburban	60-89% Rural Non-Farm	60-89% Rural Farm	90-100% Rural Non-Farm	100% Mixed Rural	90-100% Rural Farm	New England	Middle Atlantic	East North Central	West North Central	Southern	Southwest	Mountain	Pacific
Y	No answer	3.5	8.3	12.1	2.9	13.6	7.0	13.6	10.5	13.6	19.0	10.8	14.3	14.9	7.3	12.6	10.0	7.8	11.7	14.7	7.9
X	Didn't apply for Titles.	2.3	3.7	11.4	7.1	2.3	1.4	5.1	2.6	3.4	4.8	5.4	4.8	6.0	4.8	7.7	3.5	1.0	2.6	5.9	3.9
1	YES	65.1	61.1	50.7	70.0	61.4	60.6	47.5	57.9	51.7	45.2	59.5	42.9	47.8	61.8	55.7	54.7	70.6	49.4	50.0	52.6
2	NO	29.1	25.9	25.7	20.0	22.7	31.0	33.9	28.9	31.4	31.0	24.3	38.1	31.3	26.1	24.0	31.8	20.6	35.1	29.4	35.5

*Deviations from totals of 100% in each column are due to additional BSSR Keys judged by the senior author to be statistically insignificant.

BSSR Survey of 937 School Administrators on ESEA——Responses in Percentages

Question No. 27-K

Question: Below are some of the difficulties school districts have encountered with ESEA. Please indicate which have been problems for your district by checking either YES or NO for EACH statement.

Sub-Question: Provision that the indirect costs of administering programs are not reimbursable.

KEY *	SAMPLE	U.S. Total	BY SIZE OF STUDENT POPULATION									BY MEDIAN FAMILY INCOME							
			More Than 50,000 Students	25,000 to 49,999 Students	12,000 to 24,999 Students	6,000 to 11,999 Students	3,000 to 5,999 Students	1,200 to 2,999 Students	600 to 1,199 Students	300 to 599 Students	Less Than 300 Students	Less Than $3,000.	$3,000. to $4,999.	$5,000. to $6,999.	$7,000. to $8,999.	$9,000. to $11,999.	$12,000. and Over	Can't Evaluate Income	No Answer On Income
Y	No answer	10.8	.0	9.1	8.7	2.8	9.6	14.1	8.2	11.4	31.3	16.9	11.2	8.1	14.7	9.5	11.8	15.0	10.9
X	Didn't apply for Titles.	4.8	.0	.0	.0	3.8	4.1	3.7	6.4	8.8	9.4	1.7	3.1	3.1	5.2	26.2	11.8	10.0	6.3
1	YES	60.2	84.6	72.7	71.7	70.8	64.4	57.4	61.4	46.5	43.8	61.0	62.5	62.5	53.4	42.9	52.9	50.0	65.6
2	NO	24.0	15.4	18.2	19.6	22.6	20.5	24.8	24.0	33.3	15.6	20.3	22.8	26.4	26.7	21.4	23.5	20.0	17.2

*Deviations from totals of 100% in each column are due to additional BSSR Keys judged by the senior author to be statistically insignificant.

BSSR Survey of 937 School Administrators on ESEA——Responses in Percentages

Question No. 27-K

Question: Below are some of the difficulties school districts have encountered with ESEA. Please indicate which have been problems for your district by checking either YES or NO for EACH statement.

Sub-Question: Provision that the indirect costs of administering programs are not reimbursable.

		BY POPULATION MAKEUP												BY REGION							
KEY*	SAMPLE	90-100% Urban	60-89% Urban	90-100% Suburban	60-89% Suburban	Mixed Rural and Urban	Mixed Rural Urban and Suburban	Mixed Rural and Suburban	60-89% Rural Non-Farm	60-89% Rural Farm	90-100% Rural Non-Farm	100% Mixed Rural	90-100% Rural Farm	New England	Middle Atlantic	East North Central	West North Central	Southern	Southwest	Mountain	Pacific
Y	No answer	3.5	9.3	13.6	5.7	11.4	11.3	15.3	10.5	10.2	19.0	8.1	16.7	11.9	9.1	13.0	8.2	8.8	14.3	14.7	9.2
X	Didn't apply for Titles.	2.3	3.7	11.4	7.1	2.3	1.4	5.1	2.6	3.4	4.8	5.4	4.8	6.0	4.8	7.7	3.5	1.0	2.6	5.9	3.9
1	YES	62.8	63.9	55.0	67.1	62.9	64.8	52.5	59.2	61.9	42.9	62.2	54.8	52.2	67.3	57.7	62.4	72.5	55.8	47.1	48.7
2	NO	31.4	21.3	20.0	20.0	20.5	22.5	27.1	27.6	24.6	33.3	24.3	23.8	29.9	18.2	21.5	25.9	17.6	26.0	32.4	38.2

*Deviations from totals of 100% in each column are due to additional BSSR Keys judged by the senior author to be statistically insignificant.

BSSR Survey of 937 School Administrators on ESEA——Responses in Percentages

Question No. 30

Question: Have any of your project applications been denied or extensively revised?

KEY	SAMPLE	U.S. Total	BY SIZE OF STUDENT POPULATION									BY MEDIAN FAMILY INCOME							
			More Than 50,000 Students	25,000 to 49,999 Students	12,000 to 24,999 Students	6,000 to 11,999 Students	3,000 to 5,999 Students	1,200 to 2,999 Students	600 to 1,199 Students	300 to 599 Students	Less Than 300 Students	Less Than $3,000.	$3,000. to $4,999.	$5,000. to $6,999.	$7,000. to $8,999.	$9,000. to $11,999.	$12,000. and Over	Can't Evaluate Income	No Answer On Income
Y	No answer	4.5	.0	.0	4.3	.9	5.5	5.4	4.1	2.6	15.6	3.4	6.6	2.5	6.0	4.8	4.9	5.0	4.7
X	Didn't apply for any title	4.9	.0	.0	.0	3.8	4.1	3.7	6.4	8.8	12.5	1.7	3.5	3.1	5.2	26.2	11.8	10.0	6.3
0	No titles revised or denied	69.4	61.5	45.5	60.9	69.8	65.1	70.8	74.9	74.6	50.0	74.6	69.1	70.6	69.8	59.5	58.8	60.0	70.3
1	Title I revised/denied	8.5	.0	9.1	13.0	7.5	11.0	9.4	7.0	6.1	6.3	11.9	8.5	9.4	6.0	2.4	11.8	15.0	6.3
2	Title II revised/denied	.6	.0	.0	.0	.0	1.4	.3	.6	1.8	.0	.0	1.2	.6	.0	.0	5.9	.0	.0
3	Title III revised/denied	8.6	15.4	45.5	19.6	12.3	8.9	8.7	2.9	3.5	12.5	3.4	6.9	10.0	10.3	7.1	5.9	10.0	10.9
4	Can't tell which Title denied/revised	3.3	23.1	.0	2.2	5.7	3.4	1.7	4.1	2.6	3.1	5.1	4.2	3.6	2.6	.0	.0	.0	1.6
5	Both I and III revised/denied	.1	.0	.0	.0	.0	.7	.0	.0	.0	.0	.0	.0	.3	.0	.0	.0	.0	.0

BSSR Survey of 937 School Administrators on ESEA——Responses in Percentages

Question No. 30

Question: Have any of your project applications been denied or extensively revised?

KEY	SAMPLE	BY POPULATION MAKEUP												BY REGION							
		90-100% Urban	60-89% Urban	90-100% Suburban	60-89% Suburban	Mixed Rural and Urban	Mixed Rural Urban and Suburban	Mixed Rural and Suburban	60-89% Rural Non-Farm	60-89% Rural Farm	90-100% Rural Non-Farm	100% Mixed Rural	90-100% Rural Farm	New England	Middle Atlantic	East North Central	West North Central	Southern	Southwest	Mountain	Pacific
Y	No answer	1.2	5.6	4.3	.0	6.8	7.0	5.1	3.9	4.2	11.9	2.7	2.4	7.5	1.8	6.1	2.9	3.9	9.1	5.9	1.3
X	Didn't apply for any Title.	2.3	3.7	11.4	7.1	2.3	1.4	5.1	2.6	3.4	4.8	5.4	7.1	6.0	4.8	7.7	3.5	1.0	3.9	5.9	3.9
0	No titles revised/ denied	62.8	60.2	66.4	77.1	70.5	67.6	74.6	69.7	75.4	59.5	78.4	81.0	56.7	78.2	67.1	68.8	70.6	72.7	67.6	65.8
1	Title I revised/ denied	10.5	11.1	5.0	8.6	11.4	7.0	6.8	11.8	10.2	4.8	5.4	4.8	7.5	6.7	9.3	9.4	8.8	7.8	14.7	6.6
2	Title II revised/ denied	1.2	.0	1.4	.0	1.1	.0	.0	1.3	.8	.0	.0	.0	.0	.0	.0	1.8	1.0	.0	.0	2.6
3	Title III revised/ denied	19.8	13.9	10.0	4.3	5.7	9.9	6.8	6.6	3.4	14.3	.0	2.4	14.9	7.3	8.1	7.1	7.8	5.2	5.9	17.1
4	Can't tell which Title revised/denied	2.3	4.6	1.4	2.9	2.3	7.0	1.7	3.9	2.5	4.8	8.1	2.4	6.0	1.2	1.6	6.5	6.9	1.3	.0	2.6
5	Both I & III revis- ed/denied	.0	.9	.0	..0	.0	.0	.0	.0	.0	.0	.0	.0	1.5	.0	.0	.0	.0	.0	.0	.0

BSSR Survey of 937 School Administrators on ESEA——Responses in Percentages

Question No. 31

Question: The ESEA emphasizes the necessity of evaluation of all projects funded under the Act. Yet educational achievement is one of the most difficult areas to evaluate. HOW and By WHOM do you think ESEA programs should be evaluated?

KEY*	SAMPLE	U.S. Total	BY SIZE OF STUDENT POPULATION									BY MEDIAN FAMILY INCOME							
			More Than 50,000 Students	25,000 to 49,999 Students	12,000 to 24,999 Students	6,000 to 11,999 Students	3,000 to 5,999 Students	1,200 to 2,999 Students	600 to 1,199 Students	300 to 599 Students	Less Than 300 Students	Less Than $3,000.	$3,000. to $4,999.	$5,000. to $6,999.	$7,000. to $8,999.	$9,000. to $11,999.	$12,000. and Over	Can't Evaluate Income	No Answer On Income
Y	No answer	16.5	.0	18.2	8.7	11.3	17.8	17.4	19.9	16.7	18.8	13.6	16.2	15.0	16.4	26.2	17.6	15.0	23.4
1	Teachers	6.6	.0	.0	4.3	2.8	5.5	9.4	7.6	5.3	6.3	3.4	8.1	5.8	11.2	2.4	.0	5.0	4.7
2	Principals	.1	.0	.0	.0	.0	.0	.3	.0	.0	.0	.0	.4	.0	.0	.0	.0	.0	.0
3	Faculty & local administrators	9.1	15.4	.0	8.7	11.3	8.2	8.4	7.6	10.5	15.6	8.5	8.5	11.1	8.6	9.5	5.9	5.0	3.1
4	State education office	4.9	.0	27.3	2.2	3.8	2.7	5.4	4.1	4.4	18.8	5.1	5.4	4.2	5.2	4.8	5.9	5.0	6.3
5	Special consultant, universities	4.6	38.5	9.1	15.2	8.5	2.7	3.4	2.3	2.6	.0	5.1	2.3	5.8	6.9	2.4	5.9	5.0	3.1
6	Local and State combination	37.9	23.1	27.3	41.3	38.7	45.2	36.6	35.7	42.1	15.6	35.6	37.5	39.4	33.6	35.7	29.4	40.0	43.8
7	Local school system	14.5	23.1	18.2	17.4	19.8	15.1	13.4	14.6	7.9	18.8	20.3	15.8	12.8	14.7	19.0	17.6	10.0	10.9
8	Federal evaluation USOC.	.7	.0	.0	.0	.9	.0	1.0	1.2	.9	.0	.0	.8	.6	.9	.0	.0	5.0	1.6

*Deviations from totals of 100% in each column are due to additional BSSR Keys judged by the senior author to be statistically insignificant.

BSSR Survey of 937 School Administrators on ESEA——Responses in Percentages

Question No. 31

Question: The ESEA emphasizes the necessity of evaluation of all projects funded under the Act. Yet educational achievement is one of the most difficult areas to evaluate. HOW and BY WHOM do you think ESEA programs should be evaluated?

KEY*	SAMPLE	BY POPULATION MAKEUP: 90-100% Urban	60-89% Urban	90-100% Suburban	60-89% Suburban	Mixed Rural and Urban	Mixed Rural Urban and Suburban	Mixed Rural and Suburban	60-89% Rural Non-Farm	60-89% Rural Farm	90-100% Rural Non-Farm	100% Mixed Rural	90-100% Rural Farm	BY REGION: New England	Middle Atlantic	East North Central	West North Central	Southern	Southwest	Mountain	Pacific
Y	No answer	7.0	11.1	20.7	15.7	20.5	16.9	25.4	11.8	13.6	21.4	21.6	23.8	13.4	13.9	19.1	20.0	11.8	16.9	11.8	17.1
1	Teachers	4.7	4.6	4.3	8.6	9.1	2.8	10.2	11.8	10.2	.0	8.1	2.4	6.0	4.8	10.2	5.9	6.9	5.2	2.9	3.9
2	Principals	.0	.0	.0	.0	1.1	.0	.0	.0	.0	.0	.0	.0	.0	.0	.4	.0	.0	.0	.0	.0
3	Faculty and Local Administrators	12.8	9.3	9.3	7.1	9.1	1.4	15.3	9.2	9.3	7.1	10.8	7.1	16.4	10.3	8.9	9.4	8.8	6.5	.0	6.6
4	State education Office	5.8	6.5	4.3	1.4	2.3	1.4	6.8	5.3	8.5	7.1	5.4	2.4	7.5	2.4	3.3	8.2	4.9	6.5	11.8	1.3
5	Special counsultant, universities	11.6	9.3	2.9	7.1	2.3	4.2	.0	3.9	1.7	4.8	.0	4.8	10.4	4.2	4.1	1.8	2.9	5.2	2.9	10.5
6	Local and state cominbation	36.0	38.0	40.0	38.6	39.8	46.5	23.7	40.8	39.8	33.3	27.0	38.1	29.9	41.8	33.3	38.2	42.2	36.4	44.1	43.4
7	Local school system	17.4	17.6	12.1	17.1	12.5	23.9	15.3	9.2	11.0	14.3	13.5	11.9	13.4	13.9	14.2	9.4	19.6	16.9	26.5	15.8
8	Federal evaluation USOE.	.0	.0	1.4	1.4	.0	.0	1.7	1.3	.8	2.4	.0	.0	.0	1.8	1.2	.0	.0	1.3	.0	.0

*Deviation from totals of 100% in each column are due to additional BSSR Keys judged by the senior author to be statistically insignificant.

BSSR Survey of 937 School Administrators on ESEA——Responses in Percentages

Question No. 32-A

Question: Do you intend to apply under either Title I, II, or III next year (1966-67)?

Sub-Question: Title I

KEY	SAMPLE	U.S. Total	BY SIZE OF STUDENT POPULATION									BY MEDIAN FAMILY INCOME							
			More Than 50,000 Students	25,000 to 49,999 Students	12,000 to 24,999 Students	6,000 to 11,999 Students	3,000 to 5,999 Students	1,200 to 2,999 Students	600 to 1,199 Students	300 to 599 Students	Less Than 300 Students	Less Than $3,000.	$3,000. to $4,999.	$5,000. to $6,999.	$7,000. to $8,999.	$9,000. to $11,999.	$12,000. and Over	Can't Evaluate Income	No Answer On Income
Y	No answer	1.8	7.7	.0	2.2	.9	1.4	1.0	1.8	3.5	6.3	.0	1.5	1.7	.9	4.8	11.8	.0	3.1
1	YES	93.8	92.3	100.0	97.8	97.2	95.9	93.6	94.7	90.4	75.0	100.0	95.4	95.8	94.8	69.0	64.7	95.0	92.2
2	NO	3.1	.0	.0	.0	1.9	1.4	3.0	2.3	5.3	18.8	.0	2.7	1.4	4.3	19.0	11.8	.0	3.1
3	Undecided	1.3	4.0	.0	.0	.0	1.4	2.3	1.2	.9	.0	.0	.4	1.1	.0	7.1	11.8	5.0	1.6

BSSR Survey of 937 School Administrators on ESEA——Responses in Percentages

Question No. 32-A

Question: Do you intend to apply under either Title I, II, or III next year (1966-67)?

Sub-Question: Title I

KEY	SAMPLE	BY POPULATION MAKEUP												BY REGION							
		90-100% Urban	60-89% Urban	90-100% Suburban	60-89% Suburban	Mixed Rural and Urban	Mixed Rural Urban and Suburban	Mixed Rural and Suburban	60-89% Rural Non-Farm	60-89% Rural Farm	90-100% Rural Non-Farm	100% Mixed Rural	90-100% Rural Farm	New England	Middle Atlantic	East North Central	West North Central	Southern	Southwest	Mountain	Pacific
Y	No answer	1.2	2.8	2.9	1.4	1.1	.0	1.7	.0	.8	.0	5.4	7.1	1.5	1.2	2.4	2.4	.0	.0	8.8	1.3
1	YES	95.3	95.4	83.6	94.3	97.7	100.0	93.2	97.4	95.8	92.9	94.6	90.5	91.0	95.2	92.7	95.3	98.0	96.1	85.3	89.5
2	NO	2.3	.9	10.0	2.9	1.1	.0	3.4	.0	2.5	7.1	.0	2.4	4.5	1.8	4.5	2.4	.0	3.6	2.9	5.3
3	Undecided	1.2	.9	3.6	1.4	.0	.0	1.7	2.6	.8	.0	.0	.0	3.0	1.8	.4	.0	2.0	.0	2.9	3.9

BSSR Survey of 937 School Administrators on ESEA——Responses in Percentages

Question No. 32-B

Question: Do you intend to apply under either Title I, II, or III next year (1966-67)?

Sub-Question: Title II

KEY	SAMPLE	U.S. Total	BY SIZE OF STUDENT POPULATION									BY MEDIAN FAMILY INCOME							
			More Than 50,000 Students	25,000 to 49,999 Students	12,000 to 24,999 Students	6,000 to 11,999 Students	3,000 to 5,999 Students	1,200 to 2,999 Students	600 to 1,199 Students	300 to 599 Students	Less Than 300 Students	Less Than $3,000.	$3,000. to $4,999.	$5,000. to $6,999.	$7,000. to $8,999.	$9,000. to $11,999.	$12,000. and Over	Can't Evaluate Income	No Answer On Income
Y	No answer	6.4	7.7	.0	2.2	3.8	4.1	7.4	6.4	9.6	12.5	10.2	3.9	6.9	5.2	4.8	11.8	10.0	10.9
1	YES	88.7	92.3	100.0	97.8	95.3	95.2	86.6	87.7	79.8	75.0	89.8	91.5	87.8	87.9	88.1	88.2	85.0	84.4
2	NO	3.4	.0	.0	.0	.9	.7	3.0	4.7	8.8	9.4	.0	3.5	2.8	6.0	4.8	.0	5.0	4.7
3	Undecided	1.5	.0	.0	.0	.0	.0	3.0	1.2	1.8	3.1	.0	1.2	2.5	.9	2.4	.0	.0	.0

BSSR Survey of 937 School Administrators on ESEA——Responses in Percentages

Question No. 32-B

Question: Do you intend to apply under either Title I, II, or III next year (1966-67)?

Sub-Question: Title II

KEY	SAMPLE	BY POPULATION MAKEUP												BY REGION							
		90-100% Urban	60-89% Urban	90-100% Suburban	60-89% Suburban	Mixed Rural and Urban	Mixed Rural Urban and Suburban	Mixed Rural and Suburban	60-89% Rural Non-Farm	60-89% Rural Farm	90-100% Rural Non-Farm	100% Mixed Rural	90-100% Rural Farm	New England	Middle Atlantic	East North Central	West North Central	Southern	Southwest	Mountain	Pacific
Y	No answer	4.7	7.4	5.7	4.3	6.8	5.6	3.4	1.3	7.6	4.8	16.2	16.7	7.5	4.2	5.7	11.8	2.9	2.6	5.9	9.2
1	YES	93.0	88.0	89.3	90.0	89.8	91.5	86.4	94.7	83.9	92.9	83.8	76.2	91.0	92.1	90.7	75.3	95.1	94.8	85.3	89.5
2	NO	2.3	2.8	4.3	4.3	2.3	1.4	5.1	1.3	5.9	2.4	.0	7.1	.0	1.8	2.4	10.6	.0	2.6	5.9	1.3
3	Undecided	.0	1.9	.7	1.4	1.1	1.4	5.1	2.6	2.5	.0	.0	.0	1.5	1.8	1.2	2.4	2.0	.0	2.9	.0

BSSR Survey of 937 School Administrators on ESEA——Responses in Percentages

Question No. 32-C

Question: Do you intend to apply under either Title I, II, or III next year (1966-67)?

Sub-Question: Title III

KEY	SAMPLE	U.S. Total	BY SIZE OF STUDENT POPULATION									BY MEDIAN FAMILY INCOME							
			More Than 50,000 Students	25,000 to 49,999 Students	12,000 to 24,999 Students	6,000 to 11,999 Students	3,000 to 5,999 Students	1,200 to 2,999 Students	600 to 1,199 Students	300 to 599 Students	Less Than 300 Students	Less Than $3,000.	$3,000. to $4,999.	$5,000. to $6,999.	$7,000. to $8,999.	$9,000. to $11,999.	$12,000. and Over	Can't Evaluate Income	No Answer On Income
Y	No answer	15.3	.0	9.1	13.0	12.3	7.5	18.8	17.0	20.2	12.5	10.2	13.5	18.1	12.1	14.3	11.8	20.0	17.2
1	YES	48.8	92.3	90.9	69.6	70.8	56.2	42.6	34.5	36.0	59.4	57.6	47.9	47.5	54.3	45.2	64.7	45.0	40.6
2	NO	27.6	.0	.0	10.9	11.3	26.0	27.2	41.5	38.6	25.0	25.4	32.0	25.8	25.9	28.6	11.8	25.0	29.7
3	Undecided	8.3	7.7	.0	6.5	5.7	10.3	11.4	7.0	5.3	3.1	6.8	6.6	8.6	7.8	11.9	11.8	10.0	12.5

BSSR Survey of 937 School Administrators on ESEA——Responses in Percentages

Question No. 32-C

Question: Do you intend to apply under either Title I, II, or III next year (1966-67)?

Sub-Question: Title III

KEY	SAMPLE	BY POPULATION MAKEUP												BY REGION							
		90-100% Urban	60-89% Urban	90-100% Suburban	60-89% Suburban	Mixed Rural and Urban	Mixed Rural Urban and Suburban	Mixed Rural and Suburban	60-89% Rural Non-Farm	60-89% Rural Farm	90-100% Rural Non-Farm	100% Mixed Rural	90-100% Rural Farm	New England	Middle Atlantic	East North Central	West North Central	Southern	Southwest	Mountain	Pacific
Y	No answer	17. 4	16. 7	12. 1	12. 9	13. 6	14. 1	16. 9	11. 8	19. 5	11. 9	16. 2	21. 4	13. 4	10. 9	21. 1	17. 1	16. 7	5. 2	11. 8	13. 2
1	YES	59. 3	58. 3	50. 7	58. 6	46. 6	53. 3	57. 3	43. 4	35. 6	52. 4	37. 8	45. 2	64. 2	50. 9	39. 8	42. 4	55. 9	53. 2	61. 8	53. 9
2	NO	51. 1	15. 7	24. 3	22. 9	29. 5	23. 9	35. 6	38. 2	41. 5	28. 6	37. 8	26. 2	11. 9	27. 9	31. 3	34. 7	16. 7	31. 2	23. 5	26. 3
3	Undecided	8. 1	9. 3	12. 9	5. 7	0. 2	8. 5	10. 2	6. 6	3. 4	7. 1	8. 1	7. 1	10. 4	10. 3	7. 7	5. 9	10. 8	10. 4	2. 9	6. 6

Appendix D: Part I

Organization Chart, United States Office of Education
January 14, 1965 (before reorganization)

COMMISSIONER
DEPUTY COMMISSIONER

OFFICE OF LEGISLATION

OFFICE OF ADMINISTRATION

OFFICE OF INFORMATION

OFFICE OF FIELD SERVICES

PROGRAMS FOR THE EDUCATION OF THE DISADVANTAGED

OFFICE OF EQUAL EDUCATIONAL OPPORTUNITIES

OFFICE OF FEDERAL EDUCATION ACTIVITIES

OFFICE OF FEDERAL-STATE RELATIONS

BUREAU OF EDUC. RESEARCH & DEVELOPMENT
- DIVISION OF EDUC. ORG. AND ADMINISTRATION
- DIVISION OF EDUCATIONAL RESEARCH
- DIVISION OF HANDICAPPED CHILD. & YOUTH
- DIVISION OF LIBRARY SERVICES

BUREAU OF INTERNATIONAL EDUCATION
- DIVISION OF INTERNATIONAL STUDIES & SERV.
- DIV. OF TECH. ASST. & EXCH. PROGRAMS

NATIONAL CENTER FOR EDUCATIONAL STATISTICS
- DIVISION OF DATA SOURCES AND STANDARDS
- DIVISION OF STATISTICAL SERVICES
- DIVISION OF STATISTICAL ANALYSIS
- DIVISION OF OPERATIONS ANALYSIS

BUREAU OF EDUC. ASSISTANCE PROGRAMS
- DIVISION OF VOCATIONAL & TECHNICAL EDUC.
- DIV. OF SCHOOL ASST. IN FED. AFF. AREAS
- DIVISION OF STATE GRANTS
- DIV. OF COLLEGE & UNIVERSITY ASSISTANCE

BUREAU OF HIGHER EDUCATION
- DIVISION OF UNDERGRAD. ACADEMIC FAC.
- DIVISION OF GRADUATE ACADEMIC FAC.
- DIVISION OF STUDENT FINANCIAL AID

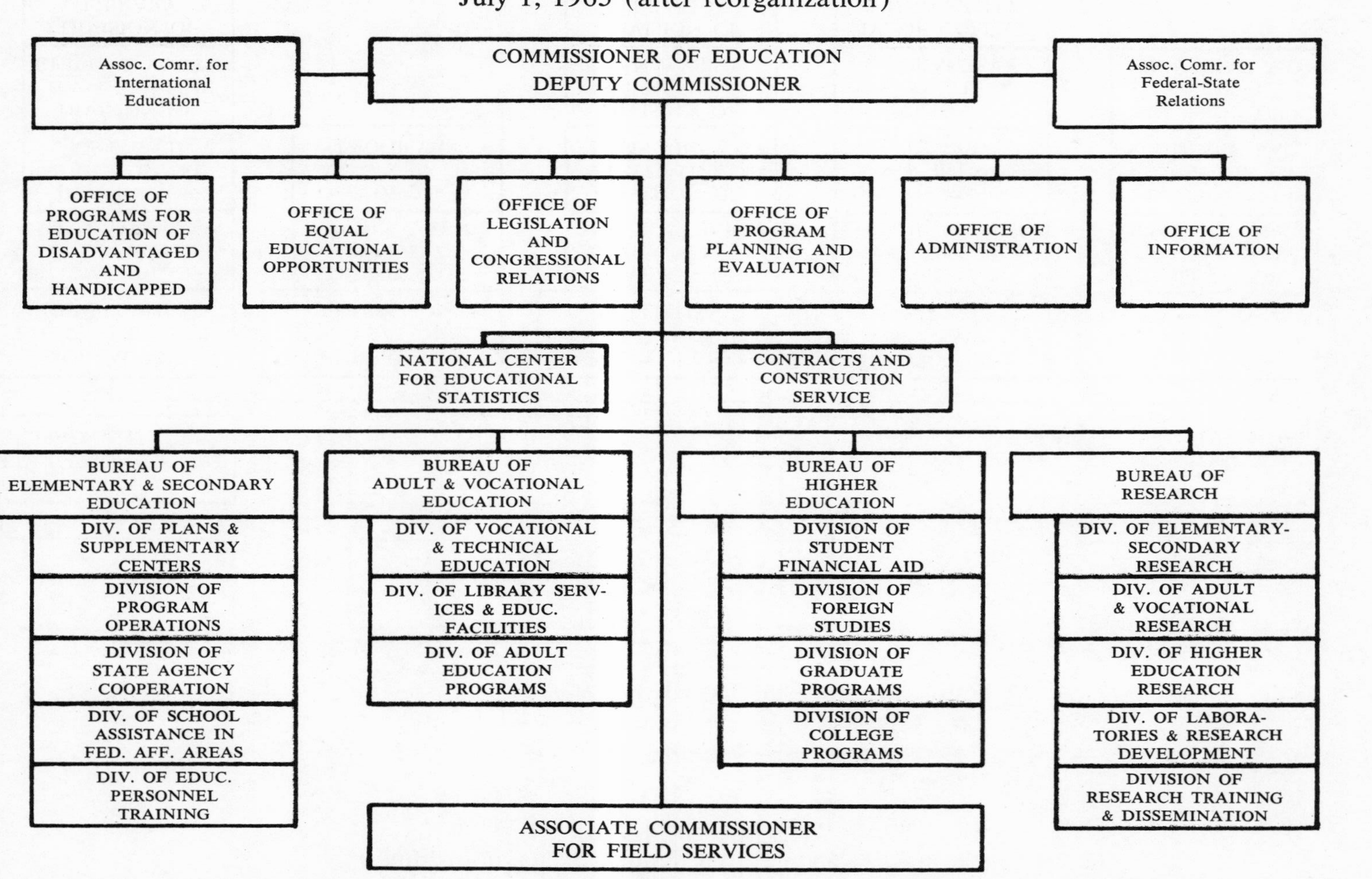
July 1, 1965 (after reorganization)
COMMISSIONER OF EDUCATION
DEPUTY COMMISSIONER
Assoc. Comr. for International Education
Assoc. Comr. for Federal-State Relations
OFFICE OF PROGRAMS FOR EDUCATION OF DISADVANTAGED AND HANDICAPPED
OFFICE OF EQUAL EDUCATIONAL OPPORTUNITIES
OFFICE OF LEGISLATION AND CONGRESSIONAL RELATIONS
OFFICE OF PROGRAM PLANNING AND EVALUATION
OFFICE OF ADMINISTRATION
OFFICE OF INFORMATION
NATIONAL CENTER FOR EDUCATIONAL STATISTICS
CONTRACTS AND CONSTRUCTION SERVICE
BUREAU OF ELEMENTARY & SECONDARY EDUCATION
DIV. OF PLANS & SUPPLEMENTARY CENTERS
DIVISION OF PROGRAM OPERATIONS
DIVISION OF STATE AGENCY COOPERATION
DIV. OF SCHOOL ASSISTANCE IN FED. AFF. AREAS
DIV. OF EDUC. PERSONNEL TRAINING
BUREAU OF ADULT & VOCATIONAL EDUCATION
DIV. OF VOCATIONAL & TECHNICAL EDUCATION
DIV. OF LIBRARY SERV- ICES & EDUC. FACILITIES
DIV. OF ADULT EDUCATION PROGRAMS
BUREAU OF HIGHER EDUCATION
DIVISION OF STUDENT FINANCIAL AID
DIVISION OF FOREIGN STUDIES
DIVISION OF GRADUATE PROGRAMS
DIVISION OF COLLEGE PROGRAMS
BUREAU OF RESEARCH
DIV. OF ELEMENTARY- SECONDARY RESEARCH
DIV. OF ADULT & VOCATIONAL RESEARCH
DIV. OF HIGHER EDUCATION RESEARCH
DIV. OF LABORA- TORIES & RESEARCH DEVELOPMENT
DIVISION OF RESEARCH TRAINING & DISSEMINATION
ASSOCIATE COMMISSIONER FOR FIELD SERVICES

APPENDIX E
MAJOR INTERVIEWS

The following names represent the major interviews conducted by the authors in connection with gathering and interpreting material for this study. The title given for each person is (as closely as possible) applicable to the period covered by the book (spring, 1964 to spring, 1966). Inevitably, some titles or positions were changed within this time period.

James E. Allen, Commissioner of Education, New York State
Roy A. Archibald, Regional Field Representative (West Coast), NEA
Charles S. Benson, Professor, University of California at Berkeley
MacKnight Black, Administrative Officer, Division of Program Operations (BESE), USOE
Louis R. Bright, Associate Commissioner for Bureau of Research, USOE
William B. Cannon, Chief of Education, Manpower, and Science Division of Bureau of the Budget; Exec. Secretary, 1964 President's Task Force on Education
William M. Capron, Assistant Director, Bureau of the Budget
Douglass Cater, Special Assistant to the President, White House
William G. Colman, Exec. Director, U.S. Advisory Commission on Intergovernmental Relations
Forrest Conner, Executive Secretary, AASA
Genevieve O. Dane, Director, Operations Branch, Division of Program Operations (BESE), USOE
Msgr. James C. Donohue, Director, Department of Education, NCWC
Gerald Elbers, Program Planner, (BESE), USOE
Emerson J. Elliott, Budget Examiner for HEW education programs, Bureau of the Budget
Rashi Fein, Member, Economic Studies Senior Staff, Brookings Institution
Ralph Flynt, Associate Commissioner for International Education, USOE
Edgar Fuller, Executive Secretary, CCSSO
Samuel Halperin, Deputy Assistant Secretary for Legislation, HEW
Arthur Harris, Associate Commissioner for Bureau of Elementary and Secondary Education, USOE
Robert Hopper, Director, Division of State Agency Cooperation (BESE), USOE
John F. Hughes, Director, Division of Program Operations (BESE), USOE
Dwight A. Ink, Director, 1965 White House Task Force on Education
Herbert Jasper, Member, 1965 White House Task Force on Education
Norman Karsh, Assistant Commissioner for Office of Administration, USOE
Francis Keppel, Commissioner of Education, USOE

Michael Kirst, Program Assistant, Division of Program Operations (BESE), USOE

Charles Lee, Member, Senate Education Subcommittee Staff

Henry Loomis, Deputy Commissioner, USOE

Michael S. March, Assistant Chief of Education, Manpower, and Science Division, Bureau of the Budget

Robert E. McKay, California Teachers Association; NEA Legislative Commission

Rufus Miles, Former Assistant Secretary for Administration, HEW

Peter Muirhead, Associate Commissioner for Bureau of Higher Education, USOE

Ewald B. Nyquist, Assistant Commissioner of Education, New York State

H. D. Reed, Jr., General Council, House Education Subcommittee Staff

Wayne Reed, Associate Commissioner for Federal-State Relations, USOE

Wilson Riles, Director of Compensatory Education, California State Department of Education

Harold Ritchie, Area Field Representative (San Francisco Office), USOE

Alice Rivlin, Deputy Assistant Secretary (Program Coordination), HEW

James E. Russell, Secretary, Educational Policies Committee, NEA

Gilbert Schulkind, Member, 1965 White House Task Force on Education

Thomas Shellhammer, Division of Compensatory Education, California State Department of Education

Martin W. Spickler, Division of Program Operations (BESE), USOE

John F. Staehle, Assistant Director for Policy and Procedures, Division of Program Operations (BESE), USOE

Ward Stewart, Director, Field Services (Bureau of Higher Education), USOE

James L. Sundquist, Member, Governmental Studies Senior Staff, Brookings Institution

Monroe Sweetland, Legislative Consultant for Western States, NEA

Ralph Tyler, Member, National Advisory Council on the Education of Disadvantaged Children

Russell Wood, Assistant Commissioner for Office of Program Planning and Evaluation, USOE

GLOSSARY

AASA American Association of School Administrators
ACE American Council on Education
AEC Atomic Energy Commission
AID Agency for International Development
BESE Bureau of Elementary and Secondary Education, U.S. Office of Education
BSSR Bureau of Social Science Research
CAA Community Action Agency
CAP Community Action Program
CCSSO Council of Chief State School Officers
CSSO Chief State School Officer
DOD Department of Defense
DPO Division of Program Operations (in BESE) (Title subsequently changed to Division of Compensatory Education)
DPSC Division of Plans and Supplementary Centers (in BESE)
EOA Economic Opportunity Act (anti-poverty) of 1964
ERIC Educational Research Information Center
ESEA Elementary and Secondary Education Act of 1965
FEB Federal Executive Board
FY Fiscal Year (*ending* June 30, of the year designated)
HEW Department of Health, Education, and Welfare
HUD Department of Housing and Urban Development
LEA Local Educational Agency
MDTA Manpower Development and Training Act
MES More Effective Schools Program
NASA National Aeronautics and Space Administration
NCEA National Catholic Education Association
NCES National Center for Educational Statistics
NCWC National Catholic Welfare Conference (now United States Catholic Conference)
NDEA National Defense Education Act
NEA National Education Association
NSBA National School Boards Association
NSF National Science Foundation
OE Office of Education (USOE)
OEO Office of Economic Opportunity

OEEO	Office of Equal Educational Opportunities (in USOE)
OPLP	Office of Program and Legislative Planning
PACE	Projects to Advance Creativity in Education (ESEA Title III)
PERT	Program Evaluation Review Techniques
POAU	Protestants and Other Americans United for the Separation of Church and State
PPBS	Program Planning and Budgeting System
PTA	National Congress of Parents and Teachers
R & D	Research and Development (R & D Centers under ESEA Title IV)
SEA	State Educational Agency
USOE	United States Office of Education
VOA	Voice of America

BIBLIOGRAPHY

BOOKS

Bailey, Stephen K. *The New Congress.* New York: St. Martins Press, 1966.

———. *The Office of Education and the Education Act of 1965.* Inter-University Case Program, #100. Indianapolis: The Bobbs-Merrill Co., 1966.

——— *et al. Schoolmen and Politics.* Syracuse: Syracuse University Press, 1962.

Benson, Charles S. *The Cheerful Prospect.* Boston: Houghton-Mifflin, 1965.

Bettelheim, Bruno. *Love is Not Enough.* New York: The Free Press, 1950.

Bloom, B., Davis, A., and Hess, R. *Compensatory Education for Cultural Deprivation.* New York: Holt, Rinehart and Winston, Inc., 1965.

Bruner, Jerome S. *The Process of Education.* (Vintage Edition.) New York: Random House, 1960.

Burkhead, Jesse. Public School Finance: Economics and Politics. Syracuse: Syracuse University Press, 1964.

——— with Fox, T. G., and Holland, J. W. *Input and Output in Large-City High Schools.* (Education in Large Cities Series.) Syracuse: Syracuse University Press, 1967.

Callahan, Raymond E. *The Cult of Efficiency: A Study of the Social Forces That Have Shaped the Administration of the Public Schools.* Chicago: University of Chicago Press, 1962.

Campbell, A. K. and Sacks, S. *Metropolitan America: Fiscal Patterns and Governmental Systems.* Glencoe: The Free Press, 1967.

Campbell, R. F., Cunningham, L. L., and McPhee, R. F. *The Organization and Control of American Schools.* Columbus: Charles E. Merrill Books, Inc., 1965.

Campbell, R. F., Sroufe, G. E., and Layton, D. H. (eds.) *Strengthening State Departments of Education.* Chicago Midwest Administration Center, University of Chicago, 1967.

Clark, Harold F. *Cost and Quality in Public Education.* Syracuse: Syracuse University Press, 1963.

Clark, Kenneth B. *Dark Ghetto.* New York: Harper and Row, 1965.

Conant, James B. *Slums and Suburbs.* New York: McGraw-Hill, 1961.

———. *The American High School Today.* New York: McGraw-Hill, 1959.

———. *Shaping Educational Policy.* New York: McGraw-Hill, 1964.

Congress and the Nation 1945–64. Washington: Congressional Quarterly Service, 1965.

The Federal Role in Education. Washington: Congressional Quarterly Service, 1965.

Fellman, David. *The Supreme Court and Education.* New York: Columbia University, Bureau of Publications, 1960.

Freund, Paul A. *Religion and the Public Schools.* Cambridge: Harvard University Press, 1965.

Garder, John W. *Excellence: Can We Be Equal and Excellent Too?* New York: Harper and Row, 1961.

———. *Excellence and Self-Renewal.* New York: Harper & Row, 1961 and 1963.

Heller, Walter W. *New Dimensions of Political Economy.* New York: W. W. Norton & Company, Inc., 1967.

Hentoff, Nat. *Our Children Are Dying.* New York: Viking Press, 1967.

Hersey, John. *The Child Buyer.* New York: Alfred A. Knopf, Inc., 1960.

Keppel, Francis. *The Necessary Revolution in American Education.* New York: Harper and Row, 1966.

Kozol, Jonathan. *Death At An Early Age: The Destruction of the Hearts and Minds of Negro Children in The Boston Schools.* Boston: Houghton-Mifflin Co., 1967.

Kursh, Harry. *The United States Office of Education.* Philadelphia: Chilton Co., 1965.

Lee, James Michael (ed.). "Catholic Education in the United States", in *Catholic Education in the Western World.* Notre Dame, Ind.: University of Notre Dame Press, 1967.

McClure, W. P. and Miller, V. *Government of Public Education for Adequate Policy Making.* Urbana: Bureau of Educational Research, College of Education, University of Illinois, 1960.

Meranto, Philip. *The Politics of Federal Aid to Education in 1965: A Study in Political Innovation.* (Education in Large Cities Series.) Syracuse: Syracuse University Press, 1967.

Mosher, Frederick C. *Program Budgeting: Theory and Practice.* Chicago: Public Administration Service, 1954.

Riesman, David. *Constraint and Variety in American Education.* New York: Doubleday & Co., 1958.

Rosenthal, R. and Jacobson, L. *Pygmalion in the Classroom.* New York: Holt, Rinehart, & Winston, 1968.

Russell, James. *Universal Opportunity for Early Childhood Education.* Washington, D.C.: National Education Association, Educational Policies Commission, 1966.

Schultz, Theodore W. *The Economic Value of Education.* New York: Columbia University Press, 1963.

Shrag, Peter. *Village School Downtown: Politics and Education—A Boston Report.* Boston: Beacon Press, 1967.

Spurlock, Clark. *Education and the Supreme Court.* Urbana: University of Illinois Press, 1955.

Tyler, Ralph W. *American Education in the Postwar Period: Curriculum Reconstruction.* Chicago: University of Chicago Press, 1945.

ARTICLES

Benson, Charles S. "Coleman Report: Why the Schools Flunk Out," *The Nation,* April 10, 1967, p. 463–466.

Bickel, Alexander. "Forcing Desegregation Through Title VI," *The New Republic,* April 9, 1966, p. 8–9.

Bowles, Samuel and Levin, Henry M. "The Determinants of Scholastic Achievement—An Appraisal of Some Recent Evidence," *Journal of Human Resources,* Winter, 1968.

Campbell, Alan K. "Educational Policy-Making Studied in Large Cities," a paper presented at the Cubberley Conference: School Boards in an Era of Conflict, (Stanford University, 1966), reprinted with other conference papers in *The American School Board Journal,* March 1967, p. 18–19.

Drew, Elizabeth Brenner. "Education's Billion Dollar Baby," *The Atlantic Monthly,* July, 1966, p. 39.

———. "HEW Grapples with PPBS," *The Public Interest,* Summer, 1967, p. 9–29.

Emmerich, Herbert. Letter to the editor, *The Washington Post,* January 29, 1967.

"Equal Educational Opportunity: A Special Issue," *Harvard Educational Review.* Winter, 1968.

Exton, Elaine. "Here's How HEW Department Applies Planning-Programming-Budgeting System," *The American School Board Journal,* December, 1965, p. 5.

Hopper, Robert L. "Strength Where It Counts," *American Education,* June, 1966.

Jenks, Christopher. "Education: The Racial Gap," *The New Republic,* October 1, 1966, p. 21–26.

Leuchtenberg, William E. "The Genesis of the Great Society," *The Reporter,* April 22, 1966, p. 36–39.

LaNoue, George R. "The Title II Trap," *Phi Delta Kappan,* June, 1966, p. 558–563, and responses, p. 564–565.

Masters, N. A. and Pettitt, L. K. "Some Changing Patterns in Educational Policy Making," *Educational Administration Quarterly,* Spring, 1966, p. 81–100.

Mayer, Martin. "What's Wrong With Our Big City Schools," *The Saturday Evening Post,* September 9, 1967, p. 21.

McKissick, Floyd. (Communication to the Editor) "Is Integration Necessary?" *The New Republic,* December 3, 1966, p. 33–36.

Miles, Rufus E. Jr. "The Case for a Federal Department of Education," *Public Administration Review,* March, 1967, p. 1.

Moynihan, Daniel P. "The Case for a Family Allowance," *The New York Times Magazine,* February 5, 1967, p. 13.

Nichols, Robert C. "Schools and the Disadvantaged," *Science,* December 9, 1966, p. 1312–1314.

Sacks, Seymour and Ranney, David C. "Suburban Education: A Fiscal Analysis," *Urban Affairs,* Fall, 1966.

Talbot, Allan R. "Needed—A New Breed of School Superintendent," *Harpers Magazine,* February, 1966, p. 81–87.

GOVERNMENT PUBLICATIONS

Beker, Jerome. *A Study of Integration in Racially Imbalanced Urban Public Schools: A Demonstration and Evaluation.* (Final Report, Project No. D-125, Public Health Service: NIMH, Grant No. R11-MH-1652.) Syracuse, N.Y.: Syracuse University Youth Development Center, 1967.

Coleman, James S., et al. *Equality of Educational Opportunity*. Washington, D.C.: U.S. Government Printing Office, 1966.

Contemporary Issues in American Education: Consultant Papers prepared for use at the White House Conference on Education, July 20–21, 1965. (Washington, D.C.: U.S. Department of Health, Education, and Welfare, Office of Education Bulletin, 1966, No. 3.)

89th Congress, 1st session. House. *Report No. 143. (Report of the Committee on Education and Labor, on the Elementary and Secondary Education Act of 1965.)*

89th Congress, 1st session. House. *Report No. 587. (Report of the Committee on Education and Labor, on School Construction in Areas Affected by Disaster.)*

89th Congress, 1st session. House, General Subcommittee on Education. *Hearings on Aid to Elementary and Secondary Education.*

89th Congress, 1st session. House, General Subcommittee on Education. *Hearings on the Elementary and Secondary School Act Formulas.*

89th Congress, 1st session, House; 1st session, Senate. *Hearings Before Subcommittee of the Appropriations Committee, on Departments of Labor and HEW Appropriations for 1966;* Departments of Labor and HEW Supplemental Appropriations for 1966.

89th Congress, 1st session. Senate, Subcommittee on Education. *Hearings on the Elementary and Secondary Education Act of 1965.*

89th Congress, 1st session. Senate, Subcommittee on Education. *Hearings on School Disaster Aid Legislation.*

89th Congress, 1st session. Senate. *Report No. 146. (Report of the Committee on Labor and Public Welfare, on the Elementary and Secondary Education Act of 1965.)*

89th Congress, 1st session. Senate. *Report No. 783. (Report of the Committee on Labor and Public Welfare, on the Elementary and Secondary Education Amendments of 1966.)*

89th Congress, 2nd session. House. *Hearings Before the Special Subcommittee on Education* (Green Committee), *on the U.S. Office of Education, 1966.*

89th Congress, 2nd session. House. *Report No. 1814. (Report of the Committee on Education and Labor, on the Elementary and Secondary Education Amendments of 1966.)*

89th Congress, 2nd session. House, General Subcommittee on Education. *Hearings on the Elementary and Secondary Education Amendments of 1966.*

89th Congress, 2nd session, House; 2nd session, Senate. *Hearings Before Subcommittee of the Appropriations Committee,* on: *Departments of Labor and HEW Appropriations for 1967; Second Supplemental Appropriations Bill for 1966; Departments of Labor and HEW Supplemental Appropriations for 1967.*

89th Congress, 2nd session. Senate. *Report No. 1674. (Report of the Committee on Labor and Public Welfare, on School Construction in Areas Affected by Disaster.)*

89th Congress, 2nd session. Senate, Subcommittee on Education. *Hearings on the Elementary and Secondary Education Act of 1966.*

90th Congress, 1st session. House, Committee on Education and Labor. *Hearings on the Elementary and Secondary Education Act Amendments of 1967.*

90th Congress, 1st session. House, Special Subcommittee on Education (Green Committee). *Study of the United States Office of Education.*

90th Congress, 1st session. Senate. *Report No. 726. (Report on appropriations procedures.)*

90th Congress, 1st session. Senate, Subcommittee on Education. *Hearings on Education Legislation, 1967.*

90th Congress, 1st session. Senate, Subcommittee on Education. *Notes and Working Papers . . . Title I of PL 89–10;* 1967.

90th Congress, 1st session. Senate, Subcommittee on Education. *Notes and Working Papers . . . Title III of PL 89–10,* April, 1967.

Elementary and Secondary Education Act Amendments of 1965 (PL 89–10).

Elementary and Secondary Education Act Amendments of 1966 (PL 89–750).

Elementary and Secondary Education Act Amendments of 1967 (PL 90–247).

Howe, Harold II. *The Human Frontier: Remarks on Equality of Education.* Washington: U.S. Government Printing Office, 1966.

National Advisory Committee on Education. *Federal Relations to Education.* Washington: U.S. Government Printing Office, 1931.

National Advisory Council on the Education of Disadvantaged Children. *First Annual Report.* Dated March 31, 1966 and other reports dated November 25, 1966, and January 31, 1967.

Novick, David, et al. *Program Budgeting: Program Analysis and the Federal Budget.* Washington, D.C.: U.S. Government Printing Office, 1965.

Recommendations of the White House Task Force on Education, Dwight A. Ink, Chairman. June 14, 1965.

Sacks, Seymour. "Fiscal Disparities in Metropolitan Areas" in *Fiscal Balance in the American Federal System.* Washington, D.C.: The Advisory Commission on Intergovernmental Relations, 1968.

U.S. Advisory Committee on Education. *Staff Study Number Two.* Washington: U.S. Government Printing Office, 1938–39.

U.S. Advisory Committee on Education. *The Federal Government and Education.* Washington: U.S. Government Printing Office, 1938.

U.S. Bureau of the Budget. Memorandum on *Planning-Programming-Budgeting,* Supplement to Bulletin No. 66–3, to Heads of Executive Departments and Establishments, February 21, 1966.

U.S. Bureau of the Budget. *Special Analysis G.* Supplement to U.S. Budget for FY '67.

U.S. Commission on Civil Rights. *Racial Isolation in the Public Schools.* (Washington, D.C.: U.S. Commission on Civil Rights, 1967).

U.S. Commission on Civil Rights. *Survey of School Desegregation in the Southern and Border States,* 1965–66. Washington, D.C., 1966.

U.S. Department of Health, Education and Welfare. *The Research and Development Centers Established Under the Cooperative Research Program of USOE.* July 14, 1967.

U.S. Department of Health, Education, and Welfare. *Trends.* Washington: U.S. Government Printing Office, 1965.

U.S. Joint Administrative Task Force (Dwight A. Ink, of HUD, Chairman). *Reducing Federal Grant-In-Aid Processing Time. An Interagency Report to the President.* September, 1967.

U.S. National Resources Planning Board. *Research—A National Resource.* Washington: U.S. Government Printing Office, 1938–41.

U.S. Department of Health, Education, and Welfare, Office of Education. *General Statement of Policies Under Title VI of the Civil Rights Act of 1964 Respecting Desegregation of Elementary and Secondary Schools,* (April, 1965), *Code of Federal Regulations.* Title 45, Part 181.

U.S. Office of Education. *A Chance for A Change*. OE-35084, Washington, D.C., 1966.

U.S. Office of Education. *Catalogue of Selected Documents on the Disadvantaged*. OE-37001. Washington: U.S. Government Printing Office, 1966.

U.S. Office of Education. *Disadvantaged Children Series*. 1965.

U.S. Office of Education. *Education, 65: A Report to the Profession*. OE-11006. Washington, D.C., 1966.

U.S. Office of Education. *Fact Book: Office of Education Programs*. Washington, D.C., 1967.

U.S. Office of Education. *Financial Management of Federal-State Education Programs*. OE-10019, 1962.

U.S. Office of Education. *First Annual Report, Title I, Elementary and Secondary Education Act of 1965*. Washington: U.S. Government Printing Office, 1967.

U.S. Office of Education. *Focus on PACE—Projects to Advance Creativity in Education; Title III: Supplementary Centers and Services*. OE-20082. Washington, D.C., 1965.

U.S. Office of Education. *Focus on Title I*. OE-35077. Washington, D.C., 1965.

U.S. Office of Education. *Focus on Title II; School Library Resources, Textbooks and Other Instructional Materials*. OE-15058. Washington, D.C., 1965.

U.S. Office of Education. *Focus on Title V: Strengthening State Departments of Education*. OE-23043. Washington, D.C., 1965.

U.S. Office of Education. *Guidelines: Special Programs for Educationally Deprived Children*. OE-35079. Washington, D.C., 1965.

U.S. Department of Health, Education, and Welfare, Office of Education. *Human Investment Programs, Elementary and Secondary Education, 1966–8*. September, 1966.

U.S. Office of Education. *Instructions for Title I, 1967 Application Forms*. OE-37003. Washington, D.C., 1966.

U.S. Office of Education. *National Conference on Education of the Disadvantaged*. OE-37004. Washington: U.S. Government Printing Office, 1966.

U.S. Office of Education. *OE 100. Highlighting the Progress of American Education*. OE-11009. Washington, D.C., 1967.

U.S. Office of Education. *Pace Setters in Innovation*. (periodic issues).

U.S. Department of Health, Education, and Welfare, Office for Civil Rights. *Policies on Elementary and Secondary School Compliance with Title VI of the Civil Rights Act of 1964* (March, 1968). *Code of Federal Regulations*, Title 45, Part 181.

U.S. Office of Education. *Profile of ESEA*. OE-20088. Washington, D.C., 1966.

U.S. Office of Education. *Program Evaluation and Review Technique: Applications in Education*. OE-12024. Washington, D.C., 1966.

U.S. Office of Education. *Programs for the Culturally Disadvantaged*. Bulletin No. 17. Washington, D.C., 1963.

U.S. Department of Health, Education, and Welfare, Office of Education. *Progress of Public Education in the United States of America*. Washington: U.S. Government Printing Office, 1964.

U.S. Department of Health, Education, and Welfare, Office of Education. *Progress Under the Elementary and Secondary Education Act of 1965* (PL 89–10) (Offset sheet), March 1966, sheet 4.

U.S. Department of Health, Education, and Welfare, Office of Education. *Projections of Educational Statistics*. Washington: U.S. Government Printing Office,1966.

U.S. Office of Education. *Projects Approved Under Title III, Elementary and Secondary Education Act*. Washington, D.C., 1966.

U.S. Department of Health, Education, and Welfare, Office of Education. *Regulations: Title I of PL 89–10, The Elementary and Secondary Education Act of 1965. Code of Federal Regulations* Title 45, Part 116.

U.S. Department of Health, Education, and Welfare, Office of Education. *Revised Statement of Policies for School Desegregation Plans Under Title VI of the Civil Rights Act of 1964,* (March 1966), *Code of Federal Regulations.* Title 45, Part 181.

U.S. Department of Health, Education, and Welfare. *State Variations in Support of Public Schools.* Washington: U.S. Government Printing Office, 1965.

U.S. Department of Health, Education, and Welfare. *Statistics of State School Systems, 1961–1962*. Washington: U.S. Government Printing Office, 1962.

U.S. Office of Education. *Summer Programs for Children of Poverty*. OE-37006. Washington, D.C., 1966.

U.S. Office of Education. *Summary of the State Interim Evaluation Reports.* (Mimeo.) Washington, D.C., 1966.

U.S. Office of Education. *Survey of Title I Supported Programs.* OE-4361. Washington, D.C., 1966.

U.S. Office of Education. *The Education of Disadvantaged Children: A Bibliography*. OE-14031-38. Washington: U.S. Government Printing Office, 1966.

U.S. Office of Education. *The First Work of These Times.* Washington, D.C., 1965.

U.S. Office of Education. *1965–66 Statistical Report of Title I Program Activities.* OE-4378. Washington, D.C., 1966.

U.S. Office of Education, Committee on Mission and Organization. *A Federal Education Agency for the Future*. OE-10010. Washington: U.S. Government Printing Office, 1961.

U.S. Office of Education, Division of Education Laboratories, Bureau of Research. *A Progress Report on the Twenty Educational Laboratories.* July 1, 1967.

U.S. Office of Education (with Office of Economic Opportunity). *Education: An Answer to Poverty*. 1965.

MISCELLANEOUS

Benson, Charles S. "Some Questions on Cost Effectiveness in Education." (Mimeo.) February 28, 1966.

Capron, William M., Assistant Director, Bureau of the Budget. *The Potential Role of Cost Effectiveness Analysis for Evaluation of Government Domestic Programs.* Address before the Symposium on Cost Effectiveness Analysis, Institute for Defense Analyses. Washington, D.C., June 15, 1965.

Chase, Francis S. *Report on Administrative Survey of the U.S. Office of Education of the Federal Security Agency*. Chicago: Public Administration Service, 1950.

Council of Chief State School Officers. *Resolution VII.* Annual Business Meeting. Honolulu, Hawaii, November 12, 1965.

Dentler, Robert A. "The Impact of Increasing Federal Aid to Education upon the Metropolitan Community," paper presented at the Session on Urban Sociology at the Annual Convention of the American Sociological Association. San Francisco, August 29, 1967.

Deutsch, Martin. *Minority Group and Class Status as Related to Social and Personality Factors and Scholastic Achievement.* Monograph #2. The Society for Applied Anthropology. Ithaca, New York, 1960.

Evaluation of ESEA Title I Projects of California Schools, 1965–66. California State Department of Education.

Green, The Honorable Edith. *Study of the Office of Education.* Speech delivered before Meeting of the Council of Chief State School Officers, Puerto Rico. November 16, 1967. (Mimeo.)

Kearney, C. Philip. *The 1964 Presidential Task Force on Education and the Elementary and Secondary Education Act of 1965.* Unpublished Ph.D. dissertation, University of Chicago, 1967.

LaNoue, George R. "Church-State Problems in the Elementary and Secondary Education Act of 1965," and "Public Funds for Parochial Schools," *The Church-State Problem Has Been Handed To You: A Guide for Community Groups.* New York: American Civil Liberties Union, 1967.

Milstein, Mike. *The Functions of the California State Department of Education as They Relate to Two Federally Funded Educational Programs.* Unpublished Ph.D. dissertation. University of California, Berkeley, 1967.

Morse, Wayne. Speech before the American Association of School Administrators. May 13, 1965.

Mosher, Edith K. *The Origins, Enactment, and Implementation of the Elementary and Secondary Education Act of 1965: A Study of Emergent National Educational Policy.* Unpublished Ph.D. dissertation. University of California, Berkeley,1967.

Munger, Frank J. *The Politics of Federal Aid to Education,* paper presented before Meeting of the American Political Science Association. Washington, D.C., 1965.

National Catholic Welfare Conference. *Questionnaire on Participation of Catholic School Children under Titles I, II and III of PL 89–10,* 1966.

National Catholic Welfare Conference, Department of Education. *Understanding the Elementary and Secondary Education Act of 1965.* 1965.

National Education Association, Department of Rural Education. *A Guide for Developing PACE,* 1966.

National Education Association, Research Division. *Estimates of School Statistics.* Research Report, 1964–R17, p. 15.

National Education Association. *School Programs for the Disadvantaged Children.* Educational Research Service Curricula No. 2. February, 1963.

New York Civil Liberties Union, *Civil Liberties in New York,* Vol. XV, No. 1. January, 1967, p. 1–2.

New York State Department of Education. *New York State Pupil Evaluation Program.* Albany, 1966.

New York State Regents Examination and Scholarship Center, Division of Educational Testing. *Test Results of the 1965 Pupil Evaluation Program in New York State: Preliminary Overview.* (and subsequent reports) Albany: January, 1967. (Mimeo.)

Nuccio, Vincent J., and Walsh, John J. *A National Level Evaluation Study of the Impact of Title I of the Elementary and Secondary Education Act of 1965 on the Participation of Non-Public School Children: Phase I.* Chestnut Hill, Mass.: Boston College, 1967. (Mimeo.)

Schweickhard, Dean M. *The Role and Policy-making Activities of State Boards of Education: Report on a Special Study Project*. Denver, Colorado: National Association of State Boards of Education, 1967.

Center for Urban Education. *Summary Report on Evaluation of the More Effective Schools Program*. New York, August, 1967.

Technomis, Inc. (Los Angeles, Calif.) *The Feasibility of Cost/Effectiveness Analysis for Title I, Public Law 89–10*. Final Report, prepared for Division of Operations Analysis, National Center for Educational Statistics. U.S. Office of Education. January 31, 1966.

Wise, Arthur E. "Is Denial of Equal Educational Opportunity Constitutional?" *Administrator's Notebook*. (University of Chicago, Mid-west Administrative Center), Vol. XIII, February, 1965, No. 6.

CONTINUING SOURCES OF INFORMATION

American Association of School Administrators. *The Hot Line*.

——— *School Management Magazine*.

Congressional Quarterly, Inc. *Weekly Report*.

Education in Large Cities Series, Alan K. Campbell, ed. Syracuse: Syracuse University Press.

National Education Association. "Washington Monitor," *Education U.S.A*. (National School Public Relations Association).

——— *National Education Association Journal*.

——— *Special Report*. (Division of Federal Relations).

——— *Washington Outlook on Education*.

National Catholic Education Association. *National Catholic Education Bulletin*.

——— *National Catholic Education Association Newsletter*.

National Committee for Support of the Public Schools. *Fact Sheet*.

National School Boards Association. *The American School Board Journal*.

Phi Delta Kappa Professional Fraternity. *Phi Delta Kappan*.

Prakken Publications, Inc. *Education Digest*.

Saturday Review, Inc. *Saturday Review*. (monthly education section).

Southern Educational Reporting Service. *Statistical Summary*.

The Catholic University of America. (School of Education). *Catholic Educational Review*.

U.S. Office of Education. *American Education*.

INDEX